S0-ADR-978

JOHN ELDREDGE

THE HEART

TWO INSPIRING BOOKS IN ONE VOLUME

DESIRE

WAKING THE DEAD

THOMAS NELSON
Since 1798

NASHVILLE   DALLAS   MEXICO CITY   RIO DE JANEIRO   BEIJING

Desire © 2000 and 2007 by John Eldredge. Formerly published as *The Journey of Desire: Searching for the Life We've Only Dreamed of.*
Waking the Dead © 2003 by John Eldredge

All rights reserved. No portion of this book may be reproduced, stored in a retrieval system, or transmitted in any form or by any means—electronic, mechanical, photocopy, recording, scanning, or other—except for brief quotations in critical reviews or articles, without the prior written permission of the publisher.

Published in Nashville, Tennessee, by Thomas Nelson. Thomas Nelson is a registered trademark of Thomas Nelson, Inc.

Published in association with Yates & Yates, www.yates2.com.

Thomas Nelson, Inc., titles may be purchased in bulk for educational, business, fund-raising, or sales promotional use. For information, please e-mail SpecialMarkets@ThomasNelson.com.

Scripture quotations noted NIV are from the HOLY BIBLE: NEW INTERNATIONAL VERSION®. © 1973, 1978, 1984 by International Bible Society. Used by permission of Zondervan Publishing House. All rights reserved.

Scripture quotations noted NKJV are from THE NEW KING JAMES VERSION. © 1982 by Thomas Nelson, Inc. Used by permission. All rights reserved.

Scripture quotations noted NLT are from the *Holy Bible,* New Living Translation. © 1996. Used by permission of Tyndale House Publishers, Inc., Wheaton, Illinois 60189. All rights reserved.

Scripture quotations noted NRSV are from the NEW REVISED STANDARD VERSION of the Bible. © 1989 by the Division of Christian Education of the National Council of the Churches of Christ in the U.S.A. All rights reserved.

Scripture quotations noted NASB are from the NEW AMERICAN STANDARD BIBLE®, © The Lockman Foundation 1960, 1962, 1963, 1968, 1971, 1972, 1973, 1975, 1977, 1995. Used by permission.

Scripture quotations noted *The Message* are from The Message by Eugene H. Peterson. © 1993, 1994, 1995, 1996, 2000. Used by permission of NavPress Publishing Group. All rights reserved.

Scripture quotations noted KJV are from the KING JAMES VERSION.

Scripture quotations noted *Moffatt* are from *The Bible: James Moffatt Translation* by James A. R. Moffatt. © 1950, 1952, 1953, 1954, by James A. R. Moffatt.

ISBN: 978-1-4002-8040-7

Printed in the United States of America
08 09 10 11 QW 6 5 4 3 2 1

CONTENTS

DESIRE

Waking *the* Dead

DESIRE

The Journey We Must Take to Find the Life God Offers

FOR BRENT

INTRODUCTION

There's an old proverb I've come to love and appreciate very much. "Above all else, guard your heart, for it is the wellspring of life" (Proverbs 4:23). The wisdom of the passage is simply this—to lose heart is to lose everything. Because everything that makes a life worth living flows from the heart. Intimacy, romance, love. Adventure and meaning and purpose. Courage and sacrifice and joy. The list could go on and on. We need this wellspring of life within us if we would live and not merely "get by."

So then, how do we guard our heart? How do we even know what our heart is up to, or how it's doing, or where it's headed? In some sense, you have to read the whole of Scripture to get a good answer. But I can give you one secret to your heart—desire. What you do with desire is what you do with your heart. How you handle your deep desires is how you handle your heart. It's that straightforward.

Desire is powerful. One of the most powerful forces in our lives.

At least, it was meant to be.

But we're not quite sure how we feel about desire, really. Or what to do with it. Desire feels . . . messy. You see those books

I

out there promising you, "The life you dream of is yours to have! Follow your desire!" It sounds good. But we've all seen people try it and fail. They leap to a new career, or open themselves up to intimacy, or start up a project they've always dreamed about. And it comes crashing down, they come limping home. Seems like the only guy who can pull it off is the author of the book making all the promises. And we wonder, "Is it worth risking, opening myself up to my desires?"

Then you've got the other camp, often coming from well-intended church folk who warn, "Don't even think about it. Desire is only going to get you into trouble." And, there's reason to believe them. We've seen the affairs, the addictions, the financial ruin and all the other heartache brought on by someone "following their desire." It looks utterly reasonable to simply kill desire. And call it sanctification. The path of maturity.

Both camps are right, in a way. And they're both wrong. Desire *can* lead us to the life we were meant to live. And, desire can get us into a heap of trouble, too. Or just profound disappointment. Desire is a lot like love in that way. When it's good, it's really good. And when it's bad, it's really bad. Many people fear love for that very reason. Just as they fear desire. But a life without love can hardly be called living. The same holds true when we abandon our heart's deep desires. Instead of guarding the wellspring of life within us, we cap it with a cement plug and try to get on with life.

It doesn't really work. You end up losing heart. And that is an awful place to find yourself.

I believe desire is a gift from God. After all, the Psalms say things like, "May he give you the desire of your heart," (20:4) and, "Praise the Lord, O my soul . . . who satisfies your desires with good things so that your youth is renewed like the eagle's" (103:5), and "You open your hand and satisfy the **desires** of every living thing" (145:16). Clearly, God is not opposed to desire. Far from it. He gave us a heart that desires deeply, and he uses those desires to draw us to himself, and to the life he created us to live.

What we need to learn is how to listen to desire, how to *interpret* it. Desire is speaking to us, all the time. It is one of the deepest voices of the heart. A voice many of us have never been taught to understand. Desire can lead us to the life we were meant to live. It can shape our hopes and dreams, fill them with passion and determination. It can sustain us in times of distress and suffering, too. It can lead us to God. If we will listen closely.

That is why we *must* take the journey of desire, the path of learning to listen to desire, and sort it through, and find in it the treasure God has for us. In fact, when I first published this book, it was called *The Journey of Desire*. But I don't think anyone understood the title. And the book came at an unfortunate time, right before the release of another book called *Wild at Heart*, which ended up eclipsing it. This little gem sort of fell between the cracks. But it has so much to offer, so much hope and guidance for this dangerous journey of the heart we call living.

To live life fully—that is to say, to live life as God meant for us to live—demands a full recovery of our heart. You need that wellspring flowing swift and clear and true. And that, my friends, waits upon how you handle your heart's desire. So, we are rereleasing this book in hopes that it will be a great gift and a blessing to you. Yes, it is risky entering into the realm of desire. "It's a dangerous business," Bilbo admitted, "going out of your door. You step into the Road, and if you don't keep your feet, there is no knowing where you might be swept off to." But it's a far, far greater risk not to. Would you spend your whole life shut up inside, gathering cobwebs and dust?

The adventure calls. The future awaits. How you handle your heart's desire will in great measure determine what becomes of your life. So let us take the journey together.

—— ONCE UPON A time there lived a sea lion who had lost the sea.

He lived in a country known as the barren lands. High on a plateau, far from any coast, it was a place so dry and dusty that it could only be called a desert. A kind of coarse grass grew in patches here and there, and a few trees were scattered across the horizon. But mostly, it was dust. And sometimes wind, which together make one very thirsty. Of course, it must seem strange to you that such a beautiful creature should wind up in a desert at all. He was, mind you, a sea lion. But things like this do happen.

How the sea lion came to the barren lands, no one could remember. It all seemed so very long ago. So long, in fact, it appeared as though he had always been there. Not that he belonged in such an arid place. How could that be? He was, after all, a sea lion. But as you know, once you have lived so long in a certain spot, no matter how odd, you come to think of it as home.

CHAPTER ONE

OUR HEART'S DEEPEST SECRET

We are never living, but hoping to live.

—PASCAL

It seems to me we can never give up longing and wishing while we are alive. There are certain things we feel to be beautiful and good, and we must hunger for them.

—GEORGE ELIOT

And I still haven't found what I'm looking for.

—U2

There is a secret set within each of our hearts. It often goes unnoticed, we rarely can put words to it, and yet it guides us throughout the days of our lives. This secret remains hidden for the most part in our deepest selves. It is the desire for life as it was meant to be. Isn't there a life you have been searching for all your days? You may not always be aware of your search, and there are times when you seem to have abandoned looking altogether. But again and again it returns to us, this yearning that cries out for the life we prize. It is elusive, to be sure. It seems to come and go at will. Seasons may pass until it surfaces again. And though it seems to taunt us, and may at times cause us great pain, we know when it returns that it is priceless. For if we could recover this desire, unearth it from beneath all other distractions, and embrace it as our deepest treasure, we would discover the secret of our existence.

You see, life comes to all of us as a mystery. We all share the same dilemma—we long for life and we're not sure where to find it. We wonder if we ever do find it, can we make it last? The longing for life within us seems incongruent with the life we find around us. What is available seems at times close to what we want, but never quite a fit. Our days come to us as a riddle, and the answers aren't handed out with our birth certificates. We must journey to find the life we prize. And the guide we have been given is the desire set deep within, the desire we often overlook or mistake for something else or even choose to ignore.

The greatest human tragedy is to give up the search. Nothing is of greater importance than the life of our deep heart. To lose heart is to lose everything. And if we are to bring our hearts along in our life's journey, we simply must not, we cannot, abandon this desire. Gerald May writes in *The Awakened Heart*,

> There is a desire within each of us, in the deep center of ourselves that we call our heart. We were born with it, it is never completely satisfied, and it never dies. We are often unaware of it, but it is always awake . . . Our true identity, our reason for being, is to be found in this desire.

The clue as to who we really are and why we are here comes to us through our heart's desire. But it comes in surprising ways, and often goes unnoticed or is misunderstood. Once in a while life comes together for us in a way that feels good and right and what we've been waiting for. These are the moments in our lives that we wish could go on forever. They aren't necessarily the

"Kodak moments," weddings and births and great achievements. More often than not they come in subtler, unexpected ways, as if to sneak up on us.

Think of times in your life that made you wish for all the world that you had the power to make time stand still. Are they not moments of love, moments of joy? Simple moments of rest and quiet when all seems to be well. Something in your heart says, *Finally—it has come. This is what I was made for!*

WHISPERS OF JOY

It was the final evening of our summer vacation. We had spent nine wonderful days in the Tetons hiking and swimming, laughing and playing, enjoying rare and wonderful time together as a family in a stunningly beautiful place. During our explorations, we had discovered a quiet pond in the woods, about a half hour's walk from camp, where wildlife would often come in the evening. This night, we planned to arrive at dusk and stay until night fell to see what nature might reveal. The sun was setting behind us as we arrived, and far off in the east massive thunderheads were building above the Absarokas, cloud upon cloud, giant castles in the sky. The fading day was slowly turning them peach, then pink, then gray.

A pair of trumpeter swans were swimming across our little pond, looking for all the world like something from a fairy tale. My wife and I sat together with our three boys on a spot of grass near the water's edge, our backs against a fallen log. Across the pond lay a meadow, the stage for the evening's drama. As light began to fade, a bull moose with a massive rack emerged from the willows directly across the meadow from where we sat. He spotted us and stopped; we held our breath. Silently, he disappeared into the trees as mysteriously as he had come. Before we could be disappointed, a cow moose and her calf appeared from another part of the meadow, wandering along grazing. We watched them as night continued to fall.

A cool breeze stirred the pines above us. Crickets began their twilight chorus. The cow lay down in the tall grass, but we could still see her calf. Sandhill cranes were calling and answering one another around the marsh with their haunting, primeval cries. The boys huddled closer to us. A beaver swam by our feet, making a V through the surface of the pond, faded with the light to a gunmetal gray. Far off in the distance, lightning was beginning within those cloud fortresses, flashes of glory. A small herd of elk came out to graze at the far end of the meadow, just as darkness was settling in. Finally, as if not to be left out, a lone coyote began to howl. It was one of the most breathtaking nights I have ever experienced in the wilderness, a living work of art. As the Scottish poet George MacDonald knew so well, something is calling to us in moments like these.

> Yet hints come to me from the realm unknown;
> Airs drift across the twilight border land,
> Odored with life;
> . . . whispers to my heart are blown
> That fill me with a joy I cannot speak,
> Yea, from whose shadow words drop faint and weak.
>
> (*Diary of an Old Soul*)

I know these years are passing quickly, and the time will come when our boys will no longer want to vacation with us. They will find other loves and form other ties, and our lives will never be the same again. Sitting there with them in the woods, clutching their flashlights, whispering to each other about each passing mystery, I would have given anything to stop the clock, turn it back if only for a few days, let us live it all again. But the seasons pass with or without our permission, and I knew in my heart we could not stay. For a moment, we were all caught up in something bigger and more beautiful than we had ever known, "suspended above the earth," as Norman MacLean says, "free from all its laws, like a work of art. And I knew just as surely and just as clearly, that life is not a work of art, and that the moment could not last."

ECHOES FROM THE PAST

Sometimes these moments go unrecognized as they unfold, but their secret comes to us years later in our longing to relive them. Aren't there times in your life that if you could, you would love to return to? I grew up in Los Angeles but spent my boyhood summers in Oregon where both my mother's and my father's parents lived. There was a beauty and innocence and excitement to those days. Woods to explore, rivers to fish, grandparents to fuss over me. My parents were young and in love, and the days were full of adventures I did not have to create or pay for, but only live in and enjoy. Rafting and swimming in the Rogue River. Playing in the park. Huckleberry pie at Becky's along the road to Crater Lake. We all have places in our past when life, if only for a moment, seemed to be coming together in the way we knew in our hearts it was always meant to be.

> There was a time when meadow, grove, and stream,
> The earth, and every common sight,
> To me did seem
> Appareled in celestial light,
> The glory and the freshness of a dream . . .
> Heaven lies about us in our infancy;

9

Shades of the prison-house begin to close
Upon the growing boy,
But he beholds the light, and whence it flows.
He sees it in his joy; . . .
At length the man perceives it die away,
And fade into the light of common day.
(*Ode, Intimations of Immortality from Recollection of Childhood*)

Wordsworth caught a glimpse of the secret in his childhood, saw in it hints from the realm unknown. We must learn the lesson of these moments, or we will not be able to bring our hearts along in our life's journey. For if these moments pass, never to be recovered again, then the life we prize is always fading from view, and our hearts with it. It isn't until the kids are out of the house that you realize how precious were those years. The inflatable pool in the backyard. The stockings hung up at Christmastime. First steps and first home runs and first dates. We fill photo albums with all these moments, trying to hang on to them somehow. We hate to see them slip away. Our losses seem to say that the life we prize will never be ours, never come to stay. But the secret is coming to us even in our greatest losses.

SHOUTS OF LAMENT

I did not know how much Brent meant to me until I lost him. He was killed last year at this time, in a climbing accident. We had taken a group of men to the mountains on a retreat, believing that to help a man recover his heart, you must take him out of the office, away from the television, and into the wild. We planned three days at a ranch in Colorado where we would bring rock climbing, fly-fishing, and horseback riding together with talks on the journey of a man's heart. Brent was leading the climbing on day two when he fell. The loss was unspeakable for many, many people. Ginny lost her husband. Ben and Drew lost their daddy. Many people lost the only man who had ever fought for their hearts.

I lost the truest friend I have ever known. Brent was more than my partner; he was for me the rarest of gifts—his heart saw what mine saw. Our friendship was a shared journey, a mutual quest, for the secret of our souls. It took us into the mountains, into literature and music, into the desperate battle raging all around for the hearts of others as well. We laughed and grieved and scorned and yearned all along the way. When he lost his son in a mountaineering accident, Nicholas Wolterstorff wrote,

> There's a hole in the world now . . . A center, like no other, of memory and hope and knowledge and affection which once inhabited this earth is gone. Only a gap remains. A perspective in this world unique in this world which once moved about in this world has been rubbed out . . . There's nobody who saw just what he saw, knows what he knew, remembers what he remembered, loves what he loved . . . Questions I have can never now get answers. The world is emptier. (*Lament for a Son*)

This is silly, really, and a little embarrassing, but I find myself turning suddenly when I see a silver gray Jeep pass by. I look to see if it is his, if he is there. Brent is gone; I know that. How I know that. But still, I find myself doing a double take when I see a Jeep like his. Something rises in me, something beyond reason. A hope that perhaps it is his, that he is driving past me again. The other day I was in a parking lot and saw a beat-up old Cherokee with a rack on top. I stopped, went over, and looked. I know in my head that this is ridiculous. Brent is gone. But my heart refuses at some level to accept it. Or rather, my yearning for things to be right is so strong that it overrides my logic and turns my head, in hope against hope, every time.

"The heart," Blaise Pascal said, "has its reasons which reason knows not of." Something in us longs, hopes, maybe even at times believes that this is not the way things were supposed to be. Our desire fights the assault of death upon life. And so people with terminal illnesses get married. Prisoners in a concentration camp plant flowers. Lovers long divorced still reach out in the night to embrace one who is no longer there. It's like the phantom pain experienced by those who have lost a limb. Feelings still emanate from that region where once was a crucial part of them, and they will sometimes find themselves being careful not to bang the corner of a table or slam the car door on a leg or an arm long since removed. Our hearts know a similar reality. At some deep level, we refuse to accept the fact that this is the way things are, or must be, or always will be.

Simone Weil was right; there are only two things that pierce the human heart: beauty and affliction. Moments we wish would last forever and moments we wish had never begun. What are we to make of these messengers? How are we to interpret what they are saying? The playwright Christopher Fry writes,

> The inescapable dramatic situation for us all is that we have no idea what our situation is. We may be mortal. What then? We may be immortal. What then? We are plunged into an existence fantastic to the point of nightmare, and however hard we rationalize, or however firm our religious faith, however closely we dog the heels of science or wheel among the starts of mysticism, we cannot really make head or tail of it. ("A Playwright Speaks: How Lost, How Amazed, How Miraculous We Are")

And what does Fry say we do with our dilemma? The worst of all possible reactions:

We get used to it. We get broken into it so gradually we scarcely notice it.

THE SAME OLD THING

Something awful has happened; something terrible. Something worse, even, than the fall of man. For in that greatest of all tragedies, we merely lost Paradise—and with it, everything that made life worth living. What has happened since is unthinkable: we've gotten used to it. We're broken in to the idea that this is just the way things are. The people who walk in great darkness have adjusted their eyes. Regardless of our religious or philosophical beliefs, most of us live as though this life is pretty much the way things are supposed to be. We dismiss the whispers of joy with a cynical "Been there, done that, bought the T-shirt." That way we won't have to deal with the haunting.

I was just talking with some friends about summer vacations, and I recommended that they visit the Tetons. "Oh, yeah, we've been there. Nice place." Dismissal. And we deaden our sorrows with cynicism as well, sporting a bumper sticker that says, "Life sucks. Then you die." Then we try to get on with life. We feed the cat, pay the bills, watch the news, and head off to bed, so we can do it all again tomorrow.

Standing before the open fridge, I'm struck by what I've just watched. Famine in Africa. Genocide . . . where? Someplace I can't even pronounce. I think it used to be part of the Soviet bloc. Corruption in Washington. Life as usual. It always ends with the anchor folding his notes and offering a pleasant "Good night." Good night? That's it? You have nothing else to say? You've just regaled us with the horrors of the world we live in, and all you can say is "Good night"? To be fair, he did promise more details—with film—at eleven. Just once I wish he would pause at the close of his report, take a long, deep breath, and then say, "How far we are from home," or "If only we had listened," or "Thank God, our sojourn here is drawing to an end." It never happens. I doubt it ever will. And not one of us gives it a second thought. It's just the way things are. Anytime I ask my neighbor how life is going, he always replies, "Same old thing."

Think with me for a moment. How has life turned out differently from the way you thought it would? If you are single, did you want to be? If you are married, is this the marriage you hoped for? Do you long to have children, or in having them, are you delighted with the course they've chosen for their lives? Your friendships—are they as rich and deep and lasting as you want? When the holidays roll around, do you look forward with eager anticipation to the time you'll spend with the people in your life? And afterward, as you pack away the decorations and clean up the mess, did the reality match your expectations?

How about your work, your place in the world—do you go to bed each night with a deep sense of having made a lasting contribution? Do you enjoy ongoing recognition for your unique successes? Are you even working in a field that fits you? Are you working at all? Now, what if I told you that this is how it will always be, that this life as you now experience it will go on forever just as it is, without improvement of any kind? Your health will stay as it is; your finances will remain as they are, your relationships, your work, all of it.

It is hell.

IN DEFENSE OF DISCONTENT

By the grace of God, we cannot quite pull it off. In the quiet moments of the day we sense a nagging within, a discontent, a hunger for something else. But because we have not solved the riddle of our existence, we assume that something is wrong—not with life, but with us. *Everyone else seems to be getting on with things. What's wrong with me?* We feel guilty about our chronic disappointment. *Why can't I just learn to be happier in my job, in my marriage, in my church, in my group of friends?* You see, even while we are doing other things, "getting on with life," we still have an eye out for the life we secretly want. When someone seems to have gotten it together, we wonder, *How did he do it?* Maybe if we read the same book, spent time with him, went to his church, things would come together for us as well. We can never entirely give up our quest. May reminds us,

> When the desire is too much to bear, we often bury it beneath frenzied thoughts and activities or escape it by dulling our immediate consciousness of living. It is possible to run away from the desire for years, even decades, at a time, but we cannot eradicate it entirely. It keeps touching us in little glimpses and hints in our dreams, our hopes, our unguarded moments. (*The Awakened Heart*)

He says that even though we sleep, our desire does not. "It is who we are." We *are desire*. It is the essence of the human soul, the secret of our existence. Absolutely nothing of human greatness is ever accomplished without it. Not a symphony has been written, a mountain climbed, an injustice fought, or a love sustained apart from desire. Desire fuels our search for the life we prize. Our desire, if we will listen to it, will save us from committing soul-suicide, the sacrifice of our hearts on the altar of "getting by." The same old thing is not enough. It never will be.

The secret that begins to solve the riddle of our lives is simply this: we are the sea lion who lost the sea. Life as usual is not the life we truly want. It is not the life we truly need. It is not the life we were made for. If we would only listen to our hearts, to what G. K. Chesterton called our "divine discontent," we would learn the secret of our existence. As he wrote in *Orthodoxy*, "We have come to the wrong star . . . That is what makes life at once so splendid and so strange. The true happiness is that we *don't* fit. We come from somewhere else. We have lost our way."

The meaning of our lives is revealed through experiences that at first seem at odds with each other—moments we wish would never end and moments we wish had never begun. Those timeless experiences we want to last forever whisper to us that *they were meant to*. We were made to live in a world of beauty and wonder, intimacy and adventure all our days. Nathaniel Hawthorne insisted, "Our Creator would never have made such lovely days, and given us the deep hearts to enjoy them, above and beyond all thought, unless we were meant to be immortal."

There is more to these days than pictures tucked away in photo albums, fading as the memory fades from view. We use a statement to try to console ourselves with what we think is the irrecoverable loss: "All good things come to an end." I hate that phrase. It's a lie. Even our troubles and our heartbreaks tell us something about our true destiny. The tragedies that strike us to the core and elicit the cry, "This isn't the way it was supposed to be!" are also telling the truth—it *isn't* the way it was supposed to be. Pascal writes,

> Man is so great that his greatness appears even in knowing himself to be miserable. A tree has no sense of its misery. It is true that to know we are miserable is to be miserable; but to know we are miserable is also to be great. Thus all the miseries of man prove his grandeur; they are the miseries of a dignified personage, the miseries of a dethroned monarch . . . What can this incessant craving, and this impotence of attainment mean,

unless there was once a happiness belonging to man, of which only the faintest traces remain, in that void which he attempts to fill with everything within his reach? (*Pensées*)

Should the king in exile pretend he is happy there? Should he not seek his own country? His miseries are his ally; they urge him on. Let them grow, if need be. But do not forsake the secret of life; do not despise those kingly desires. We abandon the most important journey of our lives when we abandon desire. We leave our hearts by the side of the road and head off in the direction of fitting in, getting by, being productive, what have you. Whatever we might gain—money, position, the approval of others, or just absence of the discontent itself—it's not worth it. "What good will it be for a man if he gains the whole world, yet forfeits his soul?" (Matt. 16:26 NIV).

TAKING UP THE QUEST

We must return to the journey. Wherever we are, whatever we are doing, we must pick up the trail and follow the map that we have at hand. Desire, both the whispers and the shouts, is the map we have been given to find the only life worth living. You may think you are following the map of desire when all you are doing is serving it slavishly, unthinkingly. It is not the same. We must *listen* to desire, look at it carefully, let it guide us through the false routes and dead ends. C. S. Lewis advises us,

I knew only too well how easily the longing accepts false objects and through what dark ways the pursuit of them leads us. But I also saw that the Desire itself contains the corrective of all these errors. The only fatal error was to pretend you had passed from desire to fruition, when, in reality, you had found either nothing, or desire itself, or the satisfaction of some different desire. The dialectic of Desire, faithfully followed, would retrieve all mistakes, head you off from all false paths, and force you to live through . . . a sort of [experiential] proof. (*The Pilgrim's Regress*)

The only fatal error is to pretend that we have found the life we prize. To mistake the water hole for the sea. To settle for the same old thing. Fry called such a life "the sleep of prisoners." You might remember the movie *The Shawshank Redemption*, the story of prison life in the Northeast in the 1940s. The film focuses on the journey of two men's hearts through the trials and temptations of incarceration. Red, the ringleader and most seasoned of the prisoners, explains what happens when you live within those walls too long: "At first, these walls, you hate them. They make you crazy. After a while you get used to 'em, don't notice 'em anymore. Then comes the day you realize you need them." That is the most tragic day of all—to prefer slavery to freedom, to prefer death to life. We must not stay in this sleep. The time has come for us to wake, to arise from our slumber. As the Scriptures say, "Wake up, O sleeper, rise from the dead" (Eph. 5:14 NIV). And so MacDonald prayed,

> When I can no more stir my soul to move,
> And life is but the ashes of a fire;
> When I can but remember that my heart
> Once used to live and love, long and aspire—
> Oh, be thou then the first, the one thou art;
> Be thou the calling, before all answering love,
> And in me wake hope, fear, boundless desire.
> (*Diary of an Old Soul*)

Bringing our heart along in our life's journey is the most important mission of our lives—and the hardest. It all turns on what we do with our desire. If you will look around, you will see that most people have abandoned the journey. They have lost heart. They are camped in places of resignation or indulgence, or trapped in prisons of despair. I understand; I have frequented all those places before and return to them even still. Life provides any number of reasons and occasions to abandon desire. Certainly, one of the primary reasons is that it creates for us our deepest dilemmas. To desire something and not to have it—is this not the source of nearly all our pain and sorrow?

THERE WAS A time, many years back, when the sea lion knew he was lost. In those days, he would stop every traveler he met to see if he might help him find his way back to the sea.

But no one seemed to know the way.

On he searched, but never finding. After years without success, the sea lion took refuge beneath a solitary tree beside a very small water hole. The tree provided refuge from the burning rays of the sun, which was very fierce in that place. And the water hole, though small and muddy, was wet, in its own way. Here he settled down and got on as best he could.

CHAPTER TWO

THE DILEMMA
OF DESIRE

I never knew the dusk could break my heart
So much longing folding in
I'd give years away to have you here
To know I can't lose you again.

—FERNANDO ORTEGA

Who needs a heart when a heart can be broken?
—TINA TURNER

I am almost committing an indecency. I am trying to rip open the
inconsolable secret in each one of you—the secret which hurts so
much that you take your revenge on it by calling it names like
Nostalgia and Romanticism and Adolescence.

—C. S. LEWIS

High on the slopes of the world's tallest mountain, slightly less than twenty-nine thousand feet above the level of the sea, the climber has halted in his tracks. He can go no farther. His whole life has come down to this. After years of planning and preparation, he has trekked halfway across the globe to a strange country high in the Himalayas. He has drained his bank account and damaged his relationships. His career has suffered. He has sacrificed everything in his life for this moment. But none of that matters now. He is exhausted. His breathing is labored. He is forced to pause after each step for three heaving breaths, followed by another step, then a pause. As he creeps along a razor's edge of snow, each move requires an agonizing amount of concentration. Oxygen deprivation reduces his mental faculties to those of a small child. Ahead of him rises the Hillary Step, a forty-foot wall of nearly vertical ice. It is all that stands between him and the goal of his life. But he is not sure he can go on.

I am haunted by the stories of people who make the summit of Everest. Such incredible devotion is required, such total focus of body, soul, and spirit. Reaching the top of the world's tallest mountain becomes for those who try the central driving force of their lives. The goal is remarkable and the journey uncertain. Many climbers have been lost on the mountain. Those who reach the summit and return safely are among a rare and elite group of mountaineers in the world. Why do they do it? *How* do they do it?

Jon Krakauer recounted the desperate tale of the ill-fated '96 expedition in his book *Into Thin Air:* "There were many, many fine reasons not to go, but attempting to climb Everest is an intrinsically irrational act—a triumph of desire over sensibility." It is a feat begun in desire that can be accomplished only through desire. Krakauer explained how one of his climbing partners attained the summit: "Yasuko had been propelled up the mountain by the unwavering intensity of her desire."

Desire—it's the only way you will ever make it. Take marriage, for instance. Or singleness. Either makes for a far more difficult and arduous ascent than Everest, in large part because it does not seem so. The struggles are not heightened and focused into one month of do or die; rather, they stretch on across a lifetime. So it is with any act of faith or of hope—anything, in other words, that makes a life worth living. How can we possibly sustain such an intrinsically irrational act as love if we've killed our desire? May honestly admits,

> Choosing love will open spaces of immense beauty and joy for you, but you will be hurt. You already know this. You have retreated from love countless times in your life because of it. We all have. We have been and will be hurt by the loss of loved ones, by what they have done to us and we to them. Even in the bliss of love there is a certain exquisite pain: the pain of too much beauty, of overwhelming magnificence. Further, no matter how perfect a love may be, it is never really satisfied . . . In both joy and pain, love is boundless. (*The Awakened Heart*)

Desire is the source of our most noble aspirations and our deepest sorrows. The pleasure and the pain go together; indeed, they emanate from the same region in our hearts. We cannot live without the yearning, and yet the yearning sets us up for disappointment—sometimes deep and devastating disappointment. One storm claimed the lives of eight of Krakauer's companions in the Everest disaster of 1996. Should they not have tried? Many have said they were foolish even to begin. Do we reach for nothing in life because our reaching opens us up to tragedy? Because of its vulnerable nature, desire begins to feel like our worst enemy.

FRIEND OR FOE?

"I'm beginning to despise the hope." We were talking about life, a friend and I, and how hard it was to keep pressing on. David had been through a series of setbacks in his career, going from earning a six-figure income at a top Wall Street firm to driving a courier van, making deliveries. It's the hardest fall a man takes. He didn't want to be there; he wanted to climb out of the slump he was in. Occasionally, an opportunity would present itself. He'd get a call or a contact through a friend. Putting on a coat and tie, David would head out into the arena. The desire for something better would resurface, only to be thwarted. The interview seemed to go well at the time, but then he'd sit by the phone and the call would never come. Each time he reached for a rung up the ladder, the rung broke, and he found himself back at the bottom. After several years of the cycle, he found himself despising hope. "It just sets me up for another fall. Why bother?"

I think of another friend, Carol, whose life has been marked over the years by one disappointing relationship after another. Just when she is ready to call it quits on loving altogether, hope appears on the horizon. She ventures out cautiously. And several months later, her heart is broken again. Over lunch yesterday she used nearly the same words: "I hate hope." Hope rouses the desire from its slumber and makes us even more vulnerable to disappointment.

As Carol and I spoke about life and love, I thought of Fantine, one of the tragic characters in Victor Hugo's novel *Les Misérables*. Fantine is a young single mother who works in a factory to support her daughter, whom she had to send away to live with an innkeeper. Fired for refusing the sexual advances of the foreman, she finds herself on the streets without a job, a place to stay, or a means of caring for her child. Those of you who have seen the musical will recall the hauntingly beautiful song she sings, entitled "I Dreamed a Dream."

> I had a dream in time gone by
> When hope was high

> And life worth living
> I dreamed that love would never die
> I dreamed that God would be forgiving.

She remembers being young and unafraid, that time in our lives when dreams are "made and used and wasted." She tells of a love that came to her, filling her days with endless wonder. He became the father of her child and then, one day, disappeared. She dreams he will return, but knows he never will. I know too many women who have lived through this nightmare. Their lives are filled with weariness, loneliness, and resignation. Fantine ends by singing,

> I had a dream my life would be
> So different from this hell I'm living
> So different now from what it seemed
> Now life has killed the dream I dreamed.

WHEN DREAMS DIE

I understand. I know the dilemma of desire. Brent was killed on the doorstep of our dreams. You see, as our friendship deepened over the years, we discovered within us a similar hope. Long before I met him, I had begun to dream of having a ranch where people could come to recover their hearts, a place of beauty and adventure where one could learn about life's journey. I was shy to even mention it; heaven knows I had hidden it from everyone for years. How stunned with delight I was to find that he held the same desire. C. S. Lewis knew:

Are not all lifelong friendships born at the moment when at last you meet another human being who has some inkling . . .

25

of that something which you were born desiring, and which, beneath the flux of other desires and in all the momentary silences between the louder passions, night and day, year by year, from childhood to old age, you are looking for, watching for, listening for? (*The Problem of Pain*)

God seemed to be affirming that dream as we partnered together, speaking at conferences, writing, counseling. Still, it felt like courage even to allow ourselves to dream. We had both known enough disappointment in our lives to be wary of hope; maybe we'd both grown more than a little resigned. Both of us had been failed deeply by key men in our lives. Dare we trust?

Yet something deeper in us urged us to move forward. Alexander Pope knew that "hope springs eternal in the human breast." We planned to begin this great ascent of our desire last May, inviting a small group of men to join us on a ranch for a long weekend of conversation and adventure. It would be the inaugural voyage, the test flight for our dream. On the afternoon of the second day, Brent was killed. The rocks on which he was standing eighty feet above the ground crumbled beneath him.

"Despair," wrote James Houston, "is the fate of the desiring soul." Or as Scripture says, "Hope deferred makes the heart sick" (Prov. 13:12 NLT). How agonizing it can be to awaken desire! Over the past year I have wrestled deeply with what it means to go on. God has come to me again and again, insisting that I not give up the dream. I have ranted and railed, fought him and dismissed him. It feels crazy to desire anymore. What does it mean to live the rest of my life without my closest friend? I think of Lewis and Clark, those inseparable wilderness explorers, how we cannot think of one without the other. Lewis said of his companion, "I could neither hope, wish, nor expect from a union with any man on earth, more perfect support or further aid in the discharge of my mission, than that, which I am confident I shall derive from being associated with yourself." I know I shall never find another like him.

But I am not alone in this. Most of you will by this time have lost a parent, a spouse, even a child. Your hopes for your career have not panned out. Your health has given way. Relationships have turned sour. We all know the dilemma of desire, how awful it feels to open our hearts to joy, only to have grief come in. They go together. We know that. What we don't know is what to do with it, how to live in this world with desire so deep in us and disappointment lurking behind every corner. After we've taken a few arrows, dare we even desire?

I have come to the point that I am able to start looking at ranches again, but I can barely open myself to friendship. Still, something in me knows that to kill desire is to kill my heart altogether. Langston Hughes wrote,

> Hold fast to dreams
> For if dreams die
> Life is a broken-winged bird
> That cannot fly.
> Hold fast to dreams
> For when dreams go
> Life is a barren field
> Frozen with snow. ("Dreams")

Do we form no friendships because our friends might be taken from us? Do we refuse to love because we may be hurt? Do we forsake our dreams because hope has been deferred? To desire is to open our hearts to the possibility of pain; to shut down our hearts is to die altogether. The full proverb reads this way:

"Hope deferred makes the heart sick, *but when dreams come true, there is life and joy*."

The road to life and joy lies through, not around, the heart-sickness of hope deferred. A good friend came to this realization recently. As we sat talking over breakfast, he put words to our dilemma: "I stand at the crossroads, and I am afraid of the desire. For forty-one years I've tried to control my life by killing the desire, but I can't. Now I know it. But to allow it to be, to let it out is frightening because I know I'll have to give up the control of my life. Is there another option?"

The option most of us have chosen is to reduce our desire to a more manageable size. We allow it out only in small doses—just what we can arrange for. Dinner out, a new sofa, a vacation to look forward to, a little too much to drink. It's not working. The tremors of the earthquake inside are beginning to break out.

THE BATTLE BETWEEN US

I haven't been the friendliest driver lately. Oh, I'm fine—until I'm provoked. When people cut me off, I'm furious. Just the other day, a car began to get on the highway as I was passing by. The fellow ignored all the rules of merging and cut in front of me as I was doing full speed. I hit my brakes to avoid him and honked my horn. He looked back, snarled, and yelled something unprintable. That did it. Only the fear of higher insurance premiums kept me from running him off the road. But oh, how I wanted to. Of course, this never happens to you. You are kind and benevolent when someone cuts you off. Why, you're practically happy when he steals your parking place, darts in right ahead of you. You smile and offer a blessing.

What is causing the quarrels and fights among you? Isn't it the whole army of evil desires at war within you? You want what you don't have, so you scheme and kill to get it. You are jealous for what others have, and you can't possess it, so you fight and quarrel to take it away from them. (James 4:1–2 NLT)

What do you make of all the road rage that's been surfacing? You don't think it's really about traffic etiquette, do you? People are shooting at each other on the freeway. This is not about bad manners or a need for driver's ed. There is something deeper, something pent up inside us. The fellow who cut me off didn't really endanger my life; but the violation felt like a symbol of a deeper, ongoing reality. Dan Allender points out,

> In every person there is a passionate, driving desire for more . . . The dilemma is that our longings for material joy are almost always partially blocked; our desires for better health and deeper relationships are never entirely possible; and the illusion of world peace seems no more attainable than the gold at the end of the rainbow. Our passion is more than usually stymied. The world simply does not bend to the desires that roar or whimper inside us. Our desires—from picking the quickest line at the bank to the overwhelming hope that our children will walk righteously with the Lord—are rarely satisfied in a way that relieves the ache of incompleteness . . . Our heart seems to rage against the ache. Our typical response to the heartbreak and sorrow of disappointment is murderous rage . . . We want someone to pay. (*Bold Love*)

The life we have is so far from the life we truly want, and it doesn't take us long to find someone to blame. In order for our longings to be filled, we need the cooperation of others. I long for a loving embrace and a kind word when I get home. I long for my boys to listen attentively when I talk about important life lessons. I want my work to be appreciated. I want my friends to be there for me in hard times. "No man is an island," wrote John Donne, and he could have been speaking of desire. We need others—it's part of our design. Very few of our desires are self-fulfilling; all our deepest longings require others to come through for us. Inevitably, someone stands in the way.

At its best, the world is indifferent to my desires. The air traffic controllers aren't the least affected when I've been traveling for a week and the plane they've chosen to cancel is my last chance to get home to my family. So long as it doesn't affect them, they couldn't care less. We suffer the violation of indifference on a daily basis, from friends, from family, from complete strangers. We think we've grown to accept it as part of life, but the effect is building inside us. We weren't made to be ignored. And though we try to pretend it doesn't really matter, the collective effect of living in a world apathetic to our existence is doing damage to our souls. Events such as bad traffic or delayed flights are merely the *occasions* for our true desperation to come out. As our desires come into direct conflict with the desires of another person, things get downright hostile.

We fought the Gulf War because Saddam Hussein wanted the rich oil fields of Kuwait. Phil and Diane fought the bedroom war over pork chops. They had invited another couple for dinner, and as Diane went out for the afternoon, she asked Phil to get the pork chops out of the freezer to thaw. He was working on the lawn mower and forgot. Dinnertime arrived, and Diane asked Phil to put the chops on the grill. He suddenly remembered that they were still hard as rocks in the freezer. You know the phrase "if looks could kill"? Diane couldn't say what she wanted to say. Their guests were sitting right there, and she had an image to maintain. She let Phil have it with a look and later that night finished the job off when they were alone.

Søren Kierkegaard said that resentment is the "constituent principle" of the modern era, this simmering anger at our blocked desires. We shove them beneath the surface for as long as possible, only to have them erupt on the freeway, in the classroom, or at home in a burst of physical or verbal retaliation. Our anger is rarely proportionate to the event. I yelled at my five-year-old son, Luke, at dinner tonight because he was being disrespectful to his mom. But is that all that was behind my stern rebuke? Aren't events like that the triggers, opening the doors to a reservoir of disappointment we pretend for the most part we have risen above? We try to get beyond the pain of desire by burying it, but it does not go away. It surfaces in other ways.

And so, Scripture says, we find ourselves in a civil war of desire. The horrors of this war go well beyond spoiled dinners and a little marital tension. We will sacrifice anything on the altar of our anger, the rage that is slowly building from a lifetime of thwarted desire—our marriages, our child's self-esteem, someone's very life. At the same moment that Krakauer's companions were battling for their lives on Everest's southeast ridge, three Indian climbers were stranded by the storm on the other side of the mountain as they attempted the summit from the northeast. Unable to work their way down, they spent the night on the face of the mountain without shelter in a howling blizzard. The following morning, two Japanese climbers ascending by the same route came across the climbers, now near death. They offered no assistance; no food or water, no bottled oxygen. They didn't even speak to them, but stepped aside and took their rest a few hundred feet beyond. The Japanese climbers made the summit; then they left the Indians to die as they passed them again on their way back down.

There is a reason Jesus chose lust and murder as examples of what happens when desire goes mad within us. He knew what our desperate hearts naturally do when our desires come into conflict. He knew to what lengths we would go to seek satisfaction of our soul's hunger. For the battle of desire rages not only between us, but *within* us.

THE BEAST WITHIN

Jeremy called and asked to see me to talk about "a little financial problem" he was having. I told him, sure, I could spare an hour of my Saturday. I thought he might need a small loan or some help with his checkbook. But when I saw the look on his face, I knew an hour wasn't going to be enough. Jeremy's little problem was that he had taken every credit card he owned to the limit, accumulating thousands of dollars in debt. Knowing he was unemployed at the time, with no prospect at all of paying off such a load, he was panic-stricken. "Good grief," I asked, "how did it happen?" The story proved more outrageous than the debt. He had booked himself a week at a five-star resort. Posing as a wealthy physician, Jeremy entertained a variety of women—"gold diggers"—purchasing their affections with lavish gifts and gourmet dinners. By the end of his self-created fantasy island trip he had lost his integrity and about ten thousand dollars.

I would never have believed it unless he himself had told me, through tears of shame and regret. He is a quiet and unassuming man, the complete opposite of some jet-setting gigolo. No one would have dreamed he was capable of such a thing. But then again, we wonder: *What am I capable of? Dare I even begin to feel my desire?* We may not go so far, but we know that there is a ravenous beast within us. Years of living in an indifferent and often hostile world create a deep sense of unsettledness within us. A friend asked the other day: "How important are feelings of desire? I ask because I have a seeming overabundance of desire, but it sometimes goes astray in a crazed and hopeless pursuit of brownies or something of the sort."

> Something has gone wrong deep within me and gets the better of me every time. It happens so regularly that it's predictable. The moment I decide to do good, sin is there to trip me up. I truly delight in God's commands, but it's pretty obvious that not all of me joins in that delight. Parts of me covertly rebel, and just when I least expect it, they take charge. (Rom. 7:20–23 *The Message*)

> For the sinful nature desires what is contrary to the Spirit, and the Spirit what is contrary to the sinful nature. They are in conflict with each other, so that you do not do what you want. (Gal. 5:17 NIV)

There is a nagging awareness inside us, warning that we'd better not feel our hunger too deeply or it will undo us. We might do something crazed, desperate. We are caught on the horns of a dilemma; our unmet desires are a source of trouble, and it feels as if it will get worse if we allow ourselves to feel how much we do desire. Not only that, we often don't even know what we desire. Dan, a passionate young friend now finishing college, just sent this e-mail:

> Chris McCandless wrote, "All hail the Phantom Bear, the beast within us all." Well the "Bear" so to speak has really been growling loud as of late. I seem to be daily wanting more out of my life than what I have been living. Leo Tolstoy wrote, "I felt in myself a superabundance of energy which found no outlet in my quiet life." And that really describes me well. I want more . . .

more of God in my life . . . more intimacy with my friends . . . and I feel bad for wanting it. Everyone seems so content here and simple . . . and also I feel like I'm longing for nothing I'm certain of.

We try food, tennis, television, or sex, going from one thing to another, never quite finding satisfaction. The reason we don't know what we want is that we're so *unacquainted* with our desire. We try to keep a safe distance between our daily lives and our heart's desire because it causes us so much trouble. We're surprised by our anger and threatened by what feels like a ravenous bear within us. Do we really want to open Pandora's box? If you remember the Greek myth, Pandora was the wife of Epimetheus, given to him by Zeus. The gods provided many gifts to her, including a mysterious box, which she was warned never to open. Eventually, her curiosity got the better of her, and she lifted the lid. Immediately, a host of evils flew out, plagues against the mind and body of mankind. She tried to close the box, but to no avail; the troubles had been loosed.

Dare we awaken our hearts to their true desires? Dare we come alive? Is it better, as the saying goes, to have loved and lost than never to have loved at all? We're not so sure. After his divorce, a friend's father decided to remain single the rest of his life. He told his son, "It's easier to stay out than to get out." Our dilemma is this: we can't seem to live with desire, and we can't live without it. In the face of this quandary most people decide to bury the whole question and put as much distance as they can between themselves and their desires. It is a logical and tragic act. The tragedy is increased tenfold when this suicide of soul is committed under the conviction that this is precisely what Christianity recommends. We have never been more mistaken.

⟶ HAD YOU JOURNEYED *in those days through the barren lands, you might have seen the sea lion for yourself. Quite often in the evening, he would go and sit upon his favorite rock, a very large boulder, which lifted him off the burning sand and allowed him a view of the entire country.*

There he would remain for hours into the night, silhouetted against the sky. And on the best nights, when the wind shifted to the east, a faint smell of salt air would come to him on the breeze. Then he would close his eyes and imagine himself once more at the sea. When he lay himself down to sleep, he would dream of a vast, deep ocean. Twisting and turning, diving and twirling, he would swim and swim and swim. When he woke, he thought he heard the sound of breakers.

The sea was calling to him.

CHAPTER THREE

Dare We Desire?

But for real proof you must look at your own longings and aspirations; you must listen to the deep themes of your own life story.

—GERALD MAY

Longing is the heart's treasury.

—AUGUSTINE

What do you want?

—JESUS OF NAZARETH

The shriveled figure lay in the sun like a pile of rags dumped there by accident. It hardly appeared to be human. But those who used the gate to go in and out of Jerusalem recognized him. It was his spot and had been for as long as anyone could remember. He was disabled, dropped off there every morning by someone in his family, and picked up again at the end of the day. Over the years, a sort of gallery of human brokenness gathered by the pool of Bethesda—the lame, the blind, the deaf, lepers, you name it. A rumor was going around that sometimes (no one really knew when) an angel would stir the waters, and the first one in would be healed. Sort of a lottery, if you will. And as with every lottery, the desperate gathered round, hoping for a miracle. So—technically speaking—the man

37

was never alone. But it had been so long since anyone had actually *spoken* to him, he thought the question was meant for someone else. Squinting upward into the sun, he didn't recognize the figure standing above him. The misshapen man asked the fellow to repeat himself; perhaps he had misheard. Although the voice was kind, the question felt harsh, even cruel.

"Do you want to get well?"

He sat speechless, blinking into the sun. Slowly, the words seeped into his consciousness, like a voice calling him out of a dream. *Do I want to get well?* Slowly, like a wheel long rusted, his mind began to turn over. *What kind of question is that? Why else would I be lying here? Why else would I have spent every day for the past thirty-eight seasons lying here? He is mocking me.* The man was familiar with mockery and had endured his share of ridicule. But now that his vision had adjusted to the glare, he could see the inquisitor's face, his eyes. There was no hint of mockery. The face was as kind as the voice he heard. Apparently, the man meant what he said, and he was waiting for an answer. "Do you want to get well? What is it that you want?"

"Hey, there, you without the legs—what are you lying here for? Wouldn't you love to get up, stretch yourself a bit, have a walk around?" Who dared ask something so callous? It was Jesus who posed the question, so there must be something we're missing here. *He is love incarnate.* Why did he ask the paraplegic such an embarrassing question? Of course the fellow wanted to get well. You don't have to be God to see the obvious. Or was it? As with most of the questions he posed, Jesus was probing for something we do not see. He knew the answer, of course—but did the man? Do we? Think of the fellow on the ground for a moment; put yourself, literally, in his shoes. His entire life has been shaped by his brokenness. All his days he has wanted one thing. Forget riches. Forget fame. Life for this man was captured in one simple, unreachable desire. When the other children ran and played, he sat and watched. When his family stood at the temple to pray, he lay on the ground. Every time he needed to have a drink or to go to the bathroom, someone had to pick him up and take him there.

So he had gone there for the past thirty-eight years, hoping to hit the jackpot. Sure, it was a long shot, but it was all he had. At what point did he begin to lose hope? First a year, then two went by. Nothing, at least for him. Maybe someone else got a miracle; that would buy him some time. What about after five years with no results? Ten? How long can we sustain desire against continual disappointment? Some hold out longer than others, but eventually, we all move to a place of resignation or cynicism or bitterness. As the years rolled on, this man, like all of us, began to lose any vital heart-connection to what he wanted. He was present, but not accounted for. The calluses had formed—not in the heart of Jesus, but over the man's heart. He had abandoned desire. Jesus took him back into the secret of his own heart. By asking him what he wanted, Jesus took the man *back into* his desire. Why?

It is where we must go if we are to meet God.

AN INVITATION TO DESIRE

This may come as a surprise to you: Christianity is not an invitation to become a moral person. It is not a program for getting us in line or for reforming society. It has a powerful effect upon our lives, but when transformation comes, it is always the *aftereffect* of something else, something at the level of our hearts. At its core, Christianity begins with an invitation to *desire*. Look again at the way Jesus relates to people. As he did with the fellow at the Sheep Gate, he is continually taking them into their hearts, to their deepest desires.

The story of the two blind men on the road to Jericho repeats the theme. Jesus is passing by the spot where these two men have sat looking for a handout for who knows how long. They learn that Jesus is going by, and they cry out for him. Though the crowd tries to shut them up, they succeed in shouting over the ruckus and capturing the Master's attention. The parade stops. Jesus steps to the side of the road, and standing there before him are two men, nothing clearer than the fact that they are blind. "What do you want me to do for you?" Again the question. Again the obvious that must not be so obvious after all.

Then there is the Samaritan woman whom Jesus meets at the well. She has come alone in the heat of the day to draw water, and they both know why. By coming when the sun is high, she is less likely to run into anyone. You see, her sexual lifestyle has earned her a "reputation." Back in those days, having one part- ner after another wasn't looked so highly upon. She's on her sixth lover, and so she'd rather bear the scorching rays of the sun than face the searing words of the "decent" women of the town who come at evening to draw water. She succeeds in avoiding the women, but runs into God instead. What does he choose to talk to her about—her immorality? No, he speaks to her about her *thirst*: "If you knew the generosity of God and who I am, you would be asking *me* for a drink, and I would give you fresh, living water" (John 4:10 *The Message*). Remarkable. He doesn't give a little sermon about purity; he doesn't even men- tion it, except to say that he knows what her life has been like: "You've had five husbands, and the man you're living with now isn't even your husband" (John 4:18 *The Message*). In other words, now that we both know it, let's talk about your heart's real thirst, since the life you've chosen obviously isn't working. "The water I give will be an artesian spring within, gushing fountains of endless life" (John 4:14 *The Message*).

Later in the gospel of John, Jesus extends the offer to anyone who realizes that his life just isn't touching his deep desire: "If you are thirsty, come to me! If you believe in me, come and drink! For the Scriptures declare that rivers of living water will flow out from within" (John 7:37–38 NLT). His message wasn't something new, but it confounded the religious leaders of the day. Surely, those scripturally learned Jews must have recalled God's long-standing invitation to them, spoken seven hundred years earlier through the prophet Isaiah:

> Come, all you who are thirsty,
>> come to the waters;
> and you who have no money,
>> come, buy and eat!
> Come, buy wine and milk
>> without money and without cost.
> Why spend money on what is not bread,
>> and your labor on what does not satisfy?
> Listen, listen to me, and eat what is good,
>> and your soul will delight in the richest of fare.
>
> (Isa. 55:1–2 NIV)

Somehow, the message had gotten lost by the time Jesus showed up on the scene. The Jews of his day were practicing a very soul-killing spirituality, a lifeless religion of duty and obligation. They had abandoned desire and replaced it with knowledge and performance as the key to life. The synagogue was the place to go to learn how to get with the program. Desire was out of the question; duty was the path that people must walk. No wonder they feared Jesus. He came along and started *appealing* to desire.

To the weary, Jesus speaks of rest. To the lost, he speaks of finding your way. Again and again and again, Jesus takes people back to their desires: "Ask and it will be given to you; seek and you will find; knock and the door will be opened to you" (Matt. 7:7 NIV). These are outrageous words, provocative words. *Ask, seek, knock*—these words invite and *arouse* desire. What is it that you *want?* They fall on deaf ears if there is nothing you want, nothing you're looking for, nothing you're hungry enough to bang on a door over.

Jesus provokes desire; he awakens it; he heightens it. The religious watchdogs accuse him of heresy. He says, "Not at all. This *is* the invitation God has been sending all along." He continues,

> You have your heads in your Bibles constantly because you think you'll find eternal life there. But you miss the forest for the trees. These Scriptures are all about *me!* And here I am, standing right before you, and you aren't willing to receive from me the life you say you want. (John 5:39–40 *The Message*)

LIFE IN ALL ITS FULLNESS

Eternal life—we tend to think of it in terms of existence that never comes to an end. And the existence it seems to imply—a sort of religious experience in the sky—leaves us wondering if we *would* want it to go on forever. But Jesus is quite clear that when he speaks of eternal life, what he means is life that is absolutely wonderful and can never be diminished or stolen from you. He says, "I have come that they may have life, and have it to the full" (John 10:10 NIV). Not, "I have come to threaten you into line," or "I have come to exhaust you with a long list of demands." Not even, "I have come primarily to forgive you." But simply, *My purpose is to bring you life in all its fullness.* Dallas Willard writes in *The Divine Conspiracy,*

Jesus offers himself as God's doorway into the life that is truly life. Confidence in him leads us today, as in other times, to become his apprentices in eternal living. "Those who come through me will be safe," he said. "They will go in and out and find all they need. I have come into their world that they may have life, and life to the limit."

In other words, eternal life is not primarily *duration* but *quality* of life, "life to the limit." It cannot be stolen from us, and so it does go on. But the focus is on the life itself. "In him was life," the apostle John said of Jesus, "and that life was the light of men" (John 1:4 NIV). Notice that the people who aren't so good at keeping up with the program but who are very aware of their souls' deep thirst are captured by Jesus' message. Common folk tear the roofs off houses to get to him. They literally trample each other in an effort to get closer to this man. I've never seen anyone acting like this in order to get a chance to serve on some church committee or to hear a sermon on why dancing is "of the devil." People act like this when it's a matter of life and death. Crowds trample each other to get out of a burning building; they press into the mob to reach a food line. When life is at stake and the answer is within reach, that's when you see human desire unmasked in all its desperation.

The Pharisees miss the boat entirely. Their hearts are hardened by the very law they claimed would bring them life. They put their hope in rules and regulations, in knowing and doing things perfectly. Having killed their souls' thirst with duty, they went on to kill their souls' only Hope, thinking they were doing their duty.

GOOD NEWS THAT'S NOT REALLY

Things appear to have come full circle. The promise of life and the invitation to desire have again been lost beneath a pile of religious teachings that put the focus on knowledge and performance.

> History has brought us to the point where the Christian mes-
> sage is thought to be essentially concerned only with how to
> deal with sin: with wrongdoing or wrong-being and its effects.
> Life, our actual existence, is not included in what is now pre-
> sented as the heart of the Christian message, or it is included
> only marginally. (*The Divine Conspiracy*)

Thus Willard describes the Gospels we have today as "gospels of sin management." Sin is the bottom line, and we have the cure. Typically, it is a system of knowledge or performance, or a mixture of both. Those in the knowledge camp put the empha- sis on getting our doctrine in line. Right belief is seen as the means to life. Desire is irrelevant; *content* is what matters. But notice this—the Pharisees knew more about the Bible than most of us ever will, and it *hardened* their hearts. Knowledge just isn't all it's cracked up to be. If you are familiar with the biblical nar- rative, you will remember that there were two special trees in Eden—the Tree of Knowledge of Good and Evil and the Tree of Life. We got the wrong tree. We got knowledge, and it hasn't done us much good. T. S. Eliot lamented,

> Endless invention, endless experiment,
> Brings knowledge of motion, but not of stillness;
> Knowledge of speech, but not of silence;
> Knowledge of words, and ignorance of the Word.
> Where is the Life we have lost in living?
> Where is the wisdom we have lost in knowledge?
> ("Choruses from the Rock")

Christianity is often presented as essentially the transfer of a body of knowledge. We learn about where the Philistines were from, and how much a drachma would be worth today, and all sorts of things about the original Greek. The information presented could not seem more irrelevant to our deepest desires.

Then there are the systems aimed at getting our behavior in line, one way or another. Regardless of where you go to church, there is nearly always an unspoken list of what you shouldn't do (tailored to your denomination and culture, but typically rather long) and a list of what you may do (usually much shorter—mostly religious activity that seems totally unrelated to our deepest desires and leaves us only exhausted).

And this, we are told, is the good news. Know the right thing; do the right thing. This is life? When it doesn't strike us as something to get excited about, we feel we must not be spiritual enough. Perhaps once we have kept the list long enough, we will understand.

We don't need more facts, and we certainly don't need more things to do. We need *Life*, and we've been looking for it ever since we lost Paradise. Jesus appeals to our desire because he came to speak to it. When we abandon desire, we no longer hear or understand what he is saying. But we have returned to the message of the synagogue; we are preaching the law. And desire is the enemy. After all, desire is the single major hindrance to the goal—getting us in line. We are told to kill desire and call it sanctification. Or as Jesus put it to the Pharisees, "You load people down with rules and regulations, nearly breaking their backs, but never lift even a finger to help" (Luke 11:46 *The Message*). As a result, Willard says, "The souls of human beings are left to shrivel and die on the plains of life because they are not introduced into the environment for which they were made."

"I began to seriously question my faith," wrote a friend, "when

I was suffering my second year of depression. People in church saw my depressed face, and they complimented me on how I was such a good Christian." I am not making this up. This poor fellow was actually cheered for doing well spiritually when it became apparent his soul was dying. "I thought the best way for a person to live is to keep his desires to a minimum so that he will be prepared to serve God." Isn't that the message? It may not be explicit (what we truly believe rarely is), but it's clear enough. Get rid of desire, and get with the program.

Compare the shriveled life held up as a model of Christian maturity with the life revealed in the book of Psalms:

> You have made known to me the path of life;
> > you will fill me with joy in your presence,
> > with eternal pleasures at your right hand.
> > > > (16:11 NIV)

> As the deer pants for streams of water,
> > so my soul pants for you, O God.
> My soul thirsts for God, for the living God.
> > When can I go and meet with God?
> > > > (42:1–2 NIV)

> > O God, you are my God,
> > > earnestly I seek you;
> > My soul thirsts for you,
> > > my body longs for you,
> > in a dry and weary land,
> > > where there is no water.
> > > > (63:1 NIV)

Ask yourself, Could this person be promoted to a position of leadership in my church? Heavens, no. He is far too unstable, too passionate, too desirous. It's all about pleasure and desire and thirst. And David, who wrote most of the psalms, was called by God a "man after his own heart" (1 Sam. 13:14 NIV).

Christianity has nothing to say to the person who is completely happy with the way things are. Its message is for those who hunger and thirst—for those who desire life as it was meant to be. Why does Jesus appeal to desire? Because it is essential to his goal: bringing us life. He heals the fellow at the pool of Bethesda, by the way. The two blind men get their sight, and the woman at the well finds the love she has been seeking. Reflecting on these events, the apostle John looked at what Jesus offered and what he delivered and said, "He who has the Son has life" (1 John 5:12 NIV).

THE STORY OF DESIRE

We misunderstand the good news Jesus announced when we hear it outside the story God is telling. Good news, a report that brings us relief and joy at the same time, is news that speaks to our dilemma. Hearing from your doctor that the lump is benign is good news. Receiving a notice from the IRS that you will not be audited after all is good news. Getting a call from the police to say that they've found your daughter is good news. Being offered tips and techniques for living a more dutiful life isn't even in the field of good news. We know in our hearts that our dilemma cannot be, "I sure wish I could be a more decent chap. What I really need is a program to improve my morals." Now, Jesus seemed to think that what he was offering really and truly spoke to our dilemma. Those who grasped what he was saying agreed. So what is our dilemma? What do we need most desperately to hear? Where are we in the story?

Let us ask the storytellers. In many ways, Hollywood has mastered the art of speaking to the human predicament. Consider the success of James Cameron's 1997 film *Titanic*. Not only did it sweep the Oscars, but the movie has become the all-time leading box office hit, passing even *Gone with the Wind*. Ticket sales have reached nearly $2 billion. I know people who have seen it not once or twice, but multiple times. It is a phenomenon whose appeal surpassed generational and cultural boundaries. Why? Christian critiques of the film missed the mark entirely, focusing almost exclusively on moral issues (sin management brought to film review). I cannot help thinking that if those reviewers were at the well when the Samaritan woman came by, they would have given her an earful.

But much more is going on here. Obviously, the film touched a nerve; it tapped into the reservoir of human longing for life. What is its story line? The film begins with romance, a story of passionate love, set within an exciting journey. Those who saw *Titanic* will recall the scene early in the film where the two lovers are standing on the prow of the great ship as it slices through a golden sea into a luscious sunset. Romance, beauty, adventure. Eden. The life we've all been searching for because it's the life we all were made for. Have we forgotten—or never been told? Once upon a time, in the beginning of humanity's sojourn on earth, we lived in a garden that was exotic and lush, inviting and full of adventure. It was "the environment for which we were made," as the sea lion was made for the sea. Now, those of you who learned about Eden in Sunday school maybe missed something here. Using flannel graphs to depict Paradise somehow doesn't do it. Picture Maui at sunset with your dearest love. A world of intimacy and beauty and adventure.

But then tragedy strikes. I'm sure I won't ruin the story for anyone if I tell you the ship goes down. How awful, how haunting are those scenes of the slow but irreversible plunge of the great ocean liner, leaving behind a sea of humanity to freeze to death in the Arctic waters. Everything is gone—the beauty, the romance, the adventure. Paradise is lost. And we know it. More than ever before, we know it. There was a time earlier in this century when we believed in the future, in something called progress. Not anymore, especially not the younger generations. I have yet to meet a young person who believes that his life will be better in a few years. As Chesterton said, we all somehow know that we are the "survivors of a wreck, the crew of a golden ship that had gone down before the beginning of the world." The ship has gone down. We are all adrift in the water, hoping to find some wreckage to crawl upon to save ourselves.

But that is not all. The secret of the film's success is found in the final scene. As the camera takes us once more to the bottom of the sea and we are given a last look at the rotting hulk of the once great ship, something happens. The *Titanic* begins to transform before our eyes. Light floods in through the windows. The rust and decay melt away as the pristine beauty of the ship is restored. The doors fly open, and there are all the great hearts of the story, not dead at all, but quite alive and rejoicing. A party is under way; a wedding party. The heroine, dressed in a beautiful white gown, ascends the staircase into the embrace of her lover. Everything is restored. Tragedy does not have the final word. Somehow, beyond all hope, Paradise has been regained.

Isn't this our dilemma? Isn't this the news we have been longing for? A return of the life we prize? Look again at what Jesus offers. There is bread enough for everyone. There is healing for every brokenness. The lost are found. The weary are given rest. There is life available—life to the limit.

I am the Gate. Anyone who goes through me will be cared for—
will freely go in and out, and find pasture. A thief is only there

to steal and kill and destroy. I came so they can have real and
eternal life, more and better life than they ever dreamed of.
(John 10:9–10 *The Message*)

DESIRE AND GOODNESS

But doesn't Christianity condemn desire—the Puritans and all
that? Not at all. Quite the contrary. Christianity takes desire seriously, far more seriously than the Stoic or the mere hedonist.
Christianity refuses to budge from the fact that man was made
for pleasure, that his beginning and his end is a paradise, and that
the goal of living is to find Life. Jesus knows the dilemma of
desire, and he speaks to it in nearly everything he says.

When it comes to the moral question, it is not simply whether
we say yes or no to desire, but always what we *do* with desire.
Christianity recognizes that we have desire gone mad within us.
But it does not seek to rectify the problem by killing desire;
rather, it seeks the healing of desire, just as it seeks the healing
of every other part of our human being.

"Two things contribute to our sanctification," wrote Pascal.
"Pains and pleasures." And while we know that our journey is
strewn with danger and difficulty, "the difficulties they meet with
are not without pleasure, *and cannot be overcome without pleasure.*"
Where do you find Jesus saying, "The problem with you people
is, you want too much. If you'd just learn to be happy with less,
we'd all get along just fine"? Not anywhere. Quite the contrary.
"My commands are for your good," he says, "always."

Something has gone wrong in us, very wrong indeed. So
wrong that we have to be told that joy is found not in having
another man's wife, but in having our own. But the point is not
the law; the point is the joy. Need I say more than this: modern
Christianity has brought an entire group of people to the point

where they have to be told that sex is, in the words of one book, "intended for pleasure."

God is realistic. He knows that ecstasy is not an option; we are made for bliss, and we must have it, one way or another. He also knows that happiness is fragile and rests upon a foundation greater than happiness. All the Christian disciplines were formulated at one time or another in an attempt to heal desire's waywardness and so, by means of obedience, bring us home to bliss. Walter Brueggemann suggests that faith on its way to maturity moves from "duty to delight." If it is not moving, then it has become stagnant. If it has changed the goal from delight to duty, it has gone backward; it is *regressing*. This is the great lost truth of the Christian faith, that correction of Judaism made by Jesus and passed on to us: the goal of morality is not morality—it is ecstasy. *You* are intended for pleasure!

WHO, THEN, CAN BE SAVED?

Look again at the story Jesus told about the prodigal son. It might be called the story of desire. Consider what each character does with his desire. You have the younger son, whose desires get him into a world of trouble. Then there is the father, whose desire for the lost boy is so deep that he sees him coming from a long way off—he has been watching, waiting. Forgiveness is assumed; it's a given. He's grateful just to have the boy home again. And then there is the older brother. He's the party pooper, if you recall. His younger brother is "back from the dead," as the father says, and the older brother won't even come in for the celebration. He stands outside, sulking. Let's pick up the story there:

> The older brother was angry and wouldn't go in. His father came
> out and begged him, but he replied, "All these years I've worked

hard for you and never once refused to do a single thing you told me to. And in all that time you never gave me even one young goat for a feast with my friends. Yet when this son of yours comes back after squandering your money on prostitutes, you celebrate by killing the finest calf we have." His father said to him, "Look, dear son, you and I are very close, and everything I have is yours. We had to celebrate this happy day. For your brother was dead and has come back to life! He was lost, but now he is found!" (Luke 15:28–32 NLT)

The older brother is the picture of the man who has lived his entire life from duty and obligation. When the wayward son returns from his shipwreck of desire, his brother is furious because he gets a party and not a trip behind the barn with the broadside of a paddle. He tells his father that he has been had; that all these years he hasn't gotten a thing in return for his life of service. The father's reply cuts to the chase: "All that is mine has always been yours." In other words, "You never asked." Rembrandt captures all this powerfully in his now-famous painting *The Return of the Prodigal Son*. In the painting, the elder brother stands a step *above* the reunion of father and son. He will not step down, enter in. He is above it all. But who receives redemption? The scandalous message of the story is this: those who kill desire—the legalists, the dutiful—are not the ones who experience the father's embrace. The question is not, Dare we desire, but dare we *not* desire?

THE SEA LION loved his rock, and he even loved waiting night after night for the sea breezes that might come. Especially he loved the dreams those memories would stir. But as you well know, even the best of dreams cannot go on, and in the morning when the sea lion woke, he was still in the barren lands. Sometimes he would close his eyes and try to fall back asleep. It never seemed to work, for the sun was always very bright.

Eventually, it became too much for him to bear. He began to visit his rock only on occasion. "I have too much to do," he told himself. "I cannot waste my time just idling about." He really did not have so much to do. The truth of it was, waking so far from home was such a disappointment, he did not want to have those wonderful dreams anymore. The day finally came when he stopped going to his rock altogether, and he no longer lifted his nose to the wind when the sea breezes blew.

CHAPTER FOUR

DISOWNED DESIRE

The danger is that the soul should persuade itself that it is not hungry. It can only persuade itself of this by lying.

—SIMONE WEIL

Everybody's got a hungry heart.

—BRUCE SPRINGSTEEN

I n his essay "Screwtape Proposes a Toast," C. S. Lewis portrays the old devil delivering the annual commencement speech for the Tempter's Training College for Young Devils. Screwtape begins his address by lamenting that "the human souls on whose anguish we have been feasting tonight were of a pretty poor quality." He laments that there are so few truly great sinners available at present; they could capture only passive milksops.

Here were vermin so muddled in mind, so passively responsive to environment, that it was very hard to raise them to that level of clarity and deliberateness at which mortal sin becomes possible. To raise them just enough; but not that fatal millimeter of "too much." For then of course all might possibly have been lost. They might have seen; they might have repented.

Screwtape decides that perhaps this is all for the best because there are real dangers when a soul is capable of deep desire. He knows what we have forgotten: "The great (and toothsome) sinners are made out of the very same material as those horrible phenomena, the great Saints."

Dare we forget King David? Yes, his passions got him in a heap of trouble—and gave us our book of *worship*, the Psalms. Sure, Peter was a hotheaded disciple always quick with a reply. Remember in the Garden of Gethsemane—he's the one who lopped off the ear of the high priest's servant. But he was also the first to acknowledge that Jesus was the Messiah, and despite his Good Friday betrayals, he became a key apostle, contributed important pieces to the Scripture, and followed Jesus all the way to his own crucifixion, asking to be nailed to the cross upside down because he was not worthy to die in the manner of his Lord. Surely, we remember that Paul was once Saul, the fiery young Pharisee "advancing in Judaism beyond many Jews of my own age and . . . extremely zealous for the traditions of my fathers" (Gal. 1:14 NIV). His zeal made him the foremost persecutor of the church. When Christ knocked him off his donkey on the Damascus road, Paul was hunting down the church, "uttering threats with every breath" (Acts 9:1 NLT). Christ captured his zeal, and after Damascus it led him to work "harder than all the other apostles" (1 Cor. 15:10 NLT).

Augustine was also a passionate young man, sexually licentious, enamored with the pleasures of Rome, "scratching the sore of lust," as he would call it after Christ got hold of him. He went on to become one of the great pillars of the church, laying the foundation for the rise of Christendom after the fall of Rome. "Tempered in the fires of his own sensuality, toughened by his arduous explorations of the heresies of the age," he became, in Malcolm Muggeridge's words, "a latter-day Noah . . . constrained to construct an ark, in his case Orthodoxy, wherein the Church could survive through the dark days that lay ahead" (*A Third Testament*).

The great saints come from the same material as the "tooth-some sinners." Desire, a burning passion for more, is at the heart of both. Those who would kill the passion altogether would murder the very essence that makes heroes of the faith. They remind me of those misguided physicians of a hundred years ago, who would attempt to cure a fever by "bleeding" their patients, cutting a vein and draining them of bowls of blood, depriving them of the very life force they needed to get better. It's a wonder so many survived. Augustine would later write,

> Give me a man in love; he knows what I mean. Give me one who yearns; give me one who is hungry; give me one far away in this desert, who is thirsty and sighs for the spring of the Eternal Country. Give me that sort of man; he knows what I mean. But if I speak to a cold man, he just doesn't know what I am talking about. (Quoted by Muggeridge in *A Third Testament*)

BLESSED ARE THE NICE?

And so Screwtape reveals the enemy's ploy—first make humans flabby, with small passions and desires, then offer a sop to those diminished passions so that their experience is one of contentment. They know nothing of great joy or great sorrow. They are merely *nice*. One young woman wrote to me,

> My parents always told me to be a "nice little girl." I simply assumed that being nice meant not getting upset or being angry with anyone . . . I was nice because I wanted to be liked, and I figured that people would like someone who was always nice. My senior year of high school I was voted "Nicest Senior" for the senior awards, and it was true. I was nice and I was proud of it. I thought there was no higher virtue than niceness.

Christianity has come to the point where we believe that there is no higher aspiration for the human soul than to be nice. We are producing a generation of men and women whose greatest virtue is that they don't offend anyone. Then we wonder why there is not more passion for Christ. How can we hunger and thirst after righteousness if we have ceased hungering and thirsting altogether? As C. S. Lewis said, "We castrate the gelding and bid him be fruitful."

The greatest enemy of holiness is not passion; it is apathy. Look at Jesus. He was no milksop. His life was charged with passion. After he drove the crooks from the temple, "his disciples remembered that it is written: 'Zeal for your house will consume me'" (John 2:17 NIV). This isn't quite the pictures we have in Sunday school, Jesus with a lamb and a child or two, looking for all the world like Mr. Rogers with a beard. The world's nicest guy. He was something far more powerful. He was holy. G. K. Chesterton wrote,

> Instead of looking at books and pictures about the New Testament I looked at the New Testament. There I found an account, not in the least of a person with His hair parted in the middle or His hands clasped in appeal, but of an extraordinary being with lips of thunder and acts of lurid decision, flinging down tables, casting out devils, passing with the wild scenery of the wind from mountain isolation to a sort of dreadful demagogy; a being who acted like an angry god—and always like a god . . . The diction used about Christ has been . . . sweet and submissive. But the diction used by Christ is quite gigantesque; it is full of camels leaping through needles and mountains hurled into the sea. (*Orthodoxy*)

If the way to avoid the murderous rage and deceptive allures of desire is to kill it, if deadness is next to godliness, then Jesus had to be the deadest person ever. But he is called the *living* God. "It is a dreadful thing," the writer of Hebrews says, "to fall into the hands of the living God . . . For our 'God is a consuming fire'" (Heb. 10:31; 12:29 NIV). And what is this consuming fire? His jealous love (Deut. 4:24). God is a deeply, profoundly passionate person. Zeal consumes him. It is the secret of his life, the writer of Hebrews says. The "joy set before him" enabled Jesus to endure the agony of the Cross (Heb. 12:2 NIV). In other words, his profound desire for something greater sustained him at the moment of his deepest trial. We cannot hope to live like him without a similar depth of passion. Many people find that the dilemma of desire is too much to live with, and so they abandon, they disown their desire. This is certainly true of a majority of Christians at present. Somehow we believe that we can get on without it. We are mistaken.

THE MAN WHO WANTED NOTHING

Initially, Gary and Jill had come to me because their marriage had become merely functional. No major issues—no one was throwing dishes; neither was having an affair. As I realized later, that would have been better, at least a sign of life. Their marriage had all the passion of yesterday's oatmeal. Jill was the one who called because she was afraid that she was losing Gary, that they were "drifting apart." It didn't take long to see why. Gary had checked out. He was still going to work, paying the bills, and cutting the grass, but that was it. There was no emotion, no investment, no reaction to anything. The more vital parts of him were shut down. I asked if he and I might spend some time just talking about his life. As the weeks rolled by, I learned that he had been a faithful church attender, never missing a Sunday. He served on a committee and offered help to those in need. But obviously, something was missing.

I was surprised, frankly, when he showed up each week. Going to counseling can feel like the emotional equivalent of attempting Everest, but I found in him nothing near the desire to make the ascent. After months of getting nowhere, I asked the obvious: "Gary, why are you a Christian?" He sat in silence for what must have been five minutes. "I don't know. I guess because it's the right thing to do." "Is there anything you're hoping to enjoy as a result of your faith?" "No . . . not really." "So what is it that you *want*, Gary?" An even longer silence. I waited patiently. "I don't desire anything." Our sessions ended shortly thereafter, and I felt bad that I was unable to help him. You cannot help someone who doesn't want a thing. All his life Gary had been a good boy. A gelding. And geldings, though they are nicer and much more well behaved than stallions, do not bring life. They are sterile.

I thought of the last story we have from the life of the prophet Elisha. Jehoash was king of Israel at the time, and he went to visit Elisha on his sickbed. He knew that without the help of the great prophet, the future of Israel was looking dim. Enemies were closing in on every side, waiting for the kill. Elisha told the king to take in hand some arrows.

> And the king took them. Elisha told him, "Strike the ground." He struck it three times and stopped. The man of God was angry with him and said, "You should have struck the ground five or six times; then you would have defeated [your enemies] completely . . . But now you will defeat [them] only three times." Elisha died and was buried. (2 Kings 13:18–20 NIV)

That's it? What a strange story! Why was the old prophet so angry? Because the king was nonchalant; he was passionless, indifferent. He gave the ground a whack or two. His heart wasn't in it. God says, in effect, "If that is how little you care about the future of your people, that is all the help you will get." In other words, if your heart's not in it, well then, neither is mine. You can't lead a country, let alone flourish in a marriage, with an attitude like that. To abandon desire is to say, "I don't really need you; I don't really want you. But I will live with you because, well, I'm supposed to." It is a grotesque corruption of what was meant to be a beautiful dance between desire and devotion.

Your heart longs, and you go to seek the one you desire. She responds to your seeking because it touches her heart's desire to be longed for. Yes, commitment plays a vital role—but only as the *expression* of desire. Duty reduces the dance to a drill. It's as if you showed up with a bouquet of flowers for your anniversary. Your wife is delighted, but then you say, "Think nothing of it, my dear. It's my obligation." John Piper opens his book *Desiring God* with this illustration, showing the deadly effect of duty on a relationship: "Dutiful roses are a contradiction in terms." A woman doesn't want to be an object of duty; she wants to be *desired*. So does God. Thus A. W. Tozer asserted, "God waits to be wanted."

At one point I had asked Gary about his prayer life. "I never ask God for anything," he replied. I wasn't surprised. You see, the real dilemma of desire is that it *humbles* us. It takes us way beyond our own resources where we need to ask for help.

FAITH AS DESIRE

You may recall the story Jesus told of the man who entrusted three of his servants with thousands of dollars (literally, "talents"), urging them to handle his affairs well while he was away. When he returned, he listened eagerly to their reports. The first two fellows went out into the marketplace and doubled their investment. As a result, they were handsomely rewarded.

The third servant was not so fortunate. His gold was taken from him, and he was thrown into "outer darkness, where there will be weeping and gnashing of teeth." My goodness. Why? All he did was bury the money under the porch until his master's return. Most of us would probably agree with the path he chose—at least the money was safe there. But listen to his reasoning. Speaking to his master, he said, "I know you are a hard man, harvesting crops you didn't plant and gathering crops you didn't cultivate. I was afraid I would lose your money, so I hid it." (See Matt. 25:14–30 NLT.) He was afraid of the master, whom he saw as a hard man. He didn't trust his master's heart.

The issue isn't capital gains—it's what we think of God. When we bury our desires, we are saying the same thing: "God, I don't dare desire because I fear you; I think you are hard-hearted."

Just yesterday evening I was taking a walk in our neighborhood, talking to the Lord about going forward and establishing the ranch I have mentioned. I had been moving toward the creation of this place of ministry in what felt like sheer obedience, dragging my heart along behind me. God had been confirming the direction with many signs and affirmations. And yet I sensed that something was wrong. I was asking him what he wanted the ranch to be. He said, *What do you want it to be? What's in your heart?* I was embarrassed by the honesty of my reply: "What do you care about my desires?" There is this hurt and angry place inside, a very old wound, that harbors some rather strong doubts about how much God really cares for me.

We all have this place. Life has not turned out the way we want, and we know God could have handled things differently. Even though we may profess at one level a genuine faith in him, at another level we are like the third servant. Our obedience is not so much out of love as it is out of carefulness. "Just tell me what to do, God, and I'll do it." Killing desire may look like sanctification, but it's really godlessness. Literally, our way of handling life without God.

"But when the Son of Man comes, will he find faith on the earth?" Jesus had been talking about prayer by telling the story of a persistent widow who wasn't getting the justice she deserved from a belligerent judge. The woman won her case because she refused to let up. Jesus used her as a picture of unrelenting desire; he urged us not only to ask, but also to keep on asking. And then he ended the parable by wondering out loud, "When I return, will I find anyone who really lives by faith?" (see Luke 18:1–8 NIV).

We know in our hearts the connection he is making, though we haven't admitted it to ourselves. To live with desire is to choose vulnerability over self-protection; to admit our desire and seek help beyond ourselves is even more vulnerable. It is an act of trust. In other words, those who know their desire and refuse to kill it, or refuse to act as though they don't need help, they are the ones who live by faith. Those who do not ask do not trust God enough to desire. *They have no faith.* The deepest moral issue is always what we, in the heart of hearts, believe about God. And nothing reveals this belief as clearly as what we do with our desire.

PRAYER AS THE LANGUAGE OF DESIRE

The book of Hebrews describes the prayer life of Jesus in the following way: "While Jesus was here on earth, he offered prayers and pleadings, with a loud cry and tears, to the one who could deliver him" (5:7 NLT). That doesn't sound like the way that prayers are offered up in most churches on a typical Sunday morning. "Dear Lord, we thank you for this day, and we ask you to be with us in all we say and do. Amen." No pleading here, no loud cries and tears. Our prayers are cordial, modest, even reverent. Eugene Peterson calls them "cut-flower prayers." They are not like Jesus' prayers or, for that matter, like the psalms. The ranting and raving, the passion and ecstasy, the fury and desolation found in the psalms are so far from our religious expression that it seems hard to believe they were given to us as our *guide* to prayer. They seem so, well, *desperate*. Yet E. M. Bounds reminds us,

> Desire gives fervor to prayer. The soul cannot be listless when some great desire fixes and inflames it . . . Strong desires make strong prayers . . . The neglect of prayer is the fearful token of dead spiritual desires . . . There can be no true praying without desire. (*E. M. Bounds: Man of Prayer*)

A young woman came to see me, as most seeking counseling do, because she was at the end of her rope. What had begun a year earlier as mild depression had sunk deeper and deeper until she found herself contemplating suicide. We met for many weeks, and I came to know a delightful woman with a poet's heart, whose soul was buried beneath years not so much of tragedy but of neglect. This one particular afternoon, we had spoken for more than an hour of how deeply she longed for love, how almost completely ignored and misunderstood she felt her entire life. It was a tender, honest, and deeply moving session. As our time drew to a close, I asked her if she would pray with me. I could hardly believe what came next. She assumed a rather bland, religious tone to her voice and said something to the effect of "God, thank you for being here. Show me what I ought to do." I found myself speechless. *You've got to be kidding me*, I thought. *That's not how you feel at all. I know your heart's true cry. You are far more desperate than that.*

I wish she'd prayed like my son Luke. He is our youngest son and very wise for all of his five years. He knows what he wants and what it means to lose it. "My life is over." Luke laid his head down on the table and sighed, a picture of lament. I had just told him he couldn't have chocolate-covered sugar bombs for breakfast, and he was devastated. There was no longer any reason to go on. Life as he knew it was over. I enjoy Luke because he has more undisguised and unadulterated desire than anyone I know. He is "out there" with his desire and his disappointments. When we go over to someone's house for dinner, the first thing he'll ask will always be, "Is there dessert?" Part of me has tried to train this out of him; part of me admires the fact that he isn't embarrassed by his desire, like the rest of us. He is unashamed. We hide our true desire and call it maturity. Jesus is not impressed. He points to the less sophisticated attitude of a child as a better way to live.

Why are we so embarrassed by our desire? Why do we pretend that we're doing fine, thank you, that we don't need a thing? The persistent widow wasn't too proud to seek help. Neither was the psalmist. Their humility allowed them to express their desire. How little we come to God with what really matters to us. How rare it is that we even admit it to ourselves. "Is there dessert?" We don't pray like Jesus because we don't allow ourselves to be nearly so *alive*. We don't allow ourselves to feel how desperate our situation truly is. We sense that our desire will undo us if we let it rise up in all its fullness. Wouldn't it be better to bury the disappointment and the yearning and just get on with life? As Larry Crabb has pointed out, pretending seems a much more reliable road to Christian maturity. The only price we pay is a loss of soul, of communion with God, a loss of direction, and a loss of hope.

DRIFTING WITHOUT DESIRE

As a teacher, counselor, and author, I love what I do for a living. But it hasn't always been so. I spent a lifetime in Washington, DC, several years ago. They were two of the most miserable years of my life. I don't like government, and I abhor politics. Harry Truman was right: "If you want a friend in Washington, buy a dog." What in the world was I doing there? I didn't really want to go; my employer talked me into accepting a transfer. But I can't put the blame on them. The truth is, I had come to a point where I didn't really know what I wanted in life. My real passion had been the theater, and for a number of years I pursued that dream with great joy. I had my own theater company and loved it. Through a series of events and what felt like betrayals, I had gotten deeply hurt. I left the theater and just went off to find a job. The Washington offer came up, and even though my heart wasn't in it, I let the opinions of people I admired dictate my course. Without a deep and burning desire of our own, we will be ruled by the desires of others.

Ann didn't know whether she should marry the man she was dating. They'd been dating for the last three years of college, and in many ways they enjoyed being together. But now that the possibility of engagement was becoming a reality, she found herself lost as to what she should do. "Do you want to marry him?" I asked. "I don't know. I guess so. I'm not sure." Ann is a very bright and energetic young woman. A youth pastor, she is rarely at a loss for ideas and energy. People regularly turn to her for counsel and encouragement. Ann always knows the "right" thing to do. But she was stumped. There was no "right" course to take. Her boyfriend was a committed Christian and a good man who loved her. She loved him too.

The problem was simply this: Ann had lived her entire life

based on what was right and had never once made a decision based on her desire. The oldest daughter in a family with some very high needs, Ann had been required to grow up much sooner than the others. She was highly responsible, and found her security in meeting the expectations and demands placed upon her. When the moment came for her to live out of her desire, she was out of practice. There was no one to tell her what to do.

I have met many Christians in the same position. I think of Charles, an attorney in his fifties who still doesn't know what he wants to be when he grows up. His wife left him last year. There is Paul, a young man in his twenties who doesn't know what to do with himself now that college is over. He focused on grades and left his heart behind. Jamie isn't sure if she should get married or stay single. Barbara hates her job but hasn't the slightest idea what she'd do if she left. They have all tried to bury their heart under the porch and seek a safer life. The poet David Whyte states,

> The hope is to stay in the background away from the fire, and wait for someone or something to come along and grant us immunity from these difficulties and sacrifices, someone to offer reassurance, saying perhaps, "Take the safe way, not the way of passion and creativity, as the path to your destiny, the life you desire. Follow it and you will never be touched . . ." [But] we cannot neglect our inner fire without damaging ourselves in the process. (*The Heart Aroused*)

The damage, of course, is a life lost unto itself. Millions of souls drifting through life, without an inner compass to give them direction. They take their cues from others and live out scripts from someone else's life. It's a high price to pay. Too high.

HOPELESS WITHOUT DESIRE

A curious warning is given to us in Peter's first epistle. There he tells us to be ready to give the reason for the hope that lies within us to everyone who asks (3:15). Now, what's strange about that passage is this: no one ever asks. When was the last time someone stopped you to inquire about the reason for the hope that lies within you? You're at the market, say, in the frozen food section. A friend you haven't seen for some time comes up to you, grasps you by both shoulders, and pleads, "Please, you've got to tell me. Be honest now. How can you live with such hope? Where does it come from? I must know the reason." In talking with hundreds of Christians, I've met only one or two who have experienced something like this.

Yet God tells us to be ready, so what's wrong? To be blunt, nothing about our lives is worth asking about. There's nothing intriguing about our hopes, nothing to make anyone curious. Not that we don't have hopes; we do. We hope we'll have enough after taxes this year to take a summer vacation. We hope our kids don't wreck the car. We hope our favorite team goes to the World Series. We hope our health doesn't give out, and so on. Nothing wrong with any of those hopes; nothing unusual, either. Everyone has hopes like that, so why bother asking us? It's life as usual. Sanctified resignation has become the new abiding place of contemporary Christians. No wonder nobody asks. Do *you* want the life of any Christian you know?

Having abandoned desire, we have lost hope. C. S. Lewis summed it up: "We can only hope for what we desire." No desire, no hope. Now, desire doesn't always translate into hope. There are many things I desire that I have little hope for. I desire to have lots more money than I do, but I see little reason to think it will come. But there isn't one thing I hope for that I don't *also* desire. This is Lewis's point. Bland assurances of the sweet by-and-by don't inflame the soul. Our hopes are deeply tied to our real desires, and so killing desire has meant a hopeless life for too many. It's as if we've already entered Dante's *Inferno*, where the sign over hell reads, "Abandon hope, all ye who enter here."

The effect has been disastrous, not only for individual Christians, but also for the message of the gospel as a whole. People aren't exactly ripping the roofs off churches to get inside. We see the enemy's ploy: drain all the life and beauty and adventure away from the gospel, bury Christians in duty, and nobody will want to take a closer look. It's so very unappealing.

THE DANGER OF DISOWNED DESIRE

Jenny fell in love in Ecuador. She wasn't looking for love, mind you. She had gone to South America on a missions trip. Her heart has long been devoted to bringing the gospel to Third World peoples, and frankly, she can be pretty intense about it. With her focus on the mission at hand, love was the last thing on her mind. It came as a great surprise. Perhaps it was the romance of being in a foreign country. The beauty of the mountains and the jungles, the exotic flowers and birds, and the intrigues of a Latin culture certainly provided a lush setting for romance to blossom. And then there was the fact that the man she was with was charming and intelligent and just a little bit dashing. Moreover, he was interested in her. His sincere questions, their shared laughter, a mutual sense of purpose added to the powerful potion. There was only one small problem: he was married.

It was with a deep sense of shame that Jenny told me her story. Nothing happened between them, but she let her heart go farther than it should. She was embarrassed, humiliated. I wasn't in the least surprised, not because Jenny is a flirt—far from it. But I've known her for a while now, and I know the story of her heart. Jenny is afraid of intimacy, and she has tried hard to live beyond her longing for love. She has known the betrayal of love and carries the wounds to prove it. Of course, she enjoyed his attention. We were made for that, remember? Like all of us, Jenny is designed for intimacy and adventure. What made me mad was that she was about to draw the wrong conclusion, a conclusion the church has long jumped to: desire gets me into trouble; I must avoid it at all costs. Jenny's story is not about the dangers of desire, but about the dangers of *disowned* desire. Just because she pretends she doesn't really want romance doesn't make the desire go away. It goes underground, to surface somewhere else at some other time.

David Whyte calls this the "devouring animal of our disowned desire." It is the reason behind most affairs in the church. The pastor lives out of duty, trying to deny his thirst for many years. One day, the young secretary smiles at him and it's over. Because he has so long been out of touch with his desire, it becomes overwhelming when it does show up. The danger of disowning desire is that it sets us up for a fall. We are unable to distinguish real life from a tempting imitation. We are fooled by the impostors. Eventually, we find some means of procuring a taste of the life we were meant for.

—— THE SEA LION was not entirely alone in those parts. For it was there he met the tortoise. Now this tortoise was an ancient creature, so weathered by his life in the barren lands that at first, the sea lion mistook him for a rock. He told the tortoise of his plight, hoping that this wise one might be able to help him. "Perhaps," the tortoise mused, "this is the sea." His eyes appeared to be shut against the bright sun, but he was watching the sea lion very closely. The sea lion swept his flippers once against his side, gliding to the end of the water hole and back. "I don't know," he said. "It isn't very deep." "Isn't it?" "Somehow, I thought the sea would be broader, deeper. At least, I hoped so."

"You must learn to be happy here," the tortoise told him one day. "For it is unlikely you shall ever find this sea of yours." Deep in his old and shriveled heart, the tortoise envied the sea lion and his sea. "But I belong to the sea. We are made for each other." "Perhaps. But you have been gone so long now, the sea has probably forgotten you." This thought had never occurred to the sea lion. But it was true, he had been gone for a long, long time. "If this is not my home, how can I ever feel at home here?" the sea lion asked. "You will, in time." The tortoise appeared to be squinting, his eyes a thin slit. "I have seen the sea, and it is no better than what you have found here." "You have seen the sea!" "Yes. Come closer," whispered the tortoise, "and I will tell you a secret. I am not a tortoise. I am a sea turtle. But I left the sea of my own accord, many years ago, in search of better things. If you stay with me, I will tell you stories of my adventures."

The stories of the ancient tortoise were enchanting and soon cast their spell upon the sea lion. As weeks passed into months, his memory of the sea faded. "The desert," whispered the tortoise, "is all that is, or was, or ever will be." When the sun grew fierce and burned his skin, the sea lion would hide in the shade of the tree, listening to the tales woven by the tortoise. When the dry winds cracked his flippers and filled his eyes with dust, the sea lion would retreat to the water hole. And so the sea lion remained, living his days between water hole and tree. The sea no longer filled his dreams.

CHAPTER FIVE

MOCKING OUR DESIRE— THE IMPOSTORS

We have sailed too close to shore; having fallen in love with life, we have lost our thirst for the waters of Life.

—SIR FRANCIS DRAKE

And my desires, like fell and cruel hounds,
E'er since pursue me.

—SHAKESPEARE

The problem with desire is, you want everything.

—PAUL SIMON

I n fourteen hundred and ninety-two, as we all remember, Columbus sailed the ocean blue. Instead of opening a trade route to Asia, he unleashed something in the European imagination when he reported discovering a New World. What followed is simply amazing. First, it was the Fountain of Youth. Ponce de León (who sailed with Columbus on his second voyage to the Caribbean) learned from the natives of a mythical island called Bimini. A spring was reported to flow there, whose waters bestowed eternal youth. He actually obtained the backing of King Ferdinand to lead a party in search of that coveted fount.

Failing to discover Bimini, Ponce de León stumbled upon Florida, which many aging Americans apparently have found to be nearly as good. Unfortunately, Ponce de León's own life was cut short by the discovery. Apparently, the natives didn't take to his attempt at conquest (and the future prospect of mobile home parks), so they killed him.

Then came El Dorado, the Lost City of Gold. As conquistadores penetrated the mainland of Central and South America, they were enchanted by a legend telling of a kingdom of unfathomable riches located somewhere in the Americas. The finder of this hidden treasure would become wealthy beyond his wildest dreams. In 1535, Sebastian de Belalcazar led a three-year search for the fabled city through the jungles of Colombia. He failed, lost control of Peru, and died of fever. You'd think his fate would have cast a chill on the whole enterprise. Not at all.

Two years later, Francisco de Orellana led an expedition down the Amazon, which also ended in disaster. About the same time, Coronado and his soldiers were marching into northern Mexico, searching for the Seven Cities of Cibola (reputed to be flowing with gold). They returned empty-handed. After a number of additional Spanish failures, Sir Walter Raleigh decided he'd give it a go. Not once, but twice he came in search of El Dorado. On his second expedition in 1616, he violated the express orders of King James I of England and attacked a Spanish settlement in Guyana. His son was killed, and Raleigh was beheaded upon his return to England.

THE SEARCH CONTINUES

What *was* it with those guys? If only Raleigh had given up on his first disappointment. But something in us will not be daunted once we've smelled the promised land. I was supposed to be writing last night, but instead sat on the couch thumbing through a Williams-Sonoma catalog. It calls itself "a catalog for cooks," but really, it's a catalog of the life we wish we had. Everything is beautiful, delicious, elegant. The kitchens portrayed are immaculate—there are no messes. Cooking there would be a joy. The tables are sumptuous with their beautiful china place settings, wine glasses brimming with nectar, gourmet foods deliciously prepared, invitingly presented. Fresh flowers abound. The homes are lovely and spacious; the view out the windows is always a mountain lake, a beach, or perhaps an English garden. Everything is as it ought to be. Glancing through its pages, you get a sense of rest. Life is good. *You see*, the images whisper, *it can be done. Life is within your grasp*. And so the quest continues. But of course. Our address used to be Paradise, remember?

And oh, how we yearn for another shot at it. Flip with me for a moment through the photo album of your heart, and collect a few of your most treasured memories. Recall a time in your life when you felt really special, a time when you *knew* you were loved. The day you got engaged perhaps. Or a childhood Christmas. Maybe a time with your grandparents. I remember one birthday in particular. My wife planned a surprise party and kept it a perfect secret. All day long, I thought everyone had forgotten me; I was thoroughly depressed. I have a hard time with birthdays anyway—the longings they rouse. I had pretty much killed my desire for something special by evening when we went to dinner at one of our favorite restaurants. There were all my friends. I was stunned, humbled, delighted all at once. It was a wonderful evening of laughter and conversation—for me, to celebrate me. A simple event, but I recall the feelings I had even still.

Hold your memory while you gather another, a time of real adventure, such as when you first learned to ride a bike, or galloped on a horse, or perhaps did something exciting on a vacation.

Stasi and I spent our tenth anniversary snorkeling in Kauai, off the Na Pali Coast. We tried to catch up to the sea turtles and grab their flippers, hoping for a ride. It was exotic and more than a little funny. I remember falling asleep that night to the sound of the waves. Now, we were meant to live in a world like that— every day. Just as our lungs are made to breathe oxygen, our souls are designed to flourish in an atmosphere rich in love and meaning, security and significance, *intimacy* and *adventure*. But we don't live in that world anymore. Far from it. Though we try to resolve the dilemma by disowning our desire, it doesn't work. It is the soul's equivalent of holding our breath. Eventually, we find ourselves gasping for air. As Allender said, "Can any human being live with a loss of soul—a loss of his or her very essence?" Of course not. Something will come along and touch those essential places in us, offering a taste of intimacy or adventure.

LOOKING FOR THE GOLDEN PERSON

"Love can touch us one time and last for a lifetime." You had to have been hibernating to have missed Celine Dion singing the theme song of *Titanic* at least once in 1998. It played constantly, in grocery stores, over the radio, and on more than nine million copies of the best-selling CD. A hauntingly beautiful song to be sure, with its Celtic strains, and made all the more powerful by the central myth of our day. Though I believe the film's success was due to its remarkable parallels to the gospel—to our longing for heroic intimacy—that is not why millions were *consciously* drawn to it. *Titanic* roused our desire for Eden, then reaffirmed the leading alternative. It offered romantic love as the answer to the heart's deepest yearnings. The idea is that someone is out there for you, and if you can find him, his love will carry you for a lifetime. How many women in particular were fueled by this film in their search for the Golden Person, their own Jack? As C. S. Lewis warned, "Another personality can become to us 'our America, our New-found-land.'"

You don't think you've been immune to all this, do you? Culture has been chanting that mantra for a long time. Of all the films, songs, television shows, musicals, dramas, poetry, and novels you've partaken of in your life, can you name more than five in which human love is *not* held up as the pinnacle of our quest? It's done so often, we don't give it a second thought when Paradise is relocated in the ideal lover. *Romeo and Juliet; Casablanca; Phantom of the Opera; The Sound of Music; Cinderella; Out of Africa; Forrest Gump*. How many couples came to the altar (or dream of coming) with this expectation? "And they all lived happily ever after." We've been fed this from childhood. Please understand me—of course, we long to be loved by another person. "It is not good for man to be alone." Most people live incredibly lonely lives. Our worst pain comes from our ever-present isolation. We are surrounded by people, but truly known by so few—if any. How we long for a soul-to-soul connection. But something else is going on here, something at the level of *worship*.

Not long ago I received a letter from a woman whose husband had left her. Having been married for ten years, she was understandably devastated. My heart broke as she poured out the pain of her divorce. But as I read on, I became more and more concerned. She said she was weeping constantly and shaking uncontrollably. She wanted to die and was seriously considering taking her own life. It was not initial shock; the letter was penned many months after their breakup. Grief is an expected and appropriate response to the loss of love. But she was reacting as though she had lost her *life*. Which is, of course, what happens when you make someone else your life.

Shortly after that, a young man whom I hadn't spoken with for a number of years called. Through his sobs, I gathered that his wife had left him and the children. He explained that she'd "met someone" on the Internet, and their relationship became her obsession. "It's my turn for love," she declared, "and I'm taking it."

If we could get some distance from it, we'd see it's no less crazy than the search for El Dorado or the Fountain of Youth. Cyber relationships have launched the search for the golden man or woman to a new level because the mystique can be maintained much longer. Internet love doesn't ever have bad breath, you don't get an STD from a terminal, and no one ever has to know. Most people don't take their search to adultery. Instead, they find other, "safer" ways to taste idyllic intimacy. It may be as subtle as that second glance or maybe never quite giving up those letters from a high school sweetheart. When that's not enough, pornography becomes the next level for men. Most women go to fantasy, fed by romance novels, soap operas, or films such as *Titanic*. How else are we to explain our revolving-door marriage policy? *It's out there*, we are told, and like those earlier explorers, we'll destroy families, homes, and careers to get it.

The potion becomes intoxicating the more openly sexual it gets. Sarah McLachlan sings in "Elsewhere,"

> I am drunk in my desire,
> I love the way your hands reach out and hold me near,
> I believe, I believe this is heaven.

You might have seen *City of Angels*, another film released in the late '90s. It tells the story of how one celestial being chooses to fall from grace into the arms of a mortal woman, who happens to be Meg Ryan. While going about his angelic duties, the angel, played by Nicolas Cage, encounters Ryan. He discovers that paradise is not where you'd expect an angel to find it (in paradise) but in her embrace. Renouncing eternity, he becomes a mortal, and they share one exquisite night together. The next morning, Ryan is killed by a bus. Even still, Cage decides it was worth it. He'd do it all again, forfeit heaven "for one smell of her perfume, one touch of her hair." It's a beautiful, powerful story, and we leave the theater with the sound track still playing in our minds, a song called "Iris" by the Goo Goo Dolls.

> And I'd give up forever to touch you,
> 'Cause I know that you feel me somehow,
> You're the closest to heaven that I'll ever be.

Sexual ecstasy has long been the leading rival to the Sacred Romance, but never has it been worshiped so blatantly. Allow me one more example.

> One dark night,
> fired with love's urgent longings
> —ah, the sheer grace!—
> I went out unseen
> my house being now stilled.
> On that glad night
> in secret, for no one saw me,
> nor did I look at anything
> with no other light or guide
> than the one that burned in my heart.
> This guided me
> more surely than the light of noon
> to where he was waiting for me
> —him I knew so well—

there in a place where no one appeared.
O guiding night!
O night more lovely than the dawn!
O night that has united
the Lover with his beloved,
transforming the beloved in her Lover.
Upon my flowering breast,
which I kept wholly for him alone.

No, this is not a recent pop hit. Nor is it the theme to yet another film celebrating human love. It is taken from *The Dark Night*, penned by St. John of the Cross in the 1500s. The Lover in the poem is God, and St. John the beloved. The passion and ecstasy expressed here by this Christian mystic come from a long tradition that finds its roots in Scripture. The psalmists sang, "My soul thirsts for you, my body longs for you. Your love is better than life, my soul clings to you. Whom have I in heaven but you? And earth has nothing I desire besides you." How far we have come. Loreena McKennitt released a CD containing a song of St. John's *Dark Night*—rewritten to adore an earthly lover. She admits that St. John wrote it to "his god" (notice the small *g*), but like all of us, she chooses another god. "How skilled you are at pursuing love!" God laments. "You have lived as a prostitute with many lovers" (Jer. 2:33; 3:1 NIV).

REACHING FOR THE GOLDEN MOMENT

We do the same thing with our hunger for adventure. I imagine there must have been great excitement at the outset for those early explorers—that is, before the mosquitoes and hostile natives became realities. Most of us are not so daring; we prefer our adventure on a more modest scale. Shopping, if you can believe it, has become for most people their experience of a sort of conquest. What do you make of the credit card debt in the U.S.? More than 1.5 billion cards in circulation, with an average balance of $5,000 on each card. (How do you explain *your* current balance?)

We say we worship money, but it's not that simple. Money is merely the means to get what we really want—clothes that give us an image of attractiveness, equipment to provide excitement. Sport-utility vehicles were the top-selling line in the past ten years, but the irony is that less than 5 percent of them are ever actually taken off road. We want the illusion of adventure without really having to risk it. There is big money in outdoor gear right now; the "look" of the expedition is in. Thirty years ago you wouldn't have found a gym in every strip mall. There, in our air-conditioned sanctuaries, we tone our bodies while watching television. We'll take our adventure *vicariously*, preferring for the most part to be voyeurs of the extreme sport rage or our favorite sports teams.

I was surprised when Steven asked to see me about a problem he was having with football. He was engaged to a wonderful young woman, and things were moving along well in their relationship. "So what's wrong?" I asked. "Well . . . her dad, you see . . . he roots for the state rival of my college football team. It's kinda becoming a big deal." I had never encountered this before. This young man had a full-blown addiction to college football. He spent Monday through Friday anticipating the games, Saturday watching the games, and Sunday talking about the outcome. He knew nearly every player's name and his stats by heart. During final exams week, he tried to get away from it by securing himself in a friend's apartment with no TV. It lasted about an hour before he dialed up the Internet and picked up live coverage of his team.

As we talked about what it all meant to him, he described the thrill of going with his dad to see their team win the national play-offs. "I have a picture at home, with all of us in it—my brothers, my dad. I've never seen him so happy, so alive." Notice how important it is that it's the *home* team. We need to feel as though we are a part of the excitement.

I had an affair of my own this past summer—with an internal frame backpack. It was outrageously expensive and totally unnecessary (I have a backpack already). But still, I became obsessed. I dreamed about it during the day. At night, I pored over the catalog, comparing it with others, deepening my conviction that this was all I needed for life to be good. As Dick Keyes has pointed out, most of our idols come in pairs. There is the "nearby idol," the thing close at hand, which gives us a sense of control over our world. And then there is the "faraway idol," which provides the taste of transcendence. In my case, the backpack was the thing within reach, which promised adventure down the road. In sexuality, we work hard on our appearance (what we can control), which in turn draws others to us, bringing, we hope, a sense of being loved. The bottom line is, we don't want to wait for the promise of God to be fulfilled.

We're not the first generation to give it a go; the spirit of it goes back at least as far as the Tower of Babel. But certainly, mankind's *options* have never been greater. The technology, the finances, and the cleverness at our disposal are unsurpassed in the history of the world. The angel may be barring our way back into Eden, but we're bound and determined to get something going on our own. Wal-Mart is open twenty-four hours a day now, with a dozen restaurants nearby. Next door, a multiplex theater with thirty screens. Or stay home—we have more than a hundred channels on the TV. Then there are computer games and the Internet. We've discovered gourmet coffee (tell your grandfather you're paying five dollars for a cup), gourmet jelly beans, gourmet popcorn—you name it. We've nearly perfected our little pleasures. When the going gets tough, the tough go shopping or fishing or out to dinner. They're all impostors—every one. But we're so taken by the dizzying array of choices, we never have to stop and take a good look at what we're doing.

THE NARCOTIC OF PLEASURE

G. K. Chesterton thought that everybody ought to get drunk once a year because if that didn't do you good, the repentance in the morning would. There's nothing like waking up to what you've done, whether it's having too much to drink or eat, or letting your anger fly. The remorse after a flagrant sin often brings a sense of clarity and resolution. (How many New Year's resolutions are made the morning after?) But if we don't quite overdo it, if we keep our indulgence at a more moderate level, such clarity never comes. We never see it in black and white, for we're always under the influence. No one stops to think about it. Pleasure isn't nearly so much about true enjoyment as it is about anesthetizing ourselves. Think about the relief your idols provide: Is your desire truly and deeply satisfied, or does the relief come more through the temporary *absence* of desire?

I've had a nagging sense I was more pleasure-oriented than might be good, but I didn't see the function of pleasure in my life until I had to face intense grief and loss. I tried every drug I could, and nothing worked. Not food. Not sleep. Not work. Not reading. Not even sex. I could not get away from the pain. And then it occurred to me: If I am trying to use pleasure as a drug in this case, how many of my so-called enjoyments are merely the same thing on a lesser scale? Reading Pascal, I found he'd already hit upon the same thing. Unable to get out of the dilemma of desire, we've found a powerful drug—distraction.

> The way to render a man happy, is to engage him with an object that will make him forget his private troubles. What can be the reason that this man, who not long ago lost his only son, and this very morning was engaged almost to distraction in a law suit, now does not give his troubles a thought? You need not be astonished; he is taken up with watching a stag, which his hounds have been in full chase after, for six hours. However great his distress may have been, in this he finds ample consolation. In short, prevail upon a man to join in any amusement whatever, and as long as that lasts he will be happy; but it will be a false and imaginary happiness, arising not from the possession of real and solid good, but from a levity of spirit that obliterates the recollection of his real miseries, and fixes his thoughts upon mean and ridiculous objects, unworthy of his attention, and still less deserving of his love. (*Pensées*)

Don't be fooled by the apparent innocence of the object you've chosen. What is its *function*? Most of our idols also have a perfectly legitimate place in our lives. That's their cover. That's how we get away with our infidelity. The prophet Isaiah gives an example when he marvels at a man who cuts down a tree in the forest and then puts it to two very different uses:

> Half of the wood he burns in the fire;
> over it he prepares his meal,
> he roasts his meat and eats his fill.

Nothing wrong here. That's the perfectly appropriate use of wood. But it doesn't end here (it rarely does):

> From the rest he makes a god, his idol;
>> he bows down to it and worships.
> He prays to it and says,
>> "Save me; you are my god."

The prophet is incredulous. *Doesn't he see what he's doing?* he wonders.

> No one stops to think,
>> no one has the knowledge or understanding to say,
>> "Half of it I used for fuel;
>> I even baked bread over its coals,
>> I roasted meat and I ate.
> Shall I make a detestable thing from what is left?
>> Shall I bow down to a block of wood?"
> He feeds on ashes, a deluded heart misleads him;
>> he cannot save himself or say,
>> "Is not this thing in my right hand a lie?"
>>>> (Isa. 44:16–17, 19–20 NIV)

So there you have it: no one stops to think. We don't want to take a good, hard look at what we are really doing, for then we might see the lie. We would expose the impostors. We would see the water hole for the muddy puddle it is. Our idols become the *means* by which we forget who we truly are and where we truly come from. They numb us. Like Hansel and Gretel, we're following a sugared path to our destruction. Or perhaps it's the Pied Piper who's got us skipping along. (There's a reason we used to tell those fairy tales. They contained wisdom we desperately need.) How else can we explain our apparent happiness when we are so far from home? Pascal observed,

> Mankind, unable to escape death, trouble and ignorance, in order to make themselves happy, have hit upon the plan of never

thinking about these things; the utmost efforts of their ingenuity can suggest no better consolation for such prodigious evils. But it is most miserable consolation, since it does not cure the evil, but merely to conceal it a little while; and by concealing it, prevents men from attempting to obtain a thorough cure. (*Pensées*)

THE ASSAULT ON OUR DESIRE

The battle of desire is not something that just takes place within us or even between us. It is also taking place *against* us, all the time. Our desire is under nearly constant attack. "We come into the world longing," says Gil Bailie, "for we know not what. We *are* desire. And desire is good, for it's what takes us to God. But our desire is not hard-wired to God."

We look to others to teach us what to desire. We are intensely imitative creatures, as Aristotle pointed out. It is how we learn language; it is how we master just about anything in life. It is also how we come to seize upon the objects of our desire. We all know this, though we don't like to admit it.

One example should suffice. I was at a garage sale, looking for some tools. There was a table saw at a wonderful price. Another fellow was sort of browsing around, standing in front of the saw but not seeming particularly interested. I opened my mouth and made the fatal error: "Wow, that's a great price on that saw." You know what happened next. Immediately, his nonchalance became intense interest, and since he was there before me, he drove off with a table saw that five minutes earlier he couldn't have given two hoots about.

Madison Avenue plays on this with a cynical brilliance. Look at fashion, for example. It lives on this dynamic. We don't wear what we want to wear; we wear what everyone else is wearing this year. The new line of cars that rolls out each year survives on this as well. Do we really imagine there's a significant difference in the actual car itself? Or notice what happens every Christmas. Quite often one toy emerges as the "must have" toy. A few years ago it was a little doll called Tickle Me Elmo, after the Sesame Street character. There was a rush on the doll. Suppliers ran out. People went mad, paying hundreds and thousands of dollars to get their hands on a little red character that retails for $29.99. Incidentally, you can go to the store tomorrow and get as many as you'd like. The mimetic fever is over—or has changed focus.

Advertisers play on this constantly, urging us to desire this and that by creating the image that "everyone who is anyone" has the object for sale, and we are surely a loser if we don't join the frenzy. Sadly, the ploy works. Bailie perceives that

> we live in a world inundated by these mimetic passions. What we call "modernity" is a world of feverishly mimetic desires and fascinations. With powers of telecommunication of which the Aztecs could not have dreamed, we are given models to emulate incessantly. We are inspired to envy, desire, compete, resent, aspire and be ambitious. (*Violence Unveiled*)

The constant effort to arouse our desire and capture it can be described only as an assault. From the time we get up to the time we go to bed, we are inundated with one underlying message: *it can be done.* The life you are longing for *can* be achieved. Only buy this product, see this movie, drive this car, take this vacation, join this gym, what have you. The only disagreement is over the means, but everyone agrees on the end: we can find life now.

I suppose the architects of Madison Avenue are for the most part motivated merely by success. It's their job to sell. But behind the whole mimetic madness is an even more brilliant schemer. The evil one has basically two ploys. If he cannot get us to kill our hearts and bury our desire, then he is delighted to seduce our desire into a trap. Once we give over our desire for life to any object other than God, we become ensnared. Think of the phrase, "She's a slave to fashion." We become slaves to any number of things, which at the outset we thought would serve us. In this light, repression of desire is a much less dangerous stage in the process. Addiction is far worse, for as May explains,

> Our addictions are our own worst enemies. They enslave us with chains that are of our own making and yet that, paradoxically, are virtually beyond our control. Addiction also makes idolaters of us all, because it forces us to worship these objects of attachment, thereby preventing us from truly, freely loving God and one another. (*Addiction and Grace*)

Like the rich young ruler, we find we cannot give up our treasured possessions, whatever they may be, even though God himself is standing before us with a better offer. If you think his sad story is not also your own, you are out of touch with yourself. I remember standing in the East River several summers ago. It was a gorgeous summer evening, and I was about to enjoy some great fly-fishing. I had just begun to cast when God spoke to me. *Put down the rod,* he said. *I'd like to spend some time with you.* I was irritated. *Now?* I replied. *You want to talk to me now? Why not later on the drive home? There's plenty of time in the car.* Good grief. What an addict I am! Thus the father of lies turns our most precious treasure—our longing for God and for his kingdom—into our worst enemy. It is truly diabolical. We wind up serving our desire slavishly or resenting it, or a little of both.

OUR TIMING IS OFF

"And envy."

It was three days after Brent's fall, and I was talking to a mutual friend of ours on the phone, telling him what I had been feeling—anger, rage, grief, numbness, exhaustion. Dan said, "And envy." He went on to describe his own feelings of a sort of jealousy, that Brent was home, that he had moved "from the battle to the banquet." I didn't reply. I didn't know what to say. I wasn't feeling envy; it hadn't even crossed my mind. Certainly, part of that can be written off to what I was going through. But not all of it.

Dan's comment exposed my basic commitment to find life here and now. It is a commitment nearly all of us share, at a far deeper level than we'd like to admit. There's something just a little hurt and angry in all of us as we find that life is not coming through. A song by Don Henley called "The End of the Innocence" captures the relation between our heartache and our use of pleasure in a very sad sort of way. The opening lines go like this:

> Remember when the days were long
> And rolled beneath a deep blue sky
> Didn't have a care in the world
> With mommy and daddy standin' by
> But "happily ever after" fails
> And we've been poisoned by these fairy tales
> The lawyers clean up all details
> Since daddy had to fly

The man in the song lost the love he was meant to know as a boy when his parents divorced. It was the end of the innocence for him, his personal encounter with life after the Fall. Hurt and angry, he searches for something now to give at least a taste of what was meant to be. Like so many men, he chooses sexual intimacy as his impostor.

> But I know a place where we can go
> Still untouched by man . . .
> So lay your head back on the ground
> Let your hair fall all round
> Offer up your best defense
> But this is the end of the innocence

Have we really been poisoned by fairy tales? No, we've merely gotten the timing wrong. Although our desire has taken us to a thousand "other lovers," we must not make a fatal error and try one more time to get rid of it. We cannot revert to killing our hearts. Instead, we must accept the first lesson in the journey of desire: ecstasy is *not* an option. We must have life. The only problem is in our refusal to wait. That is why God must rescue us from the very things we thought would save us.

IT WAS IN *May* that the winds began to blow. The sea lion had grown used to wind, and at first he did not pay much heed at all. Years of desert life had taught him to turn his back in the direction from which the wind came and cover his eyes with his flippers, so that the dust would not get in. Eventually, the winds would always pass.

But not this time. Day and night it came, howling across the barren lands. There was nothing to stop its fury, nothing to even slow it down. For forty days and forty nights the wind blew. And then, just as suddenly as it had begun, it stopped. The sea lion lifted himself to have a look around. He could hardly believe his eyes.

Every single leaf had been stripped from his tree. The branches that remained, with only a twig or two upon them, looked like an old scarecrow. And I do not need to tell you that there was no longer any shade in which to hide. But worse than this, much worse indeed, was what the sea lion saw next. The water hole was completely dry.

CHAPTER SIX

THE DIVINE THWARTER

Someone has altered the script.
My lines have been changed . . .
I thought I was writing this play.

—MADELEINE L'ENGLE

I can't get no satisfaction.

—THE ROLLING STONES

Devise your plan. It will be thwarted.

—GOD

It started five years ago with my annual fishing trip. Those of you unfamiliar with *fly*-fishing must rid your minds of the images of that other kind—guys in their lawn chairs down at the city pond, chugging cheap beer while they attempt to fool fish with fluorescent pink, garlic-flavored cheese balls beneath an enormous bobber. You wonder if they haven't met their match. To compare that with a day on a high mountain stream pursuing wild trout through the elegance and serenity of fly-fishing is like comparing the mini mart at your gas station to Nordstrom's, or professional wrestling to gymnastics, or the Simpsons to Shakespeare. Enough said.

This yearly pilgrimage has always been for me a time of consummate pleasure, a banquet of beauty with deep friendship and adventure. Then it all began to unravel. I had scheduled a few days on the Frying Pan River in Colorado in late May. The fishing there is legendary, and recent reports had been phenomenal. But as a friend and I drove up to the river, it began to rain. *Not to worry*, I thought. *Late spring often brings rain. It'll blow over in an hour or two.* As we climbed into the mountains, the rain turned into a snowstorm that lasted the entire trip.

I began to play chess with God. The following year, I planned our trip for July to eliminate all possibility of snow. I booked several days at a private ranch that caters to fly fishermen, with a guide to take us out on the upper Rio Grande. The night before we were to leave, I received a call telling me that no, it had not snowed, but thunderstorms had created mudslides and the fishing was impossible. They offered to refund my money.

I sensed that God had made a countermove, and that my king was in danger. Grabbing my phone book, I found the number of another guide on a different river and called him. Yes, the fishing was fabulous. Yes, he could take us out tomorrow. I hung up the phone with a smile. Your move, God. When we arrived early the next morning, the fellow told us sadly, "It's the strangest thing, but they opened the dam last night and the river's flooded. Sorry 'bout that."

The next year it was a drought; the year after that we still don't know what happened. High in the meadows of the Eastern Sierra, the fish had seemed to simply vanish from the San Joaquin. I was losing the game, as you can tell. But I hadn't been cornered; not yet.

Last year I was invited to speak at a conference near Bend, Oregon. It is a place very dear to me, full of memories from my childhood. The Deschutes River flows through there, and I was looking forward (can you believe my tenacity?) to some great time on the water with my new fly rod. (Country musicians use a *fiddle*, but to play Mozart, you use a *violin*. Bait fishermen use *poles*, while fly fishermen use *rods*.) I made what I felt would be my winning move. A friend arranged access for me to a private stretch of the Deschutes, a ranch visited each year by only a handful of people. The caretaker was an old master fly fisherman. When the owner of the shop in town learned where I was headed, he looked around furtively, leaned across the counter, and whispered, "Mister, that may be the best one hundred yards of fishing in the United States." Something smiled in my heart and said, *Check*.

Old Bill was a marvelous fisherman, and as we walked down to the water, he realized, "I'm thinkin' . . . let's see . . . you're the first guy to fish this since last October." *Six months ago,* I thought. *This is going to be incredible.* You know what's coming next. Nothing. We caught nothing. Bill had a funny look on his face. "John," he said, "people come from all over the world to fish this ranch. I've never had a day like this . . . ever." Feeling for all the world like Jonah, I said, "Bill, this is not about you. The fishing will be great tomorrow after I've gone." Checkmate.

CRUEL OR KIND?

This is the point at which God most feels like our enemy. It seems at times that he will go to any length to thwart the very thing we most deeply want. We can't get a job. Our attempt to find a spouse never pans out. The doctors aren't able to help us with our infertility. Isn't this precisely the reason we fear to desire in the first place? Life is hard enough as it is, but to think that God himself is working against us is more than disheartening. Job cried out, "What do you gain by oppressing me? . . . You hunt me like a lion and display your awesome power against me" (10:3, 16 NLT).

I want to state very clearly that not every trial in life is specially arranged for us by God. Much of the heartache we know comes from living in a broken world filled with broken people. And we have an enemy in the evil one who hates us deeply. But there are times when God himself seems to be set *against* us. Unless we understand our desperate hearts and our incredible tenacity to arrange for the life we want, these events will just seem cruel.

When we lived in Eden, there was virtually no restriction on the pleasure around us. We could eat *freely* from any tree in the Garden. Our desire was innocent and fully satisfied. I cannot even imagine what five minutes in total bliss would be like. We had it all, but we threw it away. By mistrusting God's heart, by reaching to take control of what we wanted, Adam and Eve set in motion a process in our hearts, a desperate grasping that can be described only as *addiction*. Desire goes mad within us. May observes, "Once they gave in to that temptation, their freedom was invaded by attachment. They experienced the need for more. God knew that they would not—*could not*—stop with just the one tree."

Our first parents are banished from Paradise as an act of mercy. The thought of the human race gaining immortality— eating from the Tree of Life—in a fallen state is too horrible to imagine. We would be evil forever. And though we are sent from the Garden, "the story of Eden is not over." Every day we reenact the Fall as we turn in our desire to the very things that will destroy us. As May reminds us,

> Addiction exists wherever persons are internally compelled to give energy to things that are not their true desires. To define it directly, addiction is a state of compulsion, obsession, or preoccupation that enslaves a person's will and desire. Addiction side-

tracks and eclipses the energy of our deepest, truest desire for love and goodness. We succumb because the energy of our desire becomes attached, nailed, to specific behaviors, objects or people. (*Addiction and Grace*)

Addiction may seem too strong a term to some of you. The woman who is serving so faithfully at church—surely, there's nothing wrong with that. And who can blame the man who stays long at the office to provide for his family? Sure, you may look forward to the next meal more than most people do, and your hobbies can be a nuisance sometimes, but to call any of this an addiction seems to stretch the word a bit too far.

I have one simple response: give it up. If you don't think you're a chess player, too, then prove it by letting go of the things that provide you with a sense of security, or comfort, or excitement, or relief. You will soon discover the tentacles of attachment deep in your soul. There will be an anxiousness; you'll begin to think about work or food or golf even more. Withdrawal will set in. If you can make it a week or two out of sheer willpower, you will find a sadness growing in your soul, a deep sense of loss. Lethargy and a lack of motivation follow.

Remember, we will make an idol of anything, especially a good thing. So distant now from Eden, we are *desperate* for life, and we come to believe that we must arrange for it as best we can, or no one will. God must thwart us to save us.

FUTILITY AND FAILURE

Adam and Eve stand before God with nothing but fig leaves to hide their shame. Knowing what has happened in our hearts, what desire can and will do divorced from its true source of happiness, God moves to intervene. With deep wisdom and kindness, he curses our lives. To Adam—and all his sons after him—God says,

> Because you listened to your wife and ate the fruit I told you not to eat, I have placed a curse on the ground. All your life you will struggle to scratch a living from it. It will grow thorns and thistles for you, though you will eat of its grains. All your life you will sweat to produce food, until your dying day. (Gen. 3:17–19 NLT)

God thwarts men where it hurts most—in the field. He strikes a blow in the arena of our labor, our strength. This is our most vulnerable spot. We draw our sense of worth from it. I am not minimizing the importance of intimacy to a man; not at all. But when men get together, they don't talk about how everyone's relationship is doing. "Did you hear about Sally and Bill? I wonder if everything's okay. Maybe we should give them a call." No, they talk about their *achievements* (typically with a little embellishment). "I bagged the Zonax account today. Yep. Won't be long now before I'm running Sales." A man's impostors are most often born out of this place in his heart. Either they offer a false sense of strength, or they relieve a man from having to be strong. Pornography, for example, does both. The woman says, "I will make you feel like a man by giving myself to you, and you don't have to do anything at all. You can have the pleasure of a woman without having to *live* with her." A man's deepest desires always relate to his strength, one way or another, and so the curse for a man strikes him at the core.

As Dan Allender has pointed out, this is obviously about more than literal thorns and thistles, or every man who is not a farmer gets to escape the curse. Those who live in an apartment and work on Wall Street would get off scot-free. If only it were that easy. If only our worst enemy were dandelions and crabgrass. But every man knows the reality of the curse because every man must face the ongoing frustration of *futility* and *failure*. No matter how much a man achieves, it is never enough. He has to go out tomorrow and do it all again. If you hit a home run in last week's game, there is such a short time of joy. Next time you're at the plate, everyone expects you to do it again. And again. Futility. And even if you do seem to beat the odds and secure yourself financially, the curse is waiting for you somewhere else in your life—in your marriage or with your children. That is why a man's worst fear is not measuring up. A woman isn't affected by defeat the way a man is. It may hurt, but typically, she bounces back from failure. Not so for a man; in some cases, failure can be debilitating for life.

LONELINESS AND HEARTACHE

When God turns to the issues of a woman's wayward heart, he brings a very different curse. To Eve and all her daughters, he says, "You will bear children with intense pain and suffering. And though your desire will be for your husband, he will be your master" (Gen. 3:16 NLT).

This is obviously about more than babies and marriage, or every single woman without children gets to escape the curse. Some of our dearest friends are in that situation, and I can tell you that they do not live in Paradise. Every woman knows the reality of the curse because every woman lives with *relational heartache* and *loneliness*. With the skill of a surgeon going after a cancer, God thwarts a woman where it matters most—in her relationships. Are not her deepest tears shed over issues of failed intimacy? When women get together, they don't talk about work, unless it's to talk about their work *relationships*. This observation is not condescending in the least. A woman's glory is her heart for others, her keen sense of interpersonal dynamics, her commitment to maintaining relational connections. A woman who knows she is deeply loved typically survives a career setback that would send a man into a tailspin.

A woman's impostors are nearly always an attempt to somehow fill that ache for love or pretend she doesn't need love. The feminist movement has tried hard to assert that women can be as tough as men; they, too, can compete, can achieve, can conquer. It's tired and overdone. Like Lady Macbeth, it was an attempt by certain women to deal with the dilemma of their desire by "unsexing" themselves. Such contempt for tenderness and vulnerability reveals only how much they fear both, how deeply they have been hurt in that place. In a backhanded way, it confirms their design.

The worst fear for a woman is *abandonment*. Like a man who refuses to play the man for fear of failing, a woman who shuns intimacy only reveals her fear of rejection by refusing to face it honestly, openly. As for the love substitutes, men aren't buying Danielle Steel romances. They have to be dragged to the next "love finally finds her" movie. Women often create colorful fantasy worlds, a kind of pornography that guarantees rich intimacy in spite of the emptiness of daily life. The writers of soaps know this tendency only too well.

THE HARDEST LESSON TO LEARN

God *promises* every man futility and failure; he *guarantees* every woman relational heartache and loneliness. We spend most of our waking hours attempting to end-run the curse. We will fight this truth with all we've got. Sure, other people suffer defeat. Other people face loneliness. But not me. I can beat the odds. We see the neighbor's kids go off the deep end, and we make a mental note: *they didn't pray for their kids every day*. And we make praying for our kids every day part of our plan. It doesn't have to happen to us. We watch a colleague suffer a financial setback, and we make another note: *he was always a little lax with his money*. We set up a rigid budget and stick to it.

Isn't there something defensive that rises up in you at the idea that you cannot make life work out? Isn't there something just a little bit stubborn, an inner voice that says, *I can do it*? Thus Pascal writes,

> All men seek happiness. This is without exception. Whatever different means they employ, they all tend to this end . . . This is the motive of every action of every man. *But example teaches us little.* No resemblance is ever so perfect that there is not some slight difference, and hence we expect that *our* hope will not be deceived on this occasion as before. And thus, while the present never satisfies us, experience dupes us and from misfortune to misfortune leads us to death. (*Pensées*)

It can't be done. No matter how hard we try, no matter how clever our plan, we cannot arrange for the life we desire. Set the book down for a moment and ask yourself this question: Will life ever be what I so deeply want it to be, in a way that cannot be lost? This is the second lesson we must learn, and in many ways the hardest to accept. We must have life; we cannot arrange for it.

People will avoid this lesson all their days, changing their plans, their jobs, even their mates, rather than facing the truth.

> You were wearied by all your ways,
>> but you would not say, "It is hopeless."
> You found renewal of your strength,
>> and so you did not faint. (Isa. 57:10 NIV)

These are the majority of folks out there, Christian and pagan, who are still giving it a go. Yes, a smaller number have collided against failure and heartache in such a devastating way that they have come to see it can't be done, but they have faded into resignation, or bitterness, or despair. They have taken their revenge on the God who has thwarted them by killing their desire.

How do we accept that *it can't be done* with an open heart? How do we sustain desire in the face of ongoing failure and loneliness? It all depends on what we do with hope.

MISPLACED HOPE

"In this world you will have trouble." No kidding. Jesus, the master of understatement, captures in one sentence the story of our lives. He adds, "But take heart! I have overcome the world" (John 16:33 NIV). Why aren't we more encouraged? (Sometimes we'll try to *feel* encouraged when we hear a "religious" passage like this, but it never really lasts.) The reason is that we are still committed to arranging for life now. Be honest. Isn't there a disappointment when you realize that I'm not going to offer you the seven secrets of a really great life today? If I wanted to make millions, that's the book I would write. The only thing is, I would have to lie. It can't be done. Not *yet*. And that *yet* makes all the difference in the world because desire cannot live without hope. But hope in what? *For* what?

"Set your hope *fully* on the grace to be given you when Jesus Christ is revealed" (1 Peter 1:13 NIV, emphasis added). I read a passage like this, and I don't know whether to laugh or to cry. Fully? We don't even set our hope *partially* on the life to come. Not really, not in the desires of our hearts. Heaven may be coming. Great. But it's a long way off and who really knows, so I'm getting what I can now. Our search is limited only by our finances, our options, and our morals. Those with fewer misgivings and greater financial discretion go farther with it. For most Christians, heaven is a backup plan. Our primary work is finding a life we can at least get a little pleasure from here. Heaven is an investment we've made, like Treasury bonds or a retirement account, which we're hoping will take care of us in the future sometime, but which we do not give much thought to at present. It's tucked away in a drawer at the back of our minds, while we throw our immediate energies into playing the stock market. God comes in like a corporate raider, ruining our plans as we watch our "stocks" go into a tailspin.

"Remember how the LORD your God led you all the way in the desert these forty years, to humble you and to test you in order to know what was in your heart . . . He humbled you, causing you to hunger" (Deut. 8:2–3 NIV). When the Israelites left Egypt, they headed across the Red Sea to Mount Sinai. From there it was only about a two-week journey into the promised land. Fourteen days turned into *forty years*. A blind camel would have found its way sooner than that. God designed a supernaturally long trail in order to deal with what was in their hearts. During my five-year chess match with God, I often wrestled with his reasons for thwarting me. *I am serving you faithfully, God. Why won't you let me have this little pleasure?* Trip after trip was supernaturally foiled. It felt to me so unfair, even cruel. I mean, we're talking about fishing, for heaven's sake. It's not as if I were trying to have an affair. Or was I?

The day after my miraculous not-even-one-little-strike disaster on the Deschutes, I was driving around the back roads of that gorgeous country in central Oregon, looking at ranches and daydreaming. For years I've had a desire for a place of my own, several hundred acres with some riverfront, maybe here in Oregon. My longing for a ranch preceded by years any thought of using it for "ministry." No, ever since I was a child, the ranch has meant to me something else, my little heaven on earth. I rolled down the windows of my four-wheel drive and drank in the beauty and the solitude, the warmth of the sun, the sight of horses grazing in the fields, and the smell of the hay meadows. As I allowed myself to feel that quiet and long-buried desire, a sentence popped up out of my heart: *I really could be happy here without God*. It was completely unlooked for and remarkably honest. The thwarting had worked; now I could see what God was after in my heart. It all fell into place, and I simply said, *Oh . . . now I understand*.

God must take away the heaven we create, or it will become our hell. You may not think your efforts to arrange for a little of what you desire are anything like heaven on earth. I certainly didn't; not, at least, in the more conscious regions of my heart. But some deep and tender part of us gets trapped there in those times and places where we have had a taste of the life we long for. There in the ranch lands of central Oregon, I realized that the real issue is this: I haven't wanted to be an eternal person. I've wanted to find life here somehow. And not somehow, but through golden days on western streams, with men I love. For it was there I felt most alive, most loved, most hopeful.

As I sat there in my Jeep, surrounded by the visions and aromas—horses in a field, the pine and sage—I was transported to a time long ago in my youth, with all the promise in the air of the day ahead. And I thought, *I would give anything to return to that time in my life*. It's as if the golden center of my heart is back there in those golden days, and God wants to free it from there, to bring it into the present for the future.

I returned home a different man. Not entirely healed, not fully delivered, but still, something deep in me had shifted. The arranging had begun to stop. My heart was beginning to lift its eyes beyond the horizon toward those eternal pastures. Two weeks later Brent was killed. I began to see the hand of God in all of it, preparing me for what was coming. I think at any time during those years of thwarting, had you asked me if I truly longed for eternity, I would have said yes. My answer would not have been dishonest, but it would not have been entirely true, either. George MacDonald explained the thwarting,

> Thy hand unloved its pleasure must restrain,
> Nor spoil both gift and child by lavishing too soon.
> (Diary of an Old Soul)

THE ULTIMATE BLOW

The phone just rang. A friend's father has died of a heart attack. One minute he is going about his business like all the other drivers on the road—like us—and the next minute is his last. He was sitting at a stoplight, waiting to make a turn, and suddenly, he was gone. It was just a few months ago that I received another call, from a different friend, telling me that her little brother had died of some complications that developed from a congenital defect. He was three years old. The day before he had been out in the yard, playing on the swings and laughing.

How can we possibly continue to bet on our arranging in the face of such an overwhelming enemy as death? It is beyond me. It certainly is a testimony to our unlimited capacity for denial. As Pascal observed, it is as if we are all under a spell.

Nothing is so important to man as his own state, nothing is so formidable to him as eternity; and thus it is not natural that there should be men indifferent to the loss of their existence, and to the perils of everlasting suffering. They are quite different with regard to all other things. They are afraid of mere trifles; they foresee them; they feel them. And this same man who spends so many days and nights in rage and despair at the loss of an office, or for some imaginary insult to his honor, is the very one who knows without anxiety and without emotion that he will lose all by death. It is a monstrous thing to see in the same heart and at the same time this sensibility to trifles and this strange insensibility to the greatest objects. It is an incomprehensible enchantment. (*Pensées*)

In the years that followed the Fall and our exile from Eden, mankind got worse and worse. Cain killed Abel; Lamech threatened to kill everybody else. The wickedness of the human heart seemed out of control and unstoppable, even by the curses. People were living for seven, eight, even nine *hundred* years. Can you imagine the arranging that one person could accomplish with that sort of time on his hands? Stubbornness seems to come with old age. Haven't you heard your grandmother sigh and say of your grandfather, "He's set in his ways"? Multiply that by a factor of eight or nine and you get the picture. So God dealt the ultimate blow. Then the Lord said, "My Spirit will not contend with man forever, for he is mortal; his days will be a hundred and twenty years" (Gen. 6:3 NIV). He cut our life short; nobody gets to pass 120. However clever we might be in our ability to conjure Paradise, we can never get around death. It is the final thwarting.

You must follow me very carefully now. We can never fully explain the reasons surrounding someone's death. We've come to accept it for the aged, and we try to console ourselves with thoughts like, *He's had a full life.* But death is *never* natural; it was not meant to be. That is why those left behind experience such excruciating pain. The agony is only worsened when the death is what we call premature, when it takes a life in full bloom, or just as the bud begins to open. Each death can begin to be understood only within the larger story God is telling. Much of that story remains for the moment a mystery.

Many people were shattered by Brent's death. I know I was. Not even on my worst enemies would I wish such pain. But I also know this: the shattering was good. Living apart from God comes naturally; all the striving and arranging is so second nature to me that to have it stopped in its tracks was a great good. I would wake in the morning in those early days of grief, and instead of my desires "rushing at me like a pack of wild animals" as Lewis said, I knew *it can't be done*. I knew it more deeply and more personally than I had ever known it before. We must learn this lesson, at whatever cost, or the spell will not be broken and we will never discover true hope.

WHAT THEN?

"There's nothing now but heaven." It was one of those truly honest moments, when my heart speaks what I most deeply believe. Stasi and I had just finished watching *A River Runs Through It*, and the warm tears rolled quietly down my face as I sat looking out the back window of our home into the night. In a subtle and unlooked-for way, the film had brought the reality of all my losses flooding back to me. The only time and place I ever really connected with my father was when we were fishing the rivers and streams of the West. But even that could not hold us together. As time passed our trips came to an end, and we drifted apart.

Years later, as a grown man, I came home distraught from a day alone on the river. I was agitated, and though I did not know why, I knew it was not because I had not caught anything. As

Stasi and I spoke about my frustration and disappointment, the words of truth slipped from my mouth: "I'll never find him out there." I hadn't known until that moment what I had been looking for in all those years of fly-fishing.

A River Runs Through It beautifully captures the author's time of boyhood innocence, and fly-fishing trips in Montana with his father, and losing it all. The story ends with the author, now an old man, standing alone in a river, fishing. "Now, all those I loved and did not understand in my youth are gone . . . But I still reach out to them." The words were true for me; they are true for all of us. It can't be done; yet the desire remains. This is the most crucial moment for our hearts. Once we come to accept that we can never find or hang on to the life we have been seeking, what then? As Dallas Willard writes, it matters for all the world to know that life is ahead of us.

> I meet many faithful Christians who, in spite of their faith, are deeply disappointed in how their lives have turned out. Sometimes it is simply a matter of how they experience aging, which they take to mean they no longer have a future. But often, due to circumstances or wrongful decisions and actions by others, what they had hoped to accomplish in life they did not . . . Much of the distress of these good people comes from a failure to realize that their life lies before them . . . the life that lies endlessly before us in the kingdom of God. (*The Divine Conspiracy*)

Pascal also observed, "We are never living, but hoping to live; and whilst we are always preparing to be happy, it is certain, we never shall be so, if we aspire to no other happiness than what can be enjoyed in this life."

Desire cannot live without hope. Yet we can only hope for

what we desire. There simply must be something more, something out there on the road ahead of us, that offers the life we
prize. To sustain the life of the heart, the life of deep desire, we
desperately need to possess a clearer picture of the life that lies
before us.

CHAPTER SEVEN

THE GREAT RESTORATION

We shall not cease from exploration
And the end of all our exploring
Will be to arrive where we started
And know the place for the first time.

—T. S. ELIOT

Look, I am making all things new!

—JESUS OF NAZARETH

See! The winter is past;
   the rains are over and gone.
Flowers appear on the earth;
   the season of singing has come.

—SONG OF SONGS 2:11–12 NIV

I was walking in the woods and fields behind our house one evening, four months after Brent's death. My heart was so aware of the loss—not only of Brent, but in some ways, of everything that mattered. I knew that one by one, I would lose everyone I cared about and the life I am still seeking. In the east, a full moon was rising, bright and beautiful and enormous as it seems when it is just above the horizon. Toward the west, the clouds were turning peach and pink against a topaz sky. Telling myself to long for eternity feels like telling myself to let go of all I love—forever. It feels like accepting the teaching of Eastern religions, a *denial* of life and all God created. We lose it all too soon, before we can begin to live and love. But what if? What if nature is speaking to us? What if sunrise and sunset tell the tale every day, remembering Eden's glory, prophesying Eden's return? What if it shall all be restored?

THE SECRET OF SPRING

Winter tarries long at six thousand feet. Here in the Rocky Mountains, spring comes late and fitfully. We had snow again last week—the second week in May. Our boys are about to get out of school for summer vacation, and it's snowing. I've come to accept that spring here is really a wrestling match between winter and summer, as if winter doesn't want to let go its grip until it absolutely has to. It makes for a long time of waiting. You see, the flowers are pretty much gone in September. The first of October, the aspens start turning gold and drop their leaves in a week or two. Come November all is gray. Initially, I don't mind. The coming of winter has its joys, and there are Thanksgiving and Christmastime to look forward to.

But after the new year, things begin to drag on. Through February and then March, the earth remains lifeless. The whole world lies shadowed in brown and gray tones, like an old photograph. Winter's novelty is long past, and by April we are longing for some sign of life—some color, some hope. Instead, we get dumped on. It's our biggest snow month. While the azaleas are coming out in full glory in Atlanta, and the dogwoods are blooming pink and white in Portland, we are shoveling several feet of snow. It's too long.

And then, just this afternoon, I rounded the corner into our neighborhood, and suddenly, the world was green again. The bluffs behind our house were transformed. What had been rock and twig and dead mulch was a rich oriental carpet of green. I was shocked, stunned. How did it happen? As if in disbelief, I got out of my car and began to walk through the woods, touching every leaf. Just yesterday the scrub oaks had the twisted, gnarled look of the hands of an old witch. Now they are beautiful, tender, supple like a maiden. The birds are back as well, waking us in the morning with their glad songs. All the chirps and cheeps and whistles and twitters, a raucous melody of simple joy. It happened suddenly. In the twinkling of an eye.

My surprise is telling. It seems natural to long for spring; it is another thing to be completely stunned by its return. I am truly and genuinely surprised, as if my reaction were, *Really? What are you doing here?* And then I realized, *I never thought I'd see you again.* I think in some deep place inside, I had accepted the fact that winter is what is really true. As I lived through the first year of my grief, I had unconsciously settled into resignation. Empty and still, the world outside seemed a confirmation, the only fitting backdrop to the world within. I am shocked by the return of spring. And I wonder, *Can the same thing happen for my soul?*

> Grief melts away
> Like snow in May
> As if there were no such cold thing.
> Who would have thought my shrivl'd heart
> Could have recover'd greennesse? It was gone
> Quite underground
>
> And now in age I bud again,
> After so many deaths I live and write;
> I once more smell the dew and rain,

> And relish versing: O my only light
> > It cannot be
> > That I am he
> On whom thy tempests fell all night.
> > ("The Flower" George Herbert)

Can it really happen? Can things in our lives be green again? No matter what our creeds may tell us, our hearts have settled into another belief. We have accepted the winter of this world as the final word and tried to get on without the hope of spring. *It will never come,* we have assumed, *and so I must find whatever life here I can.* We have been so committed to arranging for our happiness that we have missed the signs of spring. We haven't given any serious thought to what might be around the corner. Were eternity to appear tomorrow, we would be as shocked as I have been with the return of spring this week, only more so. Our practical agnosticism would be revealed. Pascal declared, "Our imagination so powerfully magnifies time, by continual reflections upon it, and so diminishes eternity . . . for want of reflection, that we make a nothing of eternity and an eternity of nothing."

MORE THAN CHURCH FOREVER

But of course we aspire to happiness we can enjoy now. Our hearts have no place else to go. We have made a nothing of eternity. If I told you that your income would triple next year, and that European vacation you've wanted is just around the corner, you'd be excited, hopeful. The future would look promising. It seems possible, *desirable.* But our ideas of heaven, while possible, aren't all that desirable. Whatever it is we think is coming in the next season of our existence, we don't think it is worth getting all that excited about. We make a nothing of eternity by enlarging the significance of this life and by diminishing the reality of what the next life is all about. Nearly every Christian I have spoken with has some idea that eternity is an unending church service. After all, the Bible says that the saints "worship God in heaven," and without giving it much more thought we have settled on an image of the never-ending sing-along in the sky, one great hymn after another, forever and ever, amen.

And our heart sinks. *Forever and ever? That's it? That's the good news?* And then we sigh and feel guilty that we are not more "spiritual." We lose heart, and we turn once more to the present to find what life we can. Eternity ends up having no bearing on our search for life whatsoever. It feels like the end of the search. And since we're not all that sure about what comes after, we search hard now. Remember, *we can only hope for what we desire.* How can the church service that never ends be more desirable than the richest experiences of life here? It would be no small difference if you knew in your heart that the life you prize is just around the corner, that your deepest desires have been whispering to you all along about what's coming. You see, Scripture tells us that God has "set eternity" in our hearts (Eccl. 3:11 NIV). Where in our hearts? In our *desires.*

The return of spring brings such relief and joy and anticipation. Life has returned, and with it sunshine, warmth, color, and the long summer days of adventure together. We break out the lawn chairs and the barbecue grill. We tend the garden and drink in all the beauty. We head off for vacations. Isn't this what we most deeply long for? To leave the winter of the world behind, what Shakespeare called "the winter of our discontent," and find ourselves suddenly in the open meadows of summer?

I am standing in my hotel room, which looks like every other hotel room I've been in over the past ten years. When you travel for a living, the excitement of hotel stays wears off pretty quickly.

There is a picture on the wall, a painting of a small harbor town. It appears to be somewhere in the Mediterranean, with its azure seas and whitewashed walls. I think of the Greek islands, perhaps Santorini. Sunlight fills the place, and small boats drift lazily in the bay. There are cafes, I am sure, filled with laughter. Along the plaza, lovers stroll hand in hand. The seas are warm and inviting. It evokes a longing, but not for vacation. Vacations end. The longing evoked by the painting is for a life that never ends.

Now . . . what if spring and summer are nature's way of expressing what Jesus was in fact trying to tell us? After all, nature is God's word to us also (Rom. 1:20). If we paid close attention, we would discover something of great joy and wonder: the restoration of the world played out before us each spring and summer is *precisely* what God is promising us about our lives. Jesus preached far more than the gospel of sin management. The good news he brought was much, much greater than forgiveness. Jesus came to announce the coming of "the kingdom of God."

> Jesus went throughout Galilee, teaching in their synagogues, preaching the good news of the kingdom. (Matt. 4:23 NIV)

> The time has come . . . The kingdom of God is near. Repent and believe the good news! (Mark 1:15 NIV)

> After this, Jesus traveled about from one town and village to another, proclaiming the good news of the kingdom of God. (Luke 8:1 NIV)

> After his suffering, he showed himself to these men and gave many convincing proofs that he was alive. He appeared to them over a period of forty days and spoke about the kingdom of God. (Acts 1:3 NIV)

And what exactly is this "kingdom of God"? What does it mean for our lives? A kingdom is a realm, quite simply, where the king's word has full sway. What the king desires is what happens. God's kingdom come means that his will is done "on *earth* as it is in heaven." Now in heaven, things are not stained or broken; everything is as it was meant to be. Think for a moment of the wonder of this. Isn't every one of our sorrows on earth the result of things *not* being as they were meant to be? And so when the kingdom of God comes to earth, wonderful things begin to unfold. Look at the evidence; watch what happens to people as they are touched by the kingdom of God through Jesus. As he went about "preaching the good news of the kingdom," Jesus was also "healing every disease and sickness among the people" (Matt. 4:23 NIV). When he "spoke to them about the kingdom of God," he "healed those who needed healing" (Luke 9:11 NIV). A direct connection is being made here. The actions of Jesus are the illustrations for the sermon.

What happens when we find ourselves in the kingdom of God? The disabled jump to their feet and start doing a jig. The deaf go out and buy themselves stereo equipment. The blind are headed to the movies. The dead are not at all dead anymore, but very much alive. They show up for dinner. In other words, human brokenness in all its forms is healed. The kingdom of God brings *restoration*. Life is restored to what it was meant to be. "In the beginning," back in Eden, all of creation was pronounced good because all of creation was exactly as God meant for it to be. For it to be good again is not for it to be destroyed, but healed, renewed, brought back to its goodness.

Those glimpses we see in the miracles of Jesus were the first-fruits. When he announces the full coming of the kingdom, Jesus says, "Look, I am making *all things* new!" (Rev. 21:5 NLT, emphasis added). He does not say, "I am making all new things." He means that the things that have been so badly broken will be restored and then some. "You mean I'll get a new pair of glasses?" my son Sam asked. "Or do you mean I'll get a new pair of eyes, so I won't need glasses?" What do you think? Jesus didn't hand out crutches to help the disabled.

THE JOY OF RESTORATION

Those of you who have been miraculously healed from a serious illness or injury will be ahead of me on this. You know firsthand the wonder and joy of restoration. But most of us have not experienced something quite so dramatic (not yet). So let me use a more common illustration, something most of you will remember—the flu. Several years ago, at Christmastime, my whole family was hit with a really vicious bug. It knocked us on our backs—literally. We brought blankets and pillows downstairs into the family room because no one had it in him to make it to his bedroom. For five days all we could do was lie on the floor, moaning. We ate nothing and drank nothing. Our house looked like an infirmary. You'll remember how awful it feels—the fever, the aches, the boredom.

One by one, we began to recover. Our first drink was simply water. It tasted like a living spring. I would have sworn it was from a different tap than we'd been using all those years. We moved up to fruit juice. It was exotic, as if we had never tasted anything like it in our lives. Each "new" food was an adventure. While I was lying in misery, I was dreaming of the day we'd go down to our favorite Mexican restaurant. It was off the charts, a sensory paradise. All things were new and absolutely delightful. It was a joy just to be alive. Our bodies had been "restored."

And going outside, after being closed in for a week, was like being released from prison. I wanted to run around, do everything all at once. I can only imagine what it would be like to walk for the very first time ever. Or to have been blind all my life and then have my sight restored. Such joy, such wonder. In *Pilgrim at Tinker Creek*, Annie Dillard recounts the stories that were reported of blind men and women who received some of the first cataract operations:

A little girl visits a garden. "She is greatly astonished, and can scarcely be persuaded to answer, stands speechless in front of the tree, which she only names on taking hold of it, and then as 'the tree with the lights in it.'" . . . One girl was eager to tell her blind friend that "men do not really look like trees at all," and astounded to discover that her every visitor had an utterly different face. Finally, a twenty-two-year-old girl was dazzled by the world's brightness and kept her eyes shut for two weeks. When at the end of that time she opened her eyes again, she did not recognize any objects, but, "the more she now directed her gaze upon everything about her, the more it could be seen how an expression of gratification and astonishment over-spread her features; she repeatedly exclaimed: 'Oh God! How beautiful!'"

How beautiful indeed. Can you imagine seeing wildflowers for the first time? Gerard Manley Hopkins was right: "The world is charged with the grandeur of God." Perhaps the reason there is reported a silence for half an hour of eternity is that we are all quite speechless (Rev. 8:1). And perhaps the gratification and astonishment that swell up afterward are the chorus of worship we are told about. "Look at this! Look there at that! Oh God! How beautiful!" Even for those of us who have always enjoyed our sight, it will be as if we are seeing for the first time. T. S. Eliot wrote in "Little Gidding,"

> The end of all our exploring
> Will be to arrive where we started
> And know the place for the first time.

OUR RESTORATION

Yes, dear friends, we are already God's children, and we can't even imagine what we will be like when Christ returns. But we do know that when he comes we will be like him, for we will see him as he really is. (1 John 3:2 NLT)

We have an expression that we use to describe someone who's out of sorts, who's not acting like the person we know her to be: "She's just not herself today." It's a marvelous, gracious phrase, for in a very real way, no one is quite himself today. There is more to us than we have seen. I know my wife is a goddess. I know she is more beautiful than she imagines. I have seen it slip out, seen moments of her glory. Suddenly, her beauty shines through, as though a veil has been lifted. It happened one night last fall.

We had slipped away from life for a long weekend in Mexico, a time to heal and rest and just be together again. We chose a hotel away from the crowds and the *turistas*. So we were almost entirely alone one evening as we ate dinner on a veranda overlooking the Sea of Cortez. Night had fallen, and the sky was so deeply black, the stars were shining right down to the horizon of the water. We sat gazing out to sea, listening to the mariachis and the breakers and our own hearts. I turned to steal a glimpse at my wife. She was beautiful, there in the moonlight, tanned from the sun, rested, serene. She was simply beautiful in a way that life often prevents her from being, but in a way she was destined to be.

All of us have moments like this, glimpses of our true creation. They come unexpectedly and then fade again. Life for the most part keeps our glory hidden, cloaked by sin, or sorrow, or merely weariness. When I see an older woman, doubled over with arthritis, the hard years etched into her face, I want to cry, *Eve, what happened?* How truly wonderful it will be to see her in her youth again, the full flower of her beauty restored.

When the disciples saw Jesus on the Mount of Transfiguration, they got a peek at his glory. He was radiant, beautiful, magnificent. He was Jesus, the Jesus they knew and loved—only *more so*. And we shall be glorious as well. Jesus called himself the Son of man to state clearly that he is what mankind was meant to be. What we see in Jesus is our personal destiny. Is this not the secret of every fairy tale? As Frederick Buechner reminds us,

> Maybe above all they are tales of transformation where all creatures are revealed in the end as what they truly are—the ugly duckling becomes a great white swan, the frog is revealed to be a prince, and the beautiful but wicked queen is unmasked in all her ugliness. They are tales of transformation where the ones who live happily ever after, as by no means everybody does in fairy tales, are transformed into what they have it in them at their best to be. (*Telling the Truth*)

I've spoken with many people who believe that we become "spirits" when we die; that we lose our bodies and float around. Some even believe we become angels. But I don't want to lose my body; I very much want it to be renewed. When we conceive of our future existence as something ghostly, mysterious, completely "other" than anything we've ever known, we place it beyond all hoping for. (You can only hope for what you desire.) The "otherness" of it takes away its power. But look at the first example—Jesus. What happens to him after he dies? He is resurrected, of course. As someone or something else? No, as himself, only healed and very much alive. Then what—float around? No, he has breakfast.

> Early in the morning, Jesus stood on the shore, but the disciples did not realize that it was Jesus. He called out to them, "Friends, haven't you any fish?" "No," they answered. He said, "Throw your net on the right side of the boat and you will find some." When they did, they were unable to haul the net in because of the large number of fish. Then the disciple whom Jesus loved said to Peter, "It is the Lord!" . . . When they landed, they saw a fire of burning coals there with fish on it, and some bread . . . Jesus said to them, "Come and have breakfast." (John 21:4–12 NIV)

Now think about this for a minute. You're the Son of God. You've just accomplished the greatest work of your life, the stunning rescue of mankind. You rose from the dead. What would you do next? Have a cookout with a few friends? It seems so unspiritual, so *ordinary*. Do you see that eternal life does not become something totally "other," but rather that life goes on—only as it should be?

Jesus did not vanish into a mystical spirituality, becoming one with the cosmic vibration. Jesus has a body, and it's *his* body. His wounds have been healed, but the scars remain—not gruesome, but lovely, a remembrance of all he did for us. His friends recognize him. They share a bite to eat. This is our future as well—our lives will be healed and we shall go on, never to taste death again. And so MacDonald writes in a letter to his wife,

> We may however say to ourselves—one day these souls of ours will blossom into the full sunshine—when all that is desirable in

the commonness of daily love, and all we long for of wonder and mystery and the look of Christmas time will be joined in one, and we shall walk as in a wondrous dream yet with more sense of reality than our most waking joy now gives us. (*The Heart of George MacDonald*)

The creation, we are told, groans for this day, the day when we—the sons and daughters of God—are revealed for who we truly are.

THE EARTH IS RESTORED

The creation waits in eager expectation for the sons of God to be revealed. For the creation was subjected to frustration, not by its own choice, but by the will of the one who subjected it, in hope that the creation itself will be liberated from its bondage to decay and brought into the glorious freedom of the children of God. (Rom. 8:19–21 NIV)

The created world itself can hardly wait for what's coming next. Everything in creation is being more or less held back. God reins it in until both creation and all the creatures are ready and can be released at the same moment into the glorious times ahead. Meanwhile, the joyful anticipation deepens. (Rom. 8:19–21 *The Message*)

How wondrous this will be! Creation can be so breathtaking *now*. What shall it be like when it is released to its full glory? Reading the journals of Lewis and Clark's journey across the West, I am filled with longing to see what they saw. The Great Plains were filled with wildlife; the buffalo dwelled in herds of hundreds of thousands. One of the first white men to see this paradise, Meriwether Lewis wrote in his journal,

I ascended to the top of the cut bluff this morning, from whence
I had a most delightful view of the country—immense herds of
buffalo, elk, deer and antelopes feeding in one common and
boundless pasture. The buffalo, elk and antelope are so gentle
that we pass near them while feeding, without appearing to
excite any alarm among them, and when we attract their attention, they frequently approach us more nearly to discover what
we are . . . The country is beautiful in the extreme.

It was the world "with dew still on it," to use MacLean's
delightful phrase. And it will be our Paradise again. We seem to
have forgotten—or perhaps we've never been told—that we get
the earth back as well. Too many of us have placed eternity
somewhere "out there," in a wispy and ethereal "heaven" that we
cannot imagine; in the clouds perhaps. "I love the earth," wrote
a friend, "and it makes me sad to think it will all be destroyed one
day." We have all probably shared in this sadness. But we needn't.
"Behold," says the Lord, "I will create new heavens and a new
earth" (Isa. 65:17; Rev. 21:1 NIV). When he says he is making all
things new, he includes the earth.

But won't the earth be destroyed, and won't we all go "up" to
heaven? Peter wrote some pretty ominous words about the end
of this age: "That day will bring about the destruction of the
heavens by fire, and the elements will melt in the heat" (2 Peter
3:12 NIV). It looks like the whole cosmos is going down in a ball
of flames. But wait—by way of comparison, Peter pointed to the
Flood of Noah's day as an allegory for the "day of the Lord." He
said about the Flood, "By these waters also the world of that time
was deluged and destroyed" (v. 6 NIV). Now, we know that the
earth was *not* destroyed by the Flood. The earth remained; the
ark didn't land on Mars. What was destroyed was all the wickedness and corruption of mankind (Gen. 6–7). The Flood *cleansed*

the earth, renewed it. Noah stepped out with his family onto a restored earth to begin again.

Fire is also used for cleansing throughout the Scriptures. Paul declared that our life's work will be tested in the fire, like gold. Only the dross is burned away (1 Cor. 3:13–15). This is the fire Peter refers to when he says, "But the day of the Lord will come like a thief. The heavens will disappear with a roar; the elements will be destroyed by fire, and the earth and everything in it will be *laid bare*" (2 Peter 3:10 NIV, emphasis added). The meaning of the word used here is not *destroyed*, but much closer translated as *revealed*. In other words, the world will be "exposed to judgment," and the earth will be cleansed of all unrighteousness. And a good scrubbing it needs. After declaring that the earth is full of the grandeur of God, Hopkins goes on to ask why we no longer see the glory of God in it.

> Generations have trod, have trod, have trod;
>> And all is seared with trade; bleared, smeared with toil;
>> And wears man's smudge and shares man's smell: the soil
> Is bare now, nor can foot feel, being shod.

All the strip mines and strip malls, all the incredibly ugly things we've done to the earth. No wonder the fire of God's jealous love will burn; he intends to cleanse the earth, once more, once and for all. Thus John (the writer of Revelation) sees the New Jerusalem not floating in the clouds, but descending from heaven *to the earth*, and he hears "a loud voice from the throne saying, 'Now the dwelling of God is with men, and he will live with them. They will be his people, and God himself will be with them and be their God'" (21:2–3 NIV). So Dallas Willard assures us, "*The life we now have as the persons we now are will continue in the universe in which we now exist.*" The earth has been our home and will be our home in eternity. This is a great consolation. When we place eternity "out there somewhere," in a place we cannot conceive of, we are left longing for home. To lose the only world we have ever known—a world so full of memories, so rich and beautiful, with so much left to explore—is to lose something deep and priceless to our hearts.

ALL SHALL BE WELL

At the end of *The Chronicles of Narnia*, Aslan seems to have brought that delightful kingdom to an end, and the children are left to mourn its loss.

"So," said Peter, "night falls on Narnia. What, Lucy! You're not *crying*? With Aslan ahead, and all of us here?" "Don't try to stop me, Peter," said Lucy, "I am sure Aslan would not. I am sure it is not wrong to mourn for Narnia. Think of all that lies dead and frozen behind that door." "Yes, and I *did* hope," said Jill, "that it might go on forever. I knew *our* world couldn't. I did think Narnia might." "Sirs," said Tirian. "The ladies do well to weep. See, I do so myself. I have seen my mother's death. What world but Narnia have I ever known? It were no virtue, but great discourtesy, if we did not mourn."

But as the children venture farther into Aslan's country, they begin to recognize every rock and stream and tree. They have been there before. And then they discover, to their wonder and joy, that Narnia exists forever in Aslan's country, that the world they loved has been preserved, though more rich and more real than ever.

It was the Unicorn who summed up what everyone was feeling. He stamped his right fore-hoof on the ground and neighed, and then cried: "I have come home at last! This is my real country! I belong here. This is the land I have been looking for all my life, though I never knew it till now. The reason why we loved the old Narnia is that it sometimes looked a little like this."

Our search for the Golden Moment is not a search in vain; not at all. We've only had the timing wrong. We do not know exactly how God will do it, but we do know this: the kingdom of God brings restoration. The only things destroyed are the things outside God's realm—sin, disease, death. But we who are God's children, the heavens and the earth he has made, will go on. "The wolf will live with the lamb, the leopard will lie down with the goat, the calf and the lion and the yearling together" (Isa. 11:6 NIV). "And Jerusalem will be known as the Desirable Place," the place of the fulfillment of all our desires (Isa. 62:12 NLT). This is significant because it touches upon the question, What will we *do* in eternity? If all we've got are halos and harps, our options are pretty limited. But to have the whole cosmos before us—wow. Thus MacDonald writes to his daughter, whom he will soon lose to tuberculosis,

I do live expecting great things in the life that is ripening for me and all mine—when we shall have all the universe for our own, and be good merry helpful children in the great house of our father. Then, darling, you and I and all will have the grand liberty wherewith Christ makes free—opening his hand to send us out like white doves to range the universe. (*The Heart of George MacDonald*)

CHAPTER EIGHT

THE GRAND AFFAIR

Thy fishes breathe but where thy waters roll;
Thy birds fly but within thy airy sea;
My soul breathes only in thy infinite soul;
I breathe, I think, I love, I live but thee.
Oh, breathe, oh, sink—O Love, live into me.

—GEORGE MACDONALD

Happiness can be found neither in ourselves nor in external
things, but in God and in ourselves as united to him.

—PASCAL

And the people came together and the people came to dance and
they danced like a wave upon the sea.

—WILLIAM BUTLER YEATS

Several years ago I gave a series of lectures on eternity to a group of career-age singles on the East Coast. Over lunch one afternoon, several of the women asked if they might have a word with me. I sensed they wanted to ask a question that they didn't feel comfortable raising during our group discussion time. After a bit of nervous hemming and hawing, they got down to the point. Though quite successful professionally, they were feeling the ache and disappointment of singleness. And as the years seemed to be racing by, they weren't feeling so young anymore. A lifetime of singleness was becoming more and more a reality for each one, though by no means her heart's desire. What I had been saying about heaven was certainly attractive, but still, they could not shake a fear that they will forever miss one of the deepest joys of human experience. "Will there be sex in heaven?" I smiled at their courage; it's a question many haven't let themselves wonder, even though they do wonder.

THE UNION THAT WE CRAVE

To understand the importance of the question, you've got to recognize the ache that seems to be met only through sexual union. When God created Eve, as you will recall, he took her straight from Adam's side. None of us have fully recovered from the surgery. There is an aloneness, an *incompleteness* that we experience every day of our lives. How often do you feel deeply and truly known? Is there another soul to whom a simple glance is all that is necessary to communicate depth of understanding? Do you have someone with whom you can commune in love? This is our inconsolable longing—to know and to be known. It is our deepest ache, which we feel to be healed only in our union with another. Even physically, there is an incompleteness until our bodies are joined together.

But let's take a closer look. What are we looking for in the opposite sex? The Beloved in Song of Songs captures something of what the heart of a woman is seeking:

> Listen! My lover!
> Look! Here he comes,
> leaping across the mountains,
> bounding over the hills.

My lover is like a gazelle or a young stag.

(2:8–9 NIV)

Picture the opening sequences of the film *Last of the Mohicans*. It is 1757. England is at war with France for possession of the American colonies. "Three men, the last of a vanishing people, are on the frontier west of the Hudson River." Before us is a vast panorama of untamed wilderness. Mountain and forest as far as the eye can see. The camera takes us down into those woods, and we discover the men, running at full speed through the deep forest. Leaping across ravines, bounding with grace and speed through the heavy undergrowth, they are clearly on a great mission.

This is our first glimpse of Nathaniel, the hero of the story. Raised by the Mohawk, he is rugged, wild, *alive*. Out here on the edge of the frontier, there is something dangerous about these men. But it does not make us afraid; rather, we are all the more drawn to them. No words are spoken in this scene; no words need to be spoken. It is an image of masculinity in motion. This is what has stirred the woman's heart in Songs—to see her man's strength. And she invites that strength to come to her in the night:

> Until the day breaks
> > and the shadows flee,
> turn, my lover,
> > and be like a gazelle
> or like a young stag
> > on the rugged hills.
> > (2:17 NIV)

There is an emptiness in the woman that only her man can fill. Is it not physically true? But it is more than just physically true. Our bodies are an outward sign of an inward reality. So,

too, the woman completes her man in a uniquely beautiful way.
Come to me, she says, and let your strength be fully expressed in
the garden of my beauty. Is this not the invitation that stirs a
man's heart? For these are the qualities of the Beloved that capti-
vate her Lover in the Song. He says,

> How beautiful you are, my darling!
> > Oh, how beautiful!
> > Your eyes behind your veil are doves . . .
> Your lips are like a scarlet ribbon;
> > your mouth is lovely . . .
> Your two breasts are like two fawns,
> > like twin fawns of a gazelle
> > that browse among the lilies.
>
> (4:1, 3, 5 NIV)

Shortly after the opening sequence of the *Mohicans* in the forest, we are given our first glimpse of Cora, the heroine of the
film. And such a contrast to the warriors she is. Cora is British;
she wears a lovely white dress, fringed with lace and flowing to
the ground. Beauty and grace have come to the frontier. She
wears a summer hat with a wide brim, which for a moment veils
her dark eyes, rich and deep as pools of water, soft as doves. She
is mysterious, but her mystery is not one that forbids. Rather, she
is captivating. Her lips are red, like the Beloved in Songs, and her
fitted bodice, in no way immodest, is alluring. Though an entire
war party of Hurons is not enough to trap Nathaniel, he is captured by Cora's femininity, "held captive" by her long black hair,
just as the Lover is in the Song.

> My lover has gone down to his garden,
> > to the beds of spices,

> to browse in the gardens
>> and to gather lilies.
> I am my lover's and my lover is mine;
>> he browses among the lilies.
>> (6:2–3 NIV)

There is no union on earth like the consummation of the love between a man and a woman. No other connection reaches as deeply as this oneness was meant to; no other passion is nearly so intense. People don't jump off bridges because they lost a grandparent. If their friend makes another friend, they don't shoot them both. No one has ruined home and career for a rendezvous at the library. Troy didn't go down in flames because somebody lost a pet. The passion that spousal love evokes is instinctive, irrational, intense, and dare I say, immortal. As the Song says,

> Love is as strong as death,
>> its jealousy unyielding as the grave.
> It burns like a blazing fire,
>> like a mighty flame.
> Many waters cannot quench love;
>> rivers cannot wash it away.
>> (8:6–7 NIV)

Small wonder that many people experience sexual passion as their highest transcendence on this earth. This love surpasses all others as the source of the world's most beautiful poetry, art, and music. Lovers reach for the stars to find words fitting enough to express what the beloved means to them and still feel those words fall short. Granted, much of it is hyperbole, expressing more the dream than the reality. But that is precisely my point. It is not merely hormones and sex drives projected outward. It is a clue to a deeper reality, a reach for something that does exist. For this exotic intimacy was given to us as a picture of something else, something truly out of this world.

OUR LOVE AFFAIR WITH GOD

After creating this stunning portrait of a total union, the man and woman becoming one, God turns the universe on its head when he tells us that this is what *he* is seeking with *us*. In fact, Paul says it is *why* God created gender and sexuality and marriage—to serve as a living metaphor. He quotes Genesis, then takes it to the nth degree: "'For this reason a man will leave his father and mother and be united to his wife, and the two will become one flesh.' This is a profound mystery—but I am talking about Christ and the church" (Eph. 5:31–32 NIV).

A profound mystery indeed. All the breathtaking things in life are. The Cross is a great mystery, but we are helped in understanding it by looking back into the Old Testament and finding there the pattern of the sacrificial lamb. Those early believers did not understand the full meaning of what they were doing, but once Christ came, the whole period of ritual sacrifice was seen in a new light, and in turn gave a richer depth to our understanding of the Cross.

We must do the same with this stunning passage; we must look back and see the Bible for what it is—the greatest romance ever written. God creates mankind for intimacy with himself, as his beloved. We see it right at the start, when he gives us the highest freedom of all—the freedom to reject him. The reason is obvious: love is possible only when it is freely chosen. True love is never constrained; our hearts cannot be taken by force. So God sets out to woo his beloved and make her his queen:

> I remember the devotion of your youth,
>> how as a bride you loved me
> and followed me through the desert,
>> through a land not sown.
> Israel was holy to the LORD,
>> the firstfruits of his harvest;
> all who devoured her were held guilty,
>> and disaster overtook them.
>>> (Jer. 2:2–3 NIV)

I gave you my solemn oath and entered into a covenant with you, declares the Sovereign LORD, and you became mine . . . I dressed you in fine linen and covered you with costly garments. I adorned you with jewelry . . . You became very beautiful and rose to be a queen. And your fame spread among the nations on account of your beauty, because the splendor I had given you made your beauty perfect. (Ezek. 16:8, 10–11, 13–14 NIV)

If you're writing a romance, love is the goal; you must allow for the possibility of betrayal. That is precisely what God calls our turning away from him. The Hebrews thought that he would be satisfied with some religious rituals and rule keeping. God calls them an "adulterous" wife, of all things:

> Long ago you broke off your yoke
>> and tore off your bonds;
>> you said, "I will not serve you!"
> Indeed, on every high hill
>> and under every spreading tree
>> you lay down as a prostitute.
>>> (Jer. 2:20 NIV)

But you trusted in your beauty and used your fame to become a prostitute. You lavished your favors on anyone who passed by and your beauty became his. (Ezek. 16:15 NIV)

The hero's heart has been broken. He rails with a jealous fury that flows only from a Lover who has been rejected:

> Because you have forgotten me
>   and trusted in false gods.
> I will pull up your skirts over your face
>   that your shame may be seen—
> your adulteries and lustful neighings,
>   your shameless prostitution!
>   (Jer. 13:25–27 NIV)

I will sentence you to the punishment of women who commit adultery and who shed blood; I will bring upon you the blood vengeance of my wrath and jealous anger. (Ezek. 16:38 NIV)

But the story does not finish with their divorce. True love never fails; it always perseveres. God will fight for his beloved. So the Old Testament ends with a promise of reconciliation:

> Therefore I will block her path with thornbushes;
>   I will wall her in so that she cannot find her way.
> She will chase after her lovers but not catch them;
>   she will look for them but not find them.
> Then she will say,
>   "I will go back to my husband as at first . . ."
> Therefore I am now going to allure her;
>   I will lead her into the desert
>   and speak tenderly to her . . .

"In that day," declares the LORD,

"you will call me 'my husband';

you will no longer call me 'my master.'"

(Hos. 2:6–7, 14, 16 NIV)

"That day" comes when Jesus appears on the scene and announces himself as the Bridegroom (Matt. 9:15). And when he says to us, "I am going there to prepare a place for you. And if I go and prepare a place for you, I will come back and take you to be with me that you also may be where I am," he is making his proposal (John 14:2–3 NIV). In the culture of the day, these are the very words a young man would say to his fiancée. Once the suitor secured the hand of his bride, he would return to his father's house and build the additional room that would be their bridal suite. (Couples moved into the home of the groom's parents.) It was "preparing a place for her." When all was ready, he would come for her and take her to be with him, so that where he is, she would also be.

We, the beloved, have become betrothed to the Bridegroom. John the Baptist said, "The bride belongs to the bridegroom. The friend who attends the bridegroom waits and listens for him, and is full of joy when he hears the bridegroom's voice" (John 3:29 NIV). We are in the time of waiting for the Bridegroom to return. By the end of the love story in Revelation 22 (vv. 17, 20 NIV), the church is practically panting for the return of Christ:

The Spirit and the bride say, "Come!" And let him who hears say, "Come!" Whoever is thirsty, let him come; and whoever wishes, let him take the free gift of the water of life . . . He who testifies to these things says, "Yes, I am coming soon." Amen. Come, Lord Jesus.

Notice that it is the *bride* who is panting. How does a bride pant? As if for a lover who has long been away. She pants like the Beloved in Song of Songs: "Come, my lover, let us go to the countryside . . . There I will give you my love" (7:11–12 NIV). We are waiting for our Love to come. Augustine declared, "The whole life of the good Christian is a holy longing. What you desire ardently, as yet you do not see . . . By withholding of the vision, God extends the longing; through longing he extends the soul, by extending he makes room in it." So, said Augustine, "let us long because we are to be filled . . . that is our life, to be exercised by longing." And when the Bridegroom of our souls comes, what then? This engagement is headed toward a consummation.

THE CONSUMMATION OF THE AFFAIR
(What Is Worship, After All?)

The older Christian wedding vows contained these amazing words: "With my body, I thee worship." Maybe our forefathers weren't so prudish after all; maybe they understood sex far better than we do. To give yourself over to another, passionately and nakedly, to adore that person body, soul, and spirit—we know there is something special, even sacramental about sex. It requires trust and abandonment, guided by a wholehearted devotion. What else can this be but worship? After all, God employs explicitly sexual language to describe faithfulness (and unfaithfulness) to him. For us creatures of the flesh, sexual intimacy is the closest parallel we have to real worship. Even the world knows this. Why else would sexual ecstasy become the number one rival to communion with God? The best impostors succeed because they are nearly indistinguishable from what they are trying to imitate. We worship sex because we don't know how to worship God. But we will. Peter Kreeft writes,

This spiritual intercourse with God is the ecstasy hinted at in all earthly intercourse, physical or spiritual. It is the ultimate reason why sexual passion is so strong, so different from other passions, so heavy with suggestions of profound meanings that just elude our grasp. (*Everything You Wanted to Know About Heaven*)

Don't let your disappointing experiences cloud your understanding of this. We have grown cynical, as a society, about whether intimacy is really possible. To the degree that we have abandoned soul-oneness, we have sought out merely sex, physical sex, to ease the pain. But the full union is no longer there; the orgasm comes incomplete; its heart has been taken away. Many have been deeply hurt. Sometimes, we must learn from what we have not known, let it teach us what *ought* to be.

God's design was that the two shall become one flesh. The physical oneness was meant to be the expression of a total interweaving of being. Is it any wonder that we crave this? Our alienation is removed, if only for a moment, and in the paradox of love, we are at the same time known and taken beyond ourselves. In *The Mystery of Marriage* Mike Mason asserts,

For many people, certainly, sex is the most powerful and moving experience that life has to offer, and more overwhelmingly holy than anything that happens in church. For great masses of people, sex is the one force which can actually tip men and women completely off their accustomed centers of gravity and lift them, however briefly, right out of themselves.

As Allender says, our hearts live for "an experience of worship that fills our beings with a joy that is so deeply in awe of the other that we are barely aware of ourselves." Many people have a hard time conceiving of this kind of intimacy with God. For their entire lives they have related to him in a distant, though reverent way. Our worship services don't get anywhere near something like our wedding nights. Men in particular have a hard time relating to the bridal imagery used in Scripture. Do we take on femininity to relate to God? What does it mean to *know* God as our Lover?

THE BEAUTY AND STRENGTH OF GOD

It is a mystery almost too great to mention, but God is the expression of the very thing we seek in each other. For do we not bear God's image? Are we not a living portrait of God? Indeed we are, and in a most surprising place—in our *gender*. "So God created man in his own image, in the image of God he created him; male and female he created them" (Gen. 1:27 NIV). Follow me closely now. Gender—masculinity and femininity—is how we bear the image of God. "I thought that there was only one kind of soul," said a shocked friend. "And God sort of poured those souls into male or female bodies." Many people believe something like that. But it contradicts the Word of God. We bear his image as men and women, and God does not have a body. So it must be at the level of the soul—the eternal part of us—that we reflect God. The text is clear; it is *as a man* or *as a woman* that the image is bestowed.

God wanted to show the world something of his strength. Is he not a great warrior? Has he not performed the daring rescue of his beloved? And this is why he gave us the sculpture that is man. Men bear the image of God in their dangerous, yet inviting strength. Women, too, bear the image of God, but in a much different way. Is not God a being of great mystery and beauty? Is there not something tender and alluring about the essence of the Divine? And this is why he gave us the sculpture that is woman.

You men will know what Mason means, though perhaps you've never made the connection:

> My wife's body is brighter and more fascinating than a flower, shier than any animal, and more breathtaking than a thousand sunsets. To me her body is the most awesome thing in creation. Trying to look at her, just trying to take in her wild, glorious beauty . . . I catch a glimpse of what it means that men and women have been made in the image of God. If even the image is this dazzling, what must the Original be like? (*The Mystery of Marriage*)

What, indeed. God is the source of all masculine power; God is also the fountain of all feminine allure. Come to think of it, he is the wellspring of everything that has ever romanced your heart. The thundering strength of a waterfall, the delicacy of a flower, the stirring capacity of music, the richness of wine. The masculine and the feminine that fill all creation come from the same heart. What we have sought, what we have tasted in part with our earthly lovers, we will come face-to-face with in our True Love. For the incompleteness that we seek to relieve in the deep embrace of our earthly love is never fully healed. The union does not last, whatever the poets and pop artists may say. Morning comes and we've got to get out of bed and off to our day, incomplete once more. But oh, to have it healed forever; to drink deeply from that fount of which we've had only a sip; to dive into that sea in which we have only waded.

And so a man like Charles Wesley can pen these words: "Jesus, Lover of my soul, let me to thy bosom fly," while Catherine of Siena can pray, "O fire surpassing every fire because you alone are the fire that burns without consuming! . . . Yet your consuming does not distress the soul but fattens her with insatiable love."

The French mystic Madame Guyon can write, "I slept not all night, because Thy love, O my God, flowed in me like delicious oil, and burned as a fire . . . I love God far more than the most affectionate lover among men loves his earthly attachment." And at the same time a monk, St. John of the Cross, can say,

> I abandoned and forgot myself,
> laying my face on my Beloved;
> all things ceased; I went out from myself
> leaving my cares
> forgotten among the lilies.

Where else are we told about oil and lilies? In Song of Songs. Is there sex in heaven? It would be better to ask, Is there worship in heaven?

THE SHARED AFFAIR

"O, rejoice beyond a common joy, and set it down with gold on lasting pillars!" This is the cry sent up at the end of Shakespeare's play *The Tempest*. What is the reason for such uncommon rejoicing? That though treason, and foul play, and a shipwreck had for so long separated families, lovers, even kingdoms, they have all been reunited. In hope against hope, they have been restored to one another.

> In one voyage
> Did Claribel her husband find at Tunis,
> And Ferdinand, her brother, found a wife
> Where he himself was lost, Prospero his dukedom
> In a poor isle, and all of us ourselves
> When no man was his own.

It is a manifestation of the humility of God that he creates a kingdom so rich in love that he should not be our all, but that others should be precious to us as well. Even in Eden, before the Fall, while Adam walked in Paradise with his God, even then God said, "It is not good for the man to be alone" (Gen. 2:18 NIV). He gives to us the joy of community, of family and friends to share in the Sacred Romance.

Is it not the nature of true love—to be generous in love? This is something of the reason that married couples long to have children; they want others to share in their happiness. The embrace of lovers does not stay confined to the lovers; rather, it builds a home, it fills a household. And so our longing for intimacy reaches beyond our "one and only." We come to discover that others mean so very much to us. There is no joy like the joy of reunion because there is no sorrow like the sorrow of separation. To lose those we love and wonder if we shall ever see them again—this is our deepest grief.

In 1991, Eric Clapton lost his only son, five-year-old Connor. The little boy fell from a window of their Manhattan apartment, plunging forty-nine stories to his death. Clapton channeled his grief into writing the heart-wrenching song "Tears in Heaven." In it he puts words to one of our deepest questions,

> Would you know my name
> If I saw you in heaven?
> Would it be the same
> If I saw you in heaven?

Oh, how much hangs on the word *if*. Jesus wept at the funeral of his dear friend Lazarus. I'm not sure we understand his tears because we do not share his strange carelessness about death. He has told us again and again not to fear it. (At the approach of his own death, he tells his closest friends to be *glad*, for heaven's sake.) On reaching Lazarus's grieving sister Martha, Jesus makes the astounding statement that those who are his will simply "never die" (John 11:26 NIV). He then comes to the grave site and weeps. Certainly, the tears are not for Lazarus, for according to Jesus, Lazarus is quite well. Jesus weeps for Martha and Mary, and for all of us who suffer loss. I think he weeps not only for our loss, but also for our inability to see beyond it. Dare I say, sometimes our refusal to see beyond it?

I have tasted grief, drunk deeply from its bitter cup. It is the most awful experience in this life. Death truly is the enemy (1 Cor. 15:26). But much of our grief comes because we have not dislodged that *if* from our hearts. As Willard explains,

> Once we have grasped our situation in God's full world, the startling disregard Jesus and the New Testament writers had for "physical death" suddenly makes sense. Paul bluntly states . . . that Jesus abolished death—simply did away with it.

> To one group of his day, who believed that "physical death" was the cessation of the individual's existence, Jesus said, "God is not the God of the dead, but of the living" (Luke 20:38). His meaning was that those who love and are loved by God are not allowed to cease to exist, because they are God's treasures. He delights in them and intends to hold onto them. He has even prepared for them an individualized eternal work in his vast universe. (*The Divine Conspiracy*)

I'll say more about that work in the next chapter. What is vital for us to grasp now, Willard says, is simply this: *"The life we now have as the persons we now are will continue in the universe in which we now exist."* By all means we shall know each other's name—not *if*—but *when* we see each other in God's great kingdom. We'll hold each other's hands, and far better than that. The naked intimacy, the real knowing that we enjoy with God, we shall enjoy with each other. George MacDonald wrote, "I think we shall be able to pass into and through each other's very souls as we please, knowing each other's thought and being, along with our own, and so being *like* God."

Brent used to call it multiple intimacy without promiscuity. It is what the ancients meant by the communion of saints. All of the joy that awaits us in the sea of God's love will be multiplied over and over as we share with each other in the Grand Affair. John Donne captures this beautifully:

> All mankind is of one author, and is one volume; when one man dies, one chapter is not torn out of the book, but translated into a better language; and every chapter must be so translated; God employs several translators: some pieces are translated by age, some by sickness, some by war, some by justice; but God's hand is in every translation; *and his hand shall bind up all our scattered leaves again,* for that library where every book shall lie open to one another.

Imagine the stories that we'll hear. And all the questions that shall finally have answers. "What were you thinking when you drove the old Ford out on the ice?" "Did you hear that Betty and Dan got back together? But of course you did—you were probably involved in that, weren't you?" "How come you never told us about your time in the war?" "Did you ever know how much I loved you?" And the answers won't be one-word answers, but story after story, a feast of wonder and laughter and glad tears.

The setting for this will be a great party, the wedding feast of the Lamb. Now, you've got to get images of Baptist receptions entirely out of your mind—folks milling around in the church gym, holding Styrofoam cups of punch, wondering what to do with themselves. You've got to picture an Italian wedding or, better, a Jewish wedding. They roll up the rugs and push back the furniture. There is *dancing*: "Then maidens will dance and be glad, young men and old as well" (Jer. 31:13 NIV). There is *feasting*: "On this mountain the LORD Almighty will prepare a feast of rich food for all peoples" (Isa. 25:6 NIV). (Can you imagine what kind of cook God must be?) And there is *drinking*—the feast God says he is preparing includes "a banquet of aged wine—the best of meats and the finest of wines." In fact, at his Last Supper our Bridegroom said he will not drink of "the fruit of the vine until the kingdom of God comes" (Luke 22:18 NIV). Then he'll pop a cork.

> And the people came together
> and the people came to dance
> and they danced like a wave upon the sea.

It was one of Brent's favorite lines from the poet Yeats. Stasi reminded me the other night of the last time Brent was in our home. For several years he and Ginny shared their lives with us and two other couples, all dear friends, in a covenant group. We'd meet twice a month or so, to talk about life. It was a place to know and be known, to come in out of the winds of the world and mend your sails. On this night, I'd asked everyone to bring a piece of art that he loved—a song, or a poem, or perhaps a film clip. Art is a glimpse into our hearts, and you can learn so much about someone when he shares with you something that has stirred his soul. Our conversation flowed from laughter to tears as we talked about each person's "window of the soul." The evening was winding to a close when Leigh offered to play the song she had brought. "It makes me think of heaven," she said, a little embarrassed. Heaven hadn't been part of the discussion 'til that moment. It was a joyful, upbeat, you've-got-to-get-up-and-dance kind of song, and soon we all were, swinging and jitter-bugging and just sort of hopping around the living room, none of us great dancers, but everyone celebrating the banquet to come. It was the last time we would all be together.

Until the Party begins.

CHAPTER NINE

THE ADVENTURE BEGINS

And in the perfect time, O perfect God,
When we are in our home, our natal home,
When joy shall carry every sacred load,
And from its life and peace no heart shall roam,
What if thou make us able to make like thee—
To light with moons, to clothe with greenery,
To hang gold sunsets o'er a rose and purple sea!

—GEORGE MACDONALD

Enter into the joy of your master.

—JESUS OF NAZARETH

We must explore one more aspect of our future if we are to recover heart for the journey of our lives. For though it will be unspeakable joy to live forever in a fully restored universe with the company of the truly intimate, it is not enough. There is something core to our being and set within our deepest desires that remains untouched. For as the nineteenth-century preacher Thomas Chalmers wrote, one of the "Grand Essentials" of human happiness is having something to *do*. I think the fear of being bored is an unspoken fear of many people about the life that is coming. After all, the never-ending sing-along in the sky isn't exactly breathtaking. Spending a weekend at the beach beats that hands down. Our lives in the coming kingdom will be surrounded with great beauty and our hearts filled with love, but what will we *do* with ourselves forever and ever? I have yet to meet a Christian who has more than the faintest notion of what his life will entail beyond the eternal church service. "I guess it will be good," sighed one friend. But guesses are not good enough in the journey of desire. We must *know*.

We've somehow overlooked a line in the parable of the talents, a single sentence that speaks volumes about the connection between our present and future life. As you'll recall, the landowner in the story has been away on a journey. In the parallel version told in Luke, the parable of the minas, he is a man of "noble birth" who has gone to "a distant country to have himself appointed king" (19:11–27 NIV). Upon his return, he rewards those faithful members of his staff in a way that at first seems, well, like no reward at all: "You have been faithful with a few things; I will put you in charge of many things." Luke's version has it this way: "Because you have been trustworthy in a very small manner, take charge of ten cities." This is their bonus— more to do? Wouldn't a vacation make a better reward? My boys clean their rooms so they can go out and play, not so they can clean the rest of the house. Yet Jesus thinks that he is sharing something delightful with us. The landowner then says, "Come and share your master's happiness." Or, as the King James has it, "Enter thou into the joy of thy lord" (Matt. 25:23). To understand what he means, we must have a closer look at God's joyful activity and our inherent design.

THE JOY OF THE MASTER

How marvelous it is to watch a master artist at work. We enjoyed a wonderful performance of Chausson's *Poeme for Violin and Orchestra* last night. The young woman who played the lead violin was simply beautiful in her long white gown, her graceful arms working the bow and strings with finesse. It was a joy just to watch her play. And the *Poeme* itself is an enchanting piece of music, almost ethereal. It fit her and the mood of the summer evening perfectly. And so it was with one accord that the audience rose in applause at the close of the performance.

Something similar happened at the opening of Genesis. As creation was unfolding from the hands of the Master, like wet clay on a potter's wheel, a great ovation erupted: "The morning stars sang together and all the angels shouted for joy" (Job 38:7 NIV). But of course. He has just finished sculpting the islands of Greece so that their white sandy beaches perfectly rim those azure seas. Then he watered the jungles of Malaysia to sustain an exotic array of orchids, after which he painted sunsets over the Sahara and hurled the Himalayas upward, treacherous peaks scraping the roof of the world.

And he doesn't stop there. Into this breathtaking setting of a thousand different habitats God places "the fish of the sea and the birds of the air and . . . every living creature that moves on the ground" (Gen. 1:28 NIV). Chameleons and caribou, porcupines and porpoises. How do we begin to describe this God whose image we bear? *Artistic* is the only word that even comes close. *Powerful, awesome, majestic*—yet *intricate, delicate, whimsical. Creative,* without a doubt. And that was just the beginning. Although God rested on the seventh day, he hasn't been lying around ever since.

Jesus said, "My Father is always at his work to this very day, and I, too, am working" (John 5:17 NIV). For many people this is a new thought—that God is still quite active. Life has led them to believe that he may have gotten things off to a great start, but then he left on vacation or perhaps went to attend to more important matters. But the creative overture recorded in Genesis was only the first movement of a great symphony that has been swelling ever since. The opening notes were not *staccato*, but *sostenuto*, ongoing, unfolding. He's not just sitting around on a throne somewhere. The psalmist proclaimed of God's work today,

> He wraps himself in light as with a garment;
>> he stretches out the heavens like a tent
>> and lays the beams of his upper chambers on their waters.
> He makes the clouds his chariot
>> and rides on the wings of the wind . . .
> He makes springs pour water into the ravines;
>> it flows between the mountains.
> They give water to all the beasts of the field;
>> the wild donkeys quench their thirst.
> The birds of the air nest by the waters;
>> they sing among the branches.
> He waters the mountains from his upper chambers;
>> the earth is satisfied by the fruit of his work.
> He makes grass grow for the cattle,
>> and plants for man to cultivate—
>> bringing forth food from the earth:
> wine that gladdens the heart of man,
>> oil to make his face shine,
>> and bread that sustains his heart.
>
> (Ps. 104:2–3, 10–15 NIV)

The only way to describe his ongoing creative activity is *extravagant*. Thunderclouds gather over the prairies, and afterward he scatters wildflowers as far as the eye can see. He fills the oceans with orcas and urchins and who knows what. A single maple leaf is woven with greater intricacy than the finest French lace—even though it will fall with the winds of autumn. New stars are born every day; a new sunset painted and swept away each night. Such magnificent generosity. No composer ever gave so many free concerts. MacDonald had it right: "Gloriously wasteful, O my Lord, art thou!"

You don't suppose he experiences his part in running the universe as drudgery, do you? Did Margot Fonteyn and Rudolf Nureyev love to dance? Does Michael Jordan love to play basketball? So God loves his work. He isn't ashamed to call it all "very good." Like a Master Craftsman offering a glimpse into his workshop, he asks Job,

> Have you ever given orders to the morning,
>   or shown the dawn its place? . . .
> Have you journeyed to the springs of the sea
>   or walked in the recesses of the deep? . . .
> Have you entered the storehouses of the snow
>   or seen the storehouses of the hail? . . .
> Can you bind the beautiful Pleiades?
>   Can you loose the cords of Orion?
> Can you bring forth the constellations in their seasons
>   or lead out the Bear with its cubs? . . .
> Do you send the lightning bolts on their way?
>   Do they report to you, "Here we are"? . . .
> Do you hunt the prey for the lioness
>   and satisfy the hunger of the lions? . . .
> Do you give the horse his strength
>   or clothe his neck with a flowing mane?
>   (Job 38:12–40; 39:19 NIV)

On and on he goes with a pride that befits his grandeur. You see, Job has come to the point where he wonders, rather loudly, whether God is "on the job" anymore. This is God's answer, and it goes on for two more chapters. The frost each morning? That's mine. The ostrich and hippo—mine too. I'm watching over the young doe when she gives birth; the eagle soars at my command. A jealous indignation characterizes these words, the sort of emotion that is aroused when someone criticizes our most cherished work. You see, it is God's *delight* to do all these things. Dallas Willard notes,

> We should, to begin with, think that God leads a very interesting life, and that he is full of joy. Undoubtedly he is the most joyous being in the universe. The abundance of his love and generosity is inseparable from his infinite joy. All of the good and beautiful things from which we occasionally drink tiny droplets of soul-exhilarating joy, God continuously experiences in all their breadth and depth . . . We are enraptured by a well-done movie sequence or by a few bars from an opera or lines from a poem. We treasure our great experiences for a lifetime, and we may have very few of them. But he is simply one great inexhaustible and eternal experience of all that is good and true and beautiful and right. This is what we must think of when we hear theologians and philosophers speak of him as a perfect being. *This is his life.* (*The Divine Conspiracy*)

And it is *this* life, with all its joyful creativity and power and unending happiness, that he says he is going to share with us. This is "the joy of your master" that we are to be welcomed into. It rather beats harps and halos, wouldn't you say? For we long to find our place in the world, caring for and developing creation in all its diverse potential. It is this for which we were made.

LITTLE GODS

"So God created man in his own image, in the image of God he created him; male and female he created them." Thus is humanity trumpeted onto the scene in verse 27 of the first chapter of Genesis (NIV). It is a passage familiar to most of us. Too familiar perhaps, for we rarely wonder about what it means. Right here, at the beginning of our existence, is the single phrase our Creator uses to characterize us, and most of us haven't the foggiest idea what it implies. If we were reading the Scripture for the story it is (and not like an encyclopedia, as many do), we would have in mind all that has transpired up to this moment. We have been watching the God whose image we bear. What do we know about him at this point? What has he been up to? Creating the heavens and the earth. Islands and caribou and wildflowers. This is what he has been doing. *This is all we know of God* when we reach the point at which we are compared to him.

If you were meeting a young man for the first time, and he was introduced to you as the "son of Einstein," you'd probably expect him to be rather bright. If you met a young woman as the "daughter of Nadia Comaneci," the Russian gymnast, you might assume she could turn a decent cartwheel. We expect greatness from the offspring of the great. To be introduced as the image bearers of God is full of anticipation. It would be as though we were introduced as the sons of a renowned artist, perhaps a Monet, or as the daughters of a graceful dancer, such as Martha Graham. It leads us to what to expect next. Jesus said, "Is it not written in your Law, 'I have said you are gods'?" (John 10:34 NIV). Why is it, then, that creativity rarely comes to mind when we think of how we reflect God? More often than not we think of godliness in moral terms. When we hear that so-and-so is a "godly person," we assume that he is devout, or perhaps self-sacrificing, and certainly more virtuous than most. But when Genesis declares we are God's image, it is describing not certain qualities of our character but *capacities of our nature*. This is why, when the essence of our likeness to God is announced, it is in the context of our *position* upon the earth, our place in creation:

> Then God said, "Let us make man in our image, in our likeness, *and let them rule* over the fish of the sea and the birds of the air, over the livestock, over all the earth, and over all the creatures that move along the ground." (Gen. 1:26 NIV, emphasis added)

In other words, we are *made* like God in our creative powers because we are to *be* like God in ruling the earth. The image implies a capacity, and the capacity assumes the creative legacy we shall carry on. "Those two phrases—'Let us make man in our Image,' and 'Let them rule'—must be taken together," says Ben Patterson. "Each modifies the other. To be like God is to rule the earth as he does. To rule the earth as he does is to be like God." Our original design was for a life of creative rule, to share in the overall care and development of God's creation. The poet writes because she is made in God's image; the builder loves to build for the same reason. Entrepreneurs risk capital ventures, baseball players go to the batting cages, and cooks experiment with spices all for the same reason. It is what we *are*.

ON MOZART AND MARTHA STEWART

"Somehow," notes Os Guinness, "we human beings are never happier than when we are expressing the deepest gifts that are truly us." Now, some children are gifted toward science, and others are born athletes. But whatever their specialty, *all* children are inherently creative. Give them a barrel of Legos and a free afternoon and my boys will produce an endless variety of spaceships and fortresses and who knows what. It comes naturally to children; it's in their *nature*, their design as little image bearers. Set a group of kindergartners down with sheets of paper and tubs of finger paint, and you don't have to provide directions. They know what to do. In fact, paint and paper aren't even necessary; chocolate pudding and a nearby wall will do nicely. A pack of boys let loose in a wood soon becomes a major Civil War reenactment. A chorus of girls, upon discovering a trunk of skirts and dresses, will burst into the *Nutcracker Suite*. The right opportunity reveals the creative nature.

This is precisely what happens when God shares with mankind his own artistic capacity and then sets us down in a paradise of unlimited potential. It is an act of creative *invitation*, like providing Monet with a studio for the summer, stocked full of brushes and oils and empty canvases. Or like giving Mozart full use of an orchestra and a concert hall for an autumn of composing. Or like setting Martha Stewart loose in a gourmet kitchen on a snowy winter weekend, just before the holidays. You needn't provide instructions or motivation; all you have to do is release them to be who they are, and remarkable things will result. As the poet Hopkins wrote, "What I do is me: for that I came."

Oh, how we long for this—for a great endeavor that draws upon our every faculty, a great "life's work" that we could throw ourselves into. "I was made for this," said one friend who after years of hesitation finally pursued his dream of becoming a high school teacher. "It energizes me." "After years in a wasteland," moaned another, "all I want is to be released to be who I am." His career had not panned out, and as he saw his most productive days slipping by, he longed to find his place. "God has created us and our gifts for a place of his choosing," says Guinness, "and we will only be ourselves when we are finally there." Our creative nature is essential to who we are as human beings—as image bearers—and it brings us great joy to live it out with freedom and skill. Even if it's a simple act such as working on your photo albums or puttering in the garden—these, too, are how we have a taste of what was meant to rule over a small part of God's great kingdom. Willard points out:

> Here is a truth that reaches into the deepest part of what it means to be a person . . . that we are made to "have dominion" within an appropriate domain of reality. This is the core of the likeness or image of God in us and is the basis of the destiny for which we were formed. We are, all of us, never-ceasing spiritual beings with a unique eternal calling to count for good in God's great universe . . . In creating human beings God made them to rule, to reign, to have dominion in a limited sphere. Only so can they be persons. (*The Divine Conspiracy*)

THE MISERIES OF A DETHRONED MONARCH

During a long layover at O'Hare, I studied the man who sells popcorn from a little stand in one of the terminal hallways. He sat silently on a stool as thousands of people rushed by. Occasionally, every fifteen minutes or so, someone would stop and buy a bag. He would scoop the popcorn from the bin, take the money, and make change—all without a word being spoken between them. When the brief encounter was over, he would resume his place on the stool, staring blankly, his shoulders hunched over. I wondered at his age; he seemed well past fifty. How long had that been his profession? Could he possibly make a living at it? His face wore a weary expression of resignation tinged with shame. *Adam,* I thought, *what happened?* Did he know how far his situation was from his true design? Somehow he knew, even if he didn't know the Story. His sadness was testimony to it. I thought of Pascal, that all our miseries prove our greatness: "They are the miseries of a dethroned monarch."

Some people love what they do. They are the fortunate souls, who have found a way to link what they are truly gifted at (and therefore what brings them joy) with a means of paying the bills. But most of the world merely toils to survive, and no one gets to use his gifts all the time. On top of that, there is the curse of thorns and thistles, the futility that tinges all human efforts at the moment. As a result, we've come to think of work as a result of the Fall. You can see our cynicism in the fact that we've chosen the cartoon character Dilbert as the icon of our working days. His is a hopeless life of futility and anonymity in the bowels of a large corporation. We don't even know what he does—only that it's meaningless. We identify with him, feeling at some deep level the apparent futility of our lives. Even if we are loved, it is not enough. We yearn to be *fruitful,* to do something of meaning and value that flows naturally out of the gifts and capacities of our souls. But of course—we were meant to be the kings and queens of the earth.

Dorothy Sayers once wrote, "Work is not, primarily, a thing one does to live, but the thing one lives to do." If only it were so; if only we could land our "dream job," where we'd be paid to do what we love. Some actually go out and do it. A friend took off several years ago to be a hunting and fishing guide in Alaska. He's having a ball. Another friend had a chance to work on Broadway; his wife said to me afterward, "John was made for this. All the experiences of his life had led up to this very thing." The rest of us look on from the sidelines with longing, held back from our dreams by fear or heartache or the demands of the life we do have. No wonder we hear the rewards in the parable with such disappointed ears—it sounds as though we'll lose even those few hours of private joy we manage to squeeze in on the weekend and take on some sort of eternal task. But what if it were the opposite? What if the master's invitation was to do, like Hopkins, what is *you*? What if you were given the *freedom* (the permission) and the *power* (all the resources necessary) to do exactly what you were always meant to do?

THE MONARCHY RESTORED

Let's come back for a moment to the restoration of the earth. In Romans 8 (NIV), Paul says something outrageous. He says that all our sufferings are "not worth comparing" with the glory that will be revealed in us. It seems hard to believe, given the way life can break your heart. The human race has seen an unspeakable amount of suffering. What can possibly make that seem like nothing? "The glory that will be revealed in us" (8:18). The Great Restoration. Paul then goes on to say, "The creation waits in eager expectation for the sons of God to be revealed" (8:19). The release of a fully restored creation is being more or less held back, waiting upon *our* restoration. Why? Because only then can we handle it. Only when we ourselves have been restored can we take our place again as the kings and queens of creation. Or did you not know? The day is coming when Christ will appoint you as one of his regents over his great and beautiful universe. This has been his plan all along.

> When the Son of Man comes in his glory, and all the angels with him, he will sit on his throne in heavenly glory. All the nations will be gathered before him, and he will separate the people one from another as a shepherd separates the sheep from the goats. He will put the sheep on his right and the goats on his left. Then

the King will say to those on his right, "Come, you who are blessed by my Father; take your inheritance, *the kingdom prepared for you since the creation of the world.*" (Matt. 25:31–34 NIV, emphasis added)

Who then is the faithful and wise servant, whom the master has put in charge of the servants in his household to give them their food at the proper time? It will be good for that servant whose master finds him doing so when he returns. I tell you the truth, *he will put him in charge of all his possessions.* (Matt. 24:45–47 NIV, emphasis added)

And they will *reign* for ever and ever. (Rev. 22:5 NIV, emphasis added)

Think for a moment. The One who created you and set all those loves and gifts in your heart, the One who has shaped all your life experiences (including the ones that seem to make no sense), this God has prepared a place for you that is a more than perfect fit for all your gifts and quirks and personality traits— even those you don't know you have. Christ is not joking when he says that we shall inherit the kingdom prepared for us and shall reign with him forever. We will take the position for which we have been uniquely made and will rule *as he does*—meaning with creativity and power.

I think back upon God's questions to Job: "Have you ever given orders to the morning? Do you hunt the prey for the lioness?" And like a young apprentice in the presence of a master, something in my heart says cautiously (yet eagerly), "No . . . but I'd like to!" And so Willard writes,

We will not sit around looking at one another or at God for eternity but will join the eternal Logos, "reign with him," in the endlessly ongoing creative work of God. It is for this that we were each individually intended, as both kings and priests (Exod. 19:6; Rev. 5:10) . . . A place in God's creative order has been reserved for each one of us from before the beginnings of cosmic existence. His plan is for us to develop, as apprentices to Jesus, to the point where we can take our place in the ongoing creativity of the universe. (*The Divine Conspiracy*)

Much of the activity of God in our lives is bringing us to the place where he can entrust us with this kind of influence. God takes our training so seriously because he fully intends to promote us. Will it be joy? Does Stephen Hawking enjoy physics? Does Mark McGwire enjoy hitting it out of the park? There are so many ways this "reigning" will be expressed—as unique and varied as there are human souls. God has quite a few "possessions," and it's going to take a lot of looking after by men and women uniquely fitted for the task.

I am not a scientist; but I am told by those who are of the great adventure in exploring the beauty revealed in the structures of physics or molecular biology. I don't go in for organizational structures and master planning, but I have friends who can talk about them for hours. To each his own—literally. Each person will live out the passion of his heart, set there by the Creator from before the beginning of time. I should like one day to paint with the grace of Monet, or plumb the wonders of physics with Einstein. Perhaps I shall. There is work enough to be done.

THE GLORIOUS FREEDOM

"Life," as a popular saying goes, "is not a dress rehearsal. Live it to the fullest." What a setup for a loss of heart. No one gets all he desires; no one even comes close. If this is it, we are lost. But what if life *is* a dress rehearsal? What if the real production is about to begin? That is precisely what Jesus says; he tells us that we are being shaped, prepared, groomed for a part in the grand drama that is coming. In *The Call*, Guinness writes about a delightful story told by Artie Shaw, a famous clarinetist during the big band era:

> Maybe twice in my life I reached what I wanted to. Once we were playing "These Foolish Things" and at the end the band stops and I play a little cadenza. That cadenza—no one can do it better. Let's say it's five bars. That's a very good thing to have done in a lifetime. An artist should be judged by his best, just as an athlete. Pick out my one or two best things and say, "That's what we did: all the rest was rehearsal."

All the rest was rehearsal—not for just a few shining moments, but for an eternity of joy. Realizing this is immensely freeing. How many of your plans take an unending future into account? "Let's see, I'm going to be alive forevermore, so . . . if I don't get this done now, I'll get to it later." This is so important, for no human life reaches its potential here.

I was talking with a playwright several years ago. His career was not panning out the way he deeply wanted it to, and he was becoming rather depressed. It wasn't a matter of being unqualified; he was, and is, a very gifted writer. But few playwrights achieve anything like success. Life wasn't inviting him to be who he was—yet. He had never once considered that he would be a great writer in the coming kingdom, and that he was merely in training now. His day was yet to come. Understanding that put his life in an entirely new light.

In Revelation 21, John describes the New Jerusalem, the city of God come to earth. It is a place of exquisite beauty and grandeur. And then he adds an odd statement: "The kings of the earth will bring *their* splendor into it" (v. 24 NIV, emphasis added). It seems hard to believe that we could add anything to the splendor God creates, but that is exactly what we are designed for and what our future involves. How amazing it will be to have our souls released into their true destiny, in a world no longer stained by sin or under the curse. To throw ourselves into some wonderful enterprise, unhindered by our own weaknesses or the frustrations typical of a broken world. Gardeners dream of a spot of ground with rich soil and not a weed or sow bug to be found. They shall have it. Architects dream of the day they shall build their own designs and not merely carry out the plans of another. They shall. Like children eager to show off our precious creations, we shall bring them to our Father in Jerusalem, for glory and praise.

The Grand Affair heals the curse of isolation. The Great Adventure heals the curse of futility. The "glorious freedom" of the children of God is the freedom of being all we were meant to be. We won't be held back by anything anymore; no, we will finally hit our stride. We all know the frustration of failure, of missing the mark—getting the equation wrong, hitting the ball into the rough, misdiagnosing the patient. And most of us at one time or another have tasted the joy of getting it right. Not only will we find our place, but we will be empowered to do the very things we aim to do, with and for God. As C. S. Lewis wrote,

The miracles that have already happened are, of course, as the Scripture often says, the first fruits of that cosmic summer which is presently coming on. Christ has risen, and so we shall rise. St. Peter for a few seconds walked on the water; and the day will come when there will be a remade universe, infinitely obedient to the will of glorified and obedient men, when we can do all things, when we shall be those gods that we are described as being in Scripture. (*The Grand Miracle*)

THREE WEEKS AFTER the wind ceased to blow, the sea lion had a dream. Now, as I told you before, there were other nights in which he had dreamed of the sea. But those were long ago and nearly forgotten. Even still, the ocean that filled his dreams this night was so beautiful and clear, so vast and deep, it was as if he were seeing it for the very first time. The sunlight glittered on its surface, and as he dived, the waters all around him shone like an emerald. If he swam quite deep, it turned to jade, cool and dark and mysterious. But he was never frightened; not at all. For I must tell you that in all his dreams of the sea, he had never before found himself in the company of other sea lions. This night there were many, round about him, diving and turning, spinning and twirling. They were playing.

Oh, how he hated to wake from that wonderful dream. The tears running down his face were the first wet thing he had felt in three weeks. But he did not pause even to wipe them away; he did not pause, in fact, for anything at all. He set his face to the east, and he began to walk as best a sea lion can.

"Where are you going?" asked the tortoise.

"I am going to find the sea."

CHAPTER TEN

ENTERING MORE DEEPLY INTO DESIRE

Blessed are those who hunger and thirst.

—JESUS OF NAZARETH

And in me wake hope, fear, boundless desire.

—GEORGE MacDONALD

The devil sleepeth not; neither is the flesh as yet dead; therefore cease not to prepare thyself for the battle; for on thy right hand and on thy left are enemies who never rest.

—THOMAS À KEMPIS

I hope by now you see why I have spent three chapters trying to bring eternity out of the clouds and into our conscious lives. The dilemma of desire is the deepest dilemma we will ever face. Its dangers are deep and potentially fatal. How, then, shall we not lose heart? If we manage to somehow hang on to our desire, how do we keep from being consumed by it? The secret is known to all of us, though we may have forgotten that we know it. Who wants to fill up with snacks on Thanksgiving Day? Who goes out to buy presents for himself on Christmas Eve? Is there anyone in his right mind who looked for someone to date at his wedding rehearsal? When we are convinced that something delicious is about to be ours, we are free to live in expectation, and it draws us on in anticipation. There are three things that we must come to terms with in our deep heart. First, we must have life. Second, we cannot arrange for it. Third, it is coming. Now we are ready to proceed on our way.

BATTLE AND JOURNEY

Life is now a battle and a journey. As Eugene Peterson reminds us, "We must fight the forces that oppose our becoming whole; we must find our way through difficult and unfamiliar territory to our true home." It's not that there aren't joy and beauty, love and adventure now—there are. The invasion of the kingdom has begun. But life in its fullness has yet to come. So we must take seriously the care of our hearts. We must watch over our desire with a fierce love and vigilance, as if we were protecting our most precious possession. We must do battle with the enemies of our hearts—those sirens that would seduce and shipwreck our desire and those arrows that aim to kill it outright. And we must journey forward, toward God, toward the Great Restoration and the Adventures to come. How awful to reach the end of life's road and find we haven't brought our hearts along with us.

So let me say it again: life is now a battle and a journey. This is the truest explanation for what is going on, the only way to rightly understand our experience. Life is not a game of striving and indulgence. It is not a long march of duty and obligation. It is not, as Henry Ford once said, "one damn thing after another." Life is a desperate quest through dangerous country to a destination that is, beyond all our wildest hopes, indescribably good. Only by conceiving of our days in this manner can we find our way safely through. You see, different roads lead different places. To find the Land of Desire, you must take the journey of desire.

You can't get there by any other means. If we are to take up the trail and get on with our quest, we've got to get our hearts back, which means getting our desire back.

RECOVERING DESIRE

I continue to be stunned by the level of deadness that most people consider normal and seem to be contented to live with. It had been more than a year since Diane and Ted first came to see me for counseling. As with most marriages, the real issues lay buried under years of just getting by, hidden beneath the way we've learned to live with each other so as not to rock the boat. Sadly, this way involves killing large regions of our hearts. And so their struggle toward intimacy required a lot of pain and hard work. But they stuck with it until they began to taste the true life of a real marriage. At this point Diane asked Ted about his deepest desires: "If I could be more of what you wanted in a woman, what do you secretly wish I would offer you?" It's a question that most men are dying to be asked. His response? Clean socks. That's all he could come up with. Life would be better, his marriage would be richer, if Diane would keep his drawer filled with clean socks. I wanted to throw him out the window.

I wasn't angry with Ted because his answer was unbelievably shallow or because it mocked all that his wife was seeking to offer him. I was angry because *it's just not true*. We are made in the image of God; we carry within us the desire for our true life of intimacy and adventure. To say we want less than that is to lie. Ted may believe that clean socks would satisfy him, but he is deceived. His satisfaction comes at the price of his soul.

When I brought up this very issue with a colleague, he sort of dismissed it all with the comment, "Not everyone longs like you do." I had to admit that much. But we were *meant* to. I thought of

The Weight of Glory, where Lewis says that "when we consider the unblushing promises of reward and the staggering nature of the rewards promised in the Gospels, it would seem that our Lord finds our desires not too strong, but too weak." My point precisely. Lewis is right:

> We are half-hearted creatures, fooling about with drink and sex and ambition, when infinite joy is offered us, like an ignorant child who wants to go on making mud pies in a slum because he cannot imagine what is meant by the offer of a holiday at the sea. We are far too easily pleased.

If only it were as strong as drink and sex and ambition. We've been bought off by clean socks and television. We'll sell our birthright for a little bit of pleasure and some peace and quiet. I understand. It hasn't taken us long to realize that life is not going to offer what we truly want, and so we've learned to reduce our desires to a more manageable size. But let's be honest about what we've done, and call it what it is: sin. The first step in the journey of desire is to stop pretending that we'd be happy with our equivalent of clean socks. Simone Weil said, "The danger is that the soul should persuade itself that it is not hungry." Recovering our true heart's desire may involve facing some very deep disappointment. Undoubtedly, it will require painful self-examination. But we do not need to fear what we will find, for our heart is our ally in this journey.

OUR DEEPEST HEART

Many committed Christians are wary about getting in touch with their desires, not because they want to settle for less, but because they fear that they will discover some dark hunger lurking in their hearts. As I've said, the father of lies takes many people out of the battle and ends their journey by keeping them in the shallows of their desire, tossing them a bone of pleasure, and thus convincing them that they are satisfied. However, once we begin to move from that place, his strategy changes. He threatens us from going into the deep waters by telling us that our core desires are evil. You might recall the scene in *Pilgrim's Progress* that takes place as Christian is making his way along the dark and dangerous trail through the Valley of the Shadow of Death:

> One thing I would not let slip; I took notice that now poor Christian was so confounded that he did not know his own voice; and thus I perceived it. One of the wicked ones got behind him, and stepped up softly to him, and whisperingly suggested many grievous blasphemies to him, which he verily thought had proceeded from his own mind. This put Christian more to it than anything that he met with before, even to think that he should now blaspheme him that he loved so much before; yet if he could have helped it, he would not have done it; but he had not the discretion either to stop his ears, or to know from whence these [thoughts] came.

The crisis for Christian is that he did not know his own voice, his true voice. He was convinced that the whispers of the enemy were his own desires. Far too many Christians today make the same dangerous assumption—that every thought and desire they experience is their own. "I could just lose myself at work." David was angry and resentful as he said this. He is struggling deeply in his marriage just now. "And no one would know the difference. I would still look married." "You are not a coward," I said. "I know you . . . that is not your heart. That is not the man you really want to be."

Listen to the promise of God to us in the new covenant: "I will give you a new heart and put a new spirit in you; I will remove from you your heart of stone and give you a heart of flesh" (Ezek. 36:26 NIV). For those who have been born of the Spirit and become new creatures in Christ, sin is no longer the truest thing about us. Since the coming of Christ, everything has changed. The joy of the new covenant is the transformation of our deepest being. As Christians, we have a new heart, and that means nothing less than this: our core desires are good. "I will put my law in their minds and write it on their hearts" (Jer. 31:33 NIV). We don't need to fear recovering our desire because our desire is from God and for God. That is what is most true about us. After several silent moments David said, "You're right. This is not what I most deeply want."

Yes, we still struggle with sin, with our tendency to kill desire or give our hearts over to false desires. But that is not who and what we truly are. If we really believe the new covenant, we'll be able to embrace our desire. So, let's come back to the simple question Jesus asks of us all: What do you want? Don't minimize it; don't try to make sure it sounds spiritual; don't worry about whether or not you can obtain it. Just stay with the question until you begin to get an answer. This is the way we keep current with our hearts.

WHAT DO YOU WANT?

"It's hard to be holy and passionate." Cindy sighed as she said this. A bright young woman and a sincerely committed follower of Christ, she's also a bit more vulnerable to men than she'd like to be. It seems that the only way Cindy can keep from chasing after physical intimacy with a man is to bury herself in grad school. But as I've said earlier, the "run from desire" approach never works, and she soon finds herself leaving the books for another compromis-

ing situation. "Why can't I get beyond this?" she asked. "I'm praying and reading my Bible every day. But still I fall." "What are you
looking for?" I asked in return. We sat in silence for a few minutes.
"I really don't know." "That's your problem . . . you don't know.
And so your unexamined desires rule you." After a few moments
she asked, "Is it pleasure? Excitement?" She was clueless. As intelligent as Cindy is, I wasn't surprised that she had no clue about
why she couldn't break her addiction to men. As a rule, most of us
live far from our hearts. We need to be much more acquainted
with them. We need to know what we want.

The path to a clearer knowledge of our desire depends on
how we've been handling it. Those who have buried desire
beneath years of duty and obligation may need to give all that a
rest so that their hearts can come to the surface. Abandon all but
the most essential duties for a while. You still have to pay the
bills, but everything you can jettison, you should. Do nothing
unless it reflects your true desire. Remember the Pharisees—
their religious activities deadened them to the point that they
couldn't even recognize God when he stood before them. When
our deepest treasure becomes our most dutiful burden, it really
kills our hearts. You might even need to give up going to church
for a while or reading your Bible. I stopped going to church for
a year; it was one of the most refreshing years of my life. I hadn't
abandoned God, and I very much sought out the company of my
spiritual companions. What I gave up was the performance of
having to show up every Sunday morning with my happy face
on. I suggested something similar to a young woman who had
really lost the joy of her faith. A few weeks later she wrote to me,
"I actually had a desire to read the Bible and pray without its
being a set time or a guilt trip! That's never happened before!"

Those who have been living to indulge desire will need to
give that a rest too. What does your heart feel when I suggest you

give up your obsession? Listen to the panic—there's something beneath it, something you need to know. Now, I understand that going cold turkey may seem overwhelming, unattainable. You may have tried that before and failed. Let me offer a more gentle approach. Simply stay in your desire for fifteen minutes longer than you usually do. When you're feeling a pull to the refrigerator or the gym or the bedroom, stop and let the desire just be; let it become more acute. Don't do anything with it. Let yourself feel it, and as you do, let your heart put some honest words to what you're feeling. You might be surprised what you find there.

I was walking down the hall at work one day, lost in my thoughts. Walking ahead of me, the same direction I was going, was a beautiful woman. I looked up and my heart said, *Wow!* Fearing that the beast of lust was rearing its ugly head, I tried to kill my reaction. It never works, and I knew it, so I decided instead to find out what was going on beneath what seemed to be an inappropriate response. Still walking along, with this beauty still in view, I asked my heart, *What do you mean by "wow"?* The next sentence literally popped out, unscripted, from someplace deep inside me: *The grand prize if you are truly a man.* I was stunned. I have lived that lie for a long time. How many young boys in our culture, just as they are entering adolescence, are introduced to sexuality as masculinity? Look at every ad designed for men. Whether it's for cars or sporting gear, clothes or beer, a beautiful siren is almost always posing seductively alongside. The message is beaten into us: if you're a man, you'll win the woman. I saw how long I had been haunted by that idea, and I also saw that what I was desiring was not an affair, but a truer sense of my masculinity.

This is something more than cognitive therapy, more than telling yourself the truth. It involves the hidden places of your heart, which are almost always revealed in your desire. But few of us take the time to look at the desire *beneath* the desire. A friend just spent thousands of dollars to undo a previous operation that tied her fallopian tubes. She wants to have another baby; no, she *needs* to have another baby. It has nothing to do with a baby. This is where she experiences being needed and wanted and loved. How many women derive their sense of self from their children? On and on it goes. Do we purchase a new home merely for more space, or does it mean security to us? We seek a better job. Might we be seeking a sense of identity, of being a successful person? It's not that the longing roused by any of these things is wrong. It's that we must learn what is actually *being* roused. The more attuned we are to our true desire, the less prone we'll be to impostors.

TEMPTATION

> Then Jesus was led by the Spirit into the desert to be tempted by the devil. After fasting forty days and forty nights, he was hungry. The tempter came to him and said, "If you are the Son of God, tell these stones to become bread." Jesus answered, "It is written: 'Man does not live on bread alone, but on every word that comes from the mouth of God.'" (Matt. 4:1–4 NIV)

We can learn many things about the journey of desire in the story of Jesus' wilderness trial. First, "he was hungry." I am so grateful for that phrase. It helps me to believe in the humanity of Jesus. He didn't just glide along through life, untouched by the dilemma of desire. Because his hunger is real, we can learn something about ours. May says, "If we think of Jesus as truly human, as a real man who was truly vulnerable to attachment, then the way he responded to Satan's temptation reveals some things that are critically important." The first thing we learn is that we're going to hunger. It's normal; expect it. Jesus' hunger validates my own. I needn't be embarrassed by it, try to hide it, or diminish it in some way. Sometimes we feel guilty about the depth of our desire, and we end up repenting of the wrong thing.

The devil sees his opportune moment. He comes to Jesus as he comes to us—in our hunger. And what he says is simply this: "You don't have to stay hungry, you know. There are options." He's not lying at this point; there usually are options. There is often something we can do about our hunger, and the options increase the more we are willing to turn away from trusting God. The lie is that the options will bring us what we most deeply want and need. They won't. Every idol is an impostor. Jesus responds, "Those options are not true life." This is the first crucial moment—facing what the options really amount to and realizing "that's not really life." A deep, robust thirst—like we feel after a long, hot hike—can be quenched only by water. To be offered a hot fudge sundae wouldn't tempt us at all. And so we see the importance of entering into desire, of knowing full well what we're craving.

I look at what my friends eat—not one-tenth of it is real food. It is all impostors—canned this, microwaved that. Bread without any nutritional value; fruit juice that boasts "10 percent real juice." Thus they slowly starve themselves while feeling full. When we are out of shape, when we are in the habit of eating poorly, truly nourishing foods don't appeal to us. Better something rich, high in fat. Those mock our need while they appease our taste. But when we are fit, when we've been working out or just working hard in the field, we know what we want. Who would trade a hearty farmhouse dinner for a plate of marshmallows? The truly healthy desire knows what it wants. Had we desired more deeply, more clearly, we would have seen the offer for what it was. Knowing full well what our heart's real thirst was, we would have looked the impostor in the face and laughed. As Jesus did.

Then the devil took him to the holy city and had him stand on the highest point of the temple. "If you are the Son of God," he said, "throw yourself down. For it is written: 'He will command his angels concerning you, and they will lift you up in their hands, so that you will not strike your foot against a stone.'" Jesus answered him, "It is also written: 'Do not put the Lord your God to the test.'" (Matt. 4:5–7 NIV)

The second trial comes after we determine not to take matters into our own hands. By refusing to turn stones to bread, Jesus chooses to trust God. That is what we are saying when we refuse our options as well. Satan's reply is, "Oh, so you're going to trust your God. Fine. Prove he cares for you." He comes with an attack on God's heart toward us. This is almost inevitable for the thirsty soul. After we have chosen to remain in our thirst for a while, the doubts begin to creep in. *God, I know you love me. But I didn't expect I'd have to wait so long for what I desire.* We begin to wonder, *Do you care for me, God?* Satan jumps all over this, throwing fuel on the fire of our doubts. Jesus' response is our only hope: "I don't need to prove that God cares for me. He cares for me *now*." There is no other place to stand. As Allender says,

> If God's goodness is looked for primarily in turns of fortune . . . then the verdict on his heart towards us will always be pending on a new set of facts. We will, then, become either a judge ("How can God be good, if he let my son die?!") or a bargainer ("God, I'll know you are good if you bring my husband back to me"). God does not seem to show his goodness to those who peer through the lens of a skeptical examiner or a demanding negotiator. The Evil One uses the pain and confusion of a fallen world to shadow doubt over God's goodness. (*Bold Love*)

Jesus came to answer once and for all our question, "Do you care for me, God?" That is why the ground before the cross is the only place we can take a firm stand against the doubts that come in the journey of desire. We don't need for God to prove his love for us; he has, at the cross.

> Again, the devil took him to a very high mountain and showed him all the kingdoms of the world and their splendor. "All this I will give you," he said, "if you will bow down and worship me." Jesus said to him, "Away from me, Satan! For it is written: 'Worship the Lord your God, and serve him only.'" Then the devil left him, and angels came and attended him. (Matt. 4:8–11 NIV)

The cat's out of the bag. Satan has revealed his true aim. "You don't have to take the route of suffering," he says. "There are shortcuts. Just give your heart away." It all comes down to worship. What will we give our hearts away to, in return for the promise of life? May says this is "the ultimate invitation to idolatry." Jesus shuts Satan down: "There are no shortcuts, and my heart belongs to God alone."

Once we realize what a precious thing this is, the heart's desire, we must see that to guard it is worth our all. To neglect it is foolishness. To kill it is suicide. To allow it to wander aimlessly, to be trapped by the seductions of the evil one, is disaster. We must be *serious* about our happiness. And so Thomas à Kempis urges,

> The greatest, and indeed the whole impediment, is that we are not disentangled from our passions and lusts, neither do we endeavor to enter into that path of perfection which the saints have walked before us; and when any small adversity befalleth us, we are too quickly dejected, and turn ourselves to human comforts. If we would endeavor, like men of courage, to stand in

the battle, surely we would feel the favorable assistance of God from heaven. For he who giveth us occasion to fight, to the end that we may get the victory, is ready to succor those that fight manfully, and do trust in his grace. (*The Imitation of Christ*)

TUNING THE INSTRUMENT

So I tell you this, and insist on it in the Lord, that you must no longer live as the Gentiles do, in the futility of their thinking. They are darkened in their understanding and separated from the life of God because of the ignorance that is in them due to the hardening of their hearts. Having lost all sensitivity, they have given themselves over to sensuality so as to indulge in every kind of impurity, with a continual lust for more. (Eph. 4:17–19 NIV)

The loss of sensitivity that Paul is referring to here is the dullness that most people accept as normal. It actually leads us into sin, to sensuality and lust. The deadened soul requires a greater and greater level of stimulation to arouse it. This is, of course, the downward spiral of any addiction. What began as an attraction to *Playboy* ends up for the porn addict in some really horrific stuff. Just look at the progression of television drama over the past thirty years. What we have now would have been considered shocking, even repulsive, to an earlier audience. Networks have to keep adding more sex, more violence, to keep our attention. We have become so sensual. This is why holiness is not numbness; it is sensitivity. It is being *more* attuned to our desires, to what we were truly made for and therefore what we truly want. Our problem is that we've grown quite used to seeking life in all kinds of things other than God.

For example, God wants to be our perfect lover, but instead we seek perfection in human relationships and are disappointed when our lovers cannot love us perfectly. God wants to provide

our ultimate security, but we seek our safety in power and possessions and then we find we must continually worry about them.
We seek satisfaction of our spiritual longing in a host of ways that
may have very little to do with God. (*Addiction and Grace*)

And so May comments, "The more we become accustomed to
seeking spiritual satisfaction through things other than God, the
more abnormal and stressful it becomes to look for God
directly." Our instrument is out of tune from years of misuse.
This is where the Law is our help. Everything in you may be saying, "But you don't understand. I *want* to eat that whole box of
chocolates (or sleep with my boyfriend, or let my anger really
fly). That's what really seems like life to me right now." God says,
"I know you do, but it'll kill you in the end. What you think is
life is not. That's not the comfort (or the love, or the significance) you are seeking. You'll wind up destroying yourself." The
commands of God become our tutor in the healing of our desire.
We need the Law because our instrument is out of tune; we're not
clear all the time on what it is we *really* desire.

And so the first command comes first. God tells us to love him
with all our hearts and all our souls, with all our minds and all our
strength. It's not a burden but a rescue, a trail out of the jungles of
desire. When we don't look for God as our true life, our desire for
him spills over into our other desires, giving them an ultimacy
and urgency they were never intended to bear. We become desperate, grasping and arranging and worrying over all kinds of
things, and once we get them, they end up ruling us. It's the difference between wants and needs. All we truly need is God. Prone
to wander from him, we find we need all sorts of other things.
Our desire becomes insatiable because we've taken our longing
for the Infinite and placed it upon finite things. God saves us from
the whole mimetic mess by turning our hearts back to him.

You may have heard an orchestra tuning up before a concert. It sounds like total chaos—oboes, cello, French horns, dozens of instruments all sounding off, everyone doing his own thing. Trills, groans, whistles, thumps—an absolute cacophony. This is how our desires seem most of the time. But then the first violin plays a long high C, and slowly, all the other instruments join in. They become focused, centered, ready to perform. Such is what happens with the chaos of our desires when we turn our souls to God in worship. All the other desires find their place as we give God his place. That is why the psalmist urges us, "Delight yourself in the LORD and he will give you the desires of your heart" (Ps. 37:4 NIV). Only as we truly delight in God is it safe to give us our desires, for then they are not likely to become idols. And by our delighting in God, he heals our false desires as our souls come true in the light of their Maker. *Worship* becomes the means by which we most deeply heal our desire.

WORSHIP—THE HEART'S HEALER

Henri Nouwen once asked Mother Teresa for spiritual direction. Spend one hour each day in adoration of your Lord, she said, and never do anything you know is wrong. Follow this, and you'll be fine. Such simple, yet profound advice. Worship is the act of the abandoned heart adoring its God. It is the union that we crave. Few of us experience anything like this on a regular basis, let alone for an hour each day. But it is what we need. Desperately. Simply showing up on Sunday is not even close to worship. Neither does singing songs with religious content pass for worship. What counts is *the posture of the soul* involved, the open heart pouring forth its love toward God and communing with him. It is a question of desire.

Worship occurs when we say to God, from the bottom of our

hearts, "You are the One whom I desire." As Thomas à Kempis prayed, "There is nothing created that can fully satisfy my desires. Make me one with You in a sure bond of heavenly love, for You alone are sufficient to Your lover, and without You all things are vain and of no substance."

I spent a year in the Psalms at the same time I was resting from the duty of Sunday morning. I wasn't studying them with my head; I was praying them from my heart. It gave me a voice for the cry of my soul—the anguish, the weariness, the joy, the sorrow. It's all there. What is remarkable is that no matter where the poet begins, he almost always ends in worship. This is no coincidence. It is where our journey must lead us. In the most often quoted phrase from Augustine, he says, "Our hearts are restless until they find their rest in Thee." He is referring to desire. Our only hope for rest from the incessant craving of our desire is in God, and us united to him. And so à Kempis prayed, "O faithful soul, make ready thy heart for this Bridegroom." He continued,

> Grant me, O most sweet and loving Jesus, to rest in thee above all creatures, above all health and beauty, above all glory and honor, above all power and dignity, above all knowledge and subtlety, above all riches and arts, above all joy and gladness, above all fame and praise, above all sweetness and comfort, above all hope and promise, above all desert and desire . . .

> Thou alone art most beautiful and loving, thou alone most noble and glorious above all things, in whom all good things together both perfectly are, and ever have been, and shall be.

The full union, of course, is coming. We rehearse for the wedding now through worship.

CHAPTER ELEVEN

LETTING GO

Grasp not at much for fear thou losest all.
— GEORGE HERBERT

For Jesus I have gladly suffered the loss of all things.
—THE APOSTLE PAUL

I f you're coming up from the south, the only way to get into the Lamar Valley in northeast Yellowstone is over Dunraven Pass. It's a narrow, winding road over the flanks of Mount Washburn and in recent years badly in need of repair. Still, I had come so far for this. It was three months after Brent's death, and I had made a sort of pilgrimage to Yellowstone. The last great adventure we shared together was here, fly-fishing among the wolves and bears in the Lamar Valley.

I had returned under the auspices of taking my family on vacation, but I sensed there was a deeper reason. Unbeknownst to them, I was on a pilgrimage, drawn here for a purpose only partially known to me. Down the desolate highways of Wyoming, across the Absarokas, up the Snake River from Jackson Hole, I had followed some inner call. There was much to see along the way, and many side trails explored with my family. But finally, we came to my real goal—the road over Dunraven Pass. It was closed.

The orange-and-white barriers stood there like a prophetic

beast out of a nightmare. ROAD CLOSED. *None shall pass.* It seems the Park Service crews had decided—that morning, with no prior warning—to close the road for repairs for the rest of the season. My journey would end here. I sat at the intersection staring dumbly at the barriers, the engine idling, cars piling up behind me. God began to speak to my sinking heart: *Your journey lies along another path. You've got to let all that go now.* I knew there was no arguing. I didn't even try to put up a fight. I've been known to plow through his barriers in the past, but not now. Remember checkmate? My grip has loosened in recent years, and I knew this was a call to loosen it even more. David Wilcox sings about this moment in "Slipping Through My Fist":

I have drifted down a ways along the shoreline,
I just watched these ropes give way
where they were tied.
I could have reached out quick when the ropes first
slipped, if I had tried,
but I was wondering where the wind was trying to take me
overnight, if I never did resist, and
what strange breezes make a sailor want to
let it come to this,
with lines untied, slipping through my fist.
It is downhill all the way to the ocean,
So of course the river wants to flow.
The river's been here longer,
It's older and stronger and knows where to go.

One thing I have come to embrace is this: we have to let it go. The more comfortable we are with mystery in our journey, the more rest we will know along the way. The Christian life is full of paradox (as if you hadn't noticed). Listen to how Paul describes his experience of the quest: "Sorrowful, yet always rejoicing; poor, yet making many rich; having nothing, and yet possessing everything" (2 Cor. 6:10 NIV). How true this is. If we will remain open to sorrow, we can know joy. Somehow being empty allows us to make others rich. And if we are willing to let go, we'll discover something most surprising—that all is ours. That is why reaching to possess is one danger of which the heart alive must be wary. Those who have given up caring aren't tempted by this. But once we *know* what we want, we must learn the grace of release.

WILLING TO THIRST

There is a widespread belief in the church that to be a Christian somehow satisfies our every desire. As one camp song has it, "I'm inright, outright, upright, downright happy all day long." What complete nonsense! Augustine emphasized, "The whole life of the good Christian is a holy longing. What you desire ardently, as yet you do not see." So, "let us long because we are to be filled . . . That is our life, to be exercised by long-ing." There's the mystery again. Longing leads to fullness some-where down the road. Meanwhile, being content is not the same thing as being full.

Paul said he had "learned the secret of being content" (Phil. 4:12 NIV), and many Christians assume he no longer experienced the thirst of his soul. But earlier in the same epistle, the old saint said that he had *not* obtained his soul's desire, or "already been made perfect." Quite the contrary. He described himself as press-ing on, "straining toward what is ahead" (Phil. 3:12–14 NIV). These are not the words of a man who no longer experienced longing because he had arrived. They are the account of a man propelled on his life quest by his desire.

Contentment is not freedom *from* desire, but freedom *of* desire. Being content is not pretending that everything is the way you wish it would be; it is not acting as though you have no wishes. Rather, it is no longer being *ruled* by your desires.

The fact is, at this point in our journey, we have only three options: (1) to be alive and thirsty, (2) to be dead, or (3) to be addicted. There are no other choices. Most of the world lives in addiction; most of the church has chosen deadness. The Christian is called to the life of holy longing. But we don't like to stay there. A. W. Tozer perceived that "there is within the human heart a tough, fibrous root of fallen life whose nature is to possess, always to possess." And why do we seek to possess? So that we do not have to live in thirst, trusting our hearts each day to the goodness of God. To live in thirst is to live with an ache. Every addiction comes from the attempt to get rid of the ache. How is it possible to satisfy an insatiable desire? Merely trying sets us on an unending chase that leads us farther and farther from home.

And thus life passes away. Men combat with a thousand difficulties for the sake of repose, and as soon as they have overcome them all, repose becomes intolerable. For their thoughts are turned either on existing evils, or on such as are impending. And when secure on all sides from danger, their inherent disquietude, destitute of objects it might just fix upon, still continues to shoot from the heart, its native soil, and overspreads the soul with its venom.

What can this incessant craving, and this impotence of attainment mean, unless there was once a happiness belonging to man, of which only the faintest traces remain, in that void which he attempts to fill with everything within his reach? But it is in vain he seeks from absent objects the relief things present cannot give, and which neither of them can give; because, in a soul that will live forever, there is an infinite void that nothing can fill, but an infinite unchangeable being. (*Pensées*)

You can be satisfied, says Pascal; you just can't be sated. There is great joy in a glass of cabernet; the whole bottle is another story. Intimate conversation satisfies a different thirst, but how awful to try to arrange for it again the next night and the night after that. The Israelites tried to hoard the manna—and it crawled with maggots. Our soul's insatiable desire becomes the venom Pascal warns of when it demands its fill here and now, through the otherwise beautiful and good gifts of our lives.

God grants us so much of our heart's desire as we delight in him: "You open your hand and satisfy the desires of every living thing" (Ps. 145:16 NIV). Not always, not on demand, but certainly more than we deserve. God delights to give good gifts to his beloved. But that old root would have us shift once more from giver to gift, and seek our rest through being full. This is the turn we must be vigilant to see, watching over our hearts with loving care. In his lovely poem "The Size," George Herbert prays,

> Content thee, greedie heart.
> Modest and moderate joys to those, that have
> Title to more hereafter when they part,
> Are passing brave.
>
> If thou hast wherewithall to spice a draught,
> When griefs prevail;
> And for the future time art heir
> To th' Isle of spices, is't not fair?
> To be in both worlds full
> Is more than God was, who was hungrie here.

Remember, pleasure is often more about drugging ourselves than it is about enjoying ourselves. And the things we do to avoid the ache are always worse in the end than the ache itself. I think of Jamie, a bright and energetic young woman who has tried so hard to know the right thing to do in every situation. She has tied herself in knots trying to figure out the will of God, solve all the theological quandaries, never miss a beat. She wrote to me recently, "I am caught in a tangle of trying to *do*, trying to live *right*. I don't know how to not think or worry or control. I don't know how to let go." It's driving her absolutely crazy. (Didn't Chesterton warn us, "Poets do not go mad; but chess-players do"?) Why can't she let go? "I want to predict what the Lord is going to do, so that it doesn't hurt so bad when it happens." Jamie grasped onto perfectionism to avoid pain and disappointment. It only made matters worse. As Carl Jung asserted, "Neurosis is always a substitute for legitimate suffering." So what do we do? How do we live with desire we cannot take care of and heartache we cannot prevent? We groan and wait.

WHAT HOPE FEELS LIKE

We know that the whole creation has been groaning as in the pains of childbirth right up to the present time. Not only so, but we ourselves, who have the firstfruits of the Spirit, groan inwardly as we wait eagerly for our adoption as sons, the redemption of our bodies. For in this hope we were saved. But hope that is seen is no hope at all. Who hopes for what he already has? But if we hope for what we do not yet have, we wait for it patiently. (Rom. 8:22–25 NIV)

Amazing. Paul is passing along to us the secret of the sojourning heart. We live in hope, and he says hoping is waiting. And groaning. When was the last time you heard that in a sermon or the title for a new book? *You, Too, Can Groan Inwardly While You Wait Eagerly!* Everything I've seen lately offers a sure-fire way to "get what you want." How to be a success at work. How to be a success at love. How to succeed in work *and* love at the same time.

Here are questions to ask yourself to see if you are a pilgrim or an arranger: What am I waiting for? Is there anything I ardently desire that I am doing nothing to secure? The first time I asked myself, I couldn't name a thing. There were many things I was working on, or fretting over, or had given up wanting. I am thankful that was some time ago. Things are different now. Now I wonder, What am I still arranging for? I should like to let it go too.

WAITING

To wait is to learn the spiritual grace of *detachment,* the freedom of desire. Not the absence of desire, but desire at rest. St. John of the Cross lamented that "the desires weary and fatigue the soul; for they are like restless and discontented children, who are ever demanding this or that from their mother, and are never contented." Detachment is coming to the place where those demanding children are at peace. As King David said,

> I have stilled and quieted my soul;
>   like a weaned child with its mother,
>   like a weaned child is my soul within me.
>
> (Ps 131:2 NIV)

Such a beautiful picture, a young one leaning against her mother's breast. There is no fussing, no insistent tears. She has learned to wait.

The word *detachment* might evoke wrong impressions. It is not a cold and indifferent attitude; not at all. May writes, "An authentic spiritual understanding of detachment devalues neither desire nor the objects of desire." Instead, it "aims at correcting one's own anxious grasping in order to free oneself for committed relationship to God."

Bethann told me this beautiful story after we both attended a conference in Denver: "After nine days of being with twelve hundred people, I wanted to breathe, to be alone, and to be free." So she went antique shopping downtown. The first shop she stepped into was very upscale. "It felt more like a museum or even cathedral than a shop. I felt out of place. Obviously, I couldn't buy anything here. I clutched my purse closely to make sure that I didn't knock anything over." Enormous English armoires, French marble fireplaces, an $18,000 Roman bathtub. Reaching the back of the store, Bethann turned into a narrow passage between pieces and was captivated by a stained glass window. "It must have come from a chalet in France. It was propped up against a window and the light that came through it seemed somehow purified; the shades of soft yellow and blue and rose flowing from an urn of profuse flowers with ribbons elegantly fluttering away. I don't know how long I stood there with my mouth open. It made my heart swell and fill and ache at the same time." Her mind began to race: How could she possess it for her own? But at $8,000, the window was beyond hoping for. "Resignation, hopelessness, and anger followed. Then out of nowhere, I rebounded. I *will* have it in my home—in heaven. Some guy making six figures may be able to have it for a few years, but I'll have it forever." It was the first time, she told me, that she saw her desires filled in the coming kingdom. *I've got the better end of the deal*, she said to herself and walked out.

As Thomas à Kempis declared, "Wait a little while, O my

soul, wait for the divine promise, and thou shalt have abundance of all good things in heaven." In this posture we discover that, indeed, we are expanded by longing. Something grows in us, a capacity if you will, for life and love and God. I think of Romans 8:24–25: "That is why waiting does not diminish us, any more than waiting diminishes a pregnant mother. We are enlarged in the waiting. We, of course, don't see what is enlarging us. But the longer we wait, the larger we become, and the more joyful our expectancy" (*The Message*). There is actually a sweet pain in longing if we will let it draw our hearts homeward.

AND GROANING

When I turned away from those barriers to the Lamar Valley, I accepted that I could not recover what had been lost. Not yet. My journey now lies along another path. And so we retreated from the road over Dunraven Pass, left Yellowstone through the south gate, and descended into the Tetons, staying there for several nights.

One morning I woke early and could not get back to sleep. My soul was agitated, restless. After what seemed like an hour of tossing and turning, I rose and slipped out of the cabin to take a walk. Waves of grief began to sweep over my soul. But it was not all about Brent or even primarily about him. His death was the lance that pierced the wound of all the ungrieved grief of my life. Sorrows from my marriage, from college days, from wounds I received as a child—all of them poured forth through this place of release. Why had I waited so many years to shed these tears? As I wept, I realized that Paul was absolutely right. How can we live without groaning? If we do not give our ache a voice, it doesn't go away. It becomes the undercurrent of our addictions. Pleasure becomes necessary in larger and larger doses, like morphine.

The paradox of grief is that it is healing; it somehow restores our souls, when all the while we thought it would leave us in despair. Control is the enemy; grief is our friend. Jamie came to realize this when her boyfriend decided he did not know if he could love her and broke off their relationship. She wrote,

> The problem is that I was already choosing to love him. How hard it was for me to let down the walls and care—risk. And it isn't that I did anything wrong in dating, so there is nothing that I can say I should have done or should not have done, besides love him. Oh, I don't know if this is making any sense, but through the breakup I have been real. I have not done my usual "cover up and pretend that I never cared in the first place." Instead I have hurt, I have embraced the pain and the reality that there is nothing that I can do besides wait for the healing. Embracing the pain has brought me to a place of more complete healing than I feel I could have known otherwise.

As she let go of her controlling, something better took its place—mourning. When the ministry of the Messiah is described in Isaiah 61, comfort for those who mourn and healing for the brokenhearted are placed at the center of his mission. None of this makes sense until we admit our brokenheartedness and give our sorrow a voice in mourning. Only then will we know his comfort. Until then, they are nice, religious-sounding words.

Solomon said that it is better to go to a house of mourning than it is to a house of feasting. I never understood this; I wrote it off as the pessimism of a depressed man. Now I think I know what he meant. Grief is good. It is cleansing. It undoes my world—and that is the best part of it. I need to be undone; simply undone. No regrouping. We need to mourn; it is the only way our hearts can remain both free and alive in this world. Why? Because it, like nothing else, puts a stop to the constant striving. Grief is the antidote to the incessant possessive demand within.

Another friend, Deborah, wrote,

How do I live in the world I have with my woundedness? How do I live as an alive woman in the world I have? I am so grateful every time God speaks deeply to my heart. I started to acknowledge my deep, deep loneliness, and when I did, everything has been happening in a rush, like a river freed, fast and tumultuous. I've been crying and it just keeps going—the kind of tears and feelings of grief that I've cried when family members have died . . . but it's oh so good, because it is also a feeling of being alive to who God made me to be and it's acknowledging the truth of how I see life and experience life.

> Those who sow in tears
> will reap with songs of joy.
> He who goes out weeping,
> carrying seed to sow,
> will return with songs of joy,
> carrying sheaves with him.
> (Ps. 126:5-6 NIV)

I believe we must add two spiritual disciplines to everyday life. The first is worship. We must adore God deliberately, regularly. The other is grief. We must allow a time for sorrow to do our own personal sowing. I see no other way to care for our hearts.

Now making time to grieve might seem strange to you. "But I don't feel grief or sorrow at all." Just because we do not feel it doesn't mean it is not there. Our pleasant experience may be the result of the thousand distractions that fill our waking moments. Kierkegaard said that despair has become so rare not because the

human race is doing suddenly better, but because we so effectively push it away. This is the "sickness unto death," to despair
without ever despairing, to mourn without ever mourning.

I've found, therefore, that quite often grief has to sneak up on
us, surprise us during our day. It may come through a song you
hear or a movie you see. It may come as you choose to allow
your soul twenty minutes of quiet during your lunch hour.
Sometimes a small disappointment can be the door into a room
of grief you never knew was there. However unexpectedly grief
shows up, let us accept it as a welcome visitor.

This is the last journal entry I made *before* going to the mountains with Brent, the weekend he was killed: *Life is loss and I must
grieve regularly, so as to give up trying to possess. I will not arrive in the
golden place until I am home with God.* The last thing Jesus said to me
before that weekend was, *Don't run from the suffering. Embrace it.* I had
no idea what was coming. I had no idea how prophetic those
words would be. I knew only the truth of them from the journey
thus far. They are truer now.

LET BEAUTY HAVE ITS SAY

*What can I possibly say to her? How can I begin to restore hope to her
life?* This is what was going through my mind as I listened to
Kathleen. It was partly about being raped, and partly about the
tensions in her marriage remaining years after, that she had come
to see me. I wondered, *What can I offer this woman? What can I say to
one who has known such terrible evil?* We sat in my office on a cold
winter afternoon; outside all was gray. Perhaps that's the reason
I first noticed the little flowers embroidered on the collar of her
denim shirt. As she told me her tragic story, my eye kept coming
back to those graceful little bouquets. Maybe I was surprised by
them, but somehow I felt they were the clue to her restoration.

Kathleen finished her story, and we sat in silence. After a few moments, I couldn't help mentioning the flowers. "Oh," she said. "Ever since the rape, beauty has meant the world to me. No one seemed to understand why. Sometimes I would spend hours just gazing at my garden and the woods behind my house. Only beauty helps."

I understand completely. As the shock of Brent's death began to wear off, the searing pain of intense grief took its place. It was too difficult to read my Bible. Conversation required more than I was able to give. Frankly, I didn't want to talk to anyone, not even God. The only thing that helped was my wife's flower garden. The solace I found there was like nothing else on earth. I wrote in my journal, *Sitting outside this evening, the Shasta daisies swaying in the gentle breeze on their long stems, the aspens shimmering without light, the full moon rising over the pine-crested bluff . . . only beauty speaks what I need to hear. Only beauty helps.*

Simone Weil was absolutely right—beauty and affliction are the only two things that can pierce our hearts. Because this is so true, we must have a measure of beauty in our lives proportionate to our affliction. No, more. Much more. Is this not God's prescription for us? Just take a look around. The sights and sounds, the aromas and sensations—the world is overflowing with beauty. God seems to be rather enamored with it. Gloriously wasteful. Apparently, he feels that there ought to be plenty of it in our lives.

I am at a loss to say what I want to say regarding beauty. Somehow, that is as it ought to be. Our experience of beauty transcends our ability to speak about it, for its magic lies beyond the power of words. Wordsworth penned these lines:

> Thanks to the human heart by which we live,
> Thanks to its tenderness, its joys, and fears,

To me the meanest flower that blows can give
Thoughts that do often lie too deep for tears.

I want to speak of beauty's healing power, of how it comforts and soothes, yet also how it stirs us, how it moves and inspires. All that sounds ridiculous. You know your own experiences of beauty. Let me call upon them then. Think of your favorite music, or tapestry, or landscape. "We have had a couple of inspiring sunsets this week." A dear friend sent this in an e-mail: "It was as if the seams of our atmosphere split for a bit of heaven to plunge into the sea. I stood and applauded . . . simultaneously I wanted to kneel and weep." Yes—that's it. All I want to do is validate those irreplaceable moments, lift any obstacle you may have to filling your life with greater and greater amounts of beauty.

We need not fear indulging here. The experience of beauty is unique to all the other pleasures in this: there is no possessive quality to it. Just because you love the landscape doesn't mean you have to acquire the real estate. Simply to behold the flower is enough; there is nothing in me that wants to consume it. Beauty is the closest thing we have to fullness without possessing on this side of eternity. It heralds the Great Restoration. Perhaps that is why it is so healing—beauty is pure gift. It helps us in our letting go.

SURRENDER

The time has come for us to quit playing chess with God over our lives. We cannot win, but we can delay the victory, dragging on the pain of grasping and the poison of possessing. You see, there are two kinds of losses in life. The first is shared by all mankind—the losses that come to us. Call them what you will— accidents, fate, acts of God. The point is that we have no control over them. We do not determine when, where, what, or even how. There is no predicting these losses; they happen *to* us. We choose only how we respond. The second kind is known only to the pilgrim. They are losses that we *choose*. A chosen loss is different from repentance, when we give up something that was never ours to have. With a chosen loss, we place on the altar something very dear to us, something innocent, whose only danger is in its goodness, that we might come to love it too much. It is the act of *consecration*, where little by little or all at once, we give over our lives to the only One who can truly keep them.

Spiritual surrender is not resignation. It is not choosing to care no longer. Nor is it Eastern mysticism, an attempt to get beyond the suffering of this life by going completely numb. As my dear friend Jan describes, "It is surrender *with* desire, or *in* desire." Desire is still present, felt, welcomed even. But the will to secure is made subject to the divine will in an act of abandoned trust. Think of Jesus in the Garden of Gethsemane. Frederick Buechner has suggested that we contrast him with a picture we have of Buddha, so that we might see the difference of true surrender:

> Buddha sits enthroned beneath the Bo-tree in the lotus position. His lips are faintly parted in the smile of one who has passed beyond every power in earth or heaven to touch him. "He who loves fifty has fifty woes, he who loves ten has ten woes, he who loves none has no woes," he has said. His eyes are closed.

> Christ, on the other hand, stands in the garden of Gethsemane, angular, beleaguered. His face is lost in the shadows so that you can't even see his lips, and before all the powers on earth or heaven he is powerless. "This is my commandment, that you love one another as I have loved you," he has said. (*Now and Then*)

Christ is weeping freely; his prayers are marked by loud cries and tears. He makes it very, very clear what he desires. Not once, but three times he begs his Father to remove this awful cup from him: "Yet not my will, but thine be done." He surrenders with desire, in desire. Making himself poor, he opens up to us the treasures of heaven. Buddha abandons his desire; Christ surrenders his will. It is no small difference.

True surrender is not an easy out, calling it quits early in the game. This kind of surrender comes only *after* the night of wrestling. It comes only after we open our hearts to care deeply. Then we choose to surrender, or give over, our deepest desires to God. And with them we give over our hearts, our deepest selves. The freedom and beauty and rest that follow are among the greatest of all surprises.

After he lost his son, Wolterstorff did not remain passive: he wept; he railed; he lamented. I suppose it was his own Gethsemane. That trail of tears brought him to a place of true surrender. This is how he describes it:

> Let me try again. All these things I still recognize. I remember delighting in them—trees, art, house, music, pink morning sky, work well done, flowers, books. I still delight in them. I'm still grateful. But the zest is gone. The passion is cooled, the striving is quieted, the longing stilled. My attachment is loosened. No longer do I set my heart on them. I can do without them. They don't matter. Instead of rowing, I float. The joy that comes my way I savor. But the seeking, the clutching, the aiming is gone. (*Lament for a Son*)

I tasted this wonderful freedom a few months ago, canoeing on a high mountain lake. My boys had already gone in for the day, and so I was alone in the canoe, paddling across this beautiful lake at dusk. That was when the trout began to rise. The surface of the water was serene in the little cove I had found, and the dimples made by feeding rainbows were too numerous to count. It is the moment fly fishermen dream about. I set down the paddle and picked up my rod to begin casting. As the line unfurled, my fly alighted gently on the water in the middle of a dozen rise-rings. First one, then two trout took my offering. I knew that if the fish continued to rise, I would have my fill before it became too dark to fish anymore. But then, a gentle breeze began to blow down the valley. It was cool and fragrant and refreshing, and though it was soft, I noticed it was strong enough to carry my canoe along. A tremor of anxiety passed through me, for I knew I could not fish and paddle at the same time. To stay in this little cove, among the rising trout, I would have to put down the rod and pick up the paddle.

I smiled and set down the rod. But I didn't take up the paddle. I let my hands rest along the gunwales and let the gentle breeze take me away, out across the surface of the lake. And as I drifted, I drank in the beauty of the mountain peaks around me, and the golden quality of the fading light, and the joy of the freedom of my desire. A little voice reminded me that fish were rising back in the cove.

But I was wondering where the wind was trying to take me
overnight, if I never did resist, and
what strange breezes make a sailor want to
let it come to this,
with lines untied, slipping through my fist.

CHAPTER TWELVE

KEEPING HEART—
TO THE END

Remember thee!
Yea, from the table of my memory
I'll wipe away all trivial fond records . . .
And thy commandment all alone shall live
Within the book and volume of my brain
Unmix'd with baser matter.

—HAMLET

Sometimes I wake, and, lo, I have forgot.
—GEORGE MacDONALD

But every now and anon a trumpet sounds from the hid battle-
ments of eternity.
—FRANCIS THOMPSON

Gabriel García Marquez's novel *One Hundred Years of Solitude* chronicles the life of the little Mexican town of Macondo and the families who call it home. At one point in their domestic journey, a plague of insomnia strikes the little village. The residents go weeks, then months without sleep. They begin to lose vital faculties. First to go is the memory—no small aspect for living. Even the simplest and most common household goods appear foreign, unfamiliar, forgotten. Aureliano, the silversmith, is working in his shop one day when he realizes he cannot remember the name for the little anvil he uses. His father, Jose, tells him the name.

Aureliano wrote the name on a piece of paper that he pasted to the base of the small anvil: *stake*. In that way he was sure of not forgetting it in the future. It did not occur to him that this was the first manifestation of a loss of memory, because the object had a difficult name to remember. But a few days later he discovered that he had trouble remembering almost every object in the laboratory. Then he marked them with their respective names so that all he had to do was read the inscription in order to identify them . . . [Jose] put it into practice all through the house and later on imposed it on the whole village. With an inked brush he marked everything with its name: *table, chair, clock, door, wall, bed, pan*. He went to the corral and marked the animals and plants: *cow, goat, pig, hen, cassava, caladium, banana*. Little by little, studying the infinite possibilities of a loss of memory, he realized that the day might come when things would be recognized by their inscriptions but that no one would remember their use. Then he was more explicit. The sign that he hung on the neck of the cow was an exemplary proof of the way in which the inhabitants of Macondo were prepared to fight against loss of memory: *This is the cow. She must be milked every morning so that she will produce milk, and the milk must be boiled in order to be mixed with coffee to make coffee and milk.*

. . . At the beginning of the road into the swamp they put up a sign that said *Macondo* and another larger one on the main street that said *God exists*.

OUR WORST ENEMY

The first time I read this story I simply laughed. But it haunted me, and on a second reading I began to realize that it's my story too. I said to myself, *It's not a bad plan. Right above my bed I think I shall hang a sign that says, GOD EXISTS.* You see, I wake most mornings an unbeliever. It seems that during the night, I slip into forgetfulness, and by the time the new day comes, I am lost. The deep and precious truths that God has brought to me over the years and even just yesterday seem a thousand miles away. It doesn't happen every morning, but enough to make it an ongoing reality. And I know I am not alone in this. As MacDonald confessed in *Diary of an Old Soul,*

> Sometimes I wake, and lo, I have forgot,
> And drifted out upon an ebbing sea!
> My soul that was at rest now resteth not,
> For I am with myself and not with thee;
> Truth seems a blind moon in a glaring morn,
> Where nothing is but sick-heart vanity.

Virtually every person I've ever counseled follows a similar pattern. Over the course of our time together, some wonderful things begin to happen. Not necessarily at first, and never on command, but God shows up. The lights turn on for these people; their heart is lifted; grateful tears flow. Suddenly, faith, hope, and love seem the only way to live. And I nearly dread the next session. When they return the following week, it is as though it never happened. The marvelous day is a distant memory. Life is hard, God is distant, and love is foolish. All is forgotten; all is sick-heart vanity. I want to grab them and shake them into sense, shouting, "Don't you *remember?* Why did you let it slip away?" Wisdom has kept me restrained so far.

Forgetting is no small problem. Of all the enemies our hearts must face, this may be the worst because it is insidious. Forgetfulness does not come against us like an enemy in full battle formation, banners waving. Nor does it come temptingly, seductively, the lady in red. It works slowly, commonly, unnoticed. My wife had a beautiful climbing rose vine that began to fill an arbor in her garden. We enjoyed the red blossoms it produced every summer. But last year, something happened. The vine suddenly turned brown, dropped its flowers, and died within the course of a week. After all that loving care we couldn't figure out what went wrong. A call to the nursery revealed that a worm had gotten into the stalk of the vine and eaten away at the life from the inside. Such is the work of forgetfulness. It cuts us off from our Life so slowly, we barely notice, until one day the blooms of our faith are suddenly gone.

BE FOREWARNED

We're certainly warned about forgetfulness in Scripture, both in word and by example. In the Old Testament, the pattern is so predictable, we come to expect it. God delivers his people from the cruel whips of Egypt by a stunning display of his power and his care—the plagues, the Passover, the Red Sea. The Israelites celebrate with singing and dancing. Three days later, they are complaining about the water supply. God provides sweet water from the bitter desert springs of Marah. They complain about the food. God drops breakfast out of the sky, every morning. Then it's the water again. God provides it from a rock. Enemies attack; God delivers. On and on it goes, for forty years. As they stand on the brink of the promised land, God issues a final warning: "Only be careful, and watch yourselves closely so that you do not forget the things your eyes have seen or *let them slip from your heart* as long as you live" (Deut. 4:9 NIV, emphasis added).

They do, of course, let it slip from their hearts. All of it. This becomes the pattern for the entire history of Israel. God shows up; he does amazing things; the people rejoice. Then they forget and go whoring after other gods. They fall under calamity and cry out for deliverance. God shows up; he does amazing things; the people rejoice—you get the picture. Round and round and round we go; where she stops, nobody knows.

And like that of the people of Macondo, their story is our story. Things aren't changed much in the New Testament, but the contrast is greater, and the stakes are even higher. God shows up *in person*, and before he leaves, he gives us the sacraments along with this plea: *Do this to remember me.*

They don't—remember him, that is. Paul is "shocked" by the Galatians: they are "turning away so soon from God, who in his love and mercy called you to share the eternal life he gives through Christ" (1:6 NLT). He has to send Timothy to the Corinthians, to "remind you of what I teach about Christ Jesus in all the churches wherever I go" (1 Cor 4:17 NLT). Peter, who knew firsthand the grief that comes from forgetting, writes his letters to combat this cancer of the soul: "So keep a firm grip on the faith. The suffering won't last forever. It won't be long before this generous God who has great plans for us in Christ—eternal and glorious plans they are!—will have you put together and on your feet for good" (1 Peter 5:10 *The Message*).

It happens to the best of us. Brent and I were having coffee with a pastor from Denver, whose wife was greatly helped by the things we wrote about in *The Sacred Romance*. He told us of her long exile in the desert of her soul, which was deepened by a bout with depression. Our words about life and God and the journey of the heart had been the means by which God had brought life to her parched heart. Her husband was truly grateful for the book, and he thanked us again and again for writing it. You would think both of us would have been quite moved. Authors live to hear such things. But Brent's comment betrayed a deeper reality: "Really? You mean, it's *true*?"

WHAT WILL WE CLING TO?

Life is a journey of the heart that requires the mind—not the other way around. The church sometimes gets this backward and makes knowing the right things the center of life. It's not; the heart is the center of life. Desire is always where the action is. However, staying alive to our desire is not enough; we know that only too well. We must bring the *truth* into our hearts to guard and to guide our desire; this is the other half of our mission. With a recovery of heart and soul taking place in many quarters, my fear now is that we will abandon the pursuit of truth and try to base our journey on our feelings and intuition. "Follow your heart" is becoming a popular message in our culture. Or as Sting sings, "Trust your soul." It will not work. Our spiritual fathers and mothers knew this only too well. In *The Imitation of Christ*, Thomas à Kempis warned, "Our own opinion and our own sense do often deceive us, and they discern but little." We must cling to the truth for dear life. And so our spiritual forbears urged us to bring *both* heart and mind together. As James Houston says in *The Heart's Desire*,

In medieval Christian thought, the idea of learning by heart was something that went far deeper than mathematical tables. It meant the re-orientation of one's life, by what Benedict called *haga*, bringing the thoughts of the mind into the heart, so that one's whole person stood in the presence of God. A Russian monk of the nineteenth century, Theophan the Recluse, gives weight to a similar idea: "The principal thing is to stand before God with the intellect in the heart, and to go on standing before him unceasingly day and night, until the end of life."

Now, not all truths help us descend with the mind into the heart. There is a way of talking about the truth that can actually deaden our hearts. Most of us were raised in the modern era, the age of reason and science. We came to believe that truth is best discovered in the scientific method—dissection. And if you will remember high school biology, we discovered quite a bit about the cat on the table before us—its respiratory system, its muscles and sinews, and all that. Only when the experiment is finished, you have nothing like a cat left at all. You have facts about a cat, but you are far from the real thing anymore. The coy, playful, aloof creature who stands waiting to be let out and walks back into the room once you've risen to open the door—the *living cat*—is gone.

Let me give another example: what is the truth of a kiss? Technically, in a modernistic sense, it is two sets of mandibles pressing together for a certain duration of time. Those of you who have experienced the wonders of a kiss will know that while true, this description is so untrue. It takes away everything beautiful and mysterious and passionate and intimate and leaves you with an icy cold fact. Those who know kissing feel robbed; those who don't are apt to say, "If that's what kissing is all about, I think I'd rather not."

We've done the same thing to theology. We have dissected God, and man, and the gospel, and we have thousands, if not millions, of facts—all of it quite dead. It's not that these insights aren't true; it's that they no longer speak. I could tell you a few facts about God, for example. He is omniscient, omnipotent, and immutable. There—don't you feel closer to him? All our statements about God forget that he is a person, and as Tozer says, "In the deep of His mighty nature He thinks, wills, enjoys, feels, loves, desires and suffers as any other person may." How do we get to know a person? Through stories. All the wild and sad and courageous tales that we tell—they are what reveal us to others. We must return to the Scriptures for the story that it is and stop approaching it as if it is an encyclopedia, looking for "tips and techniques."

Reminders of the story are everywhere—in films and novels, in children's fairy tales, in the natural world around us, and in the stories of our own lives. In fact, every story or movie or song or poem that has ever stirred your soul is telling you something you need to know about the Sacred Romance. Even nature is crying out to us of God's great heart and the drama that is unfolding. Sunrise and sunset tell the tale every day, remembering Eden's glory, prophesying Eden's return. These are the trumpet calls from the "hid battlements of eternity." We must capture them like precious treasure, and hold them close to our hearts.

HOW TO CLING

People tie strings around their fingers to offset forgetfulness. God told the Jews to bind what he told them to their foreheads. Some of them took him literally and strapped a little box to the brow in which they carried sections of Scripture. I used to read this with a sense of the ridiculous; now I read it with empathy. I need it strapped right there in front of me, every single day. *God exists.*

Blaise Pascal took it a step farther. On the night of his conversion to Christ, November 23, 1654, he penned these words to capture his encounter with the living God:

Fire. The God of Abraham, the God of Isaac, the God of Jacob . . . Certainty, Certainty, emotion, joy, peace, God of Jesus Christ. *Deum meum et Deum vestrum*, Thy God shall be my God. Oblivion of the world and of everything except God. Joy, Joy, Joy, tears of Joy!

When he died, they found this memorial sewn into his jacket, next to his heart. He had kept it there from the day of his conversion until his last breath.

We must do something similar if we are to keep our hearts with us to the end. For we lose the story every day. It is continually being stolen from us by the evil one—the ultimate deconstructionist. He twists and spins and pulls apart the truth until the fragments we have left are unrecognizable. Or we lose it ourselves in the marketplace of Vanity Fair. Bombarded by thousands of messages each day, every one of them marked urgent, we leave behind the truly important things, the only refuge for our hearts.

I remember a story from my childhood about a little pack rat named Put-it, Pick-it. He ventures out each morning with an important task to do, but then something catches his eye. It is a piece of blue glass. He drops what he is carrying and picks up the glass, determined to bring it home to show his mother. How proud she will be! Along the path, a silver sheen reflects the desert sun. He stops for a closer look. The glass is left behind, for now he has something even better—a bottle cap. On and on it goes. By the time he gets home, the true treasure is long gone.

We must be more intentional about holding on to the truth. The spiritual pilgrims who aligned themselves with St. Benedict took this task seriously—far more seriously than we do, I'm afraid. A typical day in the lives of Benedictine monks began in the middle of the night, when they arose for the Night Office. No less than twelve psalms would be said, together with three

Scripture readings, several hymns, and prayers. Sunrise brought the Morning Office, followed by six other breaks during the labors of the day for remembering: Prime, Terce, Sext, None, Vespers, and Compline in the evening. Seven times a day set aside for prayer and the recitation of psalms. Together with their night vigil, more than twenty-nine psalms would be said, not to mention numerous lessons, verses, prayers, and hymns.

Now, I'm not suggesting that we all adopt the Rule of Benedict. But think about this: these men left the distractions of the world to focus entirely on God. They lived in an environment *designed* to keep them standing before God, and what did they discover? They needed reminders every hour of the day and night! Do we, who live in the hostile chaos of the world, think we can do with an occasional visit? "Hey, Lord, I know it's been a while, but . . . um . . . thanks for being here and please help me get through this day." We are kidding ourselves if we think we can keep heart without a constant turning to the truth. So let me suggest a bit of monastic wisdom for contemporary pilgrims.

First, you must reduce the constant noise of your life. Turn off the television; it is an enemy of your heart. Having one is like inviting Vanity Fair to set up shop in your home. The whole operation runs on mimetic passion, a continual assault on your desire. Even the news is a problem because of its artificial importance. Have you noticed? Every night there's an urgency to the stories; that's what they have to do to sell the news. But if everything is urgent, then nothing is. I believe Thoreau said, "Don't read the Times; read the eternities." Given the pace of our lives, I doubt we have room for both. Simply unplug from all the clamor, and make room for eternity in your life. In *The Wisdom of the Desert*, Thomas Merton reminds us of the early Christians who fled to the deserts south of Palestine in order to draw near to God. They saw society "as a shipwreck from which every single man had to swim for his life." They believed that to "let oneself drift along, passively accepting the tenets and values of what they knew as society, was purely and simply a disaster."

TREASURES FOR OUR HEARTS

After the shepherds learn about the birth of Christ from the angels, they seek and find the Babe, lying in a manger. The whole village is astounded by their report, but Mary, we are told, "treasured up all these things and pondered them in her heart" (Luke 2:19 NIV). Later, when the boy Jesus is found in the temple holding forth with the religious leaders, we are told again that everyone is quite amazed. "But his mother treasured all these things in her heart" (Luke 2:51 NIV). It is more than a touching story of a mother's love; Mary is going to need those treasures when the tide turns against her son. At her darkest hour, when a sword pierces her soul, she does not lose heart. I believe this is why.

So if you do not have a way of seizing what God is speaking to you, begin journaling. Each year I take up a new journal in which to capture my heart's journey. *Journals* chronicle *journeys;* this is far different from simply recording the day's events in a diary, or worse still, the weekly goal sheets of the popular schedulers. A journal is about the interior life. At the back there is a section I have entitled "This New Day." There I am writing the central truths I must return to each morning (at least) to guide my desire home. My journal will be filled with all the twists and turns a year can bring, but here is the place I can go for the *interpretation* of the events and emotions and experiences. Like the Benedictines, we must keep before us the deepest truths—morning, noon, and night.

As my friend Craig and I sat in the warm sun, eating lunch

beside Four Mile Canyon, he picked up Pascal and read these words out loud: "It is awful to feel that everything we possess is hastening away, and to persist in our attachment, without being anxious, to examine if there is no object attainable that will be permanent." It was Thursday afternoon; that evening, our men's retreat was to begin. We had come up early to fish and to scout the area we would use for our rock-climbing sessions. Brent and the other guys would meet us later at the ranch.

The canyon is a beautiful place, with a lovely creek meandering through a meadow, framed on both sides by the high rock walls. It seemed strange to be talking about life slipping away when so much promise was in the air. A wonderful weekend lay ahead with some great men, doing the things I love best. I did not know why Craig had opened the *Pensées*, nor did I know the real story that was about to unfold. I would later realize that these were prophetic words, spoken to us by God at the opening of a very different scene.

God is speaking to us more often than we imagine. These are the treasures we must hide in our own hearts—sew them into our jackets if need be—for the dark hours that may come. As Buechner points out, "His word to us. is both recoverable and precious beyond telling." And so I share a few of my notes, only in the hope that they will stir you to capture and hang on to the words and images that bring the romance back to you each new day:

- *The story continues.* This simple statement reminds me that life is unfolding, that we are headed somewhere, that the story is moving toward its happy ending. "What's past is prologue," as Shakespeare said. No event is the final word. Several weeks after Brent died, as I was walking from my car to my office, I said to myself, *The story has taken a tragic turn.* Somehow it mattered immensely to say it this way because it reminded me of all the tragic stories I have known and how they made me feel, how the heroes of those stories faced their tragedies, and so it gave weight to what I was living through. But it also kept me from despair because I found the moment in its context, not a random event but as Brent would often say, "A love affair in the midst of a life-and-death struggle." I was able to allow my heart to know it is not the end—the story continues. Dan Allender notes, "Faith increases to the degree we are aware of, caught up in, enthralled by, and participating in His and our story."

- *It can't be done.* By this I remember that I can't arrange for the life I prize. I am not fully healed yet of my addictions and my tendency—which seems so second nature—to arrange for my own little Eden now. To say again and again, "It can't be done," does not discourage me; quite the contrary, it frees my heart from the grasping and plotting and fretting over my life, which always accompany arranging. It reminds me to let it go. It breaks the power of the spell the evil one is trying to weave around us.

- *It is coming.* Oh, how I forget this most of all. How easy it is to slip back into thinking that it's now or never; that if it's not here, it's not at all. The life I prize is coming. The very thing that I am aching for now, missing now, seeking now in other things is exactly what's coming to me. This is how I interpret the promises that seem to be coming through the good and beautiful gifts we have now. As you raise your glass of wine, toast to the banquet to come; as you see anything beautiful you'd like to have (Bethann's window), say to yourself, *In a little while it shall be mine forever;* as you make love, remember it is rehearsal for the Grand Affair. That way your heart will not be trapped there. I recall the end of MacDonald's novel *Phantastes*: "A great good is coming—is coming—is coming to thee."

- *Battle and journey.* We are at war, and the bloody battle is over our hearts. I am astounded how few Christians see this, how little they protect their hearts. We act as though we live in a sleepy little town during peacetime. We don't. We live in the spiritual equivalent of Bosnia or Beirut. Act like it. Watch over your heart. Don't let just anything in; don't let it go just anywhere. *What's this going to do to my heart?* is a question that I ask in every situation.

And thinking of life as a journey reminds me to stop trying to set up camp and call it home. It allows me to see life as process, with completion somewhere down the road. Thus I am freed from feeling like a failure when things are not finished, and hopeful that they will be as my journey comes to its end. I want adventure, and this reminds me I am living in it. Life is not a problem to be solved; it is an adventure to be lived.

I've written down many other thoughts and images over the years, but they couldn't possibly make sense to you. I will spare you the equivalent of looking at my home movies; I fear I have indulged myself already. But let me share one last image, captured in two words: *the meadowlark.*

- *The meadowlark.* The meadowlark has long been my favorite songbird. I suppose to many people it's a simple bird, not really all that colorful, none too spectacular in flight. But I love its song because it evokes so many summer days out in the fields and streams of the West. Because of my story, there is much romance for me in the meadowlark. Its song *means* summer, hay meadows, long lazy days, fly-fishing. More than anything else, it has become for me a symbol of hope. The meadowlark returns to Colorado in the early spring, and as I've mentioned, that typically means it arrives about the same time our major snowstorms hit. What courage; I'm sure if it were me, I'd wait until June when the weather warms up. But they come in spite of the snow, and take their place on fence posts and the tops of small trees, and begin singing. Hearing a midsummer song almost seems out of place when the flurries are whipping about your face. But that is exactly when we need it.

I heard two meadowlarks again this spring, calling and responding to each other on a cold and windy day. God began to speak through them. I heard him urging me to keep my own summer song, even though life's winter tries to throw into my spring cold wind and snow. *Do not throw away your confidence,* he said. *Do not budge from your perch, but sing your song, summer confident, sure of my great goodness toward you. You did not bring this spring, dear child; you do not have to arrange for the summer to follow. They come from thy Father's will, and they will come.* I thought of C. S. Lewis's essay, "The Grand Miracle," where he says,

> To be sure, it feels wintry enough still: but often in the very early spring it feels like that . . . the spring comes down slowly down this way; but the great thing is that the corner has been turned. There is, of course, this difference, that in the natural spring the crocus cannot choose whether it will respond or not. We can. We have the power either of withstanding the spring, and sinking back into the cosmic winter, or of going on into these "high mid-summer pomps" in which our leader, the Son of Man, already dwells, and to which he is calling us. It remains with us to follow or not, to die in this winter, or to go on into that spring and that summer.

Brent was buried on a Thursday afternoon. As we gathered by the graveside, his family and friends, Craig read these words: "I am the resurrection and the life. He who believes in me will live, even though he dies; and whoever lives and believes in me will never die" (John 11:25–26 NIV). He closed his Bible, and we all stood in silence, not really knowing what to say or do; no one wanted to leave; no one really wanted to stay. It seemed so final. At that moment, a meadowlark sang.

This is my song in return.

WAKING *the* DEAD

THE GLORY OF A HEART FULLY ALIVE

The glory of God is man fully alive.
—SAINT IRENAEUS

PART ONE

SEEING OUR WAY CLEARLY

The way through the world
Is more difficult to find than the way beyond it.
—WALLACE STEVENS

Narrow the road that leads to life, and only a few find it.
—JESUS OF NAZARETH (MATT. 7:14)

There are few things more crucial to us than our own lives.

And there are few things we are less clear about.

This journey we are taking is hardly down the yellow brick road. Then again, that's not a bad analogy at all. We may set out in the light, with hope and joy, but eventually, our path always seems to lead us into the woods, shrouded with a low-lying mist. Where is this abundant life that Christ supposedly promised? Where is God when we need him most? What is to become of us?

The cumulative effect of days upon years that we do not really understand is a subtle *erosion*. We come to doubt our place, we come to question God's intentions toward us, and we lose track of the most important things in life.

We're not fully convinced that God's offer to us *is* life. We have forgotten that the heart is central. And we had no idea that we were born into a world at war.

CHAPTER ONE

ARM YOURSELVES

The thief comes only to steal and kill and destroy;
I have come that they may have life, and have it to the full.

—JESUS OF NAZARETH (JOHN 10:10)

We and the world, my children, will always be at war.
Retreat is impossible.
Arm yourselves.

—LEIF ENGER

We were running low on fuel, and still the fog refused to lift. Icy Straight spread out below us, beautiful and threatening. I've always loved the ocean, the wilder the better. But clearly, this was no place to run out of gas. If by chance we survived ditching the small plane, we'd last about seven minutes in those waters. The nearest chance at rescue lived more than forty minutes away. *Great. This is just how it happens,* I thought. *We'll make* Reader's Digest. *"Family on vacation lost in fatal crash."* Rain and mist smeared the windshield as we strained our eyes ahead, searching for a break in the clouds. There's no radar in these planes; bush pilots fly VFR—visual flight rules. If you can't see where you're going, well, then, mister, you can't go there. And you can't keep trying forever, either; the clock that's running is the fuel gauge. Three more minutes, and we'll have to turn back.

"We'll give it one more pass."

"Fairweather Mountain" is a total misnomer. With a name like that, don't you picture some lovely place in Hawaii or maybe Costa Rica—balmy breezes, gentle green slopes, the weather always, well, *fair*? These mountains explode 15,000 feet or more above sea level, right off the coast of southeastern Alaska, sheer cliffs and foreboding glaciers. Some of the world's worst weather hangs out here.

The pilot was yelling above the drone of the engine, "They get their name 'cause you can only see 'em in fair weather."

How cute. What idiot came up with that cleverness? Raw fear had swallowed my sense of humor whole. *They ought to have named them the Peaks of Frozen Death or the Don't Even Think About It Mountains.* Fair weather? Around here, that means maybe twenty days a year—if you're lucky.

We got lucky.

And I have never seen anything more breathtaking in all my life. We banked along vertical granite walls that rose and fell thousands of feet on either side, like a sparrow gliding among the Himalayas. "Are those waterfalls?" I asked, pointing to several cascades of white falling through thin air over the black cliffs.

"Avalanches. It must be warm up here today."

Massive crevasses in the glaciers below held pools of clear water—a color I never knew existed, something between azure and cerulean blue.

"Those cracks are so big we could fly right down 'em."

I pretended not to hear. I felt we'd slipped through Death's grasp, and I didn't want to give him another swipe. The beauty that now engulfed us was enough.

IN DESPERATE NEED OF CLARITY

Twenty clear days a year—that sounds about like my life. I think I see what's really going on about that often. The rest of the time, it feels like fog, like the bathroom mirror after a hot shower. You know what I mean. What exactly are you perfectly clear on these days? How about your life? Why have things gone the way they have? Where was God in all that? And do you know what you ought to do next, with a deep, settled confidence that it will work out? Neither do I. Oh, I'd *love* to wake each morning knowing exactly who I am and where God is taking me. Zeroed in on all my relationships, undaunted in my calling. It's awesome when I do see. But for most of us, life seems more like driving along with a dirty windshield and then turning into the sun. I can sort of make out the shapes ahead, and I think the light is green.

Wouldn't a little bit of clarity go a long way right now?

Let's start with why life is so dang *hard.* You try to lose a little weight, but it never seems to happen. You think of making a shift in your career, maybe even serving God, but you never actually get to it. Perhaps a few of you do make the jump, but it rarely pans out the way you thought. You try to recover something in your marriage, and your spouse looks at you with a glance that says, "Nice try," or "Isn't it a little late for that?" and the thing actually blows up into an argument in front of the kids. Yes, we have our faith. But even there—maybe *especially* there—it all seems to fall rather short of the promise. There's talk of freedom and abundant life, of peace like a river and joy unspeakable, but we see precious little of it, to be honest.

Why is it that, as Tillich said, it's only "here and there in the world and now and then in ourselves" we see any evidence of a new creation? Here and there, now and then. In other words . . . not much. When you stand them side by side, the *description* of the Christian life practically shouted in the New Testament compared with the *actual* life of most Christians, it's . . . embarrassing. Paul sounds like a madman, and we look a little foolish, like children who've been held back a grade. Why is it that nearly every good thing, from taking the annual family vacation to planning a wedding to cultivating a relationship, takes so much work?

It's almost as if there is something set against us.

SHELL SHOCK

Some dear friends of mine just returned from a three-week vacation in France. It had been their dream for nearly twenty-five years. What could be more romantic than strolling the Champs Élysées in the evening, as lovers do? It seemed an ideal way to celebrate their twenty-fifth wedding anniversary. They'd both served God faithfully for decades, but over the years a European rendezvous seemed about as reachable as the moon. Then, late last fall, things suddenly came together.

Friends of theirs were headed to Europe and offered two tickets to come along. Time off was available. They were going to France. And right after they made it to Paris, it all fell apart. Craig came down with walking pneumonia; Lori wanted to leave the third day. All sorts of issues in their marriage surfaced, but since they were with friends, the issues mostly played themselves out in their own thoughts—which tended toward divorce. It wasn't romantic; it was *hard*. Afterward, as we talked on the phone about the whole thing, Lori said, "Life never seems to turn out the way you think it will, about 90 percent of the time." No kidding. Haven't we all got a story that goes with that little bumper sticker?

Just the day before, I received another call. That was the morning our son Blaine was to have his final cardiologist appointment, and I was anxious to hear the news. Now, I know that every parent thinks his child is head and shoulders above the rest, but I'm telling you—Blaine is a special one. He turned eleven this year, and he's one of the healthiest, happiest kids I've ever known. His heart is so good, so spiritually aware, so keen to the hearts of others. He's surprisingly compassionate for a boy his age, and he's also the most courageous one of us all. When it comes to rock climbing or cliff jumping or skiing, Blaine is always the first to go for it. He's a great athlete and a talented artist and a riot when it comes to his humor. He plays the violin; he memorizes cowboy poetry; he blows stuff up; he wants to be a Jedi knight. I love this boy.

And it's a long story of prayer and hope and worry over Blaine. When he was young, his pediatrician picked up an anomaly in his heart during a routine checkup. The cardiologist confirmed through a battery of tests that, indeed, Blaine had several holes in his heart. "He'll need surgery," he said. We opted to wait until Blaine was older, to give God a chance to intervene. The thought of putting my son under open-heart surgery gave me the shudders.

Over the course of those years we spent many nights in prayer that God would heal Blaine's heart. During one of those times, Stasi, not usually given to visions, had a picture of a light penetrating his heart. At that moment, she felt certain God had healed him. And just this morning, the day for his annual checkup, as I began to pray for Blaine, I sensed Jesus say, *I've healed him.* My heart rested, and I waited for the good report.

"Hi . . . it's me." A long silence. "Blaine needs surgery . . . right away."

Hope vanished. I felt that sick-in-the-gut feeling of an imminent free fall, that feeling you get on top of a ladder that's starting to sway under you. All kinds of thoughts and emotions rushed in. *What? Oh, no . . . Not after all this . . . I . . . I thought . . .* My heart was sinking. Despair, betrayal, abandonment by God. Failure on our part to pray enough or believe enough. I felt moments away from a total loss of heart. It seemed inevitable.

These moments aren't a rational, calculated progression of thought; they're more like being tossed out of a raft in a storm. It comes fast and furious, but the pull of the current is always toward a loss of heart. Most of the time we are swept away; we give in, lose heart, and climb out of it sometime later. Some never climb out.

EYES TO SEE

When Spillane treats injured seamen offshore, one of the first things he evaluates is their degree of consciousness. The highest level, known as "alert and oriented times four," describes almost everyone in an everyday situation. They know who they are, where they are, what time it is, and what's just happened. If someone suffers a blow to the head, the first thing they lose is recent events—"alert and oriented times three"—and the last thing they lose is their identity. A person who has lost all levels of consciousness, right down to their identity, is said to be "alert and oriented times zero." When John Spillane wakes up in the water, he is alert and oriented times zero. His understanding of the world is reduced to the fact that he exists, nothing more. Almost simultaneously, he understands that he is in excruciating pain. For a long time, that is all he knows. (*The Perfect Storm*)

John Spillane is a para-rescue jumper sent into the North Atlantic, into the worst storm of the twentieth century, the *perfect storm,* as the book and film called it, to rescue a fisherman lost at sea. When his helicopter goes down, he is forced to jump into pitch blackness from an unknown height, and when he hits the water, he's going so fast it's like hitting the pavement from eighty feet above. He is dazed and confused—just as we are when it comes to the story of our lives. It's the perfect analogy. We have no idea who we really are, why we're here, what's happened to us, or why. Honestly, most days we are alert and oriented times zero.

Has God abandoned us? Did we not pray enough? Is this just something we accept as "part of life," suck it up, even though it breaks our hearts? After a while, the accumulation of event after event that we do not like and do not understand erodes our confidence that we are part of something grand and good, and reduces us to a survivalist mind-set. I know, I know—we've been told that we matter to God. And part of us partly believes it. But life has a way of chipping away at that conviction, undermining our settled belief that he means us well. I mean, if that's true, then why didn't he _____ ? Fill in the blank. Heal your mom. Save your marriage. Get you married. Help you out more.

Either (*a*) we're blowing it, or (*b*) God is holding out on us. Or some combination of both, which is where most people land. Think about it. Isn't this where *you* land, with all the things that haven't gone the way you'd hoped and wanted? Isn't it some version of "I'm blowing it"? in that it's your fault, you could have done better, you could have been braver or wiser or more beautiful or something? Or "God is holding out on me," in that you know he *could* come through, but he hasn't come through—and what are you to make of that?

This is The Big Question, by the way, the one every philosophy and religion and denominational take on Christianity has been trying to nail down since the dawn of time. *What is really going on here?* Good grief—life is brutal. Day after day it hammers us, till we lose sight of what God intends toward us, and we haven't the foggiest idea why the things that are happening to us *are* happening to us. Then you watch lives going down with the Twin Towers, read about children starving in Ethiopia, and wham! If a good God is really in charge . . . all that.

I felt so bad that Paris wasn't what my friends hoped it would be, but I wasn't sure what to say. Like most Christians in that situation, I simply asked Lori how I could pray for them. "That we would have eyes to see what's going on." My heart leaped. Brilliant! Perfect! That is *exactly* what we need. Eyes to see. Isn't that what Jesus offered us—clarity? Recovery of sight for the blind (Luke 4:18)? We need clarity and we need it badly. A simple prayer rises from my heart: *Jesus, take away the fog and the clouds and the veil, and help me to see . . . give me eyes to really see.*

THE OFFER IS *LIFE*

The glory of God is man fully alive. (Saint Irenaeus)

When I first stumbled across this quote, my initial reaction was . . . *You're kidding me. Really?* I mean, is that what you've been told? That the purpose of God—the very thing he's staked his reputation on—is your coming fully alive? Huh. Well, that's a different take on things. It made me wonder, *What* are *God's intentions toward me? What is it I've come to believe about that?* Yes, we've been told any number of times that God does care, and there are some pretty glowing promises given to us in Scripture along those lines. But on the other hand, we have the days of our lives, and they have a way of casting a rather long shadow over our hearts when it comes to God's intentions toward *us* in particular. I read the quote again, "The glory of God is man fully alive," and something began to stir in me. *Could it be?*

I turned to the New Testament to have another look, read for myself what Jesus said he offers. "I have come that they may have life, and have it to the full" (John 10:10). Wow. That's different from saying, "I have come to forgive you. Period." Forgiveness is awesome, but Jesus says here he came to give us *life.* Hmmm. Sounds like ol' Irenaeus might be on to something. "I am the bread of life" (John 6:48). "Whoever believes in me, as the Scripture has said, streams of living water will flow from within him" (John 7:38). The more I looked, the more this whole theme of life jumped off the pages. I mean, it's *everywhere.*

Above all else, guard your heart,
    for it is the wellspring of life. (Prov. 4:23)

You have made known to me the path of life. (Ps. 16:11)

In him was life, and that life was the light of men. (John 1:4)

Come to me to have life. (John 5:40)

Tell the people the full message of this new life. (Acts 5:20)

I began to get the feeling of a man who's been robbed. I'm well aware that it's life I *need,* and it's life I'm looking for. But the offer has gotten "interpreted" by well-meaning people to say, "Oh, well. Yes, of course . . . God intends life for you. But that is *eternal* life, meaning, because of the death of Jesus Christ you can go to heaven when you die." And that's true . . . in a way. But it's like saying getting married means, "Because I've given you this ring, you will be taken care of in your retirement." And in the meantime? Isn't there a whole lot more to the relationship *in the meantime?* (It's in the meantime that we're living out our days, by the way.) Are we just lost at sea? What did Jesus mean when he promised us life? I go back to the source, and what I find is just astounding.

I am still confident of this:
    I will see the goodness of the LORD
    in the land of the living. (Ps. 27:13)

"I tell you the truth," Jesus said to them, "no one who has left home or wife or brothers or parents or children for the sake of the kingdom of God will fail to receive many times as much in this age and, in the age to come, eternal life." (Luke 18:29–30)

Jesus doesn't locate his offer to us only in some distant future after we've slogged our way through our days here on earth. He talks about a life available to us *in this age.* So does Paul: "Godliness has value for all things, holding promise for both the present life and the life to come" (1 Tim. 4:8). Our *present* life and the next. When we hear the words *eternal life,* most of us tend to interpret that as "a life that waits for us in eternity." But *eternal* means "unending," not "later." The Scriptures use the term to mean we can never lose it. It's a life that can't be taken from us. The offer is life, and that life starts *now.*

> Just as Christ was raised from the dead by the glorious power of the Father, *now* we also may live new lives. (Rom. 6:4 NLT, emphasis added)

The glory of God is man fully alive? Now? Hope unbidden rose at the thought that God's intentions toward me might be better than I'd thought. His happiness and my happiness are tied together? My coming fully alive is what he's committed to? *That's* the offer of Christianity? Wow! I mean, it would make no small difference if we knew—and I mean *really* knew—that down-deep-in-your-toes kind of knowing that no one and nothing can talk you out of—if we *knew* that our lives and God's glory were bound together. Things would start looking up. It would feel promising, like making friends on the first day of school with the biggest kid in class.

The offer is life. Make no mistake about that. So then . . . where *is* that life? Why is it so rare?

WE ARE AT WAR

> The thief comes only to steal and kill and destroy; I have come that they may have life, and have it to the full. (John 10:10)

Have you ever wondered why Jesus married those two statements? Did you even know he spoke them at the same time? I mean, he says them in one breath. And he has his reasons. By all means, God intends life for you. But right now that life is *opposed.* It doesn't just roll in on a tray. There is a thief. He comes to steal and kill and destroy. In other words, yes, the offer is life, but you're going to have to fight for it because there's an Enemy in your life with a different agenda.

There *is* something set against us.

We are at war.

How I've missed this for so long is a mystery to me. Maybe I've overlooked it; maybe I've chosen not to see. *We are at war.* I don't like that fact any more than you do, but the sooner we come to terms with it, the better hope we have of making it through to the life we do want. This is not Eden. You probably figured that out. This is not Mayberry; this is not *Seinfeld*'s world; this is not *Survivor.* The world in which we live is a combat zone, a violent clash of kingdoms, a bitter struggle unto the death. I'm sorry if I'm the one to break this news to you: you were born into a world at war, and you will live all your days in the midst of a great battle, involving all the forces of heaven and hell and played out here on earth.

Where *did* you think all this opposition was coming from?

Earlier in the Story, back in the beginning of our time on earth, a great glory was bestowed upon us. We all—men and women— were created in the image of God. Fearfully and wonderfully made, fashioned as living icons of the bravest, wisest, most stunning Person who ever lived. Those who have ever seen him fell to their knees without even thinking about it, as you find yourself breathless before the Grand Canyon or the Alps or the sea at dawn. That glory was shared with us; we were, in Chesterton's phrase, "statues of God walking about in a Garden," endowed with a strength and beauty all our own. All that we ever wished we could be, we were— and more. We were fully alive.

So God created man in his own image, in the image of God he
created him; male and female he created them. (Gen. 1:27)

When I look at the night sky and see the work of your fingers—
    the moon and the stars you have set in place—
what are mortals that you should think of us,
    mere humans that you should care for us?
For you made us only a little lower than God,
    and you crowned us with glory and honor. (Ps. 8:3–5 NLT)

I daresay we've heard a bit about original sin, but not nearly
enough about original glory, which comes *before* sin and is deeper to
our nature. We were crowned with glory and honor. Why does a
woman long to be beautiful? Why does a man hope to be found
brave? Because we remember, if only faintly, that we were once more
than we are now. The reason you doubt there could be a glory to your
life is because that glory has been the object of a long and brutal war.

For lurking in that Garden was an Enemy. This mighty angel
had once been glorious as well, the captain of the Lord's hosts,
beautiful and powerful beyond compare. But he rebelled against his
Creator, led a great battle against the forces of heaven, and was cast
down. Banished from his heavenly home, but not destroyed, he
waited for an opportunity to take his revenge. Unable to overthrow the Mighty One, he turned his sights on those who bore his
image. He lied to us about where true life was to be found, and we
believed him. We fell, and "our glory faded," as Milton said, "faded
so soon." Or as David lamented, "You turn my glory into shame"
(Ps. 4:2).

But God did not abandon us, not by a long shot. I think even a
quick read of the Old Testament would be enough to convince you
that *war* is a central theme of God's activity. There is the Exodus,
where God goes to war to set his captive people free. Blood. Hail.

Locusts. Darkness. Death. Plague after plague descends on Egypt like a boxer's one-two punch, like the blows of some great ax. Pharaoh releases his grip, but only for a moment. The fleeing slaves are pinned against the Red Sea when Egypt makes a last charge, hurtling down on them in chariots. God drowns those soldiers in the sea, every last one of them. Standing in shock and joy on the opposite shore, the Hebrews proclaim, "The LORD is a warrior!" (Ex. 15:3). Yahweh is a warrior.

Then it's war to get *to* the promised land. Moses and company have to do battle against the Amalekites; again God comes through, and Moses shouts, "The LORD will be at war against the Amalekites from generation to generation" (Ex. 17:16). Yahweh will be at war. Indeed. You ain't seen nothin' yet. Then it's war to get *into* the promised land—Joshua and the battle of Jericho, all that. After the Jews gain the promised land, it's war after war to *keep* it. Israel battles the Canaanites, the Philistines, the Midianites, the Egyptians again, the Babylonians—and on and on it goes. Deborah goes to war; Gideon goes to war; King David goes to war. Elijah wars against the prophets of Baal; Jehoshaphat battles the Edomites. Are you getting the picture?

Many people think the theme of war ends with the Old Testament. Not at all. Jesus says, "I did not come to bring peace, but a sword" (Matt. 10:34). In fact, his birth involved another battle in heaven:

> A great and wondrous sign appeared in heaven: a woman clothed with the sun, with the moon under her feet and a crown of twelve stars on her head. She was pregnant and cried out in pain as she was about to give birth. Then another sign appeared in heaven: an enormous red dragon with seven heads and ten horns and seven crowns on his heads . . . The dragon stood in front of the woman who was about to give birth, so that he might devour

her child the moment it was born. She gave birth to a son, a male child, who will rule all the nations with an iron scepter . . . And there was war in heaven. Michael and his angels fought against the dragon, and the dragon and his angels fought back. But he was not strong enough, and they lost their place in heaven . . . Then the dragon was enraged at the woman and went off to make war against the rest of her offspring—those who obey God's commandments and hold to the testimony of Jesus. (Rev. 12:1–5, 7–8, 17)

The birth of Christ was an act of war, an *invasion*. The Enemy knew it and tried to kill him as a babe (Matt. 2:13). No pale-faced altar boy, the whole life of Christ is marked by battle and confrontation. He kicks out demons with a stern command. He rebukes a fever, and it leaves Peter's mother-in-law. He rebukes a storm, and it subsides. He confronts the Pharisees time and again to set God's people free from legalism. In a loud voice he wakes Lazarus from the dead. He descends to hell, wrestles the keys of hell and death from Satan, and leads a train of captives free (Eph. 4:8–9; Rev. 1:18). And when he returns, I might point out, Jesus will come mounted on a steed of war, with his robe dipped in blood, armed for battle (Rev. 19:11–15).

War is not just one among many themes in the Bible. It is *the* backdrop for the whole Story, the context for everything else. God is at war. He is trampling out the vineyards where the grapes of wrath are stored. And what is he fighting for? Our freedom and restoration. The glory of God is man fully alive. In the meantime, Paul says, *arm yourselves,* and the first piece of equipment he urges us to don is the belt of truth (Eph. 6:10–18). We arm ourselves by getting a good, solid grip on our situation, by getting some clarity on the battle over our lives. God's intentions toward us are life. Those intentions are opposed. Forewarned is forearmed, as the saying goes.

In *Mere Christianity*, in the chapter he so rightly titled "The Invasion," C. S. Lewis tried to clarify our situation:

> One of the things that surprised me when I first read the New Testament seriously was that it talked so much about a Dark Power in the universe—a mighty evil spirit who was held to be the Power behind death and disease, and sin. The difference is that Christianity thinks this Dark Power was created by God, and was good when he was created, and went wrong. Christianity agrees . . . this universe is at war.

YOU MUST FIGHT FOR YOUR LIFE

Until we come to terms with *war* as the context of our days we will not understand life. We will misinterpret 90 percent of what is happening around us and to us. It will be very hard to believe that God's intentions toward us are life abundant; it will be even harder not to feel that somehow we are just blowing it. Worse, we will begin to accept some really awful things about God. That four-year-old girl being molested by her daddy—that is "God's *will*"? That ugly divorce that tore your family apart—God wanted that to happen too? And that plane crash that took the lives of so many—that was desired by God?

Most people get stuck at some point because God appears to have abandoned them. He is not coming through. Speaking about her life with a mixture of disappointment and cynicism, a young woman recently said to me, "God is rather silent right now." Yes, it's been awful. I don't discount that for a moment. She is unloved; she is unemployed; she is under a lot. But her attitude strikes me as deeply naive, on the level of someone caught in a cross fire who asks, rather shocked and with a sense of betrayal, "God, why won't you make them stop firing at me?" I'm sorry, but that's not where we are right now. It's not where we are in the Story. That day is coming, *later,* when the lion shall lie down with the lamb and we'll beat swords into plowshares. For now, it's bloody battle.

It sure explains a whole heckuva lot.

Before he promised us life, Jesus warned that a thief would try to steal, kill, and destroy it. How come we don't think that the thief then actually steals, kills, and destroys? You won't understand your life, you won't see clearly what has happened to you or how to live forward from here, unless you see it as *battle.* A war against your heart. And you are going to need your whole heart for what's coming next. I don't mean what's coming next in the story I'm telling. I mean what's coming next in the life you're living. There are a few things I know, and one thing I do know is this: we don't see things as clearly as we ought to. As we *need* to. We don't understand what's happening around us or to us or to those we love, and we are practically clueless when it comes to the weight of our own lives and the glory that's being . . . held back.

Some of you don't see it yet. That's all right. We have a whole book ahead of us. If it's true that there is a great and fierce battle unfolding all around us—and against us—why isn't the enemy more visible? And if there is a glory to my life, well, then, why don't I see *that*? Why do I struggle so much, and where is that life God offers?

We don't see clearly because we don't see with the eyes of our heart.

CHAPTER TWO

THE EYES OF THE HEART

I pray also that the eyes of your heart may be enlightened.

—THE APOSTLE PAUL (EPH. 1:18)

I am concerned with a certain way of looking at life, which was created in me by the fairy tales, but has since been ratified by the mere facts.

—G. K. CHESTERTON

Two men are seated across from each other in a dark room. Outside, a thunderstorm rages in the night, shaking the old house to its foundations. Flashes of lightning are dimmed by heavy curtains, which been drawn because it is a *secret* meeting. This is the first time these men have ever met, though they have been searching for each other most of their lives. Not a moment too soon, their destinies have crossed. One of them, a tall black man dressed all in black, carries the aura of a spiritual master. The younger man, trying his best to conceal the fact that he is frightened and uncertain, might become his disciple. It all depends on a decision.

MORPHEUS: I imagine that right now you're feeling a bit like Alice, tumbling down the rabbit hole?

NEO: You could say that.

MORPHEUS: I can see it in your eyes. You have the look of a man who accepts what he sees because he's expecting to wake up. Ironically, this is not far from the truth. Do you believe in fate, Neo?

NEO: No.

MORPHEUS: Why?

NEO: Because I don't like the idea that I'm not in control of my life.

MORPHEUS: I know exactly what you mean. Let me tell you why you're here. You're here because you know something. *What* you know you can't explain. You feel it. You've felt it your entire life. There's something wrong with the world. You don't know what it is. But it's there, like a splinter in your mind, driving you mad. It is this feeling that has brought you to me. Do you know what I'm talking about?

NEO: The Matrix?

MORPHEUS: Do you want to know what it is?

[*Hesitantly, Neo nods his assent.*]

MORPHEUS: The Matrix is everywhere. It is all around us. Even now in this very room. You can see it when you look out your window, or when you turn on your television. You can feel it when you go to work, when you go to church, when you pay your taxes. It is the world that has been pulled over your eyes to blind you from the truth.

NEO: What truth?

MORPHEUS: That you are a slave, Neo. Like everyone else you were born into bondage, into a prison that you cannot taste or smell or touch. A prison for your mind. Unfortunately, no one can be told what the Matrix is. You must see it for yourself.

[*In each of his open palms, held forth as an offering, the older*

*man is holding two capsules, one red, the other blue. He is offering
the younger man a chance at the truth.*]

MORPHEUS: This is your last chance. After this, there is no
turning back. You take the blue pill—the story ends, you wake
up in your bed and you believe . . . whatever you want to believe.
You take the red pill—you stay in Wonderland and I show you
how deep the rabbit hole goes.

Neo takes the red pill; Lucy steps through the wardrobe; Aladdin
rubs the lamp; Elisha prays that the eyes of his servant would be
opened; Peter, James, and John follow Jesus up to the Mount of
Transfiguration. And all of them discover that there is far more
going on here than meets the eye. The film *The Matrix* is a parable,
a metaphor—and though a dark story, it is far closer to reality and
to your life than you probably have been led to believe. (I am
referring only to the first film in the trilogy.) And the question
Morpheus asks of Neo is a question the Scriptures ask each of us:
Do you *want* to see?

How Can We Really See?

There is another man, an old man, a spiritual master. Life for him
has also been full of adventure and battle and trial by fire. He, too,
knows something that we do not. And he, too, is trying to help us
see. He writes,

Therefore we do not lose heart. Though outwardly we are wast-
ing away, yet inwardly we are being renewed day by day. For our
light and momentary troubles are achieving for us an eternal
glory that far outweighs them all. So we fix our eyes not on what
is seen, but on what is unseen. For what is seen is temporary, but
what is unseen is eternal. (2 Cor. 4:16–18)

The first line grabs me by the throat. "Therefore we do not lose heart." Somebody knows how not to lose heart? I'm all ears. For we *are* losing heart. All of us. Daily. It is the single most unifying quality shared by the human race on the planet at this time. We are losing—or we have already lost—heart. That glorious, resilient image of God in us is fading, fading, fading away. And this man claims to know a way out. Now, to appreciate the weight of his words, you need some idea of what his life has been like. He is neither wealthy nor famous; his life has not been sheltered, as the saying goes. But he has seen visions, had encounters, you might say, with something beyond the walls of this world. Ever since then, things have gotten difficult. In his own words, he has

> been in prison more frequently, been flogged more severely, and been exposed to death again and again. Five times I received . . . forty lashes minus one. Three times I was beaten with rods, once I was stoned, three times I was shipwrecked, I spent a night and a day in the open sea, I have been constantly on the move. I have been in danger from rivers, in danger from bandits, in danger from my own countrymen . . . I have known hunger and thirst and have often gone without food; I have been cold and naked. (2 Cor. 11:23–27)

Not to mention that little incident against wild beasts in Ephesus. You get the picture. His life has been hard. It has been war. His vita reads like something out of Amnesty International. Somebody has been trying to shut him up or shut him down. He knows something; he has a secret to tell. So, how, Paul—*how?* How do we not lose heart?

> So we fix our eyes not on what is seen, but on what is unseen.
> (2 Cor. 4:18)

What? I let out a sigh of disappointment. *Now that's helpful. "Look at what you cannot see."* That sounds like Eastern mysticism, that sort of wispy wisdom dripping in spirituality but completely inapplicable to our lives. Life is an illusion. Look at what you cannot see. *What can this mean?* Remembering that a little humility can take me a long way, I give it another go. This wise old seer is saying that there is a way of looking at life, and that those who discover it are able to live from the heart no matter what. How do we do this? By seeing with the eyes of the heart. "I pray . . . that the eyes of your heart may be enlightened" (Eph. 1:18).

SEEING WITH THE HEART

"A sower went out to sow some seed . . ."
"A man fell into the hands of robbers . . ."
"Suppose a woman has ten silver coins and loses one . . ."
"There were ten virgins with ten lamps . . ."

Think of it. You are the Son of the living God. You have come to earth to rescue the human race. It is your job to communicate truths without which your precious ones will be lost . . . forever. Would you do it like *this*? Really now. A treasure hidden in a field? A lump of dough? Ten virgins and something about oil? Why doesn't he come right out and say it—get to the point? What's with all the stories? Some of them rather puzzling, I might add. Jesus is not entertaining children; he is speaking to adults about the deepest things in life. And I think it's safe to say he knows quite well what he's doing. As Dallas Willard reminds us, Jesus is brilliant. He is the smartest man who ever lived. So what's up with all the stories?

We children of the Internet and the cell phone and the Weather Channel, we think we are the enlightened ones. We aren't fooled by anything—we just want the *facts*. The bottom line. So proposition has become our means of saying what is true and what is not. And proposition is helpful . . . for certain things. Sacramento is the capital of California; water freezes at 32 degrees Fahrenheit; your shoes are in the front room, under the sofa. But proposition fails when it comes to the weightier things in life. While it is a fact that the Civil War was fought between the years of 1861 and 1865 and while it is also a fact that hundreds of thousands of men died in that war, those facts hardly describe what happened at Bull Run or Antietam, at Cold Harbor or Gettysburg. You don't even begin to grasp the reality of the Civil War until you hear the stories, see pictures from the time, visit the battlefields, watch a film like *Glory*.

How much more so when it comes to the deep truths of the Christian faith. God loves you; you matter to him. That is a fact, stated as a proposition. I imagine most of you have heard it any number of times. Why, then, aren't we the happiest people on earth? It hasn't reached our hearts. Facts stay lodged in the mind, for the most part. They don't speak at the level we need to hear. Proposition speaks to the mind, but when you tell a story, you speak to the heart. We've been telling each other stories since the beginning of time. It is our way of communicating the timeless truths, passing them down.

And that's why when Jesus comes to town, he speaks in a way that will get past all our intellectual defenses and disarm our hearts. He tells a certain kind of story. As Chesterton said, "I am concerned with a certain way of looking at life, which was created in me by the fairy tales, but has since been ratified by the mere facts." And the best stories of all, the ones that bring us the Eternal Truths, they always take the form of parable or, sometimes we say, fairy tale. Better still to call them *myths*.

MYTHIC REALITY

And already I've lost many of you. For most of us rationalists, the word means "not true." Isn't that what you think when you hear someone say, "Oh, that's just a myth"? Meaning, that's not *factually* true. But myth is a story, like a parable, that speaks of Eternal Truths. I am not using *myth* in a technical way, referring to ancient Greek mythology. I am using it more broadly, more inclusively, to mean "a story that brings you a glimpse of the eternal" or "any story that awakens your heart to the deep truths of life." That is the unifying quality of all mythic stories, whether they be Sisyphus or *Sleeping Beauty* or *The Matrix*. Christian professor Rolland Hein has described it this way: "Myths are, first of all, stories: stories which confront us with something transcendent and eternal . . . a means by which the eternal expresses itself in time."

Jesus tells a story about a sower who went out to sow some seed. The year is uncertain; so is the identity of the sower in question. He and his seed are metaphors for something far more significant than a farmer and a bag of corn. In this case, they are symbols for the Son of God and the eternal Word. The story is meant for all of us, and so it transcends time and space and speaks for centuries. Myths are like that. They are stories that remind us of the transcendent and the eternal. Note the success of the *Star Wars* films or, more recently, *The Lord of the Rings* trilogy. Millions of people have enjoyed them—and more than once. It isn't because we think the stories are true in a factual sense. We don't even stop to ask the question about their historical accuracy or their scientific possibility. Their appeal lies deeper, in the realm of the heart.

Former Wheaton College professor of literature Clyde Kilby explains, "Myth is the name of a way of seeing, a way of *knowing*." Not fantasy, not lies, but things coming to us from beyond the walls of this world. Rolland Hein observes, "They are the kind of story that wakes you up, and suddenly you say, 'Yes, yes, this is what my life has really been about! Here is where my meaning and my destiny lie!'" And we need some waking up, you and I. We are, for the most part, alert and oriented times zero.

Years ago a mother wrote to C. S. Lewis regarding her son (age nine) and his love for *The Chronicles of Narnia*. The boy was feeling bad because he felt he loved Aslan (the lion hero of the story) more than Jesus. With grace and brilliance Lewis replied that he need not worry: "For the things he loves Aslan for doing or saying are simply the things that Jesus really did and said. So that when Laurence thinks he is loving Aslan, he is really loving Jesus: and perhaps loving Him more than he ever did before." Truth doesn't need a verse attached to it to be true. All that you loved about Aslan *is* Jesus.

"Systemizing flattens," says Kilby, "but myth rounds out. Systemizing drains away color and life, but myth restores. Myth is necessary because of what man is . . . because man is fundamentally mythic. His real health depends upon his knowing and living his . . . mythic nature." Mythic stories help us to see clearly, which is to say, they help us see with the eyes of the heart. So cast a wide net, and draw in all those stories that have ever stirred your soul, quickened your spirit, brought you to tears or joy or heroic imagination. You will need them all, as you shall see.

Things Are Not What They Seem

What do all the great stories and myths tell us? What do they have in common? What are they trying to get across? Wherever they may come from, whatever their shape might be, they nearly always speak to us Three Eternal Truths. First, these stories are trying to remind us that *things are not what they seem*. There is a whole lot more going on here than meets the eye. Much more. After the tornado sets her down, Dorothy wakes and steps out of her old farmhouse to find herself in a strange new world, a land of Munchkins and fairies and wicked witches. The Land of Oz. How brilliant for the filmmakers to have waited for this moment to introduce color in the movie. Up till now the story has been told in black and white; when Dorothy steps out of the house, the screen explodes in color, and she whispers to her little friend, "Toto . . . I don't think we're in Kansas anymore."

Alice falls through the rabbit hole into Wonderland. Adonos wakes to the sound of water and discovers a stream running right through his bedroom. The carpet that always looked to him like grass and flowers is, in fact, now just that—a meadow with daisies waving in a soft breeze. The ceiling above him has become the boughs of a great tree, "one of the advanced guard of a dense forest, towards which the rivulet ran. Faint traces of a footpath, much overgrown with grass and moss, were discernible along the right bank." He rightly assumes it must be the path into Fairy Land, and he rightly chooses to follow it.

Neo is awakened from the death-sleep of the Matrix to discover that the time is not 1999, but 2199, and the world he thought was real is actually a massive deception cast upon the human race to keep them prisoners. Jacob falls into a dream under the desert stars and sees a ladder "resting on the earth, with its top reaching to heaven, and the angels of God . . . ascending and descending on it" (Gen. 28:12). He wakes, more awake than he's ever been in his life, thanks to the dream, and realizes for the first time that there is more going on around him than he ever imagined. "Surely the LORD is in this place, and I was not aware of it" (28:16).

"And I was not aware of it." Isn't this the very lesson of the Emmaus Road? You recall the story—two followers of Christ are headed out of town after the Crucifixion, as dejected as two people can be, with every reason in their minds to be so and more. Their hopes have been shattered. They staked it all on the Nazarene, and now he's dead. As they slump back toward their homes, Jesus sort of sneaks up alongside, very much alive but incognito, and joins their conversation, feigning ignorance—and they not seeing it is him.

> He asked them, "What are you discussing together as you walk along?"

> They stood still, their faces downcast. One of them, named
> Cleopas, asked him, "Are you only a visitor to Jerusalem and do
> not know the things that have happened there in these days?"
>
> "What things?" he asked.
>
> "About Jesus of Nazareth," they replied. "He was a prophet,
> powerful in word and deed before God and all the people. The
> chief priests and our rulers handed him over to be sentenced to
> death, and they crucified him; but we had hoped that he was the
> one who was going to redeem Israel." (Luke 24:17–21)

"But we had hoped . . ." Ah, yes. We had hoped. I've a few
things in my life I could say that about. I imagine you could too. *I
had hoped . . .* The story is so human, so true to our lives. What is
so wonderful and hopeful and—because *we* know how it turns
out—also cracks me up is how they did not see. *They just didn't get
it.* They ignored the secret of the burning heart. For the story goes
on, as you may remember, and the mysterious Companion begins
to chide them for being "slow of heart to believe" as he reminds
them of the writings of the prophets, all the ancient wisdom. They
invite him to supper, and after another bit of feigning about need-
ing to move on, he does come in.

> When he was at the table with them, he took bread, gave thanks,
> broke it and began to give it to them. Then their eyes were
> opened and they recognized him, and he disappeared from their
> sight. They asked each other, "Were not our hearts burning
> within us while he talked with us on the road and opened the
> Scriptures to us?" (Luke 24:30–32)

Why do you suppose God gave us this story? Might it have been
to remind us that things are not what they seem? That our interpretation of events may be more than a little off? If we'll start there,
with a little humility, then we, too, might move on to have our eyes

opened to the rest of the story in *our* lives. There is more going on here than we imagined.

This is precisely what the Bible has warned us about all these years: that we live in two worlds—or better, in one world with two parts, one part that we can see and one part that we cannot. We are urged, for our own welfare, to act as though the unseen world (the rest of reality) is, in fact, more weighty and more real and more dangerous than the part of reality we can see. The lesson from the story of the Emmaus Road—the lesson the whole Bible is trying to get across—begins with this simple truth: things are not what they seem. There is more going on here than meets the eye. Far more. That is Eternal Truth Number One.

A BATTLE IS UNDER WAY

But there is another, more urgent quality to every true myth. The Second Eternal Truth brought to us comes like a broken message over the radio or an urgent e-mail from a distant country, telling us that some great struggle or quest or battle is well under way. May even be hanging in the balance. When the four children stumble into Narnia, the country and all its lovely creatures are imprisoned under the spell of the White Witch and have been for a hundred years. In another story, Jack and his mother are starving and must sell their only cow. Frodo barely makes it out of the Shire with his life and the ring of power. In the nick of time he learns that Bilbo's magic ring is the One Ring, that Sauron has discovered its whereabouts, and that the Nine Black Riders are already across the borders searching for the little hobbit with deadly intent. The future of Middle Earth hangs on a thread.

Darth Vader just about has the universe under his evil fist when a pair of droids fall into the hands of Luke Skywalker. Luke has no idea what is unfolding, what great deeds have been done on his behalf, or what will be required of him in the battle to come. Sitting in a sandstone hut with old Ben Kenobi—he does not know this is the great Jedi warrior Obi-Wan Kenobi—Luke discovers the secret message from the princess: "This is our most desperate hour. Help me, Obi-Wan Kenobi. You're my only hope."

Again, this is *exactly* what the Scriptures have been trying to wake us up to for years. "Wake up, O sleeper . . . Be very careful, then, how you live . . . because the days are evil" (Eph. 5:14–16). Or as *The Message* has it: "So watch your step. Use your head. Make the most of every chance you get. These are desperate times!" Christianity isn't a religion about going to Sunday school, potluck suppers, being nice, holding car washes, sending our secondhand clothes off to Mexico— as good as those things might be. This is a world at war. Something large and immensely dangerous is unfolding all around us, we are caught up in it, and above all we doubt we have been given a key role to play. Do you think I'm being too dramatic? Consider the tale told in the book of Daniel, chapter 10.

In 605 B.C. the notorious Babylonians sacked Jerusalem. Among the hostages taken back to the city of the hanging gardens is a young man named Daniel. He becomes a sort of counselor among the royal cabinet, largely because God favors Daniel and reveals a number of mysteries to him that had stumped everyone else on staff. You might remember the famous episode when, in the midst of a state function turned Mardi Gras, King Belshazzar sees the handwriting on the wall—literally. *Mene, Mene, Tekel, Parsin.* Actually, everyone sees it, but only Daniel can interpret what it means. The Hebrew exile is right again, the king dies that night, the Medes take over, and after a number of additional years in the dangerous world of Middle Eastern politics, Daniel has another troubling vision. Let's pick up the story there.

In the third year of Cyrus king of Persia, a revelation was given to Daniel (who was called Belteshazzar). Its message was true and it concerned a great war. The understanding of the message came to him in a vision. At that time I, Daniel, mourned for three weeks. I ate no choice food; no meat or wine touched my lips; and I used no lotions at all until the three weeks were over. (Dan. 10:1–3)

Something has happened that Daniel doesn't understand. I think we can all relate to that. We don't understand about 90 percent of what happens to us, either. Daniel is troubled. He sets out to get an answer. But three weeks of prayer and fasting produce no results. What is he to conclude? If Daniel were like most people, by this point he'd probably be headed toward one of two conclusions: *I'm blowing it*, or *God is holding out on me*. He might try confessing every sin and petty offense in hopes of opening up the lines of communication with God. Or he might withdraw into a sort of disappointed resignation, drop the fast, and turn on the television. In an effort to hang on to his faith, he might embrace the difficulty as part of "God's will for his life." He might read a book on "the silence of God." That's the way the people I know handle this sort of thing.

And he would be dead wrong.

On the twenty-first day of the fast an angel shows up, out of breath. In a sort of apology, the angel explains to Daniel that God had actually dispatched him in answer to Daniel's prayers the very first day he prayed—three weeks ago. (There goes the whole unanswered prayer thesis, right out the window.) *Three weeks ago?* What is Daniel to do with that? "The very first day? But . . . I've . . . I mean, thank you so very much, and I don't want to seem ungrateful, but . . . where have you *been*?" You haven't blown it, Daniel, and God isn't holding out on you. The angel goes on to explain that he was locked in hand-to-hand combat with a mighty fallen angel, a demonic power of dreadful strength, who kept him out of the Persian kingdom for three weeks, and he finally had to get Michael (the great archangel, the captain of the Lord's hosts) to come and help him break through enemy lines. "Now I am here, in answer to your prayer. Sorry it's taken so long."

There it is—Eternal Truth Number Two: *this is a world at war.* We live in a far more dramatic, far more dangerous story than we ever imagined. The reason we love *The Chronicles of Narnia* or *Star Wars* or *The Matrix* or *The Lord of the Rings* is that they are telling us something about our lives that we never, ever get on the evening news. Or from most pulpits. *This is our most desperate hour.* Without this burning in our hearts, we lose the meaning of our days. It all withers down to fast food and bills and voice mail and who really cares anyway? Do you see what has happened? The essence of our faith has been stripped away. The very thing that was to give our lives meaning and *protect us*—this way of seeing—has been lost. Or stolen from us. Notice that those who have tried to wake us up to this reality were usually killed for it: the prophets, Jesus, Stephen, Paul, most of the disciples, in fact. Has it ever occurred to you that someone was trying to shut them up?

Things are not what they seem. This is a world at war. Now for the most stunning news of all.

THE WEIGHT OF YOUR GLORY

Last, but not least, not by a long shot, every mythic story *shouts* to us that in this desperate hour *we have a crucial role to play.* That is the Third Eternal Truth, and it happens to be the one we most desperately need if we are ever to understand our days. For most of his life, Neo sees himself only as Thomas Anderson, a computer programmer for a large software corporation. As the drama really begins to heat up and the enemy hunts him down, he says to himself, "This is insane. Why is this happening to me? What did I do? I'm nobody. I didn't do anything." A very dangerous conviction . . . though one shared by most of you, my readers. What he later comes to realize—and not a moment too soon—is that he is "the One" who will break the power of the Matrix.

Frodo, the little Halfling from the Shire, young and naive in so many ways, "the most unlikely person imaginable," is the Ring Bearer. He, too, must learn through dangerous paths and fierce battle that a task has been appointed to him, and if he does not find a way, no one will. Dorothy is just a farm girl from Kansas, who stumbled into Oz not because she was looking for adventure but because someone had hurt her feelings and she decided to run away from home. Yet she's the one to bring down the Wicked Witch of the West. Joan of Arc was also a farm girl, illiterate, the youngest in her family, when she received her first vision from God. Just about everyone doubted her; the commander of the French army said she should be taken home and given a good whipping. Yet she ends up leading the armies to war.

You see this throughout Scripture: a little boy will slay the giant, a loudmouthed fisherman who can't hold down a job will lead the church, and a whore with a golden heart is the one to perform the deed that Jesus asked us all to tell "wherever the gospel is preached throughout the world" (Mark 14:9). Things are not what they seem. *We* are not what we seem.

Of all the Eternal Truths we don't believe, this is the one we doubt most of all. Our days are not extraordinary. They are filled with the mundane, with hassles mostly. And we? We are . . . a dime a dozen. Nothing special really. Probably a disappointment to God. But as Lewis wrote, "The value of . . . myth is that it takes all the things we know and restores to them the rich significance which has been hidden by 'the veil of familiarity.'" You are not what you think you are. There is a glory to your life that your Enemy fears, and he is hell-bent on destroying that glory before you act on it. This part of the answer will sound unbelievable at first; perhaps it will sound too good to be true; certainly, you will wonder if it is true for you. But once you begin to see with those eyes, once you have begun to know it is true from the bottom of your heart, it will change everything.

The story of your life is the story of the long and brutal assault on your heart by the one who knows what you could be and fears it.

SEEING CLEARLY

Do you think I am trying to weave a spell? Perhaps I am; but remember your fairy tales. Spells are used for breaking enchantments as well as for inducing them. And you and I have need of the strongest spell that can be found to wake us from the evil enchantment of worldliness which has been laid upon us for nearly a hundred years. (C. S. Lewis, *The Weight of Glory*)

Lewis is not being cute; he is as sober as a man can be. That evil enchantment of worldliness is the way of looking at life given to us by the Enlightenment, the Age of Reason, the modern era. Science as our interpreter. The Matrix. We all drank deeply from that cup— the church included—and now the whole kingdom lies under a spell, like Narnia in winter, like the sleeping kingdom in *Sleeping Beauty*. Or as the Bible has it, "The whole world lies under the power of the evil one" (1 John 5:19 NRSV). We've never stopped to think about it. How? *How* does the whole world lie under the power of the Evil One? They don't see. They are in a fog, under a spell. Their hearts are shrouded (2 Cor. 3:15; 4:3–6). O God, take this shroud away.

You will not think clearly about your life until you think mythically. Until you see with the eyes of your heart.

About halfway through their journey—following a great deal of hardship and facing a good deal more—Frodo's devoted friend and servant, Sam Gamgee, wonders out loud: "I wonder what sort of tale we've fallen into?" Sam is at that moment thinking mythically. He is wondering in the right way. His question assumes that there *is* a story; there is something larger going on. He also assumes that they have somehow tumbled into it, been swept up into it. This is exactly what we've lost. Things happen to you. The car breaks down, you have a fight with your spouse, or you suddenly figure out how to fix a problem at work. What is *really* happening? David Whyte says that we live our lives under a pale sky, "the lost sense that we play out our lives as part of a greater story."

What sort of tale have I fallen into? is a question that would help us all a great deal if we wondered it for ourselves. After my friend Julie saw *The Fellowship of the Ring,* she turned to the girl with her and whispered, "We've just gotten a clearer view of reality than we usually see." Yes—that's the kind of "seeing" we need; that *is* our reality. What grabbed me was the theatrical trailer for the film. In a brilliantly crafted three-minute summary, the preview captures the essential mythic elements of the story. As scene after scene races before the eyes of the viewer, and Gandalf describes the tale, these lines cross the screen:

Fate has chosen him.
A Fellowship will protect him.
Evil will hunt him.

Yes—that's it. That is the life Christianity is trying to explain to the world. Better, that is the reality into which Christianity is the door. If we could believe that about our lives, and come to *know* that it is true, everything would change. We would be so much more able to interpret the events unfolding around us, against us. We would discover the task that is ours alone to fulfill. We would find our courage. The hour is late, and you are needed. So much hangs in the balance. Where *is* your heart?

CHAPTER THREE

THE HEART OF ALL THINGS

Above all else, guard your heart,
for it is the wellspring of life.
—KING SOLOMON (PROV. 4:23)

You are never a great man when you have more mind than
heart.

—BEAUCHENE

On her journey down the yellow brick road—a journey, may I
remind you, that grows more dangerous every step she takes—
Dorothy meets a number of strange sights. She befriends the
Scarecrow, and later the two of them come upon a lumberjack
made of tin, standing utterly still in the forest, his ax frozen in
midair. At first, he seems unable to speak. Coming closer, they discover that he is trying to say something after all. *Oil . . . can.* After
a bit more misunderstanding and misinterpretation, they get the oil
can to the joints of his mouth, only to find that he can speak as well
as any man, but that he was rusted. Once he is freed from his
prison, he begins to tell them his story.

Now the movie left out a crucial point, which the author gave in his original fairy tale. The Tin Woodman had once been a *real* man, who had been in love with a beautiful maiden. It was his dream to marry her, once he could earn enough money to build them a cottage in the woods. The Wicked Witch hated his love, and she cast spells upon the man that caused him injury, so that one by one his limbs needed to be replaced with artificial ones, made of tin. At first it seemed an advantage, for his metal frame allowed him to work nearly as powerfully as a machine. With a heart of love and arms that never tired, he seemed sure to win.

> "I thought I had beaten the Wicked Witch then, and I worked harder than ever; but I little knew how cruel my enemy could be. She thought of a new way to kill my love for the beautiful Munchkin maiden, and made my axe slip again, so that it cut right through my body, splitting it into two halves. Once more the tinner came to my help and made me a body of tin. Fastening my tin arms and legs and head to it, by means of joints, so that I could move around as well as ever. But alas! I now had no heart, so that I lost all my love for the Munchkin girl, and did not care whether I married her or not . . .
>
> "My body shone so brightly in the sun that I felt very proud of it and it did not matter now if my axe slipped, for it could not cut me. There was only one danger—that my joints would rust; but I kept an oil-can in the cottage and took care to oil myself whenever I needed it. However, there came a day when I forgot to do this, and, being caught in a rainstorm, before I had thought of the danger my joints had rusted, and I was left to stand in the woods until you came to help me.
>
> "It was a terrible thing to undergo, but during the year I stood there I had time to think that the greatest loss I had known was the loss of my heart. While I was in love I was the happiest man

on earth; but no one can love who has not a heart, and so I am resolved to ask Oz to give me one. If he does, I will go back to the Munchkin maiden and marry her."

Both Dorothy and the Scarecrow had been greatly interested in the story of the Tin Woodman, and now they knew why he was so anxious to get a new heart. "All the same," said the Scarecrow, "I shall ask for brains instead of a heart; for a fool would not know what to do with a heart if he had one." "I shall take the heart," returned the Tin Woodman; "for brains do not make one happy, and happiness is the best thing in the world."

(L. Frank Baum, *The Wonderful Wizard of Oz*)

Notice, there was a man who was once real and alive and in love. But after a series of blows, his humanity was reduced to efficiency. He became a sort of machine—a hollow man. At first, he did not even notice, for his condition made him an excellent woodman, as any person can become productive like a machine when he forgoes his heart. Notice also that it was the Wicked Witch who brought the disaster upon him. Baum's mythic tale reminds us that the Enemy knows how vital the heart is, even if we do not, and all his forces are fixed upon its destruction. For if he can disable or deaden your heart, then he has effectively foiled the plan of God, which was to create a world where love reigns. By taking out your heart, the Enemy takes out *you,* and you are essential to the Story.

You'll notice he's been rather effective.

I find it almost hard to believe a case must be made that the heart is . . . well, at the heart of it all. Of life. Of each person. Of God. And of Christianity. But our Enemy has come against us, and now we are all in some way like the Tin Woodman. We, too, have suffered a series of blows over time. And we, too, have seized upon efficiency, busyness, and productivity as the life we will live instead. Now we are lost. Dazed. Alert and oriented times zero.

Sleepwalking through life. In order to find our way out of these woods, we must return to the heart.

THE HEART IS CENTRAL

The heart is central. That we would even need to be reminded of this only shows how far we have fallen from the life we were meant to live—or how powerful the spell has been. The subject of the heart is addressed in the Bible more than any other topic—more than works or service, more than belief or obedience, more than money, and even more than worship. Maybe God knows something we've forgotten. But of course—all those other things are matters of the heart. Consider a few passages:

> Love the LORD your God with all your heart and with all your soul and with all your strength. (Deut. 6:5) [Jesus called this the greatest of all the commandments—and notice that the heart comes first.]

> Man looks at the outward appearance, but the LORD looks at the heart. (1 Sam. 16:7)

> Where your treasure is, there your heart will be also. (Luke 12:34)

> Trust in the LORD with all your heart,
>   and lean not on your own understanding. (Prov. 3:5)

> Your word I have treasured in my heart,
> That I may not sin against You. (Ps. 119:11 NASB)

> These people honor me with their lips,
>   but their hearts are far from me. (Matt. 15:8)

For the eyes of the LORD range throughout the earth to strengthen
those whose hearts are fully committed to him. (2 Chron. 16:9)

All a man's ways seem right to him,
    but the LORD weighs the heart. (Prov. 21:2)

According to the Scriptures, the heart can be troubled,
wounded, pierced, grieved, even broken. How well we all know that.
Thankfully, it can also be cheerful, glad, merry, joyful, rejoicing. The
heart can be whole or divided—as in that phrase we often use, "Well,
part of me wants to, but the other part of me doesn't." It can be wise
or foolish. It can be steadfast, true, upright, stout, valiant. (All of
these descriptions can be found by perusing the listings for the word
heart in any concordance.) It can also be frightened, faint, cowardly,
melt like wax. The heart can be wandering, forgetful, dull, stubborn,
proud, hardened. Wicked and perverse. I think we know that as well.

Much to our surprise, according to Jesus, a heart can also be pure,
as in, "Blessed are the pure in heart, for they will see God" (Matt.
5:8). And even noble, as in his story about the sower: "But the seed
on good soil stands for those with a noble and good heart, who hear
the word, retain it, and by persevering produce a crop" (Luke 8:15).
The Bible sees the heart as the source of all creativity, courage, and
conviction. It is the source of our faith, our hope, and of course, our
love. It is the "wellspring of life" within us (Prov. 4:23), the very
essence of our existence, the center of our being, the fount of our life.

Think about your work life for a moment. Why are so many
people bored or frustrated with their jobs? Why do they dread
Monday morning and "thank God it's Friday"? Their hearts are not
in their work. Far from it. However they arrived at what they're
doing with their lives, it wasn't by listening to their heart. The same
holds true for their love life. Why do so many relationships fail?
Because one or both partners no longer have a heart for making it

work. On and on it goes. Why are so many people struggling with depression and discouragement? They've lost heart. Why can't we seem able to break free of our addictions? Because somewhere along the way, in a moment of carelessness or desperation, we gave our heart away, and now we can't get it back.

There is no escaping the centrality of the heart. God knows that; it's why he made it the central theme of the Bible, just as he placed the physical heart in the center of the human body. The heart is central; to find our lives, we must make it central again.

REASON AND EMOTION

The mind receives and processes *information:*

- The boiling point of water is 212 degrees Fahrenheit.
- Lincoln was our sixteenth president.
- Light travels at a speed of 186,282 miles per second.

The heart knows and wrestles with *realities:*

- Your son is missing in combat.
- God has heard your prayers.
- Your daughter is getting married tomorrow.
- You are now and always have been loved.

The mind deals in *abstractions:*

- 2+2 = 4.
- You should get an oil change every three thousand miles.
- The phone company is increasing local service charges by $1.75.

The mind takes in and processes information. It is a beautiful gift of God. Why, you are using your mind even now on your search for

God and for life. But it remains, for the most part, indifferent. Your mind tells you that it is now 2:00 A.M. and your daughter has not returned, for the car is not in the driveway. Your heart wrestles with whether or not it is cause for worry.

The heart lives in the far more bloody and magnificent realities of living and dying and loving and hating. That's why those who live from their minds are detached from life. Things don't seem to touch them very much; they puzzle at the way others are so affected by life, and they conclude others are emotional and unstable. Meanwhile, those who live from the heart find those who live from the mind . . . unavailable. Yes, they are physically present. So is your computer. This is the sorrow of many marriages, and the number one disappointment of children who feel entirely missed or misunderstood by their parents.

Yes, the heart is the source of our emotions. But we have equated the heart *with* emotion, and put it away for a messy and even dangerous guide. No doubt, many people have made a wreck of their lives by following an emotion without stopping to consider whether it was a good idea to do so. Neither adultery nor murder is a rational act. But equating the heart *with* emotion is the same nonsense as saying that love is a feeling. Surely, we know that love is more than *feeling* loving; for if Christ had followed his emotions, he would not have gone to the cross for us. Like any man would have been, he was afraid; in fact, he knew that the sins of the world would be laid upon him, and so he had even greater cause for hesitation (Mark 14:32–35). But in the hour of his greatest trial, his love overcame his fear of what loving would cost him.

Emotions are the *voice* of the heart, to borrow Chip Dodd's phrase. Not the heart, but its voice. They express the deeper movements of the heart, as when we weep over the loss of someone we love, or when we cheer at the triumph of a son's team at the state championships. The mind stands detached, but it is with the heart that we experience and respond to life in all its fullness. Francis de Sales said, "Love is the life of our heart. According to it we desire, rejoice, hope and despair, fear, take heart, hate, avoid things, feel sad, grow angry, and exult." The heart expresses itself through emotion, but it expresses itself in many other ways as well.

MOTIVES

You'll notice that those who live from the mind shed few tears. I wonder if that isn't the real reason they choose to hide there. For when we're honest, we'll admit that there are our *stated* reasons for doing any of the things we do, and then there are our *real* reasons. We call them our motives.

Your wife asks why you turned to look at the pretty young thing in the tight jeans, and you defend yourself by saying that she only reminded you of Aunt Ruth. Yes, and people put radar detectors in their cars because they want to make sure they're maintaining the speed limit. Was it out of love that you remembered your anniversary, or was it fear that you'd be in serious trouble if you didn't? You flatter your boss. Does it have anything to do with the fact that your annual review is next week? What makes the Day of Judgment so unnerving is that all our posing and all our charades will be pulled back, all secrets will be made known, and our Lord will "expose the motives of men's *hearts*" (1 Cor. 4:5, emphasis added).

This is the point of the famous Sermon on the Mount. Jesus first says we haven't a hope of heaven unless our righteousness "surpasses that of the Pharisees" (Matt. 5:20). How can that be? They were fastidious rule keepers, pillars of the church, model citizens. Yes, Jesus says, and most of it was hypocrisy. The Pharisees prayed to impress men with their spirituality. They gave to impress men with their generosity. Their actions looked good, but their motives were not. Their hearts, as the saying goes, weren't in the right place.

A person's character is determined by his motives, and motive is always a matter of the heart. This is what Scripture means when it says that man looks at the outward appearance, but God looks at the heart. God doesn't judge us by our looks or our intelligence; he judges us by our hearts.

It makes sense, then, that Scripture also locates our conscience in our hearts. Paul says that even those who do not know God's law "show that the requirements of the law are written on their hearts, their consciences also bearing witness" (Rom. 2:15), such as when your child looks guilty for having told a lie. This is why it is so dangerous to harden our hearts by silencing our consciences, and why the offer of forgiveness is such good news, to have our "hearts sprinkled clean from an evil conscience" (Heb. 10:22 NRSV). Oh, the joy of living from right motives, from a clean heart. I doubt that those who want to dismiss the heart want to dismiss our consciences, set aside the importance of character.

THE THOUGHTS OF THE HEART

This is not to say the heart is only swirling emotion, mixed motives, and dark desire, without thought or reason. Far from it. According to Scripture, the heart is also where we do our deepest thinking. "Jesus, knowing what they were thinking in their hearts," is a common phrase in the Gospels. This might be most surprising to those who have accepted the Great Modern Mistake that "the mind equals reason and the heart equals emotion." Most people believe that. I heard it again, just last night, from a very astute and devoted young man. "The mind is our reason; the heart is emotion," he said. What popular nonsense. Solomon is remembered as the wisest man ever, and it was not because of the size of his brain. Rather, when God invited him to ask for anything in all the world, Solomon asked for a wise and discerning *heart* (1 Kings 3:9).

Our deepest thoughts are held in our hearts. Scripture itself claims to be "sharper than any double-edged sword, it penetrates even to dividing soul and spirit, joints and marrow; it judges the thoughts and attitudes of the heart" (Heb. 4:12). Not the feelings of the heart, the *thoughts* of the heart. Remember, when the shepherds reported the news that a company of angels had brought them out in the field, Mary "pondered them in her heart" (Luke 2:19), as you do when some news of great import keeps you up in the middle of the night. If you have a fear of heights, no amount of reasoning will get you to go bungee jumping. And if you are asked why you're paralyzed at the thought of it, you won't be able to explain. It is not rational, but it is your conviction nonetheless. Thus, the writer of Proverbs preempts Freud by about two thousand years when he states, "As [a man] thinketh in his heart, so is he" (Prov. 23:7 KJV). It is the thoughts and intents of the *heart* that shape a person's life.

The apostle Paul drives this home when he states: "If you confess with your mouth, 'Jesus is Lord,' and believe in your heart that God raised him from the dead, you will be saved. For it is with your heart that you believe and are justified" (Rom. 10:9–10). Read that again more slowly. "It is with your *heart* that you believe." Where does saving faith come from? The heart. Which raises a troubling reality for all of us: you do not belong to God, you are not a Christian at all, until you engage your heart, believe *with your heart*. Jesus said the same when, in a moment of frustration with his own people, he cried,

For this people's heart has become calloused;
    they hardly hear with their ears,
    and they have closed their eyes.
Otherwise they might see with their eyes,
    hear with their ears,
    understand with their hearts
and turn, and I would heal them. (Matt. 13:15, emphasis added)

The mind is a faculty, and a magnificent one at that. But the heart is the dwelling place of our *true* beliefs.

MEMORY, CREATIVITY, AND COURAGE

Why is it, as Frederick Buechner said, that "a fragrance in the air, a certain passage of a song, an old photograph falling out from the pages of a book, the sound of somebody's voice in the hall . . . makes your heart leap and fills your eyes with tears"? Because the storehouse of your memory is held in your heart. We have a shard of this left in that expression we use: "I've learned it by heart," meaning, we have it inscribed into memory. But the faculty is far more than rote memorization; it is in the heart that we hang on to the most important things. In his last warning to the people of Israel, Moses urges them to "be careful, and watch yourselves closely so that you do not forget the things your eyes have seen *or let them slip from your heart* as long as you live" (Deut. 4:9, emphasis added). Memory is vital, and memory is a function of the heart.

Creativity flows from the heart as well. You can paint by the numbers, but the result will lack something essential to art. After God gave Moses detailed plans for the construction of the tabernacle—which was designed to be quite beautiful—he said, "'I have put wisdom in the hearts of all the gifted artisans, that they may make all that I have commanded you' . . . Then Moses called Bezalel and Aholiab, and every gifted artisan in whose heart the LORD had put wisdom, everyone whose heart was stirred, to come and do the work" (Ex. 31:6; 36:2 NKJV). Machines mass-produce units; but creative work flows from the heart of a person.

And then there is courage, "the first of human qualities," as Churchill knew, "because it is the quality which guarantees all the others." Indeed. It takes courage to love, doesn't it? It takes courage to trust someone with your life. It takes courage to believe what you cannot see. It takes courage to follow Christ. "Do not let your hearts be troubled and do not be afraid," he said (John 14:27). And with good reason. This life we are living takes great courage, more and more as we see what's really at stake here. "Hear, O Israel, today you are going into battle against your enemies. Do not be faint-hearted" (Deut. 20:3).

Working with a trowel in one hand and a sword in the other, the people of Israel rebuilt the wall of their fallen city: "We rebuilt the wall till all of it reached half its height, for the people worked with all their heart" (Neh. 4:6). So it is with any great project we undertake, especially this great endeavor of living. Success or failure can be pretty well predicted by the degree to which the heart is fully in it. Our word *courage* comes down to us from the Old French *cuer*, which came from the Latin *cor*, which means "heart." This battle for the heart is going to take all the courage you can muster. Heaven forbid you leave that heart behind.

THE POINT OF ALL LIVING

I love watching a herd of horses grazing in an open pasture or running free across the sage-covered plateaus in Montana. I love hiking in the high country when the wildflowers are blooming—the purple lupine and the Shasta daisies, the Indian paintbrush when it's turning magenta. I love thunderclouds, massive ones. My family loves to sit outside on summer nights and watch the lightning, hear the thunder as a storm rolls in across Colorado. I love water too—the ocean, streams, lakes, rivers, waterfalls, rain. I love jumping off high rocks into lakes with my boys. I love old barns, windmills, the West. I love vineyards. I love it when Stasi is loving something, love watching her delight. I love my boys. I love God.

Everything you love is what makes a life worth living. Take a moment, set down the book, and make a list of all the things you love. Don't edit yourself; don't worry about prioritizing or anything of that sort. Simply think of all the things you love. Whether it's the people in your life or the things that bring you joy or the places that are dear to you or your God, you could not love them if you did not have a heart. A life filled with loving is a life most like the one that God lives, which is life as it was meant to be (Eph. 5:1–2). And loving requires a heart alive and awake and free.

Of all the things that are required of us in this life, which is the most important? What is the real point of our existence? Jesus was confronted with the question point-blank one day, and he boiled it all down to two things: loving God and loving others. Do this, he said, and you will find the purpose of your life. Everything else will fall into place. Somewhere down inside we know it's true; we know love is the point. We know if we could truly love, and be loved, and never lose love, we would finally be happy. Gerald May wrote, "We are created by love, to live in love, for the sake of love." And is it even possible to love *without* your heart?

The heart is the connecting point, the meeting place between any two persons. The kind of deep soul intimacy we crave with God and with others can be experienced only from the heart. We don't want to be someone's project; we want to be the desire of their heart. May lamented, "By worshiping efficiency, the human race has achieved the highest level of efficiency in history, but how much have we grown in love?"

We've done the same to our relationship with God. Christians have spent their whole lives mastering all sorts of principles, done their duty, carried on the programs of their church . . . and never known God intimately, heart to heart. There is that troubling passage Jesus gives us when he says that in the final account of our lives, some folks who did all sorts of Christian things will be genuinely surprised not to be invited into heaven. It reads, "Many will say to me on that day, 'Lord, Lord, did we not'" do all sorts of

Christian things, amazing things? And Christ will say, "I never knew you" (Matt. 7:22–23). The point is not the activity—the point is intimacy with God. Attend a class and take in information; then use that information to change the way you live. None of that will bring you into intimacy with God, just as taking a course on anatomy won't help you love your spouse. "You will find me," God says, "when you seek me with all your heart" (Jer. 29:13).

What more can be said, what greater case could be made than this: to find God, you must look with all your heart. To remain present to God, you must remain present to your heart. To hear his voice, you must listen with your heart. To love him, you must love with all your heart. You cannot be the person God meant you to be, and you cannot live the life he meant you to live, unless you live from the heart.

THE MISSION

This is absurd. I'm trying to tell you why you should breathe. "Remember now—oxygen is crucial to your body's needs. All of the other functions depend on it. You should get plenty of oxygen every day. Inhale, exhale. Inhale, exhale. Wonderful! Now remember to do this every moment of every day." All my defense here seems so far from the actual experience of having your heart back. Go fall in love then. Do something heroic; save someone's life. Spend a month in some breathtaking spot, doing nothing productive at all. Take up painting. Have yourself a good laugh—the kind that sends tears down your face and makes you grip your side for the ache of it. Listen to a beautiful piece of music. Live with courage. Tuck your child into bed; listen to her prayers; kiss her cheek. Find God.

Then you will remember again that the heart is central. Not the mind, not the will. The heart.

So what, then, *is* the heart? "Heart in Scripture," notes Charles

Ryrie, "is considered the very center and core of life." That's right. The heart is the deep center of our life. "The innermost part of the human personality," says James Houston, "the center of those qualities that make us human." Yes, that's it. The heart is who we are. The real self. I think I like Oswald Chambers's definition most: "The use of the Bible term *heart* is best understood by simply saying 'me.'" Me. It puts us back together from all the psychological, scientific, and even theological dissection we've been handed by the Modern Era and gives us back a whole self. Me. My heart is me. The real me. Your heart is you. The deepest, truest you. That is why the heart is central, for what shall we do if we dismiss our self?

Christ did not die for an idea. He died for a person, and that person is you. But there again, we have been led astray. Ask any number of people why Christ came, and you'll receive any number of answers, but rarely the real one. "He came to bring world peace." "He came to teach us the way of love." "He came to die so that we might go to heaven." "He came to bring economic justice." On and on it goes, much of it based in a partial truth. But wouldn't it be better to let him speak for himself?

Jesus steps into the scene. He reaches back to a four-hundred-year-old prophecy to tell us why he's come. He quotes from Isaiah 61:1, which goes like this:

> The Spirit of the Sovereign LORD is on me,
>> because the LORD has anointed me
>> to preach good news to the poor.
> He has sent me to bind up the brokenhearted,
>> to proclaim freedom for the captives
>> and release from darkness for the prisoners.

The meaning of this quotation has been clouded by years of religious language and ceremonial draping. What is he saying? It has something to do with good news, with healing hearts, with setting someone free. That much is clear from the text. Permit me a translation in plain language:

> God has sent me on a mission.
> I have some great news for you.
> God has sent me to restore and release something.
> And that something is you.
> I am here to give you back your heart and set you free.

Now, Christ could have chosen any one of a thousand other passages to explain his life purpose. He is the Sacrificial Lamb, the Root of Jesse, the Morning Star. But here, at the opening moment of his ministry, he chose this passage above all others; this is the heart of his mission. Everything else he says and does finds its place under this banner. I am here to give you back your heart and set you free. *That* is why the glory of God is man fully alive: it's what he said he came to do. But of course. The opposite can't be true. "The glory of God is man barely making it, a person hardly alive." How can it bring God glory for his very image, his own children, to remain so badly marred, broken, captive? Alert and oriented times zero?

How we've overlooked this is one of the great mysteries of our times. It is simply diabolical, despicable, downright *evil* that the heart should be so misunderstood, maligned, feared, and dismissed. But there is our clue again. The war we are in would explain so great a loss. This is the *last* thing the Enemy wants you to know. His plan from the beginning was to assault the heart, just as the Wicked Witch did to the Tin Woodman. Make them so busy, they ignore the heart. Wound them so deeply, they don't want a heart. Twist their theology, so they despise the heart. Take away their courage. Destroy their creativity. Make intimacy with God impossible for them.

Of course your heart would be the object of a great and fierce battle. It is your most precious possession. Without your heart you cannot have God. Without your heart you cannot have love. Without your heart you cannot have faith. Without your heart you cannot find the work that you were meant to do. In other words, without your heart you cannot have *life*. The question is, Did Jesus keep his promise? What has he done for our hearts?

The answer will astound you.

PART TWO

THE RANSOMED HEART

"The time is coming," declares the LORD,
  "when I will make a new covenant
with the house of Israel
  and with the house of Judah.
It will not be like the covenant
  I made with their forefathers
when I took them by the hand
  to lead them out of Egypt,
because they broke my covenant,
  though I was a husband to them," declares the LORD.
"This is the covenant I will make with the house of Israel
  after that time," declares the LORD.
"I will put my law in their minds
  and write it on their hearts.
I will be their God,
  and they will be my people."

—JEREMIAH 31:31–33

I will give you a new heart and put a new spirit in you; I will
remove from you your heart of stone and give you a heart of

flesh. And I will put my Spirit in you and move you to follow
my decrees and be careful to keep my laws.

—EZEKIEL 36:26–27

This we now know: the heart is central. It matters—deeply. When
we see with the eyes of the heart, which is to say, when we see
mythically, we begin to awaken, and what we discover is that things
are not what they seem. We *are* at war. We must fight for the life
God intends for us, which is to say, we must fight for our heart, for
it is the wellspring of that life within us.

Standing in the way of the path to life—the way of the heart—
is a monstrous barrier. It has stopped far too many pilgrims dead in
their tracks, for far too long. There is a widespread belief among
Christians today that the heart is desperately wicked—even after a
person comes to Christ.

It is a crippling belief.

And it is untrue.

CHAPTER FOUR

RANSOMED AND RESTORED

Create in me a clean heart, O God.

—KING DAVID (PS. 51:10 NKJV)

I will give you a new heart.

—GOD (EZEK. 36:26)

Now Beauty feared that she had caused his death. She ran throughout the palace, sobbing loudly. After searching everywhere, she
recalled her dream and ran into the garden toward the canal,
where she had seen him in her sleep. There she found the poor
Beast stretched out unconscious. She thought he was dead.
Without concern for his horrifying looks, she threw herself on
his body and felt his heart beating. So she fetched some water
from the canal and threw it on his face.

Beast opened his eyes and said, "You forgot your promise,
Beauty. The grief I felt upon having lost you made me decide to

fast to death. But I shall die content since I have the pleasure of seeing you one more time."

"No, my dear Beast, you shall not die," said Beauty. "You will live to become my husband. I give you my hand, and I swear that I belong only to you from this moment on. Alas! I thought that I only felt friendship for you, but the torment I am feeling makes me realize that I cannot live without you."

Beauty had scarcely uttered these words when the castle radiated with light. Fireworks and music announced a feast. These attractions did not hold her attention, though. She returned her gaze to her dear Beast, whose dangerous condition made her tremble. How great was her surprise when she discovered that the Beast had disappeared, and at her feet was a prince more handsome than Eros himself, who thanked her for putting an end to his enchantment.

It is the deepest and most wonderful of all mythic truths, unveiled here in the original *Beauty and the Beast,* written by Jeanne-Marie Leprince de Beaumont. The Transformation. A creature that no one could bear to look upon is transformed into a handsome prince. That which was dark and ugly is now glorious and good. Is it not the most beautiful outcome of any story to be written? Perhaps that is because it is the deepest yearning of the human heart. Look how often this theme surfaces.

The phoenix rises from the ashes. Cinderella rises from the cinders to become a queen. The ugly duckling becomes a beautiful swan. Pinocchio becomes a real boy. The frog becomes a prince. Wretched old Scrooge becomes "as good a friend, as good a master, and as good a man as the good old city knew, or any other good old city, town or borough in the good old world." The Cowardly Lion gets his courage and the Scarecrow gets his brains and the Tin Woodman gets a new heart. In hope beyond hope, they are all transformed into the very thing they never thought they could be.

Why are we enchanted by tales of transformation? I can't think of a movie or novel or fairy tale that doesn't somehow turn on this. Why is it an essential part of any great story? Because it is the secret to Christianity, and Christianity is the secret to the universe. "You must be born again" (John 3:7). You must be transformed. Keeping the Law, following the rules, polishing up your manners—none of that will do. What counts is whether we really have been changed into new and different people (Gal. 6:15). Is this not the message of the gospel? Zacchaeus the trickster becomes Zacchaeus the Honest One. Mary the whore becomes Mary the Last of the Truly Faithful. Paul the self-righteous murderer becomes Paul the Humble Apostle.

And we? I doubt that many of us would go so far as to say we're *transformed*. Our names are written down somewhere in heaven, and we have been forgiven. Perhaps we have changed a bit in what we believe and how we act. We confess the creeds now, and we've gotten our temper under control . . . for the most part. But *transformed* seems a bit too much to claim. How about *forgiven and on our way?* That's how most Christians would describe what's happened to them. It's partly true . . . and partly *untrue*, and the part that's untrue is what's killing us. We've been told that even though we have placed our hope in Christ, even though we have become his followers, our *hearts* are still desperately wicked.

But is that what the Bible teaches?

What We Most Desperately Need

"Everything I learned about human nature I learned from me," wrote the playwright Anton Chekhov, and the characters he so vividly created—with all their selfishness, their hatred, their dark and desperate desires, their hopelessness—they do rather well to describe us all. Imagine a story whose characters are taken from *your* own inner life and blown up for all to see. Egads. Something has gone wrong with the human race, and we know it. Better said, something has gone wrong *within* the human race. It doesn't take a theologian or a psychologist to tell you that. Read a newspaper. Spend a weekend with your relatives. Simply pay attention to the movements of your own heart in a single day. Most of the misery we suffer on this planet is the fruit of the human heart gone bad.

Scripture could not be more clear on this. Yes, God created us to reflect his glory, but barely three chapters into the drama we torpedoed the whole project. Sin entered the picture and spread like a computer virus. By the sixth chapter of Genesis, our downward spiral had reached the point where God himself couldn't bear it any longer: "The LORD saw how great man's wickedness on the earth had become, and that every inclination of the thoughts of his heart was only evil all the time. The LORD was grieved that he had made man on the earth, and his heart was filled with pain" (Gen. 6:5–6). This is the first mention of God's heart in the Bible, by the way, and it's a sad beginning, to be sure. His heart is broken because ours is fallen.

Any honest person knows this. We know we are not what we were meant to be. If we'll stop shifting the blame for just a moment, stop trying to put the onus on some other person or some policy or some other race, if we will take a naked and frank assessment of ourselves as measured against the life of Christ, well, then. Most of us will squirm and dodge and admit that perhaps we fall a bit short. If we're truly honest, we'll confess that we have it in us to be the Beast, the wicked stepsister, Scrooge. Most of the world religions concur on this point. Something needs to be done.

But the usual remedies involve some sort of shaping up on our part, some sort of face-lift whereby we clean up our act and start behaving as we should. Jews try to keep the Law. Buddhists follow the Eightfold Path. Muslims live by the Five Pillars. Many Christians try church attendance and moral living. You'd think, with all the effort, humanity would be on top of things by now. Of course, the reason all those treatments ultimately fail is that we quite misdiagnosed the disease. The problem is not in our behavior; the problem is *in us*. Jesus said, "For *out of the heart* come evil thoughts, murder, adultery, sexual immorality, theft, false testimony, slander" (Matt. 15:19, emphasis added). We don't need an upgrade. We need transformation. We need a miracle.

THE LAST ADAM, THE SECOND MAN

Jesus of Nazareth is given many names in Scripture. He is called the Lion of Judah. The Bright and Morning Star. The Wonderful Counselor. The Prince of Peace. The Lamb of God. There are many, many more—each one a window into all that he truly is, all that he has done, all that he will do. But one name seems to have escaped our attention, and that might help explain our misunderstanding of the gospel. Paul refers to Jesus as the Last Adam and the Second Man (1 Cor. 15:45–47). Why is this important? Because of what happened through the *First* Adam.

Our first father, Adam, and our first mother, Eve, were destined to be the root and trunk of humanity. What they were meant to be, we were meant to be: the kings and queens of the earth, the rulers over all creation, the glorious image bearers of a glorious God. They were statues of God walking about in a Garden, radiant Man and Woman, as we were to be. Our natures and our destinies were bound up in theirs. Their choices would forever shape our lives, for good or for evil. It is deep mystery, but we see something of a hint of it in the way children so often follow in the steps of their parents. Haven't you heard it said, "He has his father's temper," or "She has her mother's wit"? As the old saying goes, the fruit doesn't fall far from the tree. In fact, we call them family trees, and Adam and Eve are the first names on the list.

Our first parents chose, and it was on the side of evil. They broke the one command, the only command, God gave to them, and what followed you can watch any night on the news. The long lament of human history. Something went wrong in their hearts, something *shifted,* and that shift was passed along to each of us. Parents will often wonder where their toddlers learned to lie or how they came into the world so self-centered. It doesn't need to be taught to them; it is inherent to human nature. Paul makes clear in Romans, "Sin entered the world through one man . . . through the disobedience of the one man the many were made sinners" (5:12, 19). Of course, I am simply restating the doctrine of original sin, a core tenet of Christianity essential to Scripture.

But that is not the end of the Story, thank God. The First Adam was only "a pattern of the one to come" (Rom. 5:14). He would foreshadow another man, the head of a new race, the firstborn of a new creation, whose life would mean transformation to those who would become joined to him: "For just as through the disobedience of the one man [Adam] the many were made sinners, so also through the obedience of the one man [Christ, the Last Adam] the many will be made righteous" (Rom. 5:19).

A man comes down from heaven, slips into our world unnoticed, as Neo does in *The Matrix,* as Maximus does in *Gladiator,* as Wallace does in *Braveheart.* Yet he is no ordinary man, and his mission no ordinary mission. He comes as a substitute, a representative, as the destroyer of one system and the seed of something new. His death and resurrection break the power of the Matrix, release the prisoners, set the captives free. It is a historic fact. It really happened. And it is more than history. It is mythic in the first degree. Lewis said, "By becoming fact, it does not cease to be myth; that is the miracle."

In the fifth chapter of the famous book of Romans, Paul asks, Was Adam effective? Did his life have far-reaching consequences? We all know it did. It was devastating. He goes on to say, Well, then, the consequences of Christ, the Last Adam, were even greater:

"For if, by the trespass of the one man, death reigned through that one man, *how much more* will those who receive God's abundant provision of grace and of the gift of righteousness reign in life through the one man, Jesus Christ" (Rom. 5:17, emphasis added).

I WILL REMOVE YOUR HEART OF STONE

Jesus of Nazareth was sentenced to death by a vain puppet of the Roman government acting as district governor of Jerusalem. He was nailed to a cross by a handful of Roman soldiers who happened to be on duty, and left there to die. He died sometime around three o'clock in the afternoon on a Friday. Of a broken heart, by the way. And we call it Good Friday, of all strange things, because of what it effected. An innocent man, the Son of God, bleeding for the sins of the world. Standing in for us, as Jack gives his life for Rose in *Titanic,* as Sydney Carton stands in to die for Charles Darnay in *A Tale of Two Cities,* or as Aslan dies on the stone table to ransom the traitor Edmund. We rebelled, and the penalty for our rebellion was death. To lose us was too great a pain for God to bear, and so he took it upon himself to rescue us. The Son of God came "to give his life as a ransom for many" (Matt. 20:28).

You have been ransomed by Christ. Your treachery is forgiven. You are entirely pardoned for every wrong thought and desire and deed. This is what the vast majority of Christians understand as the central work of Christ for us. And make no mistake about it—it is a deep and stunning truth, one that will set you free and bring you joy. For a while.

But the joy for most of us has proven fleeting because we find that we need to be forgiven again and again and again. Christ has died for us, but we remain (so we believe) deeply marred. It actually ends up producing a great deal of guilt. "After all that Christ has done for you . . . and now you're back here asking forgiveness *again?*" To be destined to a life of repeating the very things that sent our Savior to the cross can hardly be called *salvation*.

Think of it: you are a shadow of the person you were meant to be. You have nothing close to the life you were meant to have. And you have no real chance of becoming that person or finding that life. However, you are forgiven. For the rest of your days, you will fail in your attempts to become what God wants you to be. You should seek forgiveness and try again. Eventually, shame and disappointment will cloud your understanding of yourself and your God. When this ongoing hell on earth is over, you will die, and you will be taken before your God for a full account of how you didn't measure up. But you will be forgiven. After that, you'll be asked to take your place in the choir of heaven. This is what we mean by *salvation*.

The good news is . . . that is *not* Christianity. There is more. *A lot more*. And that more is what most of us have been longing for most of our lives.

Under the old covenant, a Jewish boy was to be circumcised when he was eight days old, the foreskin of his penis removed with a knife. It was intended to be symbolic, a sign of the covenant given to Abraham. Forever after, everyone, including that boy, would know that he was marked for God, set apart for God. But in that symbol lay a deeper meaning, veiled for centuries, just as the mythic is often veiled, just as the sacrificial lamb required of the ancient Jews would foreshadow the death of Christ. It would take a Jewish convert of Christ to explain the true meaning of circumcision:

> A man is not a Jew if he is only one outwardly, nor is circumcision merely outward and physical. No, a man is a Jew if he is one inwardly; and circumcision is circumcision *of the heart*, by the Spirit, not by the written code. (Rom. 2:28–29, emphasis added)

> In [Christ] you were also circumcised, in the putting off of the
> sinful nature, not with a circumcision done by the hands of men
> but with the circumcision done by Christ. (Col. 2:11)

It's not just that the Cross did something *for* us. Something deep
and profound happened *to* us in the death of Christ. Remember—the
heart is the problem. God understands this better than anyone, and
he goes for the root. God promised in the new covenant to "take away
your heart of stone." How? By joining us to the death of Christ. Our
nature was nailed to the cross with Christ; we died there, with him, in
him. Yes, it is a deep mystery—"deep magic" as Lewis called it—but
that does not make it untrue. "The death he died, he died to sin once
for all . . . In the same way, count yourselves dead to sin" (Rom.
6:10–11). Jesus was the Last Adam, the end of that terrible story.

You've been far more than forgiven. God has removed your heart
of stone. You've been delivered of what held you back from what
you were meant to be. You've been rescued from the part of you
that sabotages even your best intentions. Your heart has been circumcised to God. Your heart has been set free.

And there is even more.

AND I WILL GIVE YOU A NEW HEART

Most people assume that the Cross *is* the total work of Christ. The
two go hand in hand in our minds—Jesus Christ and the Cross; the
Cross and Jesus Christ. The Resurrection is impressive, but kind of
. . . an afterthought. It was needed, of course, to get him out of the
grave. Or the Resurrection is important because it proves Jesus was
the Son of God. His death was the *real* work on our behalf. The
Resurrection is like an epilogue to the real story; the extra point
after the touchdown; the medal ceremony after the Olympic event.
You can see which we think is more important. What image do we

put on our churches, our Bibles, our jewelry? The cross is the symbol of Christianity worldwide. However . . .

The cross was never meant to be the only or even the central symbol of Christianity.

That you are shocked by what I've just said only proves how far we've strayed from the faith of the New Testament. The cross is not the sole focal point of Christianity. Paul says so himself: "If Christ has not been raised, our preaching is useless and so is your faith . . . If Christ has not been raised, your faith is futile; you are still in your sins" (1 Cor. 15:14, 17).

> We have grown so used to the idea that the Crucifixion is the supreme symbol of Christianity, that it is a shock to realize how late in the history of Christian art its power was recognized. In the first art of Christianity it hardly appears; and the earliest example, on the doors of Santa Sabina in Rome [around A.D. 430], is stuck away in a corner, almost out of sight . . . early Christian art is concerned with miracles, healings, and with hopeful aspects of the faith like the Ascension and the Resurrection.

Art historian Kenneth Clark is telling us something so foreign to our thinking, it takes a second reading. What? Christians don't even begin to use the cross as a symbol until *four hundred years after Christ,* and then only in a minor role? *Four hundred years* of the earliest and most vibrant Christianity goes by without the cross as its rallying point?! Those who walked with Jesus, and those who walked with those who walked with Jesus—they didn't make the cross central? Why? As the record goes, what the apostles preached was the *Resurrection:*

> In those days Peter stood up among the believers (a group numbering about a hundred and twenty) and said, "Brothers, the

Scripture had to be fulfilled which the Holy Spirit spoke long ago through the mouth of David concerning Judas, who served as guide for those who arrested Jesus . . . Therefore it is necessary to choose one of the men who have been with us the whole time the Lord Jesus went in and out among us . . . For one of these must become a witness with us of his resurrection." (Acts 1:15–16, 21–22)

The priests and the captain of the temple guard and the Sadducees came up to Peter and John while they were speaking to the people. They were greatly disturbed because the apostles were teaching the people and proclaiming in Jesus the resurrection of the dead. (Acts 4:1–2)

With great power the apostles continued to testify to the resurrection of the Lord Jesus, and much grace was upon them all. (Acts 4:33)

Paul was preaching the good news about Jesus and the resurrection. (Acts 17:18)

The early Christian church symbolized the Resurrection, healings, and miracles because the church thought those things were central. The reason the first and closest friends of Jesus focused on miracles, healings, and hopeful aspects of the faith such as the Ascension and the Resurrection was simply that those are what God himself wants us to focus on. *Those are the point.* Those make Christianity such very good news. A dead man is not a great deal of help to us; a dead God is even worse. But life, real life, the power of God to *restore* you . . . now that's a whole nother matter.

We say Christ died for us, and that is true. But Christ was also *raised* for us. His resurrection was as much for us as his death was.

> For if, by the trespass of the one man [the First Adam], death reigned through that one man, how much more will those who receive God's abundant provision of grace and of the gift of righteousness *reign in life* through the one man, Jesus Christ. (Rom. 5:17, emphasis added)

> We were therefore buried with him through baptism into death in order that, just as Christ was raised from the dead through the glory of the Father, we too may live a new life . . . In the same way, count yourselves dead to sin but alive to God in Christ Jesus. (Rom. 6:4, 11)

> But because of his great love for us, God . . . made us alive with Christ. (Eph. 2:4–5)

Remember now—Adam was *a pattern* of the One to come. He was the root and trunk of our family tree. Our hearts fell when he fell. We received our sinful nature from him. So we now receive a *new* nature and a *new* heart from Christ, our Second Man. We have been made alive with the life of Christ. Just as we received our sinful nature from Adam, so we now receive a good and holy nature from Christ. It has always been God's plan not just to forgive you, but to restore you: "Make a tree good and its fruit will be good" (Matt. 12:33). Or as Milton had it,

> Their nature also to thy nature join . . .
> And live in thee transplanted, and from thee
> Receive new life.

Let me try this again. The new covenant has two parts to it: "I will give you a new heart and put a new spirit in you; I will remove from you your heart of stone and give you a heart of flesh" (Ezek.

36:26). God removed your old heart when he circumcised your heart; he gives you a new heart when he joins you to the life of Christ. That's why Paul can say "count yourselves dead to sin" *and* "alive to God in Christ Jesus" (Rom. 6:11).

> The story of the Incarnation is the story of a descent and resurrection . . . one has the picture of a diver, stripping off garment after garment, making himself naked, then flashing for a moment in the air, and then down through the green, and warm, and sunlit water into the pitch black, cold, freezing water, down into the mud and slime, then up again, his lungs almost bursting, back again to the green and warm and sunlit water, and then at last out into the sunshine, holding in his hand the dripping thing he went down to get. This thing is human nature. (C. S. Lewis, "The Grand Miracle")

The Resurrection affirms the promise Christ made. For it was *life* he offered to give us: "I have come that they may have life, and have it to the full" (John 10:10). We are saved by his life when we find that *we are able to live* the way we've always known we should live. We are free to be what he meant when he meant us. You have a new life—the life of Christ. And you have a new heart. Do you know what this means? Your heart is good.

THE DWELLING PLACE OF GOD

The year is about 1450 B.C. Somewhere in the deserts east of Sinai, a band of runaway slaves have pitched camp. In the middle of the camp, the nomads have erected a tent of goat hair and skins—a design given to them by God himself when he talked face-to-face with Moses on the mountain. The tabernacle had two parts, the Holy Place and the Most Holy Place (the Holy of

Holies). It was in the Most Holy Place that the presence of God would come: "Moses did everything just as the LORD commanded him . . . and the glory of the LORD filled the tabernacle" (Ex. 40:16, 34).

And just as Adam was a pattern of the One who was to come, just as the sacrificial lambs offered by the Jews in that tabernacle foreshadowed an even greater Sacrifice to come, so the tabernacle itself was a picture of something even more amazing. It is a kind of mythic symbol, given to us to help us understand a deeper eternal reality. Each person knows that now his *body* is the temple of God: "Do you not know that your body is a temple of the Holy Spirit, who is in you, whom you have received from God?" (1 Cor. 6:19). Indeed it is. "Don't you know that you yourselves are God's temple and that God's Spirit lives in you?" (1 Cor. 3:16). Okay—each of us is now the temple of God. So where, then, is the Holy of Holies?

Your heart.

That's right—your heart. Paul teaches us in Ephesians that "Christ may dwell in your hearts through faith" (3:17). God comes down to dwell in us, *in our hearts.* Now, we know this: God cannot dwell where there is evil. "You are not a God who takes pleasure in evil; with you the wicked cannot dwell" (Ps. 5:4). Something pretty dramatic must have happened in our hearts, then, to make them fit to be the dwelling place of a holy God.

Of course, none of this can happen for us until we give our lives back to God. We cannot know the joy or the life or the freedom of heart I've described here until we surrender our lives to Jesus and surrender them totally. Renouncing all the ways we have turned from God in our hearts, we forsake the idols we have worshiped and given our hearts over to. We turn, and give ourselves body, soul, and spirit back to God, asking him to cleanse our hearts and make them new. And he does. He gives us a new heart. And he comes to dwell there, in our hearts.

THE PROMISE FULFILLED

"If we believed that . . . we could do *anything*. We would follow him *anywhere!*"

A few of us were sitting around last week talking about the gospel, what it really promises and what it means for our lives. I was trying to make the case that the new covenant means nothing less than this: the heart is good. I was surprised to hear the protests from most of my friends, who are deeply committed followers of Jesus and who have walked with him for years. "What? That can't be! I've never heard that . . . ever." I know. Neither had I. But it's undeniable: the new covenant, accomplished through the work of Christ, means that we have a new heart. Now listen to Jesus:

> Each tree is recognized by its own fruit. People do not pick figs from thornbushes, or grapes from briers. *The good man brings good things out of the good stored up in his heart,* and the evil man brings evil things out of the evil stored up in his heart. (Luke 6:44–45, emphasis added)

Later, explaining the parable of the sower and the seed, Jesus says,

> The seed on good soil stands for those *with a noble and good heart,* who hear the word, retain it, and by persevering produce a crop. (Luke 8:15, emphasis added)

Jesus himself teaches that at least for somebody, the heart can be good and even noble. That somebody is you, if you are his. God kept his promise. Our hearts have been circumcised to God. We have new hearts. Do you know what this means? Your heart is good. Let that sink in for a moment. Your heart is *good*.

What would happen if you believed it, if you came to the place where you *knew* it was true? Your life would never be the same. My friend Lynn got it, and that's when she exclaimed, "If we believed that . . . we could do *anything*. We would follow him *anywhere!*" Exactly. It would change our lives. It would change the face of Christianity. This is the lost message of the gospel, lost at least to a great many people. Small wonder. This is the *last* thing the Enemy wants the world to know. It would change everything. Those of you who've gotten your hearts back know exactly what I mean. It's freedom. It's life.

CHAPTER FIVE

THE GLORY HIDDEN IN YOUR HEART

The LORD their God will save them on that day
  as the flock of his people.
They will sparkle in his land
  like jewels in a crown.
How attractive and beautiful they will be!

—ZECHARIAH (9:16–17)

Those who look to him are radiant;
  their faces are never covered with shame.

—KING DAVID (PS. 34:5)

"Have you no other daughters?" "No," said the man. "There is a little stunted kitchen wench which my late wife left behind her, but she cannot be the bride." The King's son said he was to send her up to him; but the step-mother answered, "Oh no, she is much too dirty, she cannot show herself!" But he absolutely insisted on it, and Cinderella had to be called. She first washed her hands and face clean, and then went and bowed down before the King's son, who gave her the golden slipper. Then she seated herself on a stool, drew her foot out of the heavy wooden shoe, and put it into the slipper, which fit like a glove. And when she rose up and the King's son looked at her face, he recognized the beautiful maiden who had danced with him and cried, "This is the true bride!" The step-mother and two sisters were horrified and became pale with rage; he, however, took Cinderella on his horse and rode away with her.

I love this part of the story—to see the heroine unveiled in all her glory. To have her, *finally,* rise up to her full height. Mocked, hated, laughed at, spit upon—Cinderella is the one the slipper fits; she's the one the prince is in love with; *she's* the true bride. Just as we are. We, the ransomed church, are the bride of the King's Son, are we not? "Come, I will show you the bride, the wife of the Lamb" (Rev. 21:9). We've been chosen by him. We are the object of his love. "You have stolen my heart with one glance of your eyes" (Song 4:9). This fairy tale is *true.* I love it that in this passage from the original "Cinderella," the king's son *insisted* she come out of hiding. Though her family would keep her in the cellar, he'll have none of that. Come out. You are mine now. Let your light shine before men.

Still, if I'm honest, I appreciate the story . . . from a distance. The thought of *me* being called out of hiding is unnerving. I don't think I want to be seen. Many years ago, during my life in the theater, I received a standing ovation for a performance. The audience was literally on its feet, cheering. What actor doesn't crave a standing ovation? So you know what I did? I *ran.* Literally. As soon as the curtain went down I bolted for the door, so I wouldn't have to talk to anyone. I didn't want to be seen. I know, it's weird, but I'll bet you feel the same about being unveiled.

You probably can't imagine there being a glory to your life, let alone one that the Enemy fears. But remember—things are not what they seem. *We* are not what we seem. You probably believed that your heart was bad too. I pray that fog of poison gas from the pit of hell is fading away in the wind of God's truth. And there is more. Not only does Christ say to you that your heart is good, he invites you now out of the shadows to unveil your glory. You have a role you never dreamed of having.

There's the beautiful scene toward the end of Joseph's life where he, too, is unveiled. The very brothers who sold him into slavery as a boy are standing before what they believe is an angry Egyptian lord, equal in power to Pharaoh himself, their knees knocking. The silver cup of this dreaded lord was found stashed away in their luggage as they headed out of town—placed there by Joseph himself as a ruse. Now Joseph interrogates them till they squirm, deepening the plot by using an interpreter as if he doesn't understand Hebrew, pressing them hard. Finally, unable to hold back his tears, he *reveals* himself: "I am Joseph; does my father still live? . . . So you shall tell my father of all my glory in Egypt . . . and you shall hurry and bring my father down here" (Gen. 45:3, 13 NKJV). This is who I really am! Tell him about my glory! Amazing.

Much to everyone's surprise, Peter is unveiled at pentecost with quite a sermon that brings three thousand converts into the church. This from the man who denied Christ, three times, in his hour of need. Peter's buddies had to have been thinking, *Whoa, where did that come from?* And of course, Jesus himself, the carpenter's son, is unveiled on the Mount of Transfiguration for who he really is—the King of glory. In a beautiful mythic parallel, Aragorn, son of Arathorn and true heir to the throne of Gondor, is finally unveiled in the third book of Tolkien's trilogy, aptly titled *The Return of the King.* For years upon end he's merely been known as Strider, a Ranger, living out in the wilds doing no one really knows what. (Can anything good come out of *Nazareth?*) The chief of the Dunedain, the last great king of the race of men, Aragorn comes forward to take his rightful place.

Thus came Aragorn son of Arathorn, Elessar, Isildur's heir, out of the Paths of the Dead, borne upon a wind from the Sea to the kingdom of Gondor; and the mirth of the Rohirrim was a torrent of laughter and a flashing of swords, and the joy and wonder of the City was a music of trumpets and a ringing of bells. But the hosts of Mordor were seized with bewilderment, and a great wizardry it seemed to them that their own ships should be filled with their foes; and a black dread fell on them, knowing that the tides of fate had turned against them and their doom was at hand . . . But before all went Aragorn with the Flame of the West, Andúril like a new fire kindled, Narsil re-forged as deadly as of old; and upon his brow was the Star of Elendil.

The day has come, and the Morning Star has risen, never to set again. This unveiling, this coming into your glory, this is inevitable for the ransomed heart. If you'll recall, Moses put a veil over his face. That, too, was a picture of a deeper reality. We all do that. We have all veiled our glory, or someone has veiled it for us. Usually, some combination of both. But the time has come to set all veils aside:

Now if the ministry that brought death, which was engraved in letters on stone, came with glory, so that the Israelites could not look steadily at the face of Moses because of its glory, fading though it was, will not the ministry of the Spirit be even more glorious? . . . Therefore, since we have such a hope, we are very bold. We are not like Moses, who would put a veil over his face to keep the Israelites from gazing at it while the radiance was fading away . . . And we, who with unveiled faces all reflect the Lord's glory, are being transformed into his likeness with ever-increasing glory, which comes from the Lord, who is the Spirit. (2 Cor. 3:7–8, 12–13, 18)

We are in the process of being unveiled. We were created to reflect God's glory, born to bear his image, and he ransomed us to reflect that glory again. Every heart was given a mythic glory, and that glory is being *restored*. Remember the mission of Christ: "I have come to give you back your heart and set you free." For as Saint Irenaeus said, "The glory of God is man fully alive." Certainly, you don't think the opposite is true. How do we bring God glory when we are sulking around in the cellar, weighed down by shame and guilt, hiding our light under a bushel? Our destiny is to come fully alive. To live with ever-*increasing* glory. This is the Third Eternal Truth every good myth has been trying to get across to us: *your heart bears a glory, and your glory is needed* . . . now. This is our desperate hour.

No Good Thing?

In an attempt to explain the biblical doctrine of sin, we've let something else creep in. You'll hear it come up almost automatically whenever Christians talk about themselves: "I'm just a sinner, saved by grace." "I'm just clothes for God to put on." "There sure isn't any good thing in me." It's so common this mind-set, this idea that we are no-good wretches, ready to sin at a moment's notice, incapable of goodness, and certainly far from any glory.

It's also unbiblical.

The passage people think they are referring to is Romans 7:18, where Paul says, "For I know that in me (that is, in my flesh,) dwelleth no good thing" (KJV). Notice the distinction he makes. He does *not* say, "There is nothing good in me. Period." What he says is that "*in my flesh* dwelleth no good thing." The flesh is the old nature, the old life, crucified with Christ. The flesh is the very thing God removed from our hearts when he circumcised them by his Spirit. In Galatians Paul goes on to explain, "Those who belong to

Christ Jesus have crucified the sinful nature [the flesh] with its passions and desires" (5:24). He does *not* say, "I am incapable of good." He says, "*In my flesh* dwelleth no good thing." In fact, just a few moments later, he discovers that "the law of the Spirit of life in Christ Jesus has made me free from the law of sin and death" (Rom. 8:2 NKJV).

Yes, we still battle with sin. *Yes,* we still have to crucify our flesh on a daily basis. "For if you live according to the flesh you will die; but if by the Spirit you put to death the deeds of the [sinful nature], you will live" (Rom. 8:13 NKJV). We have to *choose* to live from the new heart, and our old nature doesn't go down without a fight. I'll say more about that later. For now the question on the table is: Does the Bible teach that Christians are nothing but sinners—that there is nothing good in us? The answer is *no!* You have a new heart. Your heart is good. That sinful nature you battle *is not who you are.* Twice, in the famous chapter of Romans 7, where Paul presents a first-person angst about our battle against sin, he says, "But this is not my true nature. This is not my heart."

> As it is, *it is no longer I myself* who do it, but it is sin living in me.
> I know that nothing good lives in me, that is, in my sinful nature
> . . . Now if I do what I do not want to do, *it is no longer I* who do
> it, but it is sin living in me that does it . . . For in my inner being
> I delight in God's law. (vv. 17–18, 20, 22, emphasis added)

Paul is making a crucial distinction: *This is not me; this is not my true heart.* Listen to how he talks about himself in other places. He opens every letter by introducing himself as "Paul, an apostle." Not as a sinner, but as an apostle, writing to "the saints." Dump the religiosity; think about this *mythically.* Paul, appointed as a Great One in the kingdom, writing other Great Allies of the kingdom. How bold of him. There is no false humility, no groveling. He says,

> Surely you have heard about the . . . grace that was given to me
> for you, that is, the mystery made known to me by revelation, as
> I have already written briefly. In reading this, then, you will be
> able to understand my insight into the mystery of Christ, which
> was not made known to men in other generations as it has now
> been revealed [to me]. (Eph. 3:2–5)

Paul is unashamed to say that he knows things no man before
him knew. He even assumes they've heard about him, the mysteries revealed to him. That is part of his glory. His humility comes
through clearly, in that he quickly admits that it's all been a gift,
and in fact, a gift given to him *for others.*

And listen to the way he talks about us: "You shine like stars in
the universe as you hold out the word of life" (Phil. 2:15–16). As
Shawn Mullins sings, "we're born to shimmer; we're born to shine."
You are *supposed* to shimmer. "Let your light shine before men"
(Matt. 5:16). All this groveling and self-deprecation done by
Christians is often just shame masquerading as humility. Shame
says, "I'm nothing to look at. I'm not capable of goodness." Humility
says, "I bear a glory for sure, but it is a *reflected* glory. A grace given
to me." Your story does not begin with sin. It begins with a glory
bestowed upon you by God. It does not start in Genesis 3; it starts
in Genesis 1. First things first, as they say.

Certainly, you will admit that God is glorious. Is there anyone
more kind? Is there anyone more creative? Is there anyone more
valiant? Is there anyone more true? Is there anyone more daring? Is
there anyone more beautiful? Is there anyone more wise? Is there
anyone more generous? You are his offspring. His child. His reflection. His likeness. You bear *his* image. Do remember that though
he made the heavens and the earth in all their glory, the desert and
the open sea, the meadow and the Milky Way, and said, "It is
good," it was only *after* he made you that he said, "It is *very* good"

(Gen. 1:31). Think of it: your original glory was greater than anything that's ever taken your breath away in nature.

> As for the saints who are in the land,
>> they are the glorious ones in whom is all my delight. (Ps. 16:3)

God endowed you with a glory when he created you, a glory so deep and mythic that all creation pales in comparison. A glory unique to you, just as your fingerprints are unique to you, just as the way you laugh is unique to you. Somewhere down deep inside we've been looking for that glory ever since. A man wants to know that he is truly a man, that he could be brave; he longs to know that he is a warrior; and all his life he wonders, "Have I got what it takes?" A woman wants to know that she is truly a woman, that she is beautiful; she longs to know that she is captivating; and all her life she wonders, "Do I have a beauty to offer?" The poet Yeats wrote,

> If I make the lashes dark
> And the eyes more bright
> And the lips more scarlet,
> Or ask if all be right
> From mirror after mirror
> No vanity's displayed:
> I'm looking for the face I had
> Before the world was made.
> ("Before the World Was Made" from the poem "A Woman Young and Old")

Yes, that's it. When you take a second glance in the mirror, when you pause to look again at a photograph, you are looking for a glory you know you were meant to have, if only because you know you long to have it. You remember faintly that you were once more than what you have become. Your story didn't start with sin, and thank God, it does not end with sin. It ends with glory restored: "Those he justified, he also glorified" (Rom. 8:30). And "in the meantime," you have *been* transformed, and you are *being* transformed. You've been given a new heart. Now God is restoring your glory. He is bringing you fully alive. Because the glory of God is you fully alive.

UNDER A SPELL

"Well, then, if this is all true, why don't I see it?" Precisely. Exactly. Now we are reaching my point. The fact that you do not see your good heart and your glory is only proof of how effective the assault has been. We don't see ourselves clearly. Have you forgotten your fairy tales?

In *The Silver Chair* (the sixth story of the Narnia series), two English schoolchildren—Eustace and Jill—are summoned into Narnia to find the missing crown prince of that kingdom. Years earlier Prince Rilian was abducted by a witch, placed under a spell, and taken to her underground kingdom. Once a day, for an hour, the prince would wake from the magic spell and realize where he was and *who* he was and what had happened. But during those hours he was chained to a silver chair so that he could not escape. All the other hours of the day he was "free" because he was convinced that the witch was good and he was her grateful slave, a nogood wretch. Near the climax of the story the children—with the help of Puddleglum the Marsh-wiggle—free the prince from the chair and the power of the spell.

> Then he turned and surveyed his rescuers; and the something wrong, whatever it was, had vanished from his face. "What?" he cried, turning to Puddleglum. "Do I see before me a Marsh-wiggle—a real, live, honest, Narnian Marsh-wiggle?" "Oh, so you

have heard of Narnia, after all?" said Jill. "Had I forgotten it when I was under the spell?" asked the Knight. "Well, that and all other bedevilments are now over. You may well believe that I know Narnia, for I am Rilian, Prince of Narnia, and Caspian the great King is my Father." "Your Royal Highness," said Puddleglum, sinking on one knee (and the children did the same), "we have come hither for no other end than to seek you."

"How long then have I been in the power of the witch?" "It is more than ten years since your Highness was lost in the woods at the north side of Narnia." "Ten years!" said the Prince, drawing his hand across his face as if to rub away the past. "Yes, I believe you. For now that I am myself I can remember that enchanted life, though while I was enchanted I could not remember my true self."

"Though while I was enchanted I could not remember my true self." That's it exactly. We are under a spell. We are alert and oriented times zero. We have no idea who we really are. Whatever glory was bestowed, whatever glory is being restored, we thought this whole Christian thing was about . . . something else. Trying not to sin. Going to church. Being nice. Jesus says it is about healing your heart, setting it free, restoring your glory. A religious fog has tried to veil all that, put us under some sort of spell or amnesia, to keep us from coming alive. Pascal said, "It is a monstrous thing . . . an incomprehensible enchantment, and a supernatural slumber." And Paul said, It is time to take that veil away.

Whenever anyone turns to the Lord, the veil is taken away. Now the Lord is the Spirit, and where the Spirit of the Lord is, there is freedom. And we, who with unveiled faces all reflect the Lord's glory, are being transformed into his likeness with ever-increasing glory, which comes from the Lord, who is the Spirit. (2 Cor. 3:16–18)

A veil removed, bringing freedom, transformation, glory. Do you see it? I am not making this up—though I have been accused of making the gospel better than it is. The charge is laughable. Could anyone be more generous than God? Could any of us come up with a story that beats the one God has come up with? All the stories that we tell borrow their power from the Great Story he is telling. Take the movie *The Lion King*, ignore the "circle of life" stuff—the whole myth is borrowed from Christianity. There once was a beautiful kingdom. But it was stolen by the evil one. Its glory has been marred. Badly. Now it's time for the true king to come back and take over. But Simba—the lion heir to the throne—doesn't believe who he is. His father was murdered when he was young, and the enemy blamed it on Simba. Simba ran away, and after years of losing heart, he winds up living with a wart hog and a meerkat whose highest ambitions in life are breakfast, lunch, and dinner. Then, one night, Simba's father appears to him in a vision:

MUFASA: Simba.

SIMBA: Father?

MUFASA: Simba, you have forgotten me.

SIMBA: No! How could I?

MUFASA: You have forgotten who you are, and so forgotten me. Look inside yourself, Simba . . . you are more than what you have become.

SIMBA: How can I go back? I'm not who I used to be.

MUFASA: Remember who you are. You are my son, and the one true king. Remember who you are.

Simba finally throws off the veil of shame and self-reproach and goes back to take the kingdom that is rightly his. As a result, his glory and the glory of the realm are restored. Something similar happens toward the end of *The Matrix*. Neo joins the forces seeking to set the world free. He has left behind the identity of Thomas Anderson, computer guy, nobody special really. He's taken many risks, lived by faith. But the real moment of his glory comes when he finally turns to face his enemy. Up to this point everyone has run from the "agents," who are symbols of the demonic. John writes in his first epistle, "You, dear children, are from God and have overcome them, because the one who is in you is greater than the one who is in the world . . . The whole world is under the control of the evil one" (1 John 4:4; 5:19). No one has challenged them; no one has taken them on. As Neo turns to confront evil incarnate, his friends are watching, incredulous, afraid.

> TRINITY: What's he doing?
> MORPHEUS: He's beginning to believe.

What is he beginning to believe? *Who he really is.*

YOUR TRUEST SELF

> Then from on high—somewhere in the distance
> There's a voice that calls—remember who you are
> If you lose yourself—your courage soon will follow
> So be strong tonight—remember who you are
> (Gavin Greenaway and Trevor Horn, *Sound the Bugle*)

You are going to need your whole heart in all its glory for this Story you've fallen into. You'll need every ounce of courage and faith and love you can muster. So, who did God mean when he meant you? We at least know this: we know that we are not what we were meant to be. Most of us spend our energy trying to hide that fact, through all the veils we put on and the false selves we create. Our first parents thought they could hide behind fig leaves and in the bushes, and we do the same—only with more sophistication. Far better to spend our energy trying to recover the image of God and unveil it for his glory. One means that will help us is any story that helps us see with the eyes of the heart. Which brings us back to myth. Poet David Whyte says, "Myths reveal to us what we are capable of." Clyde Kilby offers this image: "Myth is a lane down which we walk in order to repossess our soul." Wow! Wouldn't you love to repossess your soul? To live with an unmasked, unveiled glory that reflects the glory of the Lord? That's worth fighting for.

The Bible is filled with characters—I don't mean people playing parts; I mean the word your grandmother uses for your grandfather, who at the age of eighty-seven just got himself his fourth speeding ticket in a month. "He's a real character." Or as you say of those folks who wear hats or sing loud or walk to the beat of a drummer nobody else is hearing. Abraham is a character; so is his wife, Sarah. King David is a character. The disciples of Jesus are all characters. Take James and John, for instance, "the sons of Zebedee." You might remember them as the ones who cornered Jesus to angle for the choice seats at his right and left hands in the kingdom. Or the time they wanted to call down fire from heaven to destroy a village that wouldn't offer Jesus a place for the night. Their buddies call them idiots; Jesus calls them the Sons of Thunder (Mark 3:17). He sees who they *really* are. It's their mythic name, their true identity. They look like fishermen out of work; they are actually the Sons of Thunder.

There are stories that you've loved; there are characters that you've resonated with down deep inside, maybe even dreamed that you could be. Do you know why? Deep is calling unto deep. They spoke to you—they speak even now—because they contain some hint or glimpse into your true self. My friend Bethann paused, then said, "Really? Could it really be that there is a hidden greatness in me?" Myth is how we discover it. Rolland Hein explains, "Whether or not people are aware of the fact, they cannot live without myth, nor can they reach full stature as people without true myths."

WHAT OUR MYTHS REVEAL

Taped across the top of my computer, just above the screen on which I am now typing this sentence, I've pasted another: "*Ego numquam pronunciare mendacium, sed ego sum homo indomitus.*" It's Latin, for those of you, like me, who don't know their Latin, a line from the movie *Braveheart.* Translated, it means "I never tell lies, but I am a savage." And there's a lot of story behind it. Personal myth. Like all stories, this one starts way back in my youth. As a young boy, I used to make up lies about myself because I didn't think there was anything special or worthy about the real me. I told my friends I was part Indian, or a robber by night, or a motorcycle racer. I made up a glory because I was convinced I had none of my own.

Fast-forward to last summer when I led a group of friends into the Wimunche Wilderness on a backpacking expedition. We were on a sort of mission. *Wild at Heart* (a book I wrote about men recovering their masculine soul) had just come out that spring, and we were sort of living it out each day. In the morning, I'd suggest a question to wrestle with, pray about as we sweated our way through the wilderness. After dinner in the evening, we'd share our thoughts and stories around the campfire, and so we processed our lives against the book. Or vice versa. On the fourth day of the trip, as we broke camp in the woods near Twin Lakes, I suggested that the issue for the day was simply this: God, who am I? What do you think of me? What's my real name?

This was The Question, the coveted question, the one we all wanted to ask on day one but knew it wouldn't come until we'd wrestled with other business, like the father wound and the role of the Woman in our lives. We had to sort of earn the right to ask this question, and after what we'd been through the day before, it seemed we'd paid our dues. (We'd lost the trail and took a three-mile detour through dense, leg-thrashing, face-lashing willows, which the elk seemed to have no trouble penetrating until I realized their legs are two feet longer than ours. We took the whole mess head-on for hours under the afternoon sun.)

Now, the day after, hoisting our packs, we headed out to cross a high pass and then down a long valley to another unknown camp. It started raining about ten minutes later, and the wind really whipped up as we climbed above the tree line. All was wetness and heather and rock and crag . . . and I was *loving* it. It reminded me of the Scottish Highlands in *Braveheart;* I felt I was hiking in a mythic reality. Then I remembered the day's mission, and I began to ask God one of the most important questions any of us will ever ask: *What do you think of me, God? Who am I to you?* The guys were strung out over a mile or two along the trail by now, and I was alone and just reaching the pass.

You are my Wallace.

Something in my heart sank. Yes, sank. *Good grief, John—look at you. You're pathetic. You're making up the voice of God. Filling in the blanks. Cooking up what you'd want him to say.* Whether or not it was the voice of God, it took only about ten seconds to shut it down with a generous dose of heartache for wanting to hear something like this ever since I was young, and contempt for thinking I'd stepped in for God to pronounce the name, and self-reproach for not being willing to just hike awhile in silence and let God speak for himself. At about this point some of the guys caught up to me, and we stopped to snap a few photos at the pass. Then we headed down.

We reached camp with about an hour to spare before the dinner chores, so I took a walk by myself out into the meadow. No, that's not exactly right. I left camp because I felt *summoned*. I knew God was waiting for me, there at the end of the day, just like a father or a friend, unwilling to let the matter slip away. As I began to tune in to my heart once more, I heard him ask me a question. (Just so you don't think I'm schizophrenic, entertaining voices, let me remind you that the heart has become the new dwelling place of God, and it is in the heart that we hear his voice. I'll say more on that in a minute.) God's question to me felt unrelated to the event at the pass.

> *Tell me what you love.*
>
> *Oh. Well . . . I loved the hike this morning. The wind and the rain and wildness of it all. The Highlands.* [Did I just say *Highlands?*]
>
> *Go on.*
>
> *Well, I love this sort of expedition too. I love leading a band of men.*
>
> *Is there anything else?* [Each question felt like it was taking me deeper into my own heart.]
>
> *I love fighting for people's freedom.*
>
> There was a moment of silence.
>
> *Are you convinced?*

God took me into the truth of the mythic name through the doorway of my own heart and my desires. I was trapped; there was no denying now that it was God who spoke that morning. I was forced to wrestle with the fact that what he spoke was true. Over the past year I have needed that mythic name and all the strength and courage it offers. The battle has been ugly, and there are many hearts to free. The Accuser laughs and mocks and throws everything he can: "You are making this up. You are a weak little man." *Ego numquam pronunciare mendacium, sed ego sum homo indomitus.* I never tell lies, but I am a savage.

EMBRACING THE GLORY

> Our deepest fear is not that we are inadequate. Our deepest fear is that we are powerful beyond measure. It is our light, not our darkness, that most frightens us. We ask ourselves, "Who am I to be brilliant, gorgeous, talented and fabulous?" Actually, who are you not to be? You are a child of God. Your playing small doesn't serve the world. There's nothing enlightened about shrinking so that other people won't feel insecure around you. We were born to manifest the glory of God that is within us . . . And as we let our own light shine, we unconsciously give other people permission to do the same. As we are liberated from our own fear, our presence automatically liberates others. (Nelson Mandela)

When I first read this quote, I thought, *No, that's not true.* We don't fear our glory. We fear we are not glorious at all. We fear that at bottom, we are going to be revealed as . . . disappointments. Mandela is just trying to make a nice speech, like a sermon, to buoy us up for a day or two. But as I thought about it more, I realized we *do* fear our glory. We fear even heading this direction because, for one thing, it seems prideful. Now pride is a bad thing, to be sure, but it's not prideful to embrace the truth that you bear the image of God. Paul says it brings glory to God. We walk in humility because we know it is a glory *bestowed*. It reflects something of the Lord's glory.

The deeper reason we fear our own glory is that once we let others see it, they will have seen the truest us, and that is nakedness indeed. We can repent of our sin. We can work on our "issues." But there is nothing to be "done" about our glory. It's so naked. It's just there—the truest us. It is an awkward thing to shimmer when everyone else around you is not, to walk in your glory with an unveiled face when everyone else is veiling his. For a woman to be truly feminine and beautiful is to invite suspicion, jealousy, mis-understanding. A friend confided in me, "When you walk into a room, every woman looks at you to see—are you prettier than they are? Are you a threat?"

And that is why living from your glory is the only loving thing to do. You cannot love another person from a false self. You cannot love another while you are still hiding. How can you help them to freedom while you remain captive? You cannot love another unless you offer her your heart. It takes courage to live from your heart. My friend Jenny said just the other day, "I desperately want to be who I am. I don't want the glory that I marvel at in others anymore. I want to be that glory which God set in me."

Finally, our deepest fear of all . . . we will need to live from it. To admit we do have a new heart and a glory from God, to begin to let it be unveiled and embrace it as true—that means the next thing God will do is ask us to live from it. Come out of the boat. Take the throne. Be what he meant us to be. And that feels risky . . . really risky. But it is also exciting. It is coming fully alive. My friend Morgan declared, "It's a risk worth taking."

> But I can cry—
> O Enemy, the maker hath not done;
> One day thou shalt behold, and from the sight wilt run.
> (George MacDonald)

PART THREE

THE FOUR STREAMS

Did you feel the darkness tremble?
When all the saints joined in one song
And all the streams flow as one river
To wash away our brokenness.

—Martin Smith, "Did You Feel
the Mountains Tremble?"

From Eden a river flowed to water the park, which on leaving the park branched into four streams.

—Genesis 2:10 (Moffatt)

In the Garden known as Eden there was a spring. Issuing from the depths of the earth, this fount became the headwaters of a mighty river, which in turn parted into four great streams. Saint Bonaventure saw in that a foreshadowing, a mythic symbol of "an ever-flowing fountain," as he called it, "that becomes a great and living river with four channels to water the garden of the entire Church." I think if you will look again at the ways in which Christ ransoms people, the *means* by which he makes a man or a woman come fully alive, you'll find he offers his life to us through Four

Streams. Those streams are Discipleship, Counseling, Healing, and Warfare.

The *terms* might sound familiar; but for so many of us they are familiar in the way that we've heard Saturn has rings around it or that Antarctica is a frozen continent. Our actual *experience* of the Four Streams is not what it could be . . . if it were, we would be "the glorious ones" by now (Ps. 16:3). It will help to think of them as walking with God, Receiving God's Intimate Counsel, Deep Restoration, and Spiritual Warfare.

Long have these streams been separated. I imagine we've sipped from only one or two. Now is the time for them to flow together again. That is how our glory is restored, how we find the life Christ offers, how we live in his Story. To discover for yourself that the glory of God *is* man fully alive, you must drink deeply from the Four Streams that Christ sends to you.

CHAPTER SIX

WALKING WITH GOD

Narrow the road that leads to life, and only a few find it.

—JESUS (MATT. 7:14)

You have made known to me the path of life.

—KING DAVID (PS. 16:11)

After the Road had run down some way, and had left Bree-hill standing tall and brown behind, they came on a narrow track that led off towards the North. "This is where we leave the open road and take to cover," said Strider.

"Not a 'short cut' I hope," said Pippin. "Our last short cut through woods nearly ended in disaster."

"Ah, but you had not got me with you then," laughed Strider. "My cuts, short or long, don't go wrong." He took a look up and down the Road. No one was in sight; and he led the way quickly down towards the wooded valley . . .

Strider guided them confidently among the many crossing paths, although left to themselves they would soon have been at a loss. He was taking a wandering course with many turns and doublings, to put off any pursuit . . . Whether because of Strider's skill or for some other reason, they saw no sign and heard no sound of any other living thing all that day . . .

They had not gone far on the fifth day when they left the last straggling pools and reed-beds of the marshes behind them. The land before them began steadily to rise again. Away in the distance eastward they could now see a line of hills. The highest of them was at the right of the line and a little separated from the others. It had a conical top, slightly flattened at the summit. "That is Weathertop," said Strider . . .

They stood for a while silent on the hill-top, near its southern edge. In that lonely place Frodo for the first time fully realized his homelessness and danger. He wished bitterly that his fortune had left him in the quiet and beloved Shire. He stared down at the hateful Road, leading back westward—to his home. Suddenly he was aware that two black specks were moving slowly along it, going westward; and looking again he saw that three others were creeping eastward to meet them. He gave a cry and clutched Strider's arm. "Look," he said, pointing downwards. At once Strider flung himself on the ground behind the ruined circle, pulling Frodo down beside him. Merry threw himself alongside.

Slowly they crawled up to the edge of the ring again, and peered through a cleft between two jagged stones. The light was no longer bright, for the clear morning had faded . . . neither Frodo nor Merry could make out their shapes for certain; yet something told them that there, far below, were Black Riders assembling on the Road beyond the foot of the hill. "Yes," said Strider, whose keener sight left him in no doubt. "The enemy is here!" (J. R. R. Tolkien, *The Fellowship of the Ring*)

GUIDED

I was downstairs early one Tuesday morning in September, a cold and foggy morning, with a blanket wrapped around me as I read, trying to capture some moments with God before the whirlwind of the day swept upon me, when I came across a passage on forgiveness. Now, I think you'll know what I mean when I say it seemed to "speak" louder or more clearly than everything else I had been reading. I could not pass on. I tried to, but I sensed that the Spirit of God was saying, *Go back to that passage—linger there.* I tried to read ahead . . . but everything after was stale. I went back and read the passage over. There it was again, that tang, that prompt, that sense of *This is what I want you to pay attention to.* The passage was warning about the dangers of an unforgiving heart, how damaging it can be.

> *Am I an unforgiving person, Lord? Is that what you are trying to say?*

> *No . . . I am warning you. Remember this. You are going to need to be forgiving.*

In less than an hour I received a phone call that can only be described in terms of Betrayal. It was devastating. Some allies we had asked to help us with a project very dear to us announced they were quitting—changing horses midstream, walking away from the battle just as it was getting hot. I was stunned, speechless. It was so out of the blue, so *unlike* them, I did not know what to say. The injury was doubled by an attempt to fix the blame on us; it was because of *our* attitudes that they had chosen to abandon ship.

Dumbfounded, blindsided, I knew this much: *This cannot bring happiness to God.* I asked if there was any way to make amends. No. Was there anything we could do to patch things up? No. As I probed the matter further, earnestly seeking a way to rebuild the friendship, their story grew increasingly thin and contradictory. They were walking away. Period. And it was *our* fault.

As the news settled in, I wanted to get angry. I was hurt. Run through with a sword. Then, like some wolf in the night sniffing at my door, I could feel Resentment trying to get in. After all, it seemed a completely justifiable response. Just as I was lifting the latch, I remembered the Lord's warning. *Oh . . . this is what you meant. Forgive.* I barred the door, refused to let Resentment in. Ten minutes later, as our conversation continued the way of the Paris Peace Talks, something else came scrounging for admittance; I was tempted to turn to Self-Reproach. Even though I really didn't think we'd done anything to earn such a betrayal, I was willing to own it nonetheless. *No . . . this is not your fault. Simply forgive them.* After more than an hour, the conversation was clearly at an impasse. Their position was making me madder than ever; I wanted to go to Pride. We were clearly in the right. *No, do not turn to Pride. Simply forgive them.*

I hung up the phone, exhausted. Then I had to call a number of closely involved parties and do my best to give a gracious and impartial account of what happened, trying to honor their stated reasons, trying to own our part in the divorce. Each new conversation brought another round of emotion: Betrayal, and with it Anger, Hurt, Resentment, Indignation, False Guilt—the whole nasty menagerie, like a pack of hungry coyotes circling the camp. *Simply forgive them.* Bar the door. Every other emotion, every other reaction felt dangerous, loaded with some further evil. Falling into bed that night, I felt as though I'd been guided by some wise Ranger like Aragorn through a dark forest, with a hundred wrong turns at every side. I felt *rescued*.

My journals are full of such stories. There must be hundreds, maybe close to a thousand by now. God has gotten me out of all sorts of tight spots—saved my life more than once, literally. He's also guided me into all sorts of beautiful surprises and adventures.

Now, it could be that I'm just a slow learner, and God is being specially gracious to a man who needs a little extra help. Lord knows, I do. But I don't think he speaks to me any more than others; I think I've just learned to expect it, need it, keep an eye out for it. It's a whole different perspective on how we approach our day. Either we wake to tackle our "to do" list, get things done, guided by our morals and whatever clarity we may at the moment have (both rather lacking to the need, I might add). Or we wake in the midst of a dangerous Story, as God's intimate ally, following him into the unknown.

If you're not pursuing a dangerous quest with your life, well, then, you don't need a Guide. If you haven't found yourself in the midst of a ferocious war, then you won't need a seasoned Captain. If you've settled in your mind to live as though this is a fairly neutral world and you are simply trying to live your life as best you can, then you can probably get by with the Christianity of tips and techniques. Maybe. I'll give you about a fifty-fifty chance. But if you intend to live in the Story that God is telling, and if you want the life he offers, then you are going to need more than a handful of principles, however noble they may be. There are too many twists and turns in the road ahead, too many ambushes waiting only God knows where, too much at stake. You cannot possibly prepare yourself for every situation. Narrow is the way, said Jesus. How shall we be sure to find it? We need God intimately, and we need him desperately.

"You have made known to me the path of life," David said (Ps. 16:11). Yes—that's it. In all the ins and outs of this thing we call living, there is one narrow path to life, and we need help finding it.

What Is Discipleship?

On the other hand, there is what we have come to accept as discipleship. A friend of mine recently handed me a program from a large and successful church somewhere in the Midwest. It's a rather exemplary model of what the idea has fallen to. Their plan for discipleship involves, first, becoming a member of this particular church. Then they encourage you to take a course on doctrine. Be "faithful" in attending the Sunday morning service and a small group fellowship. Complete a special course on Christian growth. Live a life that demonstrates clear evidence of spiritual growth. Complete a class on evangelism. Consistently look for opportunities to evangelize. Complete a course on finances, one on marriage, and another on parenting (provided that you are married or a parent). Complete a leadership training course, a hermeneutics course, a course on spiritual gifts, and another on biblical counseling. Participate in missions. Carry a significant local church ministry "load."

You're probably surprised that I would question this sort of program; most churches are trying to get their folks to complete something like this, one way or another. No doubt a great deal of helpful information is passed on. My goodness, you could earn an MBA with less effort. But let me ask you: A program like this—does it teach a person how to apply principles, or how to walk with God? They are not the same thing. Change the content and any cult could do this. I mean, Gandhi was a remarkable man; so was Lao-tzu, Confucius, or Thomas Jefferson. They all had *principles* for a better life. But only Christianity can teach you to walk with God.

We forfeit that birthright when we take folks through a discipleship program whereby they master any number of Christian precepts and miss the most important thing of all, the very thing for which we were created: intimacy with God. There are, after all, those troubling words Jesus spoke to those who were doing all the "right" things: "Then I will tell them plainly, 'I never knew you'" (Matt 7:23). Knowing God. That's the point.

You might recall the old proverb: "Give a man a fish and you feed him for a day; teach a man to fish and you feed him for a lifetime." The same holds true here. Teach a man a rule and you help him solve a problem; teach a man to walk with God and you help him solve the rest of his life. Truth be told, you couldn't master enough principles to see you safely through this Story. There are too many surprises, ambiguities, exceptions to the rule. Things are hard at work—is it time to make a move? What *has* God called you to do with your life? Things are hard at home—is this just a phase your son is going through, or should you be more concerned? You can't seem to shake this depression—is it medical or something darker? What does the future hold for you—and how should you respond?

Only by walking with God can we hope to find the path that leads to life. *That* is what it means to be a disciple. After all—aren't we "followers of Christ"? Then by all means, let's actually *follow* him. Not ideas about him. Not just his principles. Him.

By Wisdom

A personal walk with God comes to us through wisdom and revelation. You will soon discover that we need both.

For a moment the King's grief and anger were so great that he could not speak. Then he said: "Come, friends. We must go up river and find the villains who have done this, with all the speed we may. I will not leave one of them alive." "Sire, with a good will," said Jewel. But Roonwit said, "Sire, be wary in your just wrath. There are strange doings on foot. If there should be rebels in arms further up the valley, we three are too few to meet them. If it would please you to wait while . . ." "I will not wait the tenth part of a second," said the King. "But while Jewel and I go forward, do you gallop as hard as you may to Cair Paravel . . . we must go on and take the adventure that comes to us." "It is the only thing left for us to do, Sire," said the Unicorn. He did not see at the moment how foolish it was for two of them to go on alone; nor did the

King. They were too angry to think clearly. But much evil came
of their rashness in the end. (C. S. Lewis, *The Last Battle*)

King Tirian of Narnia has a good heart. But he also has an
unwise heart—an untrained heart. I'd say that's true for most of us.
Our heart has been made good by the work of Christ, but we
haven't learned how to live from it. Young and naive it remains. It's
as though we've been handed a golden harp or a shining sword.
Even the most gifted musician still has to take lessons; even the
bravest of warriors must be trained. We are unfamiliar, unpracticed
with the ways of the heart. This is actually a very dangerous part of
the journey. Launching out with an untrained heart can bring
much hurt and ruin, and afterward we will be shamed back into the
gospel of Sin Management, having concluded that our heart is
bad. It isn't bad; it's just young and unwise. The poet George
Herbert warned,

> Go not abroad at every quest or call
>   of an untrained hope or passion.

When the apostles needed the help of some good men to shepherd the exploding new church, they chose men "full of the Spirit
and wisdom" (Acts 6:3). The two go together; we need both. We
need to walk by the inspiration of the Spirit, and we need wisdom
as well. Wisdom and revelation. Early on in our journey, I think we
should lean more into wisdom. It takes time to learn to walk with
God in a deeply intimate way, and many challenges face us before
we are accustomed to the way of the heart. We must practice our
chords; we must do our drills.

> For the waywardness of the simple will kill them,
>   and the complacency of fools will destroy them;

but whoever listens to me will live in safety
and be at ease, without fear of harm . . .
Then you will understand what is right and just
and fair—every good path.
For wisdom will enter *your heart*,
and knowledge will be pleasant to your soul.
Discretion will protect you,
and understanding will guard you. (Prov. 1:32–33; 2:9–11, emphasis added)

A friend of mine wanted to teach English as a second language in an Asian country as a way of becoming a sort of undercover missionary. A beautiful dream, one that I'm sure she would have been excellent in fulfilling. But she rushed to the field unprepared in many ways. I don't mean finances and language skills; I mean in the ways of the heart. Lurking down in her soul were some deep and unresolved issues that would set her up for a fall: among them shame and guilt from an abusive past. The team she joined was totally unfamiliar with the new heart, and they doubted its goodness; as with too many Christian ministries, shame and guilt were often used as motivators. Their old covenant theology would play right into Susan's issues, shut down her young heart. Finally, she was unpracticed in spiritual warfare, ill-equipped for what hell would throw at her. The devil is a master at shame and guilt. She went; she got hammered; she came home, defeated. Her friends wonder if she'll ever try it again.

The disaster could have been avoided. Wisdom was crying out: do not rush the field (Luke 14:31); train yourself to discern good and evil (Heb. 5:14); live as though your life is at stake, and the enemy is waiting to outwit you (Matt. 10:16). God has given us all sorts of counsel and direction in his written Word; thank God, we have it written down in black and white. We would do well to be familiar with it, study it with all the intensity of the men who studied the maps of the Normandy coastline before they hit the beaches on D-Day. The more that wisdom enters our hearts, the more we will be able to trust our hearts in difficult situations. Notice that wisdom is not cramming our heads with principles. It is developing a discerning *heart*. What made Solomon such a sharp guy was his wise and discerning heart (1 Kings 3:9).

We don't seek wisdom because it's a good idea; we seek wisdom because we're dead if we don't. We seek wisdom because the trail is narrow and hard to find. It is a cruel thing to tell someone to follow her dreams without also warning her what hell will come against her. High school and college commencement speeches are full of such naïveté. Reach for the stars; follow your dreams; find yourself. It's not that the advice is bad; it is, however, woefully inadequate. That's like a thirteen-year-old falling in love. Her motives may be lovely, but she is in for a painful fall. Will she ever love again with such abandon?

AND REVELATION

Wisdom is crucial. But wisdom is not enough. Many well-meaning evangelicals rely on it exclusively. That is why their lives remain where they are—rather short of all Christ promised. Okay—way short. Wisdom is essential . . . and insufficient.

Saul of Tarsus was headed to Damascus, "breathing out murderous threats against the Lord's disciples," with official documents granting him permission to arrest all Christians in the city and have them sent to prison (Acts 9:1–2). Now, you and I know that Jesus changed Saul's agenda radically before he ever reached the city— the blinding light, the voice from heaven, the total realignment of his worldview. But the believers in Damascus don't know all this. As they wait in fear for Saul's arrival, God speaks to one of them, a man named Ananias, and tells him to go to the house where Saul is staying, lay hands on him, and pray for him. Understandably, Ananias suggests this is not such a good idea: "Lord . . . I have heard many reports about this man and all the harm he has done to your saints in Jerusalem. And he has come here with authority from the chief priests to arrest all who call on your name" (9:13–14). It's okay, God says, he's my man now. Against wisdom Ananias goes, and the greatest of all the apostles is launched.

The Bible is full of such counterintuitive direction from God. Would you counsel a father to sacrifice his only child, the only hope for the promised nation? Certainly, it wasn't wisdom that compelled a fugitive to walk back into the country where he was wanted for murder, a land where all his kin were held as slaves, march into Pharaoh's palace and demand their release. Was it reasonable to take a fortified city by marching around it blowing trumpets? What's the sense of slashing the ranks of your army from 32,000 to 300, just before battle? It was dangerous advice, indeed, to send the young maiden before her king unbidden, and even worse to send a boy against a trained mercenary. And frankly, it looked like perfect madness for Jesus to give himself up to the authorities, let himself get killed.

Somewhere in our hearts I think we'd all love to have a role like that, be used by God so dramatically. To find it, wisdom is just not enough—may even hold us *back* from doing the will of God. The particular foolishness of the church in the past century was Reason above all else. The result has been a faith stripped of the supernatural, the Christianity of tips and techniques. The commonsense life, which, as Oswald Chambers warned, can be the enemy of the supernatural life. Many of the ministries and churches I've known made their decisions by principles and expedience. We have our morals and we have our precepts, but where is the living God? How will we hear him call us out of Ur, lead us to our own promised land, bring us through our own Calvary? Putting all our confidence

320 THE FOUR STREAMS

in human reason was naive, and it left us in a very dangerous position. The only way out of this mess is to turn to our Guide, our Captain, to learn to walk with God.

REVELATION: LISTENING FOR HIS VOICE

We begin by assuming that God is still speaking.

An old hymn celebrating the wonderful Scriptures has a line that goes something like this: "What more can he say, than to you he has said?" The implication being that God has said all he has to say to us in the Bible. Period. It sounds orthodox. Except that's not what the Bible says: "I have much more to say to you, more than you can now bear. But when he, the Spirit of truth, comes, he will guide you into all truth" (John 16:12–13). There's more that Jesus wants to say to you, much more, and now that his Spirit resides in your heart, the conversation can continue. Many good people never hear God speak to them personally for the simple fact that they've never been told that he *does*. But he does—generously, intimately. "He who belongs to God hears what God says" (John 8:47).

> The man who enters by the gate is the shepherd of his sheep. The watchman opens the gate for him, and the sheep listen to his voice. He calls his own sheep by name and leads them out. When he has brought out all his own, he goes on ahead of them, and his sheep follow him because they know his voice . . . I am the good shepherd. (John 10:2–4, 11)

You don't just leave sheep to find their way in the world. They are famous for getting lost, attacked by wild animals, falling into some pit, and that is why they must stay close to the shepherd, follow his voice. And no shepherd could be called good unless he personally guided his flock through danger. But that is precisely what he promises to do. He *wants* to speak to you; he wants to lead you to good pasture. Now, it doesn't happen in an instant. Walking with God is a way of life. It's something to be learned; our ability to hear God's voice and discern his word to us grows over time. As Brother Lawrence had it, we "practice the presence of God." We have an eye out for his particular word to us, and we learn as we go along. At first Frodo wasn't sure he could trust Strider; some of his choices seemed unwise. Frodo said, "I was afraid of him at first . . . but I have become very fond of him."

Two years ago we spent a wonderful family vacation at a ranch here in Colorado—horseback riding, campfires, porch swings, home cookin'. It was one of the best weeks we'd had together in a long time. So when it came to making plans for this past summer, it seemed like a no-brainer. We just assumed we'd go back and do it again. Heck, it would be even *better* the second time around because we would be familiar with the place. And wouldn't it be neat to build a family tradition? But as we asked God about it, Stasi and I sensed him saying, *Not this year.* It was hard counsel to accept; everybody wanted to go back. Three times we asked God about it, and each time he said *No.* When the Hayman Fire burned 137,000 acres of Colorado in June, we looked at each other and realized that was the week we would have been at the ranch. It was almost totally engulfed in flames. He made known to us the path of life.

Notice that we must *ask.* And we will sometimes struggle *to* hear and struggle with *what* we hear. But personally, it's worth it. I'm after the path of life—and he alone knows it.

In fact, walking with God is how he led me into the Four Streams. I was sitting upstairs one Saturday morning, having some time with God, when he spoke to me two words: *Jack Hayford.* I paused, waiting to hear what the Lord wanted to say. That was it. Jack Hayford. I said, "Yes, Lord . . . anything else?" Silence. I sort of shrugged it off as my weirdness. A random thought. About an hour later, the phone rang. My friend Joni was calling from the lobby of a conference here in town.

"John, I know this is late notice and it's Saturday and all . . . but I think you're supposed to be at this conference . . . so I bought you a ticket."

I was silent. Truth is, I was bugged. This was my day off.

"Jack Hayford is speaking next," she added.

"I'll be right there."

It was a powerful and balanced talk Jack gave that day, on how we bring the life of Christ to people. As almost a side comment, he said, "All the streams are coming together now in the church—Healing, Counseling, Deliverance, and Discipleship." My heart leapt. *Yes. That's it! That's what we need in order to see people come alive—to see them set free.*

Let me share a more troubling example. In the fall of 2001 I was scheduled to take the gospel to Edinburgh, Scotland, and Dublin, Ireland. It was a mission I felt very called to, and I was very much looking forward to it. Stasi and the boys were coming along. Our flight plan had us departing on September 11. Several weeks beforehand we were impressed that we should leave earlier. As we prayed, we sensed God was saying, *Leave on the tenth.* Against all normal procedures, our agent was able to change our outbound flight. As you know, had we stayed with the eleventh, we wouldn't have gone anywhere. The terrorist attacks of that day shut down all international flights.

I know—the story raises some troubling questions. Why didn't God warn the people aboard the planes that crashed on September 11, 2001? Perhaps he did. God told David not to number the fighting men of Israel; David did anyway and 70,000 men died (1 Chron. 21). There is no searching out the mystery of an event like that. James was martyred; Peter was sprung from jail (Acts 12). We cannot solve the depths of God's work in this world. All we can do is stay very close by his side and listen for his voice, obey his counsel. More depends on it than we know. Those meetings in Scotland and Ireland were remarkable, by the way, and many, many hearts were set free.

PAY ATTENTION TO YOUR HEART

Second, we pay attention to our hearts.

When we set out to hear God's voice, we do not listen as though it will come from somewhere above us or in the room around us. It comes to us from *within,* in the heart, the dwelling place of God. Now, most of us haven't been trained in this, and it's going to take a little practice "tuning in" to all that's going on in there. And there's a lot going on in there, by the way. Many things are trying to play upon the beautiful instrument of the heart. Advertisers are constantly trying to pull on your heartstrings. So is your boss. The devil is a master at manipulating the heart. So are many people— though they would never admit that is what they are doing. How will you know what is compelling you? "Who can map out the various forces at play in one soul?" asked Augustine, a man who was the first to write out the story of listening to his heart. "Man is a great depth, O Lord . . . but the hairs of his head are easier by far to count than . . . the movements of his heart."

This can be distressing at times. All sorts of awful things can seem to issue from your heart—anger, lust, fear, petty jealousies. If you think it's you, a reflection of what's really going on in your heart, it will disable you. It could stop your journey dead in its tracks. What you've encountered is either the voice of your flesh or an attempt of the Enemy to distress you by throwing all sorts of thoughts your way and blaming you for it. You must proceed on this assumption: your heart is good. If it seems that some foul thing is at work there, say to yourself, *Well, then—this is not my heart. My heart is good. I reject this.* Remember Paul in Romans 7? This is not me. *This is not me.* And carry on in your journey. Over time you'll grow familiar with the movements of your heart, and who is trying to influence you there.

We do the same with any counsel or word that presents itself as being from God, but contradicts what he has said to us in his written Word. We walk with wisdom and revelation. When I hear something that seems really unwise, I test it again and again before I launch out. The flesh will try to use your "freedom" to get you to do things you shouldn't do. And now that the Enemy knows you are trying to walk with God and tune in to your heart, he'll play the ventriloquist and try to deceive you there. Any "word" or suggestion that brings discouragement, condemnation, accusation—that is not from God. Neither is confusion, nor any counsel that would lead you to disobey what you do know. Reject it all, and carry on in your journey. Yes, of course, God needs to convict us of sin, warn us of wrong movements in the soul, discipline us for our own good—but the voice of God is never condemning (Rom. 8:1), never harsh or accusing. His conviction brings a desire for repentance; Satan's accusation kills our hearts (2 Cor. 7:10).

Often before I head out on a mission of some sort, I will ask God for his "advance words" to me. It's proven to be a vital part of staying close to him and avoiding disaster. Last fall I was finishing a brutal tour of twenty-eight different trips. As I was heading out for the final engagement—reluctantly, I might add (I asked God to cancel the flight, bring a snowstorm, anything so I didn't have to go)—God said, *Do not give way to cynicism.* I wrote it down in my journal because I forget stuff like this when the forest grows dim and the other voices begin to chatter and chant. But to be honest, I wasn't really sure why he said that.

The trip turned into an ordeal. My flight was delayed; I missed my connection; I missed my ride to the hotel. When I finally got there—around midnight—I hadn't eaten all day. No restaurants were open; I couldn't get to a fast-food joint; the vending machine in the hotel swallowed my last two quarters. The key I was handed led to the last room in the place, overlooking the trash bins. It smelled of thirty years of cigarettes and cheap beer. ("I'm sorry, sir, but the nonsmoking rooms have all been taken. You should have gotten here sooner.") A bare lightbulb hung from the ceiling; the hot water tap didn't work. All sorts of thoughts and impulses began to occur to me: *What a lousy day. Boy, it's great to be in God's service. What a stinking room! This is how this ministry takes care of guests? No wonder nobody wants to come here. I wish I hadn't even come. What a waste of time!* My attitude was going south on a greased pole. Then I remembered God's warning: *Do not give way to cynicism.* Oh. This is what he meant.

I fought cynicism through the hours of the night, battling for my heart. The new day brought a series of beautiful sessions. Rescued again.

STAY CLOSE TO HIS FRIENDS

Third, we get alongside those who walk with God.

I'll say a whole lot more about living in a community that practices the Four Streams later in the book. Put simply, that is what church is supposed to be about. Would that it were. I hope you will find a few folks who walk with God to also walk with you through the seasons of your life. But honesty—and Scripture—forces me to admit they are a rare breed. Few there are who find it. All the more reason for you to make the number less scarce by becoming someone who walks with God and teaches others how.

Look to those who have walked with God down through the ages. Certainly, that is why the Bible is given to us. If God had intended it to be a textbook of doctrine, well, then, he would have written it like one. Oh, yes, we learn many crucial things about doctrine and Christian character in the Scripture, along with a great deal of wisdom. But if you'll flip from cover to cover, you'll notice that it's overwhelmingly a book of stories—tales of men and women who walked with God. Approach the Scriptures not so much as a manual of Christian principles but as the testimony of God's friends on what it means to walk with him through a thousand different episodes. When you are at war, when you are in love, when you have sinned, when you have been given a great gift—this is how you walk with God. Do you see what a different mind-set this is? It's really quite exciting.

And there are those who have walked with God since the canon of Scripture closed. Here is an Athanasius, a Bonaventure, a Julian of Norwich, a Brother Lawrence, an A. W. Tozer—here is how they walked with God. When it comes to time and place, temperament and situation, they could not be more different. Julian lived in a cloister; Tozer lived in Chicago. Athanasius fled to the desert; Lawrence worked in the kitchen. But there is a flavor, a tang, an authenticity to their writings that underlies whatever it is they are trying at the moment to say. Here is someone who knew God, really knew him. This is what it's like to walk with God, and that is what it's like as well.

OTHERWISE . . .

"Most of us are afraid of our guidance, our intuition, our 'hunches,'" warns Agnes Sanford. "We try to close our minds to them, thereby increasing our restlessness and losing the benefit of the heavenly warning that would tell us when and how to pray." My friend Bart is a private pilot. Two weeks ago he flew out to Colorado to take us into a crucial mission of rescuing some of the great warriors of the kingdom. This is the e-mail I received from him afterward:

Had a great flight back to California—a glorious time flying over some of the world's most beautiful country, from the peaks of the San Juans to the depths of the Grand Canyon. But is also very dangerous country to fly over. A loss of flight control would leave few options.

The next day I called maintenance and asked them to take care of a few squawks we identified before I went to Colorado. (The maintenance personnel cleared the safety of the aircraft for this last trip and assured me everything they checked was OK.) As I gave them the airplane to have those items checked again, I asked them something I cannot explain, something I have very seldom thought of and never in the eight years I've owned 17PG have had done. I asked to have the prop balanced. Richard, the manager, said they'd have to send for a specialist to do this, but I said, "Let's have it done."

Yesterday Richard called back. His first words were, "Good call on having the prop balanced. Bart, we found the spinner cracked." (The spinner is the bullet-shaped point in front of the prop.) It is extremely rare for this to occur, and the prop had been replaced just 350 hours ago, which would have yielded this problem at that time. Richard went on to say the points of attachment were cracked almost all the way through the metal, creating a very dangerous situation. If the spinner had detached, it would have been disaster, come right through the windshield. The point of all this is that something or Someone "nudged" me to ask for something to be done on that airplane I have almost never thought of. John, my prayers will be *deliberate* and *often* as I realize how real this battle is going on all around. Thank you for "waking" me to this reality.

Bart

CHAPTER SEVEN

RECEIVING GOD'S
INTIMATE COUNSEL

They dress the wound of my people
as though it were not serious.

—GOD (JER. 6:14)

Let us beware of tinkering with our inner life.

—A. W. TOZER

And being very tired and having nothing inside him, he felt so sorry for himself that the tears rolled down his cheeks. What put a stop to all this was a sudden fright. Shasta discovered that someone or somebody was walking beside him. It was pitch dark and he could see nothing. And the Thing (or Person) was going so quietly that he could hardly hear any footfalls. What he could hear was breathing. His invisible companion seemed to breathe on a very large scale . . .

If the horse had been any good—or if he had known how to get any good out of the horse—he would have risked everything on a breakaway and a wild gallop. But he knew he couldn't make that horse gallop. So he went on at a walking pace and the unseen companion walked and breathed beside him. At last he could bear it no longer. "Who are you?" he said, scarcely above a whisper.

"One who has waited long for you to speak," said the Thing. Its voice was not loud, but very large and deep . . .

"Oh please—please do go away. What harm have I ever done you? Oh, I am the unluckiest person in the whole world!" Once more he felt the warm breath of the Thing on his hand and face. "There," it said, "that is not the breath of a ghost. Tell me your sorrows." Shasta was a little reassured by the breath: so he told how he had never known his real father or mother and had been brought up sternly by the fisherman. And then he told the story of his escape and how they were chased by lions and forced to swim for their lives; and of all their dangers in Tashbaan and about his night among the tombs and how the beasts howled at him out of the desert. And he told about the heat and thirst of their desert journey and how they were almost at their goal when another lion chased them and wounded Aravis. And also, how very long it was since he had had anything to eat.

"I do not call you unfortunate," said the Large Voice. "Don't you think it was bad luck to meet so many lions?" said Shasta. "There was only one lion," said the Voice. "What on earth do you mean? I've just told you there were at least two the first night, and . . ." "There was only one; but he was swift of foot." "How do you know?"

"I was the lion."

And as Shasta gaped with open mouth and said nothing, the Voice continued. "I was the lion who forced you to join with Aravis. I was the cat who comforted you among the houses of the dead. I was the lion who drove the jackals from you while you slept. I was the lion who gave the Horses the new strength of fear for the last mile so that you should reach King Lune in time. And I was the lion you do not remember who pushed the boat in which you lay, a child near death, so that it came to shore where a man sat, wakeful at midnight, to receive you."

"Then it was you who wounded Aravis?"

"It was I."

"But what for?"

"Child," said the Voice, "I am telling you your story, not hers."

(C. S. Lewis, *The Horse and His Boy*)

Our Story

Our life is a story. A rather long and complicated story that has unfolded over time. There are many scenes, large and small, and many "firsts." Your first step; your first word; your first day of school. There was your first best friend; your first recital; your first date; your first love; your first kiss; your first heartbreak. If you stop and think of it, your heart has lived through quite a story thus far. And over the course of that story your heart has learned many things. Some of what you learned is true; much of it is not. Not when it comes to the core questions about your heart and the heart of God. Is your heart good? Does your heart really matter? What has life taught you about that? Imagine for a moment that God is walking softly beside you. You sense his presence, feel his warm breath. He says, "Tell me your sorrows." What would you say in reply?

"And I will ask the Father, and he will give you another Counselor to be with you forever—the Spirit of truth" (John 14:16–17). Come again? How would you feel if your spouse or a friend said to you, "I think you need some counseling, and so I've arranged for it. You start tomorrow; it'll probably take years"? I've got five bucks that says you'd get more than a little defensive. The combination of our pride—*I don't need any therapy, thank you very much*—and the fact that it's become a *profession*—Freud and Prozac and all that—has kept most of us from realizing that, in fact, we do need counseling. All of us. Jesus sends us his Spirit as Counselor; that ought to make it clear. In fact, we apparently need quite a lot of counsel—the Spirit isn't just stopping in to give us a tune-up; not even an annual checkup. He has come to stay.

Remember, the purpose of this thing called the Christian life is that our hearts might be restored and set free. That's the deal. That's what Jesus came to do, by his own announcement. Jesus wants Life for us, Life with a capital *L*, and that Life comes to us through our hearts. But restoring and releasing the heart is no easy project. God doesn't just throw a switch and poof—it's done. He sends his Counselor to walk with us instead. That tells us it's going to be a *process*. All sorts of damage has been done to your heart over the years, all sorts of terrible things taken in—by sin, by those who should have known better, and by our Enemy, who seeks to steal and kill and destroy the image bearers of God. At best, "hope deferred makes the heart sick" (Prov. 13:12). Certainly, there's been a bit of that in your life. "Even in laughter the heart may ache" (Prov. 14:13), which is to say, things may look fine on the outside, but inside it's another story.

We're told to "trust in the LORD" with all our hearts (Prov. 3:5), but frankly, we find it hard to do. Does trust come easily for you? I would *love* to trust God wholeheartedly. Why is it almost second nature to worry about things? We're told to love one another deeply, "from the heart" (1 Peter 1:22), but that's even more rare. Why is it so easy to get angry at, or to resent, or simply to grow indifferent toward the very people we once loved? The answers lie down in the heart. "For it is with your heart that you believe," Paul says (Rom. 10:10). And in Proverbs we read, "The heart of a man is like deep water, but a man of understanding draws it out" (20:5 NASB). Our deepest convictions—the ones that really shape our lives—they are down there somewhere in the depths of our hearts.

You see, we don't really develop our core convictions so much as they develop within us, when we are young. Down deep, in the inmost parts they form, down in deep water, like the shifting of the continental plates. Certainly, we'd reject the more disabling beliefs if we could; but they form when we are vulnerable, without our really knowing it, like a handprint in wet cement, and over time the cement hardens and there you have it. Think of it this way: Have you always known down deep inside, down to the tips of your toes, that *your* heart is good and that *your* heart matters to God? Me neither. No, what we've come to believe about those ultimate issues was handed to us early on, in most cases by our families.

Assaulted from Our Youth

Joseph had a dream, and when he told it to his brothers, they hated him all the more. He said to them, "Listen to this dream I had: We were binding sheaves of grain out in the field when suddenly my sheaf rose and stood upright, while your sheaves gathered around mine and bowed down to it." His brothers said to him, "Do you intend to reign over us? Will you actually rule us?" And they hated him all the more because of his dream and what he had said . . .

Now his brothers had gone to graze their father's flocks near Shechem, and Israel said to Joseph, "As you know, your brothers are grazing the flocks near Shechem. Come, I am going to send you to them . . . See if all is well with your brothers and with the flocks, and bring word back to me" . . .

So Joseph went after his brothers and found them near Dothan. But they saw him in the distance, and before he reached them, they plotted to kill him. "Here comes that dreamer!" they said to each other. "Come now, let's kill him and throw him into one of these cisterns and say that a ferocious animal devoured him. Then we'll see what comes of his dreams." (Gen. 37:5–8, 12–14, 17–20)

Joseph stands out, as we were all meant to stand out, each in his or her own way. Instead of celebrating his glory, his brothers want to destroy it. A common story, I'm sorry to say. The worst blows typically come from family. That's where we start our journey of the heart, and that's where we are most vulnerable. What we learned from our parents and siblings about our heart defines us the rest of our days; it becomes the script we live out, for good or for ill. Cinderella's father calls her "a little stunted kitchen wench which my late wife left behind," and her stepmother sees her as "much too dirty, she cannot show herself!" What do you suppose she learned about her heart from growing up in *that* home?

The reason Cinderella's story has stayed with us so many years is that her story is the story of so many little girls. Listen to my friend Abby:

> The assault started as a young girl. There was something about me that seemed to aggravate my father—something about me. Something that seemed to annoy him and repel him. As I grew older, I only seemed to become more frustrating to him. I would ask him a question about how he was doing, and I would watch as the look of annoyance filled his eyes. And I began to suspect that there was something deeply wrong with me, something that made me unlovable, undesirable, something that was "too much" and "not enough," all at once. I tried endlessly to edit my personality, trying to figure out the "right" way to be, the "right" thing to say in every context, in every relationship. And I lived mostly in fear that I was going to "blow" it, and that at any moment the person I loved was going to turn on me, filled with contempt and disdain.

A little girl longs to know that her daddy delights in her, that she is "daddy's girl." What do scenes like this teach a young heart? Abby concluded there was something wrong with her. Most of us believe that, down deep inside. She learned her heart must be bad; certainly, it's not worth fighting for. And God? Well, her heart mustn't really matter to him, either. After all, he let it happen. He didn't intervene.

> Even after receiving Jesus into my heart, this suspicion of something "dark and wrong" haunted me. I began to find myself especially anxious around animals and children, certain that in their piercing intuition they would sense this darkness in me and my vain attempts to cover it up. And I would be exposed. One time, while horseback riding, my horse knocked me against the limb of the tree. The limb ripped me off my saddle and I tumbled down onto the ground. My eyes filled with hot tears and my heart with waves of self-contempt. The voice within me said, *See, there really is something dark about you. That horse sensed it and he just wanted to get you off of him, whatever it took.*

There is David, whose heart of glory rises like the sun, full of faith and courage when he sees that no one will take on Goliath. Though he is only a youth, untrained for war, he is outraged that an "uncircumcised Philistine" has dared to taunt the armies of the living God. He announces, "Let no one lose heart on account of this Philistine; your servant will go and fight him" (1 Sam. 17:32). David's oldest brother was among the soldiers of Israel who *should* have had the heart to face Goliath but rehearsed his excuses instead. His cowardice is exposed by David's bravery after he lashes out: "Why have you come down here? And with whom did you leave those few sheep in the desert? I know how conceited you are and how wicked your heart is; you came down only to watch the battle" (1 Sam. 17:28). Ah, family.

The worst blows tend to come from those who know us well and should have loved us. In the German myth, Siegfried was a great warrior; he slew a terrible dragon; he was fearless in battle. Siegfried was invincible—except for a small place on his back, between his shoulders. There, he could be wounded. An uncle discovered Siegfried's "weak spot" and murdered him. Stabbed in the back. By family. Small wonder this tale has endured through time.

MISUNDERSTOOD

Even Jesus endured this sort of assault—not the open accusation that he had a wicked heart, but the more subtle kind, the seemingly "innocent" arrows that come through "misunderstanding."

> After this, Jesus went around in Galilee, purposely staying away from Judea because the Jews there were waiting to take his life. But when the Jewish Feast of Tabernacles was near, Jesus' brothers said to him, "You ought to leave here and go to Judea, so that your disciples may see the miracles you do. No one who wants to become a public figure acts in secret. Since you are doing these things, show yourself to the world." For even his own brothers did not believe in him. (John 7:1–5)

I think we can relate to that. Did your family believe in you? Some did—but far too many more believe in the person *they* wanted you to be. Did they even notice your heart at all? Have they been thrilled in your choices, or has their disappointment made it clear that you just aren't what you're supposed to be? At another point in his ministry, Jesus' family shows up to collect him. "Your mother and brothers are standing outside, wanting to see you" (Luke 8:20). They think he's lost it, and they've come to bring him home, poor man. Misunderstanding is damaging, more insidious because we don't identify it as an attack on the heart. How subtly it comes, sowing doubt and discouragement where there should have been validation and support. There must be something wrong with us.

I'm not big on computer games personally. But my eldest son, Sam, is an absolute crackerjack at them. It's a point of tension in our relationship. I don't think he ought to spend so much time there, and he thinks he's not given enough. Though I try to hide my distaste because I know how much he loves playing Off Road Fury and Delta Force, it's pretty obvious when I never play with him. Just yesterday Sam said to me, "You and Mom don't like computer games, so I feel like you don't like me." Ouch. I missed a part of his glory, shamed a part of his heart. How many an artist has been crushed in a family that prefers a "rational" approach to life? How many an engineer dismissed by a family of musicians? How many of us are lost in life simply because no one in our early world saw our glory and affirmed it?

"How long, O men, will you turn my glory into shame?" (Ps. 4:2). These blows aren't random or incidental. They strike directly at some part of the heart, turn the very thing God created to be a source of celebration into a source of shame. And so you can at least begin to discover your glory by looking more closely at what you were shamed for. Look at what's been assaulted, used, abused. As Bernard of Clairvaux declared, "Through the heart's wound, I see its secret."

Let me put it this way: What has life taught you about your God-given glory? What have you believed about your heart over the years? "That it's not worth anyone's time," said a woman. Her parents were too busy to really want to know her. "That it's weak," confided a friend. He suffered several emasculating blows as a boy, and his father simply shamed him for it. "That I shouldn't trust it to anyone." "That it's selfish and self-centered." "That it's bad." And you . . . what have you believed?

Those accusations you heard growing up, those core convictions that formed about your heart, will remain down there until someone comes to dislodge them, run them out of Dodge.

THE WONDERFUL COUNSELOR

None of this was your fault.

I was visiting my parents a year ago last summer, and as you well know, that has a way of stirring the pot, bringing all sorts of debris to the surface. For many people, family is like kryptonite. You remember, the one substance that zapped Superman's strength. It seems that no matter how much we've grown, how long we've been away, how far we've traveled in our own journeys, when we go back to family, we are suddenly children again. All the old dynamics, the patterns, the messages—they're all back, trying to pull us down. So you'll understand when I made up some excuse about running to the market for a few things. I simply had to get out of the house, take a drive. I needed some air.

I drove to the neighborhood of an old girlfriend, my first girl-friend, who years upon years ago broke my heart. The first cut is the deepest, as the saying goes. It wasn't simply what happened with her that I wanted to remember; our breakup happened at the time in my life when everything else was coming down around me like a house of cards. My father's alcoholism. The collapse of my family. When it rains, it pours. I thought I had found in my first love a refuge from all that. And I did . . . for a time. Then she sent me away, for no reason I could find out. All the arrows landed in the same place in my heart: you don't matter; you're not worth fighting for; there's something wrong with you.

For years now I've lived with the fear that at some point, everyone is going to leave, and I will be left alone. For no reason I can say, in no way I can prevent, I am going to wind up alone. I can't really explain why, but I know it's my fault. It lingers there, down under the surface, like a chronic backache or a low-grade fever. But it colors everything I say and do; it shapes every relationship. I remain guarded, distant. I feel I ought to do more, be more. So it becomes a self-fulfilling prophecy. And I'm sick of it.

I parked the car and simply let the tears come, allowed the memories to take me to the place in my heart that was pierced by the loss of those I loved, "loved but did not understand in my youth," as Norman MacLean said. Somehow, being in the old neighborhoods again, smelling all the old familiar smells, hearing the voices of the past, brought this unhealed place to the surface. And Jesus walked softly beside.

None of this was your fault.

Now, you must understand, I didn't know that for all those years I had believed it *was* my fault. I didn't think about it much at all. But down in the deep waters of my soul that conviction had settled, grown, like barnacles on a shipwreck, lies clinging to my heart. *This all happened because my heart is bad; it's my fault.* And down the Spirit went to speak the words to break those lies. *None of this was your fault.* And something of my heart came free that night.

> I'm standing before my old high school.
> It's been ten years since I touched the door.
> But to heal the old pain we must face it again
> so I'll walk down that hallway once more.
> I have come to this ten year reunion
> for my heart is still prisoner of war.
> That's what I came back here for. (David Wilcox, "Last Chance Waltz")

ASK GOD

Peter was one of Jesus' closest friends, one of only three invited into his innermost circle. Christ brought him up to the Mount of

Transfiguration to see his glory unveiled. Only two others got to see this (James and John); the rest of the gang waited at the base. They waited outside the door as well, when Christ went in to raise Jairus's daughter from the dead. But Peter got to come in with him. In Gethsemane, at his hour of greatest need, Jesus again took Peter aside, poured his heart out to him; he looked to Peter for strength. Three years of this, and who knows how many other stories. Peter must have known, *I have a special place in Jesus' heart.* So, how do you suppose Peter felt after he denied Christ—not just once, but three times? It must have been devastating.

After the Resurrection, Jesus is on the beach with Peter and the others. It's a touching reunion. Following a night of lousy fishing, Christ yells out to the guys to let their nets down for a catch—just as he did that morning he first called them. Again, their nets are bursting with the load. Just like the good old days. Peter leaps from the boat and swims to Christ. They have breakfast together. Reunited, laughing about the catch, relaxed, warmed by the fire, and stuffed from breakfast, Jesus then turns to Peter.

> When they had finished eating, Jesus said to Simon Peter, "Simon son of John, do you truly love me more than these?" "Yes, Lord," he said, "you know that I love you." Jesus said, "Feed my lambs." Again Jesus said, "Simon son of John, do you truly love me?" He answered, "Yes, Lord, you know that I love you." Jesus said, "Take care of my sheep." The third time he said to him, "Simon son of John, do you love me?" Peter was hurt because Jesus asked him the third time, "Do you love me?" He said, "Lord, you know all things; you know that I love you." Jesus said, "Feed my sheep." (John 21:15–17)

What a beautiful story. Notice first that Christ does not let Peter sweep the whole matter under the rug. If this issue isn't addressed, it will haunt the old fisherman for the rest of his life. A nagging guilt will make it hard to pray. That sense of *Who are you kidding?* will be there every time Peter tries to tell others about Jesus. No, this must be spoken to. Most of us simply try to "put things behind us," get past it, forget the pain as quickly as we can. Really—denial is a favorite method of coping for many Christians. But not with Jesus. He wants truth in the inmost being, and to get it there he's got to *take us into* our inmost being. One way he'll do this is by bringing up an old memory. You'll be driving down the road and suddenly remember something from your childhood. Or maybe you'll have a dream about a long-forgotten person, event, or place. However he brings it up, go with him there. He has something to say to you.

Notice also that Jesus asks Peter the penetrating question three times—once for every betrayal. Peter is hurt by it, and that is the point. The lessons that have been laid down in pain can be accessed only in pain. Christ must open the wound, not just bandage it over. Sometimes he'll take us there by having an event repeat itself years later, only with new characters in the current situation. We find ourselves overlooked for a job, just as we were overlooked by our parents. Or we experience fear again, just as we felt those lonely nights in our room upstairs. These are all *invitations* to go with him into the deep waters of the heart, uncover the lies buried down there, and bring in the truth that will set us free. Don't just bury it quickly; ask God what he is wanting to speak to.

There are two things we need to know, maybe above all else. We need to know that our heart is good, and that our heart matters to God. I've found that for most folks, this is what's been most assaulted; this is what we most doubt. We can't just talk ourselves into this; Jesus must show us. He must take us there, as he did with Peter. So ask him. Ask God to show you that your heart is good, and that you do matter to him. I recently received this e-mail from a young woman who took my advice:

On Monday, I ventured over to the park for just some time in beauty. The sun was slowly making its way down, and as I watched, my heart just ached to receive what God was whispering: "Karen, yes your heart is good, ever since you let me come in and dwell there . . . but." And I stopped there. It was getting dark, and I had things to do. So I made my way back to my car . . . slowly. A few steps later, I heard God say that He wouldn't let me leave without hearing the rest of it. But I kept walking, until I just couldn't go any further—dang it. I knew that He wanted to be with me in a place that was not comfortable, was not "safe," not in my car where no one could see me. Oh no . . . it had to be there in a public wilderness. For that was part of the freedom that my heart needed—release from trying to "save" face and release from caring so much what people think of me (the lies that killed my heart as a leader in the church).

The tears of grief flowed freely down my face. He began to show me and I let Him. I was reminded of all of the recurring assaults, and with each arrow He spoke to me His shield, "You see, Karen, that lie? That was the assault to keep you from connecting. That lie? That one was to make you fearful and anxious. That brutal arrow? That was to keep you from glorifying ME. Ah . . . but Karen, in the places where those lies targeted . . . your heart was good. It is good." As God spoke, I wept. I've so needed to grieve where my heart has been lost. I've needed to find it! I got mad at the lies and strategies that Satan has used on me. Wow. Little did I know that a huge part of the freedom God has been aching for me to experience would come from asking our Abba to "show me that my heart is good."

I have a number of stories like that as well; they are beautiful and precious to me. It might be one of the hardest and richest things you ever do. Ask God to reveal to you that the new covenant is true. Your heart is good. And your heart matters. Deeply.

THE HELP OF OTHERS

Now I was indeed in a pitiful plight. There was literally nothing in the tower but my shadow and me. The walls rose right up to the roof; in which, as I had seen from without, there was one little square opening. This I now knew to be the only window the tower possessed. I sat down on the floor, in listless wretchedness.

More earnestly than ever, I longed for freedom; more drearily than ever, crept on the next wretched day. I measured by the sunbeams, caught through the little window in the trap of my tower, how it went by, waiting only for the dreams of night.

About noon, I started as if something foreign to all my senses and all my experience had suddenly invaded me; yet it was only the voice of a woman singing. My whole frame quivered with joy, surprise, and the sensation of the unforeseen. Like a living soul, like an incarnation of Nature, the song entered my prison-house. Each tone folded its wings, and laid itself, like a caressing bird, upon my heart. It bathed me like a sea; enrapt me like an odorous vapor; entered my soul like a long draught of clear spring water; shone upon me like essential sunlight; soothed me like a mother's voice and hand.

Hardly knowing what I did, I opened the door. Why had I not done so before? I do not know. At first I could see no one; but when I forced myself past the tree which grew across the entrance, I saw, seated on the ground and leaning against the tree, with her back to my prison, a beautiful woman. She looked up at me and smiled. "Ah! Were you the prisoner there? I am very glad I have wiled you out." (George MacDonald, *Phantastes*)

I want to be careful, lest I have painted a wrong picture here. This stream of Counseling doesn't just flow to us directly from Christ, *only* from him. It flows through his people as well. We need others—and need them deeply. Yes, the Spirit was sent to be our Counselor. Yes, Jesus speaks to us personally. But often he works through another human being. The fact is, we are usually too close to our lives to see what's going on. Because it's *our* story we're trying to understand, we sometimes don't know what's true or false, what's real and imagined. We can't see the forest for the trees. It often takes the eyes of someone to whom we can tell our story, bare our souls. The more dire our straits, the more difficult it can be to hear directly from God.

In every great story the hero or heroine must turn to someone older or wiser for the answer to some riddle. Dorothy seeks the Wizard; Frodo turns to Gandalf; Neo has Morpheus; and Curdie is helped by the Lady of the Silver Moon. Several years ago there was a woman who wiled me out of my prison, a prison of my own making. It was in my final year of graduate studies for a degree in counseling. Naturally, I thought by this time I pretty much had it all together. Why, I was about to become a professional counselor. Danger sign number one. Pride is so blinding. Her name was Joy, and she was . . . eventually. But first she had to cut through my facade.

As a part of our course requirement, we had to meet with a graduate assistant for an hour each week. This being a Christian program, I thought she would go after my sin. Instead, she went after my glory. No one had ever done that before.

"Why are you holding back?" she asked.

I hesitated, stalled. "I'm not sure what you're talking about."

"Yes, you do. You are holding back, playing it safe."

I was squirming. Is this what Adam felt as he heard the voice of God coming closer to his hiding place in the bushes? *Where are you?*

"Now, you're gifted enough to pull it off, make it *look* like you're engaged with us. But you are running on only six cylinders; I know you have eight. Come forward and lead us."

It was more than a little unnerving. I'd been seen; I'd been found out. But not as a disappointment, not as a bad heart exposed. Rather, it was my glory that had been seen, and it was being asked for. What do you do with *that*?

Over the course of several months my whole system of perfectionism-so-as-not-to-be-seen unraveled. *Maybe* . . . the thought began to creep in . . . *maybe the world has been wrong about me.* "The world has been wrong about you. They've hated your glory— just as the Evil One hates the glory of God. But we need your gift. Come forth." I began to believe the truth, and it set me free. The doctrine I knew—kind of. But having a doctrine pass before the mind is not what the Bible means by knowing the truth. It's only when it reaches down deep into the heart that the truth begins to set us free, just as a key must penetrate a lock to turn it, or as rainfall must saturate the earth down to the roots in order for your garden to grow.

Listen to the rest of Abby's story:

> God has given me a new name, a name that is so perfectly and wondrously opposite of the lie that had controlled so much of my life. And he is healing my heart. A year ago, a wise woman whom I deeply respect was praying for me. She heard God call me "My Sunshine and my delight." *Really . . . really?* My heart responded. *Sunshine? Not darkness? Not object of my contempt?* This was so precious to me, so beyond my wildest hopes for who I was to my God, that I kept it to myself. Over the next several months, two friends wrote to me completely independent of one another, and in their letters they both described that I was like "sunshine" in their lives. Still, I kept this in my heart. Then, my boss and dear friend began to call me "Sunshine." I could barely believe it! And finally, a dear friend saw a painting of a young girl and instantly "recognized" my face in it. The young girl had a

look of confidence and mischief, and utter security in who she was and to whom she belonged. The name of the painting was "Jessica of the Sunlight Ranch."

God was calling to me—God was calling to me to believe that truly I was "his sunshine and his delight." Calling me to believe that there was something beautiful and valiant that he had placed deep within me that my husband, my friends, that this world needs. Calling me to believe that the effect of my life is "goodness and light and *life*"; not darkness and contempt and irritation. And so I've started offering my heart. I've started saying no to the voice of my enemy that calls me to fearfully tone down, edit, control my words and my actions for fear of "offending" or bringing on rejection and shame. Instead, I've been stepping out. I've been sharing what I see of my God and in my friends. I've chosen to offer my presence, my heart, and my love, instead of trying endlessly to figure out what else I should offer. I've chosen to believe I am loved and safe with my God.

"Behold, You desire truth in the innermost being" (Ps. 51:6 NASB). Getting it there is the work of the stream we'll call Counseling—Receiving God's Intimate Counsel.

CHAPTER EIGHT

DEEP RESTORATION

He heals the brokenhearted
    and binds up their wounds.

—PSALM 147:3

Look at me—I'm shattered.

—THE ROLLING STONES

For at that moment a curious little procession was approaching—eleven Mice, six of whom carried between them something on a litter made of branches, but the litter was no bigger than a large atlas. No one has ever seen mice more woebegone than these. They were plastered with mud—some with blood too—and their ears were down and their whiskers drooped and their tails dragged in the grass, and their leader piped on his slender pipe a melancholy tune. On the litter lay what seemed little better than a damp heap of fur; all that was left of Reepicheep. He was still breathing, but more dead than alive, gashed with innu-

merable wounds, one paw crushed, and, where his tail had been,
a bandaged stump.

"Now, Lucy," said Aslan.

Lucy had her diamond bottle out in a moment. Though only
a drop was needed on each of Reepicheep's wounds, the wounds
were so many that there was a long and anxious silence before she
had finished and the Master Mouse sprang from the litter. His
hand went at once to his sword hilt, with the other he twirled his
whiskers. He bowed.

"Hail, Aslan!" (C. S. Lewis, *Prince Caspian*)

A House Divided

Yes, we have all been wounded in this battle. And we will be
wounded again. But something deeper has happened to us than
mere wounds.

I expect that all of us at one time or another have said, "Well,
part of me wants to, and another part of me doesn't." You know
the feeling—part of you pulled one direction, part of you the
other. Part of me loves writing and genuinely looks forward to a
day at my desk. But not all of me. Sometimes I'm also afraid of it.
Part of me fears that I will fail—that I am simply stating what is
painfully obvious, or saying something vital but incoherent. I'm
drawn to it, and I also feel ambivalent about it. Come to think of
it, I feel that way about a lot of things. Part of me wants to go
ahead and dive into friendship, take the risk. I'm tired of living
alone. Another part says, *Stay away—you'll get hurt. Nobody really
cares anyway.* Part of me says, *Wow! Maybe God really is going to
come through for me.* Another voice rises up and says, *You are on
your own.*

Don't you sometimes feel like a house divided?

Take your little phobias. Why are you afraid of heights or intimacy or public speaking? All the discipline in the world wouldn't get you to go skydiving, share something really personal in a small group, or take the pulpit next Sunday. Why do you hate it when people touch you or criticize you? And what about those little "idiosyncrasies" you can't give up to save your life? Why do you bite your nails? Why do you work so many hours? Why do you get irritated at these questions? You won't go out unless your makeup is perfect—why is that? Other women don't mind being seen in their grubbies. Something in you "freezes" when your dad calls—what's that all about? You clean and organize; you demand perfection—did you ever wonder *why*?

I think we've just assumed all that stuff is our battle with "the flesh." And yes, there is a civil war waged between the new heart and the old nature. Romans 7–8 describes it quite well. Part of me doesn't want to love my neighbor—not when his son just backed his car into my Jeep and smashed it up. I want to take the little brat to court. Part of me knows that prayer is essential; another part of me would rather turn on the TV and check out. And that whole bit about being long-suffering—no way. Part of me wants to just get drunk. And that is the part I must crucify daily, give no ground to, make no alliance with. It's not the true me (Rom. 7:22). It's my battle with the flesh. We all know that battle well. But that is not what I'm wanting to explore here.

No, there's something else we are describing when we say, "Well, part of me wants to and part of me doesn't." It's more than a figure of speech. We might not know it, but something really significant is being revealed in those remarks. There are these places that we cannot seem to get beyond. Everything is going along just fine, and then—boom. Something suddenly brings you to tears or makes you furious, depressed, or anxious, and you cannot say why. I'll tell you why.

We are not wholehearted.

BROKENHEARTED

A few years ago a woman pulled me aside to tell me that her marriage was in trouble. Her husband, a kind and patient man, had simply reached his limit with her obsessive-compulsive behavior. Their home was being overrun by puppies—not the live version, but the stuffed little critters. She collected them ravenously, hundreds of doggies, large and small. In fact, she snatched up *anything* that had a puppy on it—plates, pictures, pillows, posters. For several years she was able to contain it to her bedroom, but it had eventually overrun the entire house. Now, I think a stuffed dog or two are probably good things to have around, but having more than a hundred does raise some concerns. Anytime we find ourselves doing something we wish we could stop but cannot, it ought to raise some concerns. For that matter, anytime we find ourselves *unable* to do the very thing we want to do, it also ought to raise some concerns.

She told me that when she was a very young girl of four or five, she had a little toy puppy that was her playmate. You know how that goes—they went everywhere together. The two of them had tea parties. He went to kindergarten in her backpack. He took all the family trips with her. This little puppy—Scruffy was his name—had the place of honor in her bedroom, upon her pillow every night. He was her special friend. That is, until the day her father in a fit of rage ripped the head off Scruffy while she stood crying before him, begging her daddy not to hurt him. It was the kind of blow that shatters a little girl's heart. It's not just about a stuffed animal, of course. The assault brought terror into her relationship with her daddy, cast a shadow over her whole young world, shattered all security. Fifty-some years later, she is unable to make herself stop collecting puppies, and she cannot tell you why.

When Isaiah promised that the Messiah will come to heal the brokenhearted, he was not speaking poetically. The Bible does use metaphor, as in when Jesus says, "I am the gate" (John 10:9). Of course, he is not an *actual* gate like the kind you slammed yesterday; he has no hinges on his body, no knob you turn. He is using metaphor. But when Isaiah talks about the brokenhearted, God is not using metaphor. The Hebrew is *leb shabar* (*leb* for "heart," *shabar* for "broken"). Isaiah uses the word *shabar* to describe a bush whose "twigs are dry, they are broken off" (27:11); to describe the idols of Babylon lying "shattered on the ground" (21:9), as a statue shatters into a thousand pieces when you knock it off the table; or to describe a broken bone (38:13). God is speaking literally here. He says, "Your heart is now in many pieces. I want to heal it."

The heart can be broken—literally. Just like a branch or a statue or a bone. Can you name any precious thing that *can't*? Certainly, we've seen that the mind can be broken—or what are all those mental institutions for? Most of the wandering, muttering "homeless" people pushing a shopping cart along have a broken mind. The will can be broken too. Have you seen photos of concentration camp prisoners? Their eyes are cast down; something in them is defeated. They will do whatever they are told. But somehow we have overlooked the fact that this treasure called the heart can also be broken, *has* been broken, and now lies in pieces down under the surface. When it comes to "habits" we cannot quit or patterns we cannot stop, anger that flies out of nowhere, fears we cannot overcome or weaknesses we hate to admit—much of what troubles us comes out of the broken places in our hearts crying out for relief.

In the case of the woman obsessed with puppies, part of her heart was broken when she was five, and that part of her *remains* young and afraid and desperate for someone to come and protect her, restore her puppy to her. Those aren't the actions of a fifty-something woman; they are the cries of a five-year-old heart. Surely, there are things you do that you cannot provide a reasonable explanation for. Those of you unable to resist a jelly donut—certainly, that is a hunger for more than sweets. Love, perhaps? Comfort? The drive that keeps you late at the office—what is it you are hoping for? Approval? For someone to finally say, "We're so very proud of you"?

I know losing a toy puppy seems rather innocuous, given the horrifying things done to some children. And some of you are thinking, *I wish all I was doing was collecting puppies,* given the dark and dangerous things some people find themselves doing. The mother who passes out in front of her children for love of alcohol. The young man dying of AIDS for the love he's been seeking with other men. But there is something common in all these stories. Something inside is compelling them to do things they do not want to do. What that usually indicates is a broken heart. Those actions are attempts to nurse or repair a rift in the soul.

A fine young man I know is absolutely beside himself with anxiety whenever he begins to care deeply for another person. Now, this is not a man given over to fits of weeping. He is for the most part a fine, upstanding Christian man. But when he draws near to love, this tough construction worker starts to shake all over and cry uncontrollably for reasons he cannot explain. When he was young, his father walked out on him and his mom. It was, as it should have been, devastating. Later on, a girlfriend did the exact same thing to him. Now, he's prayed lots about this; he's had some counseling; he's memorized lots of Scripture on the faithfulness of God and all that. It hasn't changed things. He's still absolutely undone at the approach of possible abandonment. It's like an earthquake in the soul. There's some rift or fault line down there.

Yet another indication of a house divided is the "on again, off again" personality. One day you are kind; the next day you are sullen and angry. One day you are inspired by Christ, captured for his purposes; the next day, you are completely driven by the world. Sure—we all have bad days. Lord knows, PMS and traffic jams can bring on some dramatic changes. But I'm talking about a pattern that is repeated again and again.

I know a man just like that; he's so hard to read, you never know what you're going to get. He'll be completely committed to following Christ one moment, and the next he's watching his stocks and totally absorbed in his businesses. It's not bad to keep an eye on things; but being so totally absorbed to the point that everything else—*everyone* else—suffers, that's not so good. It's like somebody threw a switch inside him. Not a Dr. Jekyll–Mr. Hyde, just a man so completely different depending on what part of his heart he's living out of. He is not wholehearted.

It doesn't take a major assault like sexual abuse to create a broken heart, by the way. This is so important to understand, for many good people assume they haven't any real brokenness because they haven't endured the horrors they read about in the paper or watch on TV. Depending on the age or circumstances, it can be an embarrassing moment like stuttering in front of the class or hearing a harsh word from your mother. The bottom line is, Jesus speaks as though we are all the brokenhearted. We would do well to trust his perspective on this.

THE STREAM OF HEALING OR DEEP RESTORATION

> For this people's heart has become calloused;
>> they hardly hear with their ears,
>> and they have closed their eyes.
> Otherwise they might see with their eyes,
>> hear with their ears,
>> understand with their hearts
> and turn, and I would heal them. (Matt. 13:15)

"And I would heal them." That's a different offer from: "And I would forgive them." It's a different offer from: "And I will give them a place in heaven." No, Jesus is offering *healing* to us. Look at what he does to people who are broken. How does he handle them? The blind are able to see like a hawk. The deaf are able to hear a pin drop. The lame do hurdles. The corroding skin of the leper is cleansed and made new. The woman with the issue of blood stops hemorrhaging. The paralyzed servant hops out of bed. They are, every last one of them, healed. Now follow this closely: everything Jesus *did* was to illustrate what he was trying to *say*. Here—look at this—this is what I'm offering to do for you. Not just for your body, but more important, for your soul. I can heal your heart. I can restore your soul.

> The LORD is my shepherd, I shall not be in want.
>> He makes me lie down in green pastures,
> he leads me beside quiet waters,
>> he restores my soul. (Ps. 23:1–3)

> He heals the brokenhearted
>> and binds up their wounds. (Ps. 147:3)

> Heal me, O LORD, and I will be healed;
>> save me and I will be saved,
>> for you are the one I praise. (Jer. 17:14)

> For you who revere my name, the sun of righteousness will rise with healing in its wings. (Mal. 4:2)

> He welcomed them and spoke to them about the kingdom of God, and healed those who needed healing. (Luke 9:11)

For some reason, this has been lost in much of the recent offerings of Christianity. Perhaps it has been our pride, which has kept us from admitting that we are broken. Lord knows, I've done that for years—probably am still doing it now. Perhaps it is our fear of getting our hopes up; it seems too good to be true. Perhaps it's been the almost total focus on sin and the Cross. But the Scripture is abundant and clear: Christ came not only to pardon us, but also to heal us. He wants the glory restored. So, put the book down for just a moment, and let this sink in: Jesus can, and wants to, heal your heart. What does that rouse in you? Is it hope? Is it cynicism? Is it "I tried that—it doesn't work"?

It was only a few months ago that I woke in the wee hours of the morning to fear . . . again. How many other times had I simply jumped into my day as fast as I could—shower, shave, rush off to work—hounded by a nameless fear, trying to bury it with a heap of busyness? I thought somehow that if I just ran hard enough, it wouldn't catch up to me. Perfectionism was my refuge. But this morning, thank God, was different. I'm tired of running, like the prodigal, I suppose. Sooner or later you're just going to have to turn and face things. I lay there in bed and let the fear rise up, let it come. And as it came, I began to ask a question of both myself and God: *What am I afraid of?* The sense I had was that *I'm going to blow it—badly. I'm about to make a mess of things.* Now, there was nothing in my life at the time on the brink of falling apart. Things were going well. But staying with it, I invited Christ to come into the fear and speak to me there. *Jesus, what is this all about?*

When have you felt like this before?

Two memories came to me. The feeling of *I'm blowing it badly* took me there. The first was the day I got arrested for "breaking and entering," police jargon for robbing a house. I was fifteen years old at the time, spinning out of control, my family falling apart at home. It was a deeply shameful experience, and no one talked to me about it; no one showed me the way out. The second memory came quickly on the heels of the first, as if it had to come now or I'd never let it: the day my girlfriend got an abortion. It might be the most horrifying day of my life. I don't think we really knew what we were doing, but somewhere deeper in my soul I knew whatever was happening, it was really, really bad. That one was so dark I just buried it deep and never, ever spoke of it again.

As each event came back to me, all I could do was invite Jesus in. *Yes, Lord, thank you for bringing this back. Come in and meet me here; speak to me here.* I asked his forgiveness for my part in the burglary and in the abortion. I asked him to come and heal those wounds and bring what was true about my heart *to* my heart. And he did; he counseled me deeply. But that wasn't the end of it. Several weeks later the fear came back. A month after that it came again. There was something broken in me, something that allowed the fear to keep returning, no matter how many comforting things Christ said. I needed a different stream.

A PERSONAL HEALING

A remarkable and unlooked-for healing came to me the same day I nearly killed myself in the Collegiate Peaks Wilderness in Colorado. It was early summer, when the melting snows began to give us back the high country, and I had gone into the wilderness on a four-day backpacking trip. I went alone—well, that is to say, I went without another human companion. Scout, my golden retriever, came along, much to his boundless joy. It had been a very emotionally and spiritually intense spring, and I desperately needed to find my heart and God again. (The two go hand in hand, of course. Without your heart you cannot hope to find God, for the heart is his dwelling place. If you ignore your heart, it's like looking for him everywhere but at home.)

On the third day I tried to cross a ridge between two valleys. No trail existed there, but I thought from the map that it could be done, and I'd even talked to a ranger at the trailhead on my first day who told me he'd heard of people crossing that pass. I began to negotiate my way down the far side of the ridge on what seemed to be an ancient game trail, but after about one hundred feet the ground beneath me disappeared; below me a cliff simply dropped straight down for more than seven hundred feet. I was forced to backtrack, climbing my way back to the top of the pass with a sixty-pound pack and a very reluctant retriever. It became so dangerous I was forced to leave Scout on a ledge, climb to the top to dump my pack, and make a second trip down for the dog. Hours later we slumped back into the very camp we'd broken that morning—tails dragging, exhausted, frightened, confused.

The air grew chill as the sun began to set, so I went and sat on a rock in the last rays to get warm. Tears began to flow, though I could not have told you why. I sensed the presence of Jesus with me, felt he was speaking to some young and frightened place in my heart. At first the movements of God in me were inarticulate, deeper than words. Then, slowly, I began to tune in to what seemed like a conversation between Jesus and a sort of young place in my soul. It was as if I was eavesdropping; Jesus had just asked a question, and my heart—it felt like the heart of a very young boy— replied, *He's always doing that to me.* Oops. I knew the "he" in question was me, and "that" was what happened up on the ridge. I felt like an older brother caught making his younger brother jump off the roof.

Will you let me heal you?

I wasn't sure whether the question was for the "young" me or the "old" me, so I waited and listened in humbled silence. Jesus was speaking to the young and frightened place in my heart. (How many years have I lived in fear? Far too many.) This is what he nearly always does when he comes to mend those rifts in our hearts.

He brings his comfort and mercy to those times and places where we suffered the shattering blow, and the heart in that place often feels the same age as it was at the time of the event, even though it might have been decades ago. More tears.

It might be a surprise that Christ asks our permission to come in and heal, but you may remember that famous passage from Revelation, "Behold, I stand at the door and knock" (3:20 NKJV). He doesn't force his way in, and the principle remains true after we have given Christ the initial access to our hearts that we call salvation. There are rooms we have kept locked up, places he has not had access to by our own will, and in order to experience his healing, we must also give him permission to come in there. *Will you let me heal you?* Something in me . . . hesitated. *Only if he'll stop doing that to me.*

Then it was as if the gaze of Christ had turned to me—the "older" me—and what he said was, *It's true, John. You know you are very hard on your heart. You are not merciful with those broken places within you.* He's right, of course—I'm not. They are a nuisance. I don't like feeling as though there is a young and fearful boy inside, and I handle that by shoving those fears down and pushing myself on. I think that's how most of us handle the young and broken places within; we simply try to get past them, push them down, hide them as much as possible, and get on with life. Thank God, Jesus is much more compassionate. I felt I needed to repent of my drivenness, and after a prayer to that effect, I sensed the young part give Christ permission to come in.

The work of Christ in healing the soul is a deep mystery, more amazing than open-heart surgery. A friend described his experience as having Christ "holding the broken parts of my heart in his hands, and bringing them all together, holding them tenderly until his life brought a wholeness or a oneness to what was many pieces." Yes— that's it. That idea of "binding up" our brokenness involves bringing all the shattered pieces back together into one whole heart.

Reintegrating those places broken off by tragedy or assault. It was as if Jesus took this broken part of me and loved me there, brought me into the safety of his presence, brought this part "home."

The sun set. All was quiet. I felt . . . lighter. Gladder. The fear was gone. In its place came a great surprise—joy. Something had been healed, restored, mended. I went around the woods gathering firewood while singing a sort of make-it-up-as-you-go kind of song a young boy would sing when he was happy. It was but one event in an amazing journey that began several years ago when I prayed this simple but earnest prayer: *Jesus, I want my whole heart back*.

TOWARD RESTORATION

> We simply invoke His Presence, then invite Him into our hearts. He shows us our hearts. In prayer for the healing of memories, we simply ask our Lord to come present to that place where we were so wounded (or perhaps wounded another). Forgiving others, and receiving forgiveness, occurs. In prayer for the healing of the heart from fears, bitterness, etc., we see primal fears as well as lesser ones dealt with immediately: those fears that the sufferer often has not been aware of, never been able to name—they only know that their lives have been seriously restricted and shaped because of them. (Leanne Payne, *The Healing Presence*)

Walking with God leads to receiving his intimate counsel, and counseling leads to deep restoration. As we learn to walk with God and hear his voice, he is able to bring up issues in our hearts that need speaking to. Some of those wounds were enough to break our hearts, create a rift in the soul, and so we need his healing as well. This is something Jesus walks us into—sometimes through the help of another person who can listen and pray with us, sometimes with God alone. As David said in Psalm 23, he leads us away, to a quiet place, to restore the soul. Our first choice is to go with him there—to slow down, unplug, accept the invitation to come aside. You won't find healing in the midst of the Matrix. We need time in the presence of God. This often comes on the heels of God's raising some issue in our hearts or after we've just relived an event that takes us straight to that broken place, or waking as I did to a raw emotion.

> Teach me your way, O LORD,
> > and I will walk in your truth;
> give me an undivided heart,
> > that I may fear your name.
> I will praise you, O Lord my God, with all my heart;
> > I will glorify your name forever. (Ps. 86:11–12)

When we are in the presence of God, removed from distractions, we are able to hear him more clearly, and a secure environment has been established for the young and broken places in our hearts to surface. We ask God to surround us with his presence. We give ourselves back over to him, come under his authority, for as Paul warns, it is possible to lose connection with our Head, who is Christ (Col. 2:19). We declare the authority of Jesus over our hearts, for he made our hearts (Ps. 33:15) and he has redeemed our hearts (Rom. 2:29).

> *Jesus, I come into your presence now, and I ask you to surround me. I come under your authority and your claim upon my life. I give myself to you—body, soul, and spirit. I give my heart to you, in every way—including the broken places in me. I declare your authority over my heart, for you made my heart and you have redeemed my heart.*

Then we invite Christ in. We ask Jesus to come into the emotion, the memory, this broken place within us. We give him permission; we give him access. We open the door to this particular place in our hearts. "If you hear me calling and open the door, I will come in" (Rev. 3:20 NLT). Truth be told, there are probably many broken places within us. Stay with one at a time, the one connected with the event or the emotion or the habit you can't seem to escape. Ask Jesus to bring his light there. "For God, who said, 'Let light shine out of darkness,' made his light shine in our hearts" (2 Cor. 4:6). Ask him to make it clear to you. *What's going on here, Jesus? What is this all about? Shine your light in my heart.*

> *Jesus, I invite you into this broken place within me (this wound, this memory). I give you total access to my heart. Come, Lord, shine your light here. Reveal to me all that is going on here. What is this about, Jesus? Come and show me, meet me here, in this place.*

Sometimes he will take us back to a memory, a time and place where a shattering blow was given. Other times he will make us aware of a young place in our hearts. Just the other evening, Stasi and I were in the living room together, reading. She told me she had been sad for several days, but she wasn't sure why. There wasn't anything sad going on in her life—quite the contrary. It had been a good several weeks with many blessings. But as she prayed about it, tuned in to her heart, she became aware of a place in her heart that felt as if it was weeping. Anytime someone says, "I feel like there's this part of me . . . ," my radar lights up. We asked Jesus about it, and sure enough, there was a part of Stasi's heart, about seventeen years old, that was grieving. We asked Jesus to come in and lead us in prayer for this brokenness.

We ask Jesus what he is saying to this wounded part of us, listening, as Payne puts it, "for the healing word that God is always sending to the wounded." He will often bring words of love and kindness, or comfort, specifically to this place in our hearts: "You have the words of real life" (John 6:68 *The Message*). Sometimes he will ask a question: *Why are you frightened?* or *Will you let me heal you?* He is drawing this place in our hearts out from the shadows, out from hiding; he is bringing our brokenness into the place of assurance.

> *Jesus, come and lead me in healing this brokenness in my heart. Speak to me here, Lord. What are you saying to me? Give me ears to hear and eyes to see what you are revealing. Let no other voice speak but you, my Lord Jesus, and you alone.*

Now, I think it is safe to say that we all have mishandled these places in our hearts. We push them down, as I did. Or we turn to something or someone we hope will bring comfort, like food or sex. If we have done that, Jesus will often make that clear to us as we pray. As he does, we confess our sins, renounce them (often a great act of the will), and ask him to cleanse our hearts (1 John 1:9).

> *Jesus, forgive me for the ways I've mishandled my brokenness. You alone make me dwell in safety. Forgive me for all my self-protection and self-redemption, and for all my false comforters. (You'll want to renounce specific sins you are aware of here.) Cleanse my heart of every sin by your shed blood.*

Oftentimes these young and broken places have become sites of spiritual strongholds. (This will make a great deal more sense after you read the next chapter.) All of the streams flow together for our healing; we must use the stream of Warfare as well. Our sins give the Enemy a certain claim to our lives (Rom. 6:16). As we renounce any sin, we also renounce any claim we've given to Satan in our lives. This often comes in the form of "agreements"—Satan has suggested something to us, and we have said, "Yes." He might have said, *Don't ever trust anyone,* or *Your heart is bad—never show it to anyone,* or *You are dirty . . . lustful . . . addicted and never will get free.* Whatever we have agreed with, we renounce those agreements. We ask God to cleanse us by the blood of Christ; we command our Enemy to flee (James 4:7).

I now break every agreement I have made with Satan and his lies. (Get specific here. What have you believed, bought into?) I renounce any claim I have given to my Enemy, and in the name of Jesus I command him to flee.

And then we ask Jesus to do for us the very thing he said he came to do: we ask him to heal this brokenness, to bind up our hearts. Sometimes he will ask us to take his hand in this shattered place, follow him into his heart and his presence within us. These places are often isolated from the life and the love of God in us; he draws them back into his presence and heals them through union with himself, *in* our hearts. Our part is to listen and follow where he is leading, and to welcome that part of our heart home. This is so important because many of us *sent* that part away. We welcome back the despised, forsaken part, just as Jesus embraces us.

Jesus, come now and do as you promised to do—heal my broken heart and set me free. (Listen here for what Jesus is saying.) Bring this place into your love and healing, bring this place home. I welcome your healing, and I welcome this part of my heart home. Come, bind me up and make me whole.

Carry On the Journey

"Healing prayer," says Payne, "is not the 'instant fix,' nor the bypassing of slow and steady growth. It is that which clears the path and makes such progress possible." Brokenness keeps so many people from walking the path that God has for them. "Make straight paths for your feet, so that the limb which is lame may not be put out of joint, but rather be healed" (Heb. 12:13 NASB). As long as we have these unhealed places within us, these rifts in the soul, we will find it next to impossible to live in freedom and victory. No matter how much we demand of ourselves, applying discipline and doctrine, it will not work. It has not worked. Those places keep undermining us at crucial moments, cutting us off at the knees. And our Enemy knows them well and uses them against us with disabling effect. I'll say more about that in a moment. We desperately need the stream of Healing, so that we may go on to walk this journey with Christ.

Then Gandalf said: "Let us not stay at the door, for the time is urgent. Let us enter! For it is only in the coming of Aragorn that any hope remains for the sick that lie in the House. Thus spake Ioreth, wise-woman of Gondor: *The hands of the king are the hands of a healer, and so shall the rightful king be known . . ."*

Now Aragorn knelt by Faramir, and held a hand upon his brow. And those that watched felt that some great struggle was going on. For Aragorn's face grew grey with weariness; and ever and anon he called the name of Faramir, but each time more faintly to their hearing, as if Aragorn himself was removed from them, and walked afar in some dark vale, calling for one that was lost.

And at last Bergil came running in, and he bore six leaves in a cloth. "It is kingsfoil, Sir," he said; "but not fresh, I fear. It must have been culled two weeks ago at the least. I hope it will serve, Sir?" Then looking at Faramir he burst into tears.

But Aragorn smiled. "It will serve," he said. "The worst is now over. Stay and be comforted!" Then taking two leaves, he laid them on his hands and breathed on them, and then he crushed them, and straightaway a living freshness filled the room, as if the air itself awoke and tingled, sparkling with joy . . .

Suddenly Faramir stirred, and he opened his eyes, and he looked on Aragorn who bent over him; and a light of knowledge and love was kindled in his eyes, and he spoke, softly. "My lord, you called me. I come. What does the king command?" "Walk no more in the shadows, but awake!" said Aragorn . . . "I will, my lord," said Faramir. "For who would lie idle when the king has returned?" (J. R. R. Tolkien, *The Return of the King*)

CHAPTER NINE

SPIRITUAL WARFARE: FIGHTING FOR YOUR HEART

It is the image of God reflected in you that so enrages hell;
it is this at which the demons hurl their mightiest weapons.

—WILLIAM GURNALL

Awake, awake, O Zion,
    clothe yourself with strength . . .
Shake off your dust;
    rise up, sit enthroned, O Jerusalem.
Free yourself from the chains on your neck,
    O captive Daughter of Zion.

—GOD (ISA. 52:1–2)

Wolfgang Amadeus Mozart was a glorious man. An image bearer. You remember from your youth the little song "Twinkle, Twinkle, Little Star"? Mozart wrote that melody when he was three. He composed his first symphony when he was twelve. And Mozart's music has *endured,* enchanting the world for centuries. He is probably played more often than any other classical composer. Yet this brilliant man died young—we don't really know how or why. Impoverished, alone, his body was dumped in a common grave. The movie *Amadeus* is Peter Shaffer's attempt to tell that tale.

It's a story of genius and jealousy, leading to murder. Shaffer creates a villain worthy of the devil himself in the character of the court composer Salieri. A musician of lesser note, Salieri is tormented by envy of Mozart's greatness. Like Joseph's brothers. He embodies what must have been Lucifer's jealousy of God's glory, which brought the angel to his ruin. There is a remarkable scene in the film that depicts the day Mozart's wife brings his music to Salieri, in hopes of getting her husband a job. She does not yet know that he is a wolf in sheep's clothing. Glancing through the pages of Mozart's portfolio, Salieri is captivated by the work of his rival's hand.

SALIERI: These . . . are *originals?*

FRAU MOZART: Yes, sir. He doesn't make copies.

[*As the astonished composer begins to read the sheets before him, he narrates the tale.*]

SALIERI: Astounding. It was actually . . . beyond belief. These were first, and *only* drafts of music. But they showed no correction of any kind. Not one. He had simply written down music already finished . . . in his *head!* Page after page of it, as if he were just taking dictation! And music . . . finished like no music is ever finished. Displace one note and there would be diminishment. Displace one phrase and the structure would fall. It was clear to me . . . that sound I had heard in the Archbishop's palace had been no accident. Here again was the very voice of God. I was staring through the cage of those meticulous ink strokes at an absolute beauty.

[*Salieri is enraptured, and the sheets fall to the floor from his limp hands.*]

FRAU MOZART: Is it not good?

SALIERI: [*Clearly wounded*] It is . . . miraculous.

FRAU MOZART: Yes . . . he's very proud of his work. So you will help us?

[*Sullen, determined, Salieri simply leaves the room in silence.*

The scene shifts to his private chambers. Salieri is taking down a cru-cifix from the wall and placing it in the fire.]

SALIERI: From now on we are enemies, You and I. Because You choose for Your instrument a boastful, lustful, smutty, infantile boy . . . and give me only the ability to recognize the Incarnation. Because You are *unjust . . . unfair . . . unkind!* I will block You. I swear it. I will hinder and harm Your creature here on earth as far as I am able. [*Shaking his fist in the air*] I will ruin Your incarnation.

OUR SITUATION

This is the heart of our Enemy. He is determined to hinder and harm and ruin God's image bearers. To steal and kill and destroy. So, let me say this again: the story of your life is the story of the long and brutal assault on your heart by the one who knows what you could be and fears it. I hope you are beginning to see that more clearly now. Otherwise, much of the Bible will not make sense to you. Much of your *life* will not make sense to you.

> I will go before you
>   and will level the mountains;
> I will break down gates of bronze
>   and cut through bars of iron.
> I will give you the treasures of darkness,
>   riches stored in secret places,
> so that you may know that I am the LORD,
>   the God of Israel, who summons you by name. (Isa. 45:2–3)

Doesn't the language of the Bible sometimes sound . . . overblown? Really now—God is going to level mountains for us? We'd be happy if he just helped us get through the week. What's all that about breaking down gates of bronze and cutting through bars of iron? I mean, it sounds heroic, but, well, who's really in need of that? This isn't ancient Samaria. We'd settle for a parking place at the mall. Now, I like the part about treasures of darkness and riches stored in secret places—it reminds me of *Treasure Island* and Long John Silver and all that. What boy hasn't wanted to find buried treasure? And, in fact, those associations make the passage seem like fantasy as well—good poetry, meant to inspire. But not much more.

What if we looked at the passage through the eyes of the heart? That language makes perfect sense if we are living a reality on the mythic level of *Amadeus* or *The Lord of the Rings*. In those stories, gates must be broken down, riches are hidden in darkness, and precious friends must be set free. If we *are* in an epic battle, then the language of the Bible fits perfectly. Things are not what they seem. We are at war. That war is against your heart, your glory. Once more, look at Isaiah 61:1:

> He has sent me to bind up the brokenhearted,
> to proclaim freedom for the captives
> and release from darkness for the prisoners.

This is God's personal mission for his people; the offer is for us all. So, we must all be held prisoner to some form of darkness. We didn't know it—that's proof enough. In the darkness we can't see. And what is this hidden treasure? Our *hearts*—they are the treasures hidden by darkness. They are not darkness; they are *hidden* by darkness, pinned down, held away in secret places like a hostage held for ransom. Prisoners of war. That is a given. That is assumed. The question is not, *Are* we spiritually oppressed, but *Where* and *How?*

Think of it—why does every story have a villain?

Little Red Riding Hood is attacked by a wolf. Dorothy must face and bring down the Wicked Witch of the West. Qui-Gon Jinn and Obi-Wan Kenobi go hand to hand against Darth Maul. To release the captives of the Matrix, Neo battles the powerful "agents." Frodo is hunted by the Black Riders. (The Morgul blade that the Black Riders pierced Frodo with in the battle on Weathertop—it was aimed at his heart.) Beowulf kills the monster Grendel, and then he has to battle Grendel's mother. Saint George slays the dragon. The children who stumbled into Narnia are called upon by Aslan to battle the White Witch and her armies so that Narnia might be free.

Every story has a villain because *yours* does. You were born into a world at war. When Satan lost the battle against Michael and his angels, "he was hurled to the earth, and his angels with him" (Rev. 12:9). That means that right now, on this earth, there are hundreds of thousands, if not millions, of fallen angels, foul spirits, bent on our destruction. And what is Satan's mood? "He is filled with fury, because he knows that his time is short" (v. 12). So what does he spend every day and every night of his sleepless, untiring existence doing? "Then the dragon was enraged at the woman and went off to make war against . . . those who obey God's commandments and hold to the testimony of Jesus" (v. 17). He has you in his crosshairs, and he isn't smiling.

You have an Enemy. He is trying to steal your freedom, kill your heart, destroy your life. As Satan said through Salieri, "I will hinder and harm Your creature here on earth as far as I am able. I will ruin Your incarnation." Very, very few people live like that. The alarm goes off, and they hit the snooze button, catch a few extra winks, gulp down a cup of coffee on their way to work, wonder why there are so many hassles, grab some lunch, work some more, come home under a sort of cloud, look at the mail, have dinner, watch a little TV, feed the cat, and fall into bed—without once even wondering how the Enemy might be attacking them. All they know is, they sure aren't enjoying that abundant life Christ talked about.

To find the freedom and the life offered by Christ, we must live in all Four Streams. To be restored as a man or a woman fully alive, we must live in all Four Streams. This, the fourth, may be the most neglected of all. And frankly, it may be the most critical. To live in ignorance of spiritual warfare is the most naive and dangerous thing a person can do. It's like skipping through the worst part of town, late at night, waving your wallet above your head. It's like walking into an al-Qaida training camp, wearing an "I love the United States" T-shirt. It's like swimming with great white sharks, dressed as a wounded sea lion and smeared with blood. And let me tell you something: you don't escape spiritual warfare simply because you choose not to believe it exists or because you refuse to fight it.

The bottom line is, you are going to have to fight for your heart. Remember John 10:10—the thief is trying to steal the life God wants to give.

SUBTLE ATTACK—LOOKING FOR AGREEMENTS

The devil has more temptations than an actor has costumes for the stage. And one of his all-time favorite disguises is that of a lying spirit, to abuse your tender heart with the worst news he can deliver—that you do not really love Jesus Christ and that you are only pretending, you are only deceiving yourself. (William Gurnall)

Satan is called in Scripture the Father of Lies (John 8:44). His very first attack against the human race was to lie to Eve and Adam about God, and where life is to be found, and what the consequences of certain actions would and would not be. He is a master at this. He suggests to us—as he suggested to Adam and Eve—some sort of idea or inclination or impression, and what he is seeking is a sort of "agreement" on our part. He's hoping we'll buy into whatever he's saying, offering, insinuating. Our first parents bought into it, and look what disaster came of it. But that story is not over. The Evil One is still lying to us, seeking our agreement every single day.

Your heart is good. Your heart matters to God. These are the two hardest things to hang on to. I'm serious—try it. Try to hold this up for even a day. *My heart is good. My heart matters to God.* You will be amazed at how much accusation you live under. You have an argument with your daughter on the way to school; as you drive off, you have a nagging sense of, *Well, you really blew that one.* If your heart agrees—*Yeah, I really did*—without taking the issue to Jesus, then the Enemy will try to go for more. *You're always blowing it with her.* Another agreement is made. *It's true. I'm such a lousy parent.* Keep this up and your whole day is tanked in about five minutes. The Enemy will take any small victory he can get. It moves from *You did a bad thing* to *You are bad.* Or weak. Or ugly. Or prideful. You know how it goes. After a while it just becomes a cloud we live under, accept as normal.

My friend Aaron decided to get into shape. He went out and took a run. First, the Enemy tried discouragement to get him to quit. *Look how far you have to go. You can't do this—you'll die out there. Give it up.* Aaron thought, *Gee—it is a long way. I'm not sure I can do this.* But then he recognized what was going on and pressed into it. The attack became more personal, more vicious. He was running along, and he was hearing stuff like this: *You're just a fat pig. You always have been.* A gorgeous woman in fabulous shape approached from the other direction. *She'd never be attracted to a slob like you.* "By the time I got back to my car," he said, "it felt like I'd been assaulted. But this time, I knew what it was and I won. I made no agreements."

This sort of thing goes on all the time. But unlike Aaron, most of the time we don't recognize it as an attack. At first it tends to be vague—not voices in the head, not an obvious assault, but more of a "sense" we have, an impression, a feeling that comes over us. The power of *suggestion.* Now, if some demon were standing in front of us, telling us, "Here, drink this rat poison," we'd tell him where to go. But because we do not live as though we are at war, well, we just assume these impressions are our own, and we accept them, agree with them, live under them like slaves under a task master. Listen carefully: any movement toward freedom and life, any movement toward God or others, *will be opposed.* Marriage, friendship, beauty, rest—the thief wants it all. A. W. Tozer wrote:

> So, it becomes the devil's business to keep the Christian's spirit imprisoned. He knows that the believing and justified Christian has been raised up out of the grave of his sins and trespasses. From that point on, Satan works that much harder to keep us bound and gagged, actually imprisoned in our own grave clothes. He knows that if we continue in this kind of bondage . . . we are not much better off than when we were spiritually dead.

Sadly, many of these accusations will actually be spoken by Christians. Having dismissed a warfare worldview, they do not know who is stirring them to say certain things. The Enemy used David, who apparently wasn't watching for it, to do his evil: "Satan rose up against Israel and incited David to take a census of Israel" (1 Chron. 21:1). He tried to use Peter too. "From that time on Jesus began to explain to his disciples that he must go to Jerusalem and suffer many things . . . Peter took him aside and began to rebuke him. 'Never, Lord!' he said. 'This shall never happen to you!' Jesus turned and said to Peter, 'Get behind me, Satan!'" (Matt. 16:21–23). Heads up—these words will come from anywhere. Be careful what or who you are agreeing with.

The whole plan is based on agreements. When we make those agreements with the demonic forces suggesting things to us, we come under their influence. It becomes a kind of permission we give the Enemy, sort of like a contract. The bronze gates start clanging shut around us. I'm serious—maybe half the stuff people are trying to "work through" in counseling offices, or pray about in their quiet times, is simply agreements they've made with the Enemy. Some foul spirit whispers, *I'm such a stupid idiot,* and they agree with it; then they spend months and years trying to sort through feelings of insignificance. They'd end their agony if they'd treat it for the warfare it is, break the agreement they've made, send the Enemy packing.

If you are having trouble taking in all of this, let me ask you: Have you had this experience? Something bad happens, and you start telling yourself what a jerk you are. Do you really think the source of that is just you? Or God? Think about it this way: Who would take the most delight in it? Take it all real slow if you need to. Start by simply entertaining the notion that the source might be something besides your "low self-esteem."

I don't mean to suggest it's easy. This can get really nasty.

We've been looking for a house for four years. A long story, one we haven't time for here, but those have been four years of ups and downs and promises and hopes and finally, just this last Sunday afternoon, we found it. It was not only beautiful and private; it was perfect for holding the many fellowship events that are the centerpiece of our community. A perfect fit for our family. The only property we'd seen that met our criteria and made our hearts beat faster, and it was vacant—we could move in immediately. After a long, hard journey, we found a place of rest, a respite from the battle. We wrote up what we thought would be a slam-dunk offer. As our agent drove to deliver our contract, he received a call that another offer came in before us by twenty minutes. Some agent in his office saw our offer and sneaked one in ahead of ours designed to beat us out.

It felt like a perfect setup. Our hearts were so hopeful, open, vulnerable. I can equate it only to something like parents waiting for four years to adopt, and finally the opportunity opens for them. God says, *This is your turn. This is my gift to your hearts.* They are promised a baby, but on the day they are supposed to receive her, she's given to another couple. We really thought this house was a gift from God. Not getting it was a direct, intentional wound to our hearts. It wasn't just about a *house,* for heaven's sake. That sounds silly. It was about our relationship with God, our walk with him . . . and therefore, about all the other things in our lives that flow from that. The wound came in at the most intimate place of our lives—our walk with God.

And a whole lot of other crap rushed in as well. Just as sharks can smell blood in the water from miles away, the enemies of our souls smell woundedness, and they close in for the kill. Suddenly, betrayal felt true. *God has betrayed you.* Desolation felt true. *None of what you believe is true.* Apostasy, abandoning all faith felt true. *Why walk with God if you can't trust him?* We were reeling. Thoughts went through my heart about how to get out of this book contract because I can't write except out of my walk with God . . . and that had been pierced. Stasi was crying. Our middle son was crying. I felt like I'd been . . . hit by a truck.

If Jesus said the thief comes to steal and kill and destroy, well, then, why don't we think the thief ever *actually comes* to steal and kill and destroy? Good grief—the things people just roll over and accept as "God's will." The house was just the move to steal; the Enemy wanted to kill our hearts and destroy our faith and all that flows from it. I think that's nearly always true. The particular attack is not the issue; he'll steal anything to kill and destroy.

During an assault like that, you must remember: *make no agreements.* The Enemy will suggest all sorts of things. *You see— God doesn't care. You're not worth fighting for. Your heart doesn't matter. You can't trust him.* He is trying to kill your heart, destroy the glory of your life. It will feel hard—really hard, almost impossible—but whatever you do, make no agreements. You have to start there.

OPEN ASSAULT

Stephen came to us because he was at the end of his rope. I liked him right away. He was an honest, insightful man, earnestly seeking the life of God. At one time he had been an alive and passionate friend of Jesus. He wrote music, led worship in his church. He had a Bible study in his home. Many people received specific words of encouragement and guidance from God through Stephen. He shared his faith with anyone. He walked with God. But that was long ago. It had been years since he'd been able to write any music; worship was as dead as your great-great-grandmother. He could not pray, could not read the Bible, could not hear from God. This man had been taken out.

During the first few years of his ordeal, Stephen sought the streams he knew to seek. Asked his pastor for counseling. Tried his best to push through it with discipline and prayer. Went to conferences, tried to hear from God. Nothing. He thought maybe it was that whole "silence of God" thing, thought if he just waited it out, it would lift. It didn't. No, it sat there like a great weight upon his spirit, a stone someone had rolled over his heart. After five years he'd almost given up. Thank God, he turned to the stream of Warfare.

As Stephen told me his story, this is what emerged: in his younger years as a boy, he had taken some serious wounds of rejection, the first one coming at the age of three from his father. The result was a vow never to let anyone hurt him again. He did, however, keep his heart open to his mother, from whom he received mercy and kindness. They were friends. She was the only relational connection he had. Stephen came to Christ as a young man. Shortly after, his mother grew very ill. He prayed and prayed she would not die. You know what's coming. She did. Understandably, a sense of betrayal and abandonment rode in on the wings of that pain. But he hung in there with his faith.

He tried to reach out again and trust others, especially men. He knew he needed to have that place in his heart healed, and he bravely sought to enter into a few deep relationships with men he trusted and respected. There were three of them; two he considered mentors, one a close friend. Both mentors ended up having affairs, one of them with a woman in Stephen's home group. The wounds pierced deeply, and what do you suppose came with them? Yep: betrayal and abandonment. He sought direction from his pastor over one of the affairs; since the woman was in his fellowship, Stephen felt a burden to at least confront the two. His pastor wounded him again, suggesting that Stephen was prideful and arrogant, and was making up part of the story. More betrayal, more abandonment. The Enemy will arrange to have others do to you what he is doing to you.

If we could have seen what happened in the spiritual realm, I think we would have seen some foul spirit at work right from the beginning. Paul warns us in Ephesians: "Do not let the sun go down while you are still angry, and do not give the devil a foothold" (4:26–27). Paul is writing to Christians here, and he makes it clear that a believer can have a stronghold of Satan in his life. It's not just about anger; it can happen through all sorts of issues. The Devil will try to use your wounds and unresolved emotional issues to pin down your heart under a spiritual stronghold. The wounds we take are not accidental. It was no doubt at Satan's suggestion that Stephen made that first vow never to let anyone in. Clearly, he seized the opportunity of the death of Stephen's mom to bring in all those feelings and thoughts of betrayal and abandonment.

Now, it was Stephen who made the agreements with the Enemy. People make choices, and they are responsible before God for those choices. But through those agreements the Evil One secured a beachhead (a "foothold" in Paul's words), then waited for an opportunity to take even greater dominion. In Stephen's case, the unresolved hurt and betrayal were there, and the addition of the affairs was just what the Enemy needed; no doubt he had some hand in those as well. The bronze gates closed over Stephen's heart, now a treasure hidden in darkness.

There Is No Escaping This War

Stephen's story is really quite common. Remember, when Jesus boiled his whole mission down to healing the brokenhearted and setting prisoners free from darkness, he was referring to *all* of us. Our modern, scientific, Enlightenment worldview has simply removed spiritual warfare as a practical category, and so it shouldn't surprise us that we can't see spiritual strongholds after we say they don't really exist. It took all Four Streams to set Stephen free, but the clincher was the stream of Warfare. I'll explain in the next chapter how we did it. Now, he is free, I'm grateful to say. His heart is back. A few months later he said to me, "If we hadn't used all Four Streams, I'd probably have lived the rest of my life in that prison."

And that's true, dear friends. He probably would have.

If you deny the battle raging against your heart, well, then, the thief just gets to steal and kill and destroy. Some friends of mine started a Christian school together a few years ago. It had been their shared dream for nearly all their adult lives. After years of praying and talking and dreaming, it finally happened. Then the assault came . . . but they would not see it as such. It was "hassles" and "misunderstanding" at first. As it grew worse, it became a rift between them. A mutual friend warned them of the warfare, urged them to fight it as such. "No," they insisted, "this is about *us*. We just don't see eye-to-eye." I'm sorry to say their school shut its doors a few months ago, and the two aren't speaking to each other. Because they refused to fight it for the warfare it was, they got taken out. I could tell you many, many stories like that.

There is no war is the subtle—but pervasive—lie sown by an enemy so familiar to us we don't even see him. For too long he has infiltrated the ranks of the church, and we haven't even recognized him.

THE RELIGIOUS SPIRIT

I was reading the prophet Jeremiah a few weeks ago when I ran across a passage that referred to God as "the Lord Almighty." To be honest, it didn't resonate. There's something too religious about the phrase; it sounds churchy, sanctimonious. The *Lawd Almiiiighty*. It sounds like something your grandmother would say when you came into her kitchen covered in mud. I found myself curious about what the *actual* phrase means in Hebrew. Might we have lost something in the translation? So I turned to the front of the version I was using for an explanation. Here is what the editors said:

> Because for most readers today the phrases "the Lord of hosts" and "God of hosts" have little meaning, this version renders them "the Lord Almighty" and "God Almighty." These renderings convey the sense of the Hebrew, namely, "he who is sovereign over all the 'hosts' (powers) in heaven and on earth, especially over the 'hosts' (armies) of Israel."

No, they don't. They don't even come close. The Hebrew means "the God of angel armies," "the God of the armies who fight for his people." *The God who is at war.* Does "Lord Almighty" convey "the God who is at war"? Not to me, it doesn't. Not to anyone I've asked. It sounds like "the God who is up there but still in charge." Powerful, in control. The God of angel armies sounds like the one who would roll up his sleeves, take up sword and shield to break down gates of bronze, and cut through bars of iron to rescue me. Compare "Joe is a good man who is in control" to "Joe is a Navy Seal." It changes the way you think about Joe and what he's up to. Why don't "most readers today" understand about the God of angel armies? Could it be because we have abandoned a warfare worldview? Who sold us that crock of sanctimonious puff-and-fluff?

For that matter, who has kept the new covenant so effectively under wraps that most Christians still believe their hearts are evil? It happened again just the other night—a leader in their church told friends of mine, in a very direct way, "The heart is desperately wicked." Dear God—they hold to that lie as a core doctrine of their *faith*. To say your heart is good still sounds like heresy. Whose PR campaign made that so effective?

Let me ask you another question: Who did Jesus tangle with more than any other group or type of person? Who started the rumors about him to try to discredit his ministry? Who kept trying to put him on the spot with their loaded questions? And when it became clear they could not shame or intimidate him back into place, where did the open opposition to Christ come from? Who paid Judas the thirty pieces of silver? Who got the crowd to yell for Barabbas when Pilate was ready to let Jesus go?

Religion and its defenders have always been the most insidious enemy of the true faith precisely because they are not glaring opponents; they are *impostors*. A raving pagan is easier to dismiss than an elder in your church. Before Jesus came along, the Pharisees ran the show. Everybody took what they said as gospel—even though it didn't sound like good news at all. But we wrestle not against flesh and blood. The Pharisees and their brethren down through the ages have merely acted—unknowingly, for the most part—as puppets, the mouthpiece of the Enemy.

Satan realized he couldn't stop the church. Oh, he tried. He arranged to have Jesus killed as a babe (Matt. 2:16). He tried to seduce him as a man. He tried to marginalize his message by having

the religious establishment discredit him. Finally, he had him crucified. It backfired. Badly. Then he tried to stop the young church
through intimidation and through death, having most of them
killed. It also backfired. So he turned to a backup plan. If you
can't beat 'em . . . join 'em. Infiltrate their ranks dressed as an
angel of light (Gal. 1:8). Then slowly bring a veil over all that is
good and beautiful and true. Take them captive through their
own religion.

Where are the Four Streams? The Religious Spirit has turned
discipleship into a soul-killing exercise of principles. Most folks
don't even know they can walk with God, hear his voice. The
Religious Spirit has stigmatized counseling as a profession for sick
patients, and so the wounds of our hearts never get healed. He's
taken healing away from us almost entirely so that we sit in pews as
broken people, feeling guilty because we can't live the life we're supposed to live. And he takes warfare and mocks it, stigmatizes it as
well so that most of the church knows almost nothing about how
to break strongholds, set captives free.

Finally, the Religious Spirit makes it next to impossible for a person to break free by spreading the lie that *there is no war*. Be honest.
How many Christians do you know who practice spiritual warfare
as a normal, necessary, daily part of the Christian life? Some of my
dearest friends pull back from this stream and sort of cast a concerned look over me when I suggest it's going on. Onward, Christian
soldiers, marching as to war? You've got to be kidding me. We gave
up the hymn not so much for reasons of musical fashion but
because we felt ridiculous singing it, as you do when asked to sing
"Happy Birthday" in a restaurant to a perfect stranger. We don't
sing it 'cause it ain't true. We have acquiesced. We have surrendered
without a fight.

We've exchanged that great hymn for a subtle but telling substitute, a song that is currently being taught to thousands of children

in Sunday school each week, which goes something like this (sung in a very happy, upbeat tune):

> I may never march in the infantry,
>> ride in the cavalry,
>> shoot the artillery,
> I may never fly over the enemy
>> but I'm in the Lord's army, yes, sir!

There is no battle and there is no war and there is no Enemy and your life is not at stake and you are not desperately needed this very hour, but you're in the Lord's army. Yes, sir. Doing *what*? may I ask.

The reason I bring this up is that if you want the real deal, if you want the life and freedom that Jesus offers, then you are going to have to break free of this religious fog in particular. "It is for freedom that Christ has set us free. Stand firm, then, and do not let yourselves be burdened again by a yoke of slavery" (Gal. 5:1). So here's a bottom-line test to expose the Religious Spirit: if it doesn't bring freedom and it doesn't bring life, it's not Christianity. If it doesn't restore the image of God and rejoice in the heart, it's not Christianity.

The ministry of Jesus is summarized by one of those who knew him best when Peter brings the gospel to the Gentiles: "God anointed Jesus of Nazareth with the Holy Spirit and power, and . . . he went around doing good and healing all who were under the power of the devil, because God was with him" (Acts 10:38). In 1 John 3:8 (NKJV), we read, "For this purpose the Son of God was manifested, that He might destroy the works of the devil." The stream of Spiritual Warfare was essential to Jesus' life and ministry. It follows that it must be essential to ours if we would be his followers.

CHAPTER TEN

SETTING HEARTS FREE: INTEGRATING THE FOUR STREAMS

Can plunder be taken from warriors,
　　or captives rescued from the fierce?
But this is what the LORD says:
"Yes, captives will be taken from warriors,
　　and plunder retrieved from the fierce;
I will contend with those who contend with you,
　　and your children I will save.
I will make your oppressors eat their own flesh;
　　they will be drunk on their own blood, as with wine.
Then all mankind will know
　　that I, the LORD, am your Savior,
　　your Redeemer, the Mighty One of Jacob.
　　　　　　　　　　　　　　—ISAIAH (49:24–26)

They were about twice our height, and armed to the teeth. Through the visors of their helmets their monstrous eyes shone with a horrible ferocity. I was in the middle position, and middle giant approached me. My eyes were busy with his armor, and I was not a moment in settling the mode of attack. I saw that his body-armor was somewhat clumsily made, and that the overlappings in the lower part had more play than necessary, and I hoped that, in a fortunate moment, some joint would open a little, in a visible and accessible part. I stood till he came near enough to aim a blow at me with the mace, which has been, in all ages, the favorite weapon of giants, when, of course, I leaped aside, and let the blow fall upon the spot where I had been standing. Full of fury, he made at me again; but I kept him busy, constantly eluding his blows, and hoping thus to fatigue him. He did not seem to fear any assault from me, and I attempted none as yet. At length, as if somewhat fatigued, he paused for a moment, and drew himself slightly up; I bounded forward, foot and hand, ran my rapier through to the armor of his back, let go the hilt, and passing under his right arm, turned as he fell, and flew at him with my saber. At one happy blow I divided the band of his helmet, which fell off, and allowed me, with a second cut across the eyes, to blind him. After which I clove his head.

I stood exhausted amidst the dead, after the first worthy deed of my life.

I searched the giants, and found the keys of their castle, to which I repaired . . . I released the prisoners, knights and ladies, all in a sad condition, from the cruelties of the giants. (George MacDonald, *Phantastes*)

FIERCE MASTERY

Let's come back for a moment to original glory, the glory of God given to us when we were created in his image. So much light could be shed on our lives if we would explore what we were *meant* to be before things started going wrong. What were we created to *do*? What was our original job description?

Then God said, "Let us make man in our image, in our likeness, and let them rule over the fish of the sea and the birds of the air, over the livestock, over all the earth, and over all the creatures that move along the ground." So God created man in his own image, in the image of God he created him; male and female he created them. God blessed them and said to them, "Be fruitful and increase in number; fill the earth and subdue it. Rule." (Gen. 1:26–28)

And let them *rule*. Like a foreman runs a ranch or like a skipper runs his ship. Better still, like a king rules a kingdom, God appoints us as the governors of his domain. We were created to be the kings and queens of the earth (small *k*, small *q*). Hebrew scholar Robert Alter has looked long and hard at this passage, mining it for its riches. He says the idea of *rule* means "a fierce exercise of mastery." It is active, engaged, passionate. It is *fierce*. I suppose such language doesn't really fit if we were created to spend our days singing in the choir ("I may never march in the infantry"). But it makes perfect sense if we were born into a world at war. God says, "It will not be easy going. This is no Sunday school hour. Rule fiercely in my name." We were meant to rule, as he—the God of angel armies—rules.

Now—what will be our role in the kingdom of God to come? What does he have in store for us in the future? Let's take the parable of the talents as one example. A landowner is going away for a while, and he appoints his servants to take care of the place while he's gone. Some do, and some don't. When he returns, he rewards those who ruled well in his absence by giving them even greater authority over his estate. He says, "Well done, good and faithful servant! You have been faithful with a few things; I will put you in charge of many things" (Matt. 25:21). Jesus teaches that in the coming kingdom, we will be promoted to positions of authority, and we will reign with him there. The ranch hand is promoted to foreman; the manager gets the vice president's office; the prince becomes king.

To drive the point home, Jesus follows this parable with another, a story about some sheep and goats. The sheep are the good guys in this tale, and their reward is really amazing. Jesus says, "Then the King will say to those on his right, 'Come, you who are blessed by my Father; take your inheritance, the kingdom prepared for you since the creation of the world'" (Matt. 25:34). He doesn't say, "Good job. Now, come and sing songs in heaven forever." He gives them an entire kingdom to rule over—a kingdom waiting for them since the beginning of time. That was the plan all along. That's why we read in Revelation 22:5, "And they [meaning the saints] will reign for ever and ever." We will rule, just as we were always meant to.

And in the meantime? What is God up to with us in the meantime? Training us to do what we're made to do: rule. In the gospel of Luke, chapter 10, there is a sort of test flight for this whole idea. Christ appoints seventy-two of his disciples—not the apostles, just regular folks like you and me—to go out and prepare the way for his ministry. (The story will make more sense if we remember that his ministry is healing the brokenhearted and setting the captives free.) Jesus sets the stage by saying, "I am sending you out like lambs among wolves" (10:3). In other words, this could get vicious. It's no rummage sale.

Now, when the seventy-two return, they are blown away by what happened: "The seventy-two returned with joy and said, 'Lord, even the demons submit to us in your name'" (10:17). Christ gives his followers his authority, and they go out to set captives free. Jesus listens carefully to the report, and then he says, "I saw Satan fall like lightning from heaven" (v. 18). In other words, "You see, you guys? It works! It *works!* Satan's days are numbered!" But the battle is not over; it's just beginning to heat up. Jesus then goes on to say, "I have given you authority to . . . overcome all the power of the enemy" (v. 19). There's more to be done. This was only a trial run. After his resurrection, Jesus sends us *all* out to do what he did: "As the Father has sent me, so I send you" (John 20:21 NRSV). And he gives us his authority to do it: "All authority in heaven and on earth has been given to me. Therefore go" (Matt. 28:18–19). Why else would he have given us his authority if we weren't supposed to *use* it?

The attitude of so many Christians today is anything *but* fierce. We're passive, acquiescent. We're acting as if the battle is over, as if the wolf and the lamb are now fast friends. Good grief—we're beating swords into plowshares as the armies of the Evil One descend upon us. We've bought the lie of the Religious Spirit, which says, "You don't need to fight the Enemy. Let Jesus do that." It's nonsense. It's unbiblical. It's like a private in Vietnam saying, "My commander will do all the fighting for me; I don't even need to fire my weapon." We are *commanded* to "resist the devil, and he will flee from you" (James 4:7). We are told, "Your enemy the devil prowls around like a roaring lion looking for someone to devour. Resist him" (1 Peter 5:8–9); "Fight the good fight" (1 Tim. 1:18); "Rescue those being led away to death" (Prov. 24:11).

Seriously, just this morning a man said to me, "We don't need to fight the Enemy. Jesus has won." *Yes,* Jesus has won the victory over Satan and his kingdom. *However,* the battle is not over. Look at 1 Corinthians 15:24–25: "Then the end will come, when he [Jesus] hands over the kingdom to God the Father after he has destroyed all dominion, authority and power. For he must reign until he has put all his enemies under his feet." *After* he has destroyed the rest of the Enemy's works. *Until* then, he must reign by bringing his enemies under his feet. Jesus is still at war, and he calls us to join him.

Leanne Payne recounts a story from the life of Catherine of Sienna that helped her see the battle for her heart and trained her to fight it. In the story, Catherine has gone up to a secret place to pray:

As she began to pray, her ears were assaulted by blasphemous words, and she cried out to God, "Oh, look, Lord, I came up

here to give you my day. Now look what is happening." And the
Lord said, "Does this please you, Catherine?" "Oh no, Lord," she
said. And the Lord said, "It is because I indwell you that this dis-
pleases you so." These words brought instant understanding of
my plight . . . I also knew that the problem was not a state or
condition of my mind or my heart, but that it was harassment
from without, from the accuser of my soul. I knew beyond all
shadow of a doubt that "Greater is he who is in you, than he who
is in the world." I then cried out to God, "Take it away, Lord.
Send this filthy, horrible thing away." But the Lord said, "No,
you do it." It was then that I learned spiritual authority. Centered
in God and He in me, I took authority over the evil spirit when
it manifested itself and commanded it to leave. After several
months of this, a concentrated training in moving from the center where Christ dwells, I was utterly free of this harassment.

Notice, first, that the victory came when she realized that those
awful thoughts were *not* from her; her heart is good. The assault
came from *outside,* from the Enemy. That is the turning point,
when we begin to operate as if the heart is good, and we are at war.
Second, notice that Jesus told *her* to send it away. "You do it." *We*
must exercise our authority in Christ. *We* are to resist. Finally,
notice that it took several months of battle for a final victory.
During that period of time, she was not blowing it, nor was God
holding out on her. It was *training.* We are made to rule. We need
to learn how. Spiritual warfare is a great deal of our training.

SETTING CAPTIVES FREE

Let me come back now to Stephen's story and use it to show how
the Four Streams work together to set us free. You might recall that
I asked Stephen to first tell me his story. We need to hear a person's

story to get some understanding and context of what's going on in their heart and life. This is the stream of Counseling. I always listen carefully for the wounds, for how we mishandle them, and for where the Enemy has probably come in. Stephen's wounds had a clear theme to them (as do ours). In his case, it was betrayal and abandonment.

But there is another piece of evidence that we often overlook. As we began to help Stephen, there was a strong pull on me to drop him altogether, a vague but strong sense that felt like, *C'mon, John. This isn't worth it. You can't help him. Back off.* In other words, betray and abandon him. The Enemy will always try to get you to do to someone what he is doing to that person. I've seen this *so* many times. A woman came into my office and immediately I felt this pull toward lust and *Use her—she's available.* Her story centered around the wounds of sexual abuse. That's where the Enemy had a stronghold. A man came in with a deep wound of emasculation. *Despise him* was the pull, and it took a serious conscious effort not to do so. There is a gravitational field the Enemy creates around a person that pulls everyone in her life to do to her what he is doing to her. Heads up— it's not you, and being aware of it becomes a *very* helpful diagnostic.

We prayed and listened to God on behalf of Stephen—listening to God, walking with God throughout the entire process, as his disciples. Jesus confirmed that there were spirits of Betrayal and Abandonment pinning down his heart, along with a spirit of Desolation. (Anytime someone totally loses his sense of God, can't worship, can't pray, loses faith, Desolation is usually a part of things.)

Yes—spirits have personalities and specific functions. Michael (whose name means "who is like God?") is an archangel, the captain of the Lord's hosts, with special duties to protect God's people (Rev. 12:7; Dan. 10:13, 21). Gabriel's name means "strong man of God," and he is often given the role of messenger (Dan. 8:16; Luke 1:19, 26). Fallen angels have similar qualities, though twisted for evil. Jesus rebukes a "deaf and mute spirit" from a boy (Mark 9:25), and Legion from a tormented man (Mark 5:1–13). Paul casts out from a fortune-teller a spirit of divination (Acts 16:18).

Now I know—there is a great deal of debate today around the issue of a Christian's being "possessed" by a demon. I am not saying that Stephen was possessed. I am saying that there were spiritual enemies present in his life—set *against* him, trying to make an illegitimate claim over him. Paul teaches in Ephesians that unresolved emotional issues can create spiritual strongholds in our lives—"'In your anger do not sin: Do not let the sun go down while you are still angry, and do not give the devil a foothold" (4:26–27). The word means more than just "opportunity"; it conveys a place of influence, even strong influence. The New International Version and *The Message* translate it as "foothold"; the New Living Translation has it as "mighty foothold." Paul is not writing about non-Christians; he is clearly speaking to believers and he is making it clear that we can have demonic footholds in our lives.

That is why, before we could go after those enemies of Stephen's heart, he first had to confess his part in the mess. God honors our will (remember God's words to Catherine—"you do it"). Stephen had to renounce the vow he'd made as a young boy never to let anyone get close to him again. Childhood vows are very dangerous things; they act as major agreements with the Enemy, give him permission to enter some part of our lives. Stephen also had to confess the bitterness he held toward God for not saving his mother, and toward those two men who had betrayed him. (Bitterness is one example of "letting the sun go down" on an issue, and giving the devil a foothold). By bringing those sins under the blood of Christ, the Enemy lost his hold (Col. 2:13–15; Rev. 12:11).

Now, the apostle Peter teaches us, *we* are to resist the devil because he "prowls around like a roaring lion looking for someone to devour" (1 Peter 5:8). Not just tempt. *Devour.* That idea has a vicious connotation to it, as in "really harm." Maul. And Peter goes on to clarify that this "someone" includes Christians because he says we are to "resist him, standing firm in the faith, because you know that your brothers throughout the world are undergoing the same kind of sufferings" (v. 9). He is writing to Christians, and using other Christians as examples that we can and will be spiritually assaulted—sometimes in very vicious ways. We *must* resist.

It was time for us to get fierce. Time for the stream of Warfare. You'll notice that sometimes Jesus had to command foul spirits with a *stern* voice (Luke 4:35). In fact, when he first tried to deliver the man with Legion in him, the demon didn't leave—and *Christ* was doing the commanding! He had to get more information, in that case, the name and number of the demons present (Mark 5:1–13).

Now, I know—setting people free from demonic oppression might seem really weird to our modern, scientific world, but it has been a normal part of Christian ministry ever since Jesus modeled it for us. (Remember—things are not what they seem. We are at war.) The disciples made it an essential part of their ministry too. "Crowds gathered from the towns around Jerusalem, bringing their sick and those tormented by evil spirits, and all of them were healed" (Acts 5:16). The early church fathers saw it as an essential part of their ministry too. Listen to this prayer, one of many deliverance prayers penned by John Chrysostom, archbishop of Constantinople:

> Satan, the Lord rebukes you by his frightful name! Shudder, tremble, be afraid, depart, be utterly destroyed, be banished! You who fell from heaven and together with you all evil spirits: every evil spirit of lust, the spirit of evil . . . an imaginative spirit, and encountering spirit . . . or one altering the mind of man. Depart swiftly from this creature of the Creator Christ our God! And be gone from this servant of God, from his mind, from his soul, from his heart, from his reins, from his

senses, from all his members, that he might become whole and sound and free, knowing God.

Notice that St. John is rebuking foul spirits by name, on behalf of a believer ("this servant of God"). One at a time, we brought the authority of Jesus Christ, who is Lord, and the fullness of the Cross, Resurrection, and Ascension against all three foul spirits set against Stephen. We commanded them to release their claim on him, and to go to their judgment in the name of Jesus. After a fierce battle, they left. Stephen was free.

But that was not the end of the work for Stephen.

We then turned to the issue of his broken heart. We moved from the stream of Warfare to the stream of Healing, for to leave those places unhealed is only to invite the Enemy to return in another form, another day. We prayed with Stephen in the way I described at the end of Chapter 8, bringing the broken places into the healing presence of Jesus. It was dramatic, it was beautiful, and *it worked*. He is writing music again, hearing God's voice, and starting another fellowship group. He is free.

FIFTEEN MINUTES TO FREEDOM

With every morn my life afresh must break
The crust of self, gathered about me fresh;
That thy wind-spirit may rush in and shake
The darkness out of me, and rend the mesh
The spider-devils spin out of the flesh—
Eager to net the soul before it wake,
That it may slumberous lie, and listen to the snake.
(George MacDonald)

A few years ago, as Stasi and I really began to wake up and have our eyes opened to the spiritual battle raging against us and those we love, she said, "Quick little prayers just aren't going to do it anymore." I'm smiling and shaking my head as I recall this. How true it was; how true it has become. If we would do what Jesus did—heal all those who are under the power of the devil—and if we would find the life that he offers us, we have to fight for it. Fiercely. That is where we are now in this great Story.

All spiritual warfare follows the simple pattern given us in James 4:7: submit, and resist. We always start by submitting ourselves to Christ, and then resist whatever has come against us or against those we love. I've found that it is best to do this daily. There is a "dailyness" to our walk with Christ that follows these themes. So what I offer here is a walk through the prayer that Stasi and I, and our ministry team, pray every day. I'm going to unpack it for you as we go along, to help you understand why we pray this way. This is *not* a formula, but a model, an *example*. It might seem a bit more involved than the prayer most of us shoot up to God as we run out the door, but I promise you, this is fifteen minutes toward *freedom*! Quick little prayers aren't going to do it anymore.

First, we have to *choose* to abide in Christ. It's not something that happens automatically, and we can lose connection with our Head (Col. 2:19). Not a loss of salvation, but a loss of that intimate connection to the Vine through which we receive his life. Every morning we bring our lives fully back to Christ and under his lordship. It's important that we consecrate our whole being to Christ—body (Rom. 12:1), soul (Luke 10:27), and spirit (1 Cor. 6:17).

My dear Lord Jesus, I come to you now to be restored in you—to renew my place in you, my allegiance to you, and to receive from you all the grace and mercy I so desperately need this day. I honor you as my sovereign Lord, and I surrender every aspect of my life totally and completely to you. I give you my body as a living sacrifice; I give you my heart, soul, mind, and strength; and I give you my spirit as well.

Okay. Having consecrated ourselves, we cleanse our lives with the blood of Christ—a very powerful weapon in this war. It washes us from our sins and the sins of others against us (1 John 1:9). It also disarms Satan (Rev. 12:11). Next, the whole spiritual realm works under authority, so as we take our place under the headship of Christ, we extend our authority and covering over those who are under us. You might remember that Jesus was astounded by the faith of the centurion: "I have not found anyone in Israel with such great faith" (Matt. 8:10). Do you know what it was that the commander understood? *Authority.*

> *I cover myself with your blood—my spirit, my soul, and my body. And I ask your Holy Spirit to restore my union with you, seal me in you, and guide me in this time of prayer. In all that I now pray, I include (my wife, and/or my children, by name). Acting as their head, I bring them under my authority and covering, and I come under your authority and covering. Holy Spirit, apply to them all that I now pray on their behalf.*

The major ways we give claim to the Enemy in our lives are through sin and through making agreements with him. Most of our sins fall under the category of pride (independence from God, self-sufficiency) and idolatry (giving our devotion or our fear or any part of the heart to something other than God). In this part of the prayer we humble ourselves by declaring God's rightful place in our lives. And we ask him to search us so that we might confess any sin or agreement we've unknowingly made with our Enemy.

> *Dear God, holy and victorious Trinity, you alone are worthy of all my worship, my heart's devotion, all my praise and all my trust and all the glory of my life. I worship you, bow to you, and give myself over to you in my heart's search for life. You alone are Life, and you have become my life. I renounce all other gods, all idols, and I give*

you the place in my heart and in my life that you truly deserve. I con-
fess here and now that it is all about you, God, and not about me.
You are the Hero of this story, and I belong to you. Forgive me, God,
for my every sin. Search me and know me and reveal to me any
aspect of my life that is not pleasing to you, expose any agreements I
have made, and grant me the grace of a deep and true repentance.

God is Trinity, and we must learn to relate to him as such. We begin with our Father, who has done so much for us in Jesus Christ. Part of the way the saints overcome the Evil One in Revelation 12:11 is by "the word of their testimony." It's so powerful to declare again what is true, what God is to us, and what he has done on our behalf. (There's so much Scripture in this prayer, I've added notes, which you'll find at the end of this chapter, so that it doesn't distract from the actual praying. But you'll find it worthwhile to go over the passages at some point.)

Heavenly Father, thank you for loving me and choosing me before
you made the world.[1] You are my true Father—my Creator, my
Redeemer, my Sustainer, and the true end of all things, including my
life. I love you; I trust you; I worship you. Thank you for proving your
love for me by sending your only Son, Jesus, to be my substitute and
representative.[2] I receive him and all his life and all his work, which
you ordained for me. Thank you for including me in Christ,[3] for for-
giving me my sins,[4] for granting me his righteousness,[5] for making me
complete in him.[6] Thank you for making me alive with Christ,[7] rais-
ing me with him,[8] seating me with him at your right hand,[9] granting
me his authority,[10] and anointing me with your Holy Spirit.[11] I receive
it all with thanks and give it total claim to my life.

Now we turn to the Son and to his three great works on our behalf, starting with the Cross. There is so much more that the

Cross has accomplished than our forgiveness, but the constant barrage of the Enemy's lies wears us down over time, and we forget what is true. By entering into the work of Christ daily, we appropriate in a fresh way all he has already done for us. After all, Christ told us to take up our cross daily, for we must "put to death the misdeeds" of the flesh (Luke 9:23; Rom. 8:13).

> *Jesus, thank you for coming for me, for ransoming me with your own life.[12] I honor you as my Lord; I love you, worship you, trust you. I sincerely receive you as my redemption, and I receive all the work and triumph of your crucifixion, whereby I am cleansed from all my sin through your shed blood,[13] my old nature is removed,[14] my heart is circumcised unto God,[15] and every claim being made against me is disarmed.[16] I take my place in your cross and death, whereby I have died with you to sin and to my flesh,[17] to the world,[18] and to the Evil One.[19] I am crucified with Christ, and I have crucified my flesh with all its passions and desires.[20] I take up my cross and crucify my flesh with all its pride, unbelief, and idolatry. I put off the old man.[21] I now bring the cross of Christ between me and all people, all spirits, all things. Holy Spirit, apply to me (my wife and/or children) the fullness of the work of the crucifixion of Jesus Christ for me. I receive it with thanks and give it total claim to my life.*

Having put off the old man, we are told to put on the new (Eph. 4:24). The Resurrection astounded the first several centuries of the church; they saw it as central to living the Christian life. It's *life* that he promised, and it's *life* that we need. The Resurrection gives us that life. How awesome to begin to discover that through the power of the life of Christ in us, we *are* saved by his life (Rom. 5:10). We do, indeed, "reign in life" through him (Rom. 5:17).

> *Jesus, I also sincerely receive you as my new life, my holiness and sanctification, and I receive all the work and triumph of your resurrection, whereby I have been raised with you to a new life,[22] to walk in newness of life, dead to sin and alive to God.[23] I am crucified with Christ, and it is no longer I who live but Christ who lives in me.[24] I now take my place in your resurrection, whereby I have been made alive with you,[25] I reign in life through you.[26] I now put on the new man in all holiness and humility, in all righteousness and purity and truth. Christ is now my life,[27] the one who strengthens me.[28] Holy Spirit, apply to me (my wife and/or my children) the fullness of the resurrection of Jesus Christ for me. I receive it with thanks and give it total claim to my life.*

Finally, we turn to the ascension of Christ, whereby he was given all authority in heaven and earth. By the grace of God, we share that authority with Jesus. It was Adam who gave it away, and it was Christ who won it back. Satan and his emissaries bank an awful lot of their work on the fact that Christians don't know the power and authority we now have in Christ. When we begin to exercise that fierce mastery, everything begins to change.

> *Jesus, I also sincerely receive you as my authority and rule, my everlasting victory over Satan and his kingdom, and I receive all the work and triumph of your ascension, whereby Satan has been judged and cast down,[29] his rulers and authorities disarmed,[30] all authority in heaven and on earth given to you, Jesus,[31] and I have been given fullness in you, the Head over all.[32] I take my place in your ascension, whereby I have been raised with you to the right hand of the Father and established with you in all authority.[33] I bring your authority and your kingdom rule over my life, my family, my household, and my domain.*
>
> *And now I bring the fullness of your work—your cross, resurrection,*

and ascension—against Satan, against his kingdom, and against all his emissaries and all their work warring against me and my domain. Greater is he who is in me than he who is in the world.[34] *Christ has given me authority to overcome all the power of the Evil One, and I claim that authority now over and against every enemy, and I banish them in the name of Jesus Christ.*[35] *Holy Spirit, apply to me (my wife and my children) the fullness of the work of the ascension of Jesus Christ for me. I receive it with thanks and give it total claim to my life.*

Now we turn to the third member of the Trinity, the Holy Spirit. For as the Bible says, "Now the Lord is the Spirit, and where the Spirit of the Lord is, there is freedom" (2 Cor. 3:17). We want all of the freedom that the Spirit of God gives to us, and we want all of his work in our lives. So we honor him as Lord, and choose to walk in step with him at all times. You don't have to be Pentecostal to appreciate all that the Holy Spirit was meant to be toward us. Personally, I don't consider myself a charismatic, but I do need and want all that the Spirit of God offers me. After all, Christ sent him to us . . . at pentecost (Acts 2).

Holy Spirit, I sincerely receive you as my Counselor, my Comforter, my Strength, and my Guide.[36] *Thank you for sealing me in Christ.*[37] *I honor you as my Lord, and I ask you to lead me into all truth, to anoint me for all of my life and walk and calling, and to lead me deeper into Jesus today.*[38] *I fully open my life to you in every dimension and aspect—my body, my soul, and my spirit— choosing to be filled with you, to walk in step with you in all things.*[39] *Apply to me, blessed Holy Spirit, all of the work and all of the gifts in pentecost.*[40] *Fill me afresh, blessed Holy Spirit. I receive you with thanks and give you total claim to my life (and my wife and/or children).*

Having given the triune God his rightful place in our lives, and having received all that God has done for us, we turn now to some final preparations for the day:

Heavenly Father, thank you for granting to me every spiritual blessing in the heavenlies in Christ Jesus.[41]

I receive those blessings into my life today, and I ask the Holy Spirit to bring all those blessings into my life this day. Thank you for the blood of Jesus. Wash me once more with his blood from every sin and stain and evil device. I put on your armor—the belt of truth, the breastplate of righteousness, the shoes of the readiness of the gospel of peace, the helmet of salvation. I take up the shield of faith and the sword of the Spirit, the Word of God, and I wield these weapons against the Evil One in the power of God. I choose to pray at all times in the Spirit, to be strong in you, Lord, and in your might.[42]

Father, thank you for your angels. I summon them in the authority of Jesus Christ and release them to war for me and my household.[43] *May they guard me at all times this day. Thank you for those who pray for me; I confess I need their prayers, and I ask you to send forth your Spirit and rouse them, unite them, raising up the full canopy of prayer and intercession for me.*[44] *I call forth the kingdom of the Lord Jesus Christ this day throughout my home, my family, my life, and my domain. I pray all of this in the name of Jesus Christ, with all glory and honor and thanks to him.*

We've been praying along these lines for several years now. Every time we do it's like a fog lifting—the clouds break, and suddenly, faith is obvious, God is near, we see again, and we can breathe. Give it a week or two—you'll see. (For your convenience, the prayer has been duplicated at the back of this book, intact and without footnotes.) Walking in the stream of Warfare will draw you close to Christ, for there is no other safe place to abide. It will make you holy because you'll find that the Enemy will try to seize any open door—sort of like a presidential campaign. They look for "dirt" on you, go through old files. As the attack comes, it causes you to sanctify yourself even more deeply, close those doors, break those agreements. And it will deepen your appreciation for the work of Christ on your behalf. He has not left you on your own; he *did* come through. Mightily.

In the second film of *The Lord of the Rings* trilogy—*The Two Towers*—there is a king who is reluctant to go to war. Theoden, lord of the horse warriors of Rohan, is fearful and timid. An army is marching through his lands, an army bred for a single purpose: to destroy the world of men. Villages fall; women and children are slain. Still Theoden balks: "I will not risk open war." "Open war is upon you," says Aragorn, "whether you would risk it or not." As I watched this scene I could not help thinking of the church. It made me so sad. I love the Bride of Christ. I hate to see her captive in any way. *The primary reason* most people do not know the freedom and life Christ promised is that they won't fight for it, or they have been told not to fight for it. Friends, we are now in the midst of an epic battle, a brutal and vicious war against an Enemy who knows his time is short. Open war is upon you, whether you would risk it or not.

NOTES
1. Ephesians 1:4.
2. Romans 5:8.
3. 1 Corinthians 1:30.
4. Colossians 2:13.
5. 2 Corinthians 5:21.
6. Colossians 2:10.
7. Colossians 2:13.
8. Colossians 3:1.
9. Ephesians 2:6.
10. Luke 10:19; Ephesians 2:6.

11. Ephesians 1:13.
12. Matthew 20:28.
13. 1 John 1:9.
14. Colossians 2:11.
15. Romans 2:29.
16. Colossians 2:15.
17. Romans 6:11.
18. Galatians 6:14.
19. Colossians 1:13.
20. Galatians 2:20.
21. Ephesians 4:22.
22. Romans 6:4.
23. Romans 6:11.
24. Galatians 2:20.
25. Ephesians 2:5.
26. Romans 5:17.
27. Colossians 3:4.
28. Philippians 4:13.
29. John 12:31.
30. Colossians 2:15.
31. Matthew 28:18.
32. Colossians 2:10.
33. Ephesians 2:6.
34. 1 John 4:4.
35. Luke 10:19.
36. John 14:16; Acts 9:31.
37. Ephesians 1:13.
38. John 15:26; 16:13.
39. Galatians 5:25.
40. Ephesians 4:8.
41. Ephesians 1:3.
42. Ephesians 6:10–18.
43. Hebrews 1:14.
44. 2 Corinthians 1:8–11.

PART FOUR

THE WAY OF THE HEART

Rise, heart
Thy Lord is risen.
—GEORGE HERBERT

If all of this is true (and it is true), there are some deep and urgent implications. Many of those have probably begun to occur to you already. But there are two I must unveil.

You might remember that the first Christians were called "followers of the Way" (Acts 9:2; 18:25–26). They had found the Way of Life and had given themselves over to it. They lived together, ate together, fought together, celebrated together. They were intimate allies; it was a fellowship of the heart. How wonderful it would be if we could find the same. How dangerous it will be if we do not.

Finally, let me ask you a question: How would you live differently if you believed your heart was the treasure of the kingdom? Because we are at war, the business of guarding the heart is a most serious business indeed. It is precisely because we do not know what the next turn of the page will bring that we nourish our hearts *now*, knowing at least this much: we will need our whole hearts for whatever is coming next. Above all else, you must care for your heart. For without your heart . . . well, have a look around.

CHAPTER ELEVEN

FELLOWSHIPS OF THE HEART

All the believers were one in heart.

—LUKE THE PHYSICIAN (ACTS 4:32)

Elrond summoned the hobbits to him. He looked gravely at Frodo. "The time has come," he said.

"The Company of the Ring shall be Nine; and the Nine Walkers shall be set against the Nine Riders that are evil. With you and your faithful servant, Gandalf will go; for this shall be his great task, and maybe the end of his labors. For the rest, they shall represent the other Free Peoples of the World: Elves, Dwarves, and Men. Legolas shall be for the Elves; and Gimli son of Glóin for the Dwarves. They are willing to go at least to the passes of the Mountains, and maybe beyond. For men you shall have Aragorn son of Arathorn, for the Ring of Isildur concerns him closely."

"Strider!" cried Frodo. "Yes," he said with a smile. "I ask leave once again to be your companion, Frodo." "I would have begged you to come," said Frodo, "only I thought you were going to Minis Tirith with Boromir." "I am," said Aragorn. "And the Sword-that-was-Broken shall be re-forged ere I set out to war. But your road and our road lie together for many hundreds of miles. Therefore Boromir will also be in the Company. He is a valiant man."

"There remain two more to be found," said Elrond. "These I will consider. Of my household I may find some that it seems good for me to send." "But that will leave no place for us!" cried Pippin in dismay. "We don't want to be left behind. We want to go with Frodo." "That is because you do not understand and cannot imagine what lies ahead," said Elrond. "Neither does Frodo," said Gandalf, unexpectedly supporting Pippin. "Nor do any of us see clearly. It is true that if these hobbits understood the danger, they would not dare to go. But they would still wish to go, or wish they had dared, and be shamed and unhappy. I think, Elrond, that in this matter it would be well to trust rather to their friendship than to great wisdom."

"Let it be so, then. You shall go," said Elrond, and he sighed. "Now the tale of Nine is filled. In seven days the Company must depart." (J. R. R. Tolkien, *The Fellowship of the Ring*)

We Happy Few

Once more, lend a mythic eye to your situation. Let your heart ponder this:

You awake to find yourself in the midst of a great and terrible war. It is, in fact, our most desperate hour. Your King and dearest Friend calls you forth. Awake, come fully alive, your good heart set free and blazing for him and for those yet to be rescued. You have a glory that is needed. You are given a quest, a mission that will take you deep into the heart of the kingdom of darkness, to break down gates of bronze and cut through bars of iron so that your people might be set free from their bleak prisons. He asks that you heal them. Of course, you will face many dangers; you will be hunted.

Would you try to do this *alone?*

Something stronger than fate *has* chosen you. Evil *will* hunt you. And so a fellowship *must* protect you. Honestly, though he is a very brave and true hobbit, Frodo hasn't a chance without Sam, Merry, Pippin, Gandalf, Aragorn, Legolas, and Gimli. He has no real idea what dangers and trials lie ahead. The dark mines of Moria; the Balrog that awaits him there; the evil orcs called the Urak-hai that will hunt him; the wastes of the Emyn Muil. He will need his friends. And you will need yours. You must cling to those you have; you must search wide and far for those you do not yet have. *You must not go alone.* From the beginning, right there in Eden, the Enemy's strategy has relied upon a simple aim: divide and conquer. Get them isolated, and take them out.

When Neo is set free from the Matrix, he joins the crew of the *Nebuchadnezzar*—the little hovercraft that is the headquarters and ship of the small fellowship called to set the captives free. There are nine of them in all, each a character in his own way, but nonetheless a company of the heart, a "band of brothers," a family bound together in a single fate. Together, they train for battle. Together, they plan their path. When they go back into the Matrix to set others free, each one has a role, a gifting, a glory. They function as a team. And they watch each other's back. Neo is fast, really fast, but he still would have been taken out if it hadn't been for Trinity. Morpheus is more gifted than them all, but it took the others to rescue him.

You see this sort of thing at the center of every great story. Dorothy takes her journey with the Scarecrow, the Tin Woodman, the Lion, and of course, Toto. Prince Caspian is joined by the last few faithful Narnians, and together they overthrow the wicked king Miraz. Though in the eyes of the world they are only gladiator-slaves, walking dead men, Maximus rallies his little band and triumphs over the greatest empire on earth. When Captain John Miller is sent deep behind enemy lines to save Private Ryan, he goes in with a squad of eight rangers. And, of course, Jesus had the Twelve. This is written so deeply on our hearts: *You must not go alone.* The Scriptures are full of such warnings, but until we see our desperate situation, we hear it as an optional religious assembly for an hour on Sunday mornings.

Think again of Frodo or Neo or Caspian or Jesus. Imagine you are surrounded by a small company of friends who know you well (characters, to be sure, but they love you, and you have come to love them). They understand that we all are at war, know that the purposes of God are to bring a man or a woman fully alive, and are living by sheer necessity and joy in the Four Streams. They fight for you, and you for them. Imagine you *could* have a little fellowship of the heart. Would you want it if it were available?

This Is Available

Leigh was born to dance.

But the story of her life is the story of that glory assaulted, stolen, and given up for lost. (This is *always* the story.) She was actually the first woman ever to win a scholarship to her university for dance. That might tell you how gifted she is. But talent alone is never enough to overcome wounds, and brokenness, and whatever hell has thrown at you from your childhood. Shame and Judgment hunted Leigh from her youth; they seemed larger than her heart to dance. She dropped out of school, married, had children, went on with her life. Still, the longing would not go away. When no one else was around, Leigh would dance alone in her house, like a writer composing poetry from prison, or like a dolphin swimming round and round its tank in captivity. From behind those infamous gates and bars, Leigh's heart cried out to be free to do what she was meant to do.

Thirty years of seclusion went by. Thirty. Then Leigh took a risk. She joined the dance ministry of her church. And she shone. Even though she's old enough by now to be the mother of the other dancers, Leigh stood out. She shone so much, in fact, that others were threatened by her glory. You can hear it coming. Remember Joseph's brothers? Cinderella's stepsisters? Satan seized the opportunity—accused Leigh of "pride" in the hearts of some of the members of the team, who turned on Leigh and shamed her openly. (The attack always comes to "your heart is bad.") Not wanting to be a source of strife, Leigh withdrew.

It became more and more obvious to us that Leigh would never step into her glory unless someone fought for her. Fiercely. Over the years her husband, Gary, fought valiantly for her, but more was needed. Jesus reassures us: "I tell you the truth, whatever you bind on earth will be bound in heaven . . . if two of you on earth agree" (Matt. 18:18–19). Off and on, over the course of maybe a year, we battled spiritual warfare for Leigh. One Saturday morning three of us men spent more than three hours coming against her tormentors, who were strong. Shame was there. So was Judgment. On another night Stasi had a vision of a huge serpent binding Leigh's feet. Aaron sent it to hell. Can captives be rescued from "the fierce" (Isa. 49:24)? You betcha.

Leigh persevered. During our evenings together, there arose opportunities for prayer for the healing of childhood memories, too, and the mending of her broken heart. This all took place in the normal life of our community. At another point the women gathered to celebrate Leigh's birthday. Their gift: dance shoes (something she could never bring herself to spend money on). Their words of love and encouragement might have been the greater gift, though. "You can do this, Leigh. We are for you." Those words meant something because they *knew* her. Words of life. Then, from within the fellowship, an opportunity came up for Leigh to dance—solo—before two thousand people. Understandably . . . she hesitated. Should she take the risk again? Was it a setup for disaster?

Leigh asked us to pray and listen to God on her behalf. *Is this the one, Lord?* It's so hard to hear from God when your own story is tangled up in it, and the Enemy has long assaulted the very thing you are wondering about. *Yes, it is time.* As Leigh practiced for the Big Day, she continued to be assaulted. She lost the rehearsal room. Her choreographer bailed. She pulled a hamstring. One physical injury after another. The Enemy laughed and mocked and threw the book at her. But her fellowship would not let her go. We slew the orcs; we found the trail; we stuck together.

After all those years, Leigh finally danced.

And she was glorious. I mean, it was *powerful.* Her performance launched other opportunities to dance. And *it would not have happened* without her friends.

I could fill a book with stories like that one, involving each member of our fellowship and the way we live in the Four Streams on behalf of one another. It's really quite normal, as ordinary as sending out for Chinese food or chatting on the phone.

It Must Be Small

When he left Rivendell, Frodo didn't head out with a thousand Elves. He had eight companions. Jesus didn't march around backed by hundreds of followers, either. He had twelve men—knuckleheads, every last one of them, but they were a band of brothers. This is the way of the kingdom of God. Though we are part of a great company, we are meant to live in little platoons. The little companies we form must be small enough for each of the members to know one another as friends and allies. Is it possible for five thousand people who gather for an hour on a Sunday morning to really and truly *know* each other? Okay, how about five hundred? One hundred and eighty? It can't be done. They can't possibly be intimate allies. It can be inspiring and encouraging to celebrate with a big ol' crowd of people, but who will fight for your heart?

Who will fight for your heart?

How can we offer the stream of Counseling to one another unless we actually *know* one another, know one another's stories? Counseling became a hired relationship between two people primarily because we couldn't find it anywhere else; we haven't formed the sort of small fellowships that would allow the stream to flow quite naturally. Is it possible to offer rich and penetrating words to someone you barely know, in the lobby of your church, as you dash to pick up the kids? And what about warfare? Would you feel comfortable turning to the person in the pew next to you and, as you pass the offering plate, asking him to bind a demon that is sitting on your head?

Where will you find the Four Streams?

The Four Streams are something we learn, and grow into, and offer one another, within a small fellowship. We hear each other's stories. We discover each other's glories. We learn to walk with God together. We pray for each other's healing. We cover each other's back. This small core fellowship is the essential ingredient for the Christian life. Jesus modeled it for us *for a reason*. Sure, he spoke to the masses. But he *lived* in a little platoon, a small fellowship of friends and allies. His followers took his example and lived this way too: "They broke bread in their homes and ate together with glad and sincere hearts" (Acts 2:46); "Aquila and Priscilla greet you warmly in the Lord, and so does the church that meets at their house" (1 Cor. 16:19); "Give my greetings to the brothers at Laodicea, and to Nympha and the church in her house" (Col. 4:15).

Church is not a building. Church is not an event that takes place on Sundays. I know, it's how we've come to think of it. "I go to First Baptist." "We are members of St. Luke's." "Is it time to go to church?" Much to our surprise, that is *not* how the Bible uses the term. Not at all. Certainly, the body of Christ is a vast throng, millions of people around the globe. But when Scripture talks about church, it means *community*. The little fellowships of the heart that are outposts of the kingdom. A shared life. They worship together, eat together, pray for one another, go on quests together. They hang out together, in each other's homes. When Peter was sprung from prison, "he went to the house of Mary the mother of John" where the church had gathered to pray for his release (Acts 12:12).

Anytime an army goes to war or an expedition takes to the field, it breaks down into little platoons and squads. And *every* chronicle of war or quest will tell you that the men and women who fought so bravely fought *for each other*. That's where the acts of heroism and sacrifice take place because that's where the devotion is. You simply cannot be devoted to a mass of people; devotion takes place in small units, just as in a family.

> We have stopped short of being an organization; we are an organism instead, a living and spontaneous association of individuals who know one another intimately, care for each other deeply, and feel a kind of respect for one another that makes rules and bylaws unnecessary. A group is the right size, I would guess, when each member can pray for every other member, individually and by name.

The preceding is the wisdom of Brother Andrew, who smuggled Bibles into Communist countries for decades. It's the model, frankly, of the church in nearly every country but the U.S. Now, I'm not suggesting you not do whatever it is you do on Sunday mornings. I'm simply helping you accept reality—whatever else you do, you *must* have a small fellowship to walk with you and fight with you and bandage your wounds. Remember, the path is narrow, and *few* find it. *Few* means "small in number," as opposed to, say, massive. This is essential. This is what the Scriptures urge us to do. First. Foremost. Not as an addition to Sunday. *Before* anything else.

It Must Be Intimate

Of course, small groups have become a part of the programming that most churches offer their people. For the most part, they are short-lived. There are two reasons. First, you can't just throw a random group of people together for a twelve-week study of some kind and expect them to become intimate allies. The sort of devotion we want and need takes place within a shared life. Over the years our fellowship has gone camping together. We play together; help one another move; paint a room; find work. We throw great parties. We fight for each other, live in the Four Streams. This is how it was meant to be.

I love this description of the early church: "All the believers were one in heart" (Acts 4:32). A camaraderie was being expressed there, a bond, an esprit de corps. It means they all loved the same thing, they all wanted the same thing, and they were bonded together to find it, come hell or high water. And hell or high water *will* come, friends, and this will be the test of whether or not your band will make it: if you are one in heart. Judas betrayed the brothers because his heart was never really with them, just as Cipher betrays the company on the *Nebuchadnezzar* and as Boromir betrays the fellowship of the Ring. My goodness—churches split over the size of the parking lot or what instruments to use during worship. Most churches are *not* "one in heart."

Second, most small groups are anything but redemptive powerhouses because, while the wineskin might be the right size, they don't have the right wine. You can do some study till you're blue in the face, and it won't heal the brokenhearted or set the captives free. We come; we learn; we leave. It is not enough. Those hearts remain buried, broken, untouched, *unknown*. It is the Way of the Heart and the Four Streams that turns a small fellowship into a redemptive community. It is knowing that you are at war, that God has chosen you and evil is hunting you, and so a fellowship like Frodo's must protect you. How many small groups have you been a part of where what we did for Leigh is what happens all the time?

On a Tuesday evening last January, those of us in our fellowship were sitting around talking about our need to see the rest of the picture, how we cannot make good decisions or even know what's really going on without eyes to *see*. That led into a conversation about the power of myth to open the eyes of our hearts. I suggested we do this: "Write down on a piece of paper five words or phrases that capture your life right now. What does it feel like? Don't edit. Don't make it sound better than it is. How are you doing?" It began an incredibly eye-opening journey.

Once we had our words or phrases (many of us couldn't keep it to five), I then asked, "What stories or scenes or characters help you *interpret* those words, help you see what's going on, give a context to your words for your life right now?" You see, no experience or feeling provides its own interpretation. You feel besieged on all sides. Are you Elijah on Mount Carmel, on the brink of great victory? Or are you Paul in Thessalonica, and you'd better get out of town, *fast*? We have to find something that gives our experiences meaning and context. And that's when the really good stuff took place. First, we shared our words and the stories that we felt interpreted them for us. Then, the fellowship offered to each other the characters and scenes that *we* saw for each other.

Misty had moved to our community a year earlier and had gone through a pretty tough time. New apartment, new job, all that.

Would she fit in? Does she really have anything to offer? Her words were: "Newness, uncharted territory, yellow brick road, fighting, a page turned, warfare." She thought that, maybe, there *might* be some truth for her in Dorothy from *The Wizard of Oz,* at least early in the story: "She sees things in others and calls them forth, but she's desperate to come home." The other story Misty chose felt more true; she really felt like the young woman in *Ever After* who "poses as royalty to save a servant friend, but she is exposed as less than royalty." As we listened first to her words and then to her interpretation, we all quietly jotted down our own stories for her.

When it was our chance to offer comments, five different people said, "Arwen," from *The Lord of the Rings.* It fit perfectly. She is beautiful (what woman doesn't long to hear this?), she is a warrior, and she is regal. And that is so true of Misty—all of it. Three folks also chose Dorothy from *Oz;* not because she's lost, but because she is right where she needs to be, and especially because she has a heart of gold. (By this point Misty is in tears. Did I mention she moved here from *Kansas?*) Then a real home run came—at least two of us offered Joan of Arc. I was one of them, and I had no idea where it came from. Misty was speechless. "I'm reading a book on her life right now. She's who I so *want* to be." God was speaking. What made it so powerful was that we saw her, she knew she was exposed to us, and what we saw was her glory. She felt called into something Great and Weighty, with beauty and courage to match.

"Longing, fear, lonely, waiting, thwarted." Those were Aaron's words. He chose Boromir from *The Fellowship of the Ring* "because he's the one that gets taken out, he's unstable, a mess." Aaron has fought a long, hard battle against a lot of oppression—some pretty fierce stuff. And his deep brokenness has often made him feel like he's just a mess. It's not true—but you know how when you're in need, it feels so shameful, like you're always in need. There was a moment of silence. Then every last one of us said, almost in the same breath, "Strider—Aragorn." Early in the story, isn't he also longing, lonely, waiting, thwarted? Aaron was speechless. "You're a good man, Aaron. You've walked a lonely trail, fought many hard battles. But your heart is good. You *are* Strider." Very, very quietly, like the dawn, he said, "That's who I want to be."

Stasi's words for her life were "persevering, hidden, misunderstood, weary, mundane tasks." She chose Lucy from *The Lion, the Witch and the Wardrobe* "because she wants to be faithful and true." (You'll recall that Lucy was also rather plain and not too pretty.) She also wrote down Lucilla, the empress in *Gladiator,* "because I long to be a beautiful, courageous empress." Notice that nearly always *our* interpretation of our days will reveal what we long to be but fear we really are not. Then it was our turn. Someone offered Cinderella, and *everyone* said, "Oh, my gosh. Yes!" She, too, was persevering, hidden, misunderstood, given mundane tasks. But she was also beautiful and didn't know it. We know Stasi's story; her glory *has* been assaulted. Remember how the wicked stepsisters tore the gown off Cinderella, so she couldn't go to the ball? I reminded Stasi of the time her sisters actually did that very thing to her. She burst into tears. "I forgot all about that . . . Oh, my." The truth was reaching her heart.

It was an incredible evening. All of us had chosen words that were hard (life is *hard*), and all our interpretations of our own lives were off. Each of us was in the process of making subtle agreements with the Enemy, and we weren't even aware of it. It was only through the eyes of our friends that we recovered our hearts, our true place, reality. But the real power of living in community is, we remembered those stories for months, and we used them for each other at crucial moments in the battle ahead. Jenny later said, "What makes this community so powerful is that you remember my story for me. I don't have to carry the burden of remembering alone." I tell you about that night because that's the kind of intimacy you need. It wouldn't have been possible to offer that to one another in a larger gathering. We need *intimate* allies.

IT WILL BE MESSY

The family is . . . like a little kingdom, and, like most other little kingdoms, is generally in a state of something resembling anarchy.

G. K. Chesterton could have been talking about a little fellowship (our *true* family, because it is the family of God). It is a royal mess. I will not whitewash this. It is *disruptive*. Going to church with hundreds of other people to sit and hear a sermon doesn't ask much of you. It certainly will never expose you. That's why most folks prefer it. Because community will. It will reveal where you have yet to become holy, right at the very moment you are so keenly aware of how *they* have yet to become holy. It will bring you close and you will be *seen* and you will be *known,* and therein lies the power and therein lies the danger. Aren't there moments when all those little companies, in all those stories, hang by a thread? Galadriel says to Frodo, "Your quest stands upon the edge of a knife. Stray but a little and it will fail, to the ruin of all. Yet hope remains while the Company is true."

We've experienced incredible disappointments in our fellowship. We have, every last one of us, hurt one another. Sometimes deeply. Last year there was a night when Stasi and I laid out a vision for where we thought things should be going—our lifelong dream for redemptive community. We hoped the Company would leap to it with loud hurrahs. "Hurrah for John and Stasi!" Far from it. Their response was more on the level of blank stares. Our dream was mishandled—badly. Stasi was sick to her stomach; she wanted to leave the room and throw up. I was . . . stunned. Disappointed. I felt the dive toward a total loss of heart. The following day I could feel my heart being pulled toward resentment. Moments like that usually toll the beginning of the end for most attempts at community.

Seriously now—how often have you seen this sort of intimate community work? It is *rare*. Because it is hard, and it is fiercely *opposed*. The Enemy hates this sort of thing; he knows how powerful it can be, for God and his kingdom. For our hearts. It is devastating to him. Remember divide and conquer? Most churches survive because everyone keeps a polite distance from the others. We keep our meetings short, our conversations superficial. "So, Ted, how's everything going on the Stewardship Committee?" "Oh, just great, Nancy. We've got a big goal to reach this year, but I think we'll be able to get that gym after all." No one is really being set free, but no one is really at odds with each other, either. We have settled for safety in numbers—a comfortable, anonymous distance. An army that keeps meeting for briefings, but never breaks into platoons and goes to war.

Living in community is like camping together. For a month. In the desert. Without tents. All your stuff is scattered out there for everyone to see. C'mon—anybody can look captured for Christ an hour a week, from a distance, in his Sunday best. But your life is open to those you live in community with. Some philosopher described it like a pack of porcupines on a winter night. You come together because of the cold, and you are forced apart because of the spines. *Here we go again. Why does Jim always have to be discouraged? I'm sick of encouraging him. And what is it with Mary and her inability to stop talking about herself? Why is Brian always so guarded? These people* bug *me.*

However, there are two things you now have that you didn't have before, and they enable this sort of fellowship to work. First, you know the heart is good. That is the missing key in most fellowships. Your heart is good, and the others' hearts are good. This makes it so much easier to trust and to forgive. Whatever may be happening in the moment, whatever the misunderstanding might be, I know that our hearts toward one another are good, and that we are for one another. Craig says something that stings. If I thought, *You know, he meant that; he's trying to hurt me,* it would pretty quickly trash the relationship. But I know that is not his heart toward me; that is not who he truly is. If I thought it was, why, I'd turn tail and run.

Second, we know we are at war. The thought that says, *Oh, brother, here goes Frank again. Why can't he just drop it about his mother? What is it with these people? They're not really my friends. I'm outta here.* That's the Enemy. You *must* remember that the Enemy is always trying to pull everyone else to do to you what *he* is doing to you. As I said earlier, he creates a kind of force field, a gravitational pull around you that draws others into the plot without their even knowing it. Gary walks into the room and, suddenly, I'm irritated at him. It's not me, and it's not him. I have to know that. His lifelong assault has been, "If you can't get it right, we don't want to be with you." It's a lie. It's the Enemy. I don't feel that way toward him *really.* But unless I live with this awareness, keep a watchful eye out for it, and resist, I'll get sucked into the pull, start making agreements with it, and there goes the friendship.

Fight for It

> Be kind, for everyone you know is facing a great battle. (Philo of Alexandria)

A true community is something you'll have to fight for. You'll have to fight to get one, and you'll have to fight to keep it afloat. But you fight for it as you bail out a life raft during a storm at sea. You want this thing to work. You *need* this thing to work. You can't ditch it and jump back on the cruise ship. This *is* the church; this is all you have. Without it, you'll go down. Or back to captivity. This is the reason those small house fellowships thrive in other countries: they *need* each other. There are no other options.

Suddenly, all those *one another*'s in Scripture make sense. Love one another. Bear one another's burdens. Forgive one another. Acts of kindness become deeply meaningful because we know we are at war. Knowing full well that we all are facing battles of our own, we give one another the benefit of the doubt. *Leigh isn't intentionally being distant from me—she's probably under an assault.* That's why you must know each other's stories, know how to "read" each other. A word of encouragement can heal a wound; a choice to forgive can destroy a stronghold. You never knew your simple acts were so *weighty*. It's what we've come to call "lifestyle warfare."

We check in regularly with one another, not out of paranoia ("Do you still like me?"), but out of a desire to watch over one another's hearts. "How are you doing?" But be careful about what you are looking for from community. For if you bring your every need to it, it will collapse. Community is no substitute for God. I left our annual camping trip absolutely exhausted and disappointed. As we drove home, I realized I was looking to them to validate me, appreciate me, fill this aching void in my heart. Only once in ten days did I take time to be away with God, alone. I was too busy trying to get my needs met through them. Which is why community cannot live without solitude.

I was so struck by the layout of the early Irish and Scottish monasteries when we visited there last year. First, they knew they *had* to live in community. They needed each other. But in every single location, set apart from the community buildings by about a twenty-minute walk, you'd find little "cells," small stone huts designed for one member to get alone and be with God. They knew community could not survive without solitude. There is a rhythm to life together, as Bonhoeffer said. We first go to God, alone, so that we have something to bring back to the community. This is part of lifestyle warfare. I know my community needs me; everyone is coming over tonight. So I'd better get with God this afternoon. I want to contribute. I want to play a vital role.

THE TIME HAS COME AGAIN

It's the little platoons that change the world. This has always been true.

In 564 Saint Columba (Columcille in Gaelic) left his beloved Ireland in a coracle, sail unfurled, willing to let God lead him wherever he might for the sake of the gospel. With him were twelve disciples, friends, warrior-monks as they would later be called. They landed on a small island off the coast of Scotland (at the time a dark, vicious, pagan country), and there they established what they called a "little heavenly community." The place was Iona, and it became the center of a new and vibrant Christianity.

Now, in order to realize what Iona was and what it means for us, you must understand the context of that moment in history. First, the world around them had grown very dark. Night had fallen with the fall of Rome; the Vandals and the Goths and the Visigoths and all those predatory gangs had swept down upon Europe and basically ransacked the place. Western Europe was like L.A. during the riots. Paganism flourished; law and order were long gone. It was barbarous.

But you must also know that at the time of Iona, the Christian church based in Rome was already becoming institutionalized, hierarchical, far more an organization than it was an organism. That living and spontaneous association of individuals who know one another intimately and care for one another deeply was giving way to a large, centralized, bureaucratic church where rules and bylaws become necessary. Sad, but true. And so I hope you see that it was a time very much like our own. A world, come to think of it, very much like the one the early church also found itself in. The synagogue was dead, and the cultures around them pagan indeed. What did they do? They came together into little fellowships of the heart.

Iona and its warrior-monks began to carry their light into that darkness. Columba won to Christ the king of the Picts, the notorious pagan warriors of northern Scotland who painted their faces blue before battle (the precursors of *Braveheart*). In winning him, Columba won over a great deal of Scotland. Iona also became the staging point for missionary raids into England and deep into Europe. In this way, Irish monasticism and Celtic Christianity began to change the world. Everywhere they went, they established communities like their own, little "fellowships of the heart" along the way. It was the book of Acts all over again. It was a spirituality of the heart, based in a community that knew it was at war, and it was unstoppable. Historian Thomas Cahill said Iona "forever changed the course of western history."

> Celtic spirituality is not a top-down form of church, but bottom-up. It allows spirituality to flow from the heart. It allows the five senses to be used. It's creative. It's a flowering of creative arts. It's an expression of Christianity which believes that to be Christian is to be fully human. (Ray Simpson, Lindisfarne Community)

They believed that the glory of God is man fully alive.

Our trip to Iona last year was a sort of pilgrimage, and I can tell you, it is still a remarkable place. The veil between the worlds is very thin there. As we strolled among the ruins, read their accounts, looked at their way of life, I realized that this was not the faith of some good people applying biblical principles to their lives in a fairly benign, though disappointing and fallen world. Here was the burning-heart conviction of a group of increasingly glorious men and women who wanted the freedom and life and restoration Christ promised, and who were willing to fight for it because they knew this is a world at war. A community of people living in the Four Streams because they knew the Christian life as an *epic*, no less than the greatest myths the world has ever known.

We paused by one of the ancient Celtic crosses. God spoke, and this is what he said:

I am doing this again.

God is calling together little communities of the heart, to fight for one another and for the hearts of those who have not yet been set free. That camaraderie, that intimacy, that incredible impact by a few stouthearted souls—that is available. It is the Christian life as Jesus gave it to us. It is completely normal.

CHAPTER TWELVE

LIKE THE TREASURES
OF THE KINGDOM

Arise, shine, for your light has come,
    and the glory of the LORD rises upon you.
See, darkness covers the earth
    and thick darkness is over the peoples,
but the LORD rises upon you
    and his glory appears over you.

—ISAIAH (60:1–2)

And then my soul, awaking with the morn
Shall be a waking joy, eternally new-born.

—GEORGE MACDONALD

Jesus, once more deeply moved, came to the tomb. It was a cave with a stone laid across the entrance. "Take away the stone," he said. "But, Lord," said Martha, the sister of the dead man, "by this time there is a bad odor, for he has been there four days." Then Jesus said, "Did I not tell you that if you believed, you would see the glory of God?" So they took away the stone. Then Jesus looked up and said, "Father, I thank you that you have heard me. I knew that you always hear me, but I said this for the benefit of the people standing here, that they may believe that you sent me." When he had said this, Jesus called in a loud voice, "Lazarus, come out!" The dead man came out, his hands and feet wrapped with strips of linen, and a cloth around his face. Jesus said to them, "Take off the grave clothes and let him go." (John 11:38–44)

And when Jesus had cried out again in a loud voice, he gave up his spirit. At that moment the curtain of the temple was torn in two from top to bottom. The earth shook and the rocks split. The tombs broke open and the bodies of many holy people who had died were raised to life. They came out of the tombs, and after Jesus' resurrection they went into the holy city and appeared to many people. (Matt. 27:50–53)

ARISE

I awoke in the desert on Easter morning.

Through the window of my tent, I could see branches of a pinion pine, the sharp tines of a yucca, and beyond them soft, rolling sandstone—in full daylight the color of oatmeal, but glowing golden now with first light. The birds were up, rejoicing, flitting to and fro in the pinion, but, thanks be to God, not another living thing could be seen or heard. I had awakened on my fifth morning in Arches National Park, hidden near the northeast corner of Utah, but it could have been Palestine around A.D. 33. This desert is not a wasteland, as many people wrongly picture when they hear the word, but a vibrant place full of grasses, cacti, juniper and pinion, and wildflowers scattered across the landscape, a place where you can find puma prints in the soft, wet sand down in the canyons, where springs nearly reach the surface. A place of life in many ways.

It was cold enough to see my breath when I stepped out of the tent, so I cranked the Coleman stove to set water boiling for coffee and cocoa before I roused the boys, cocooned head-and-all down in their sleeping bags. Savoring moments that were mine alone, I climbed to the top of the rocks behind our camp, to drink in the vast beauty of the desert at dawn. To the west, gigantic mesas, Navajo sandstone, rose like ancient fortresses from the desert floor, their sheer red cliffs radiating back the rays that had not reached the sands at their feet.

I turned to the east to take the glad warmth of the new day head-on, surprised to see the La Sal Mountains covered in snow, a hundred miles away. My heart was at home in this place of wild beauty and staggering vistas. But it was an awkward time to have come. On this resurrection morn, Stasi was in Los Angeles, holding the hand of her dying mother. She would be gone in less than a month. Strange timing to up and go camping. But God brought me here.

Like many pilgrims down through the ages, I discovered my spiritual life in the desert. I found solitude and silence in the Mojave of southern California, far from the numbing sameness and suffocating density of the suburbs that warehouse millions of people. The desert awakened my heart, and I discovered freedom of spirit walking across the arroyos for hours upon end, haunted by stark beauty and the thin veil of heaven there. No wonder Moses, Elijah, and John the Baptist spent their free time in the desert. And though the desert meant so much to me, spoke to my heart, I left it behind many years ago. You know how life pickpockets you of these things, slipping them away so subtly you never even notice they are gone. I simply stopped going.

In the spring of 2001, Stasi was making frequent trips to southern California to be with her mom, whom we were losing to multiple myeloma, and I was doing my best with the boys and the bills back home in Colorado. To be honest, we were simply waiting for "the call," when we would jump a flight to attend Jane's funeral. So I did not believe it was God when first I heard him say, *Go to Moab. Go to the desert.* It took several confirmations to get my attention. At a coffeehouse I ran into a young gal who in the midst of chitchat simply dropped into the conversation that she'd just returned from Moab. I did a sort of double take, then asked calmly, "How was it?" "Great," she said. "You have to go." The next day I was on the phone with a pastor from Denver, making plans for a men's retreat. "I just got back from Moab," he said, out of the blue. "It was awesome." I'm simply confessing that I came to the desert borne not on the wings of my own wisdom, but hesitantly, reluctantly, pushed along by God.

Moab. Okay. The boys are missing Mom and the distraction would be good and there's really nothing more we can do from here anyway except pray, which I might give more devotion to out in the wild, and so we came. I was surprised at the level of warfare I had to fight through. For about five hours of the drive I was forced to bring the work of Christ against an overwhelming oppression that made it hard to concentrate, a really awful veil over my spirit. Over a *camping* trip? It seemed so stupid. But the thief comes to steal and kill and destroy *any* movement toward freedom and life. We battled through, got there late, and discovered that God had held the last campsite for us.

I'm not sure I can even put into words all that Jesus restored to me in those five days, but some part of my heart long forgotten was given back, along with some deep words I desperately needed. I came alive in the vast, wild desert. And it began to sink in. *My heart matters to God. My heart has always mattered to him.* It is one thing to say we believe that; it is another thing to *discover* it is true. This was a gift unique to my heart, and it could not have been given in any other place. I awoke that Easter morning more alive than I have been in a long, long time.

TREATING YOUR HEART FOR THE TREASURE IT IS

"Above all else, guard your heart" (Prov. 4:23). We usually hear this with a sense of "keep an eye on that heart of yours," in the way you'd warn a deputy watching over some dangerous outlaw, or a bad dog the neighbors let run. "Don't let him out of your sight." Having so long believed our hearts are evil, we assume the warning is to keep us out of trouble. So we lock up our hearts and throw away the key, and then try to get on with our living. But that isn't the spirit of the command at all. It doesn't say guard your heart because it's criminal; it says guard your heart because it is the well-spring of your life, because it is a *treasure*, because everything else depends on it. How kind of God to give us this warning, like some-one's entrusting to a friend something precious to him, with the words: "Be careful with this—it means a lot to me."

Above all else? Good grief—we don't even do it once in a while. We might as well leave our life savings on the seat of the car with the windows rolled down—we're that careless with our hearts. "If not for my careless heart," sang Roy Orbison, and it might be the anthem for our lives. Things would be different. I would be farther along. My faith would be much deeper. My relationships so much better. My life would be on the path God meant for me . . . if not for my careless heart. We live completely backward. "All else" is above our hearts. I'll wager that caring for your heart isn't even a category you think in. "Let's see—I've got to get the kids to soccer, the car needs to be dropped off at the shop, and I need to take a couple of hours for *my* heart this week." It probably sounds unbib-lical, even after all we've covered.

Seriously now—what do you do on a daily basis to care for your heart? Okay, that wasn't fair. How about weekly? *Monthly?*

Yes, we do have a cultural scrap of this called vacation. Most working-class folks get a week or two off each year, and that is the only time they actually plan to do something that might be good for their souls. Or they squander the scrap on some place like Miami, as a poor man spends his last dollar on a lottery ticket. And you know how it goes when you get back. The attitude among your family, friends, and colleagues is usually something like, "Great! You're back! Hope you had a good time 'cause, boy, everything fell apart while you were gone and we're expecting—now that you're rested up—that you'll really put your nose to the grindstone." Whatever that week gave you is devoured in a matter of moments or days.

But God intends that we treat our hearts as the treasures of the kingdom, ransomed at tremendous cost, as if they really *do* matter, and matter deeply.

STORING UP TO OVERFLOW

> If then you are wise, you will show yourself rather as a reservoir than as a canal. A canal spreads abroad water as it receives it, but a reservoir waits until it is filled before overflowing, and thus without loss to itself [it shares] its superabundant water. (Bernard of Clairvaux)

A beautiful picture. The canal runs dry so quickly, shortly after the rains subside. Like a dry streambed in the desert. But a reservoir is a vast and deep reserve of life. We are called to live in a way that we store up reserves in our hearts and *then* offer from a place of abundance. Jesus said, "Every teacher of the law who has been instructed about the kingdom of heaven is like the owner of a house who brings out of his storeroom new treasures as well as old" (Matt. 13:52). I'm thinking, *Storeroom? What storeroom?* "The good man brings good things out of the good stored up *in his heart* . . . For out of the overflow of his heart his mouth speaks" (Luke 6:45, emphasis added).

I'm afraid I live spiritually the same way I live financially—I get a little and go spend it. I live like a canal. I *look* like a reservoir when the rains come, but shortly after, I'm dried up again. (My financially responsible readers have just congratulated themselves on living a more disciplined life. But may I ask, Are you using those reserves to do things that nourish your heart? Many a Scrooge has filled his coffers while starving his soul.) "There are very many canals in the church today," laments Julia Gatta, "but few reservoirs." One woman deeply involved in ministry wrote to me recently that she is "burned out to a crackling crunch." She has been a canal. She hasn't cared for her heart. She is not alone.

How would you live differently if you believed your heart was the treasure of the kingdom?

This is what God tells us to do, above all else, as the passage says. Last week over breakfast I asked a small group of friends—men who fight for the hearts of others all the time—"What are you doing these days to care for your heart?" They fell silent, eyes roaming the floor, staring at their eggs, examining their nails as if they were pondering a really good answer, but nothing ever came. I was saddened, but not surprised. Our hearts are always the first things to go.

But did you know that God gives out of the *abundance* of his heart? One of the first things John tells us about his dear friend Jesus is that "from the fullness of his grace we have all received one blessing after another" (John 1:16). From God's *fullness*, we receive blessing. Or as Paul prays in Ephesians, "I pray that out of his glorious riches he may strengthen you" (3:16), which is to say, out of the riches God has stored up in his great heart, he gives to ours. Dallas Willard reminds us,

> He is full of joy. Undoubtedly he is the most joyous being in the universe. The abundance of his love and generosity is inseparable from his infinite joy. All of the good and beautiful things from which we occasionally drink [Willard includes the sea in all its beauty, or a wonderful movie, or music] . . . God continuously experiences in all their breadth and depth and richness.

Has it ever occurred to you that God is such a loving and generous person *because* his heart is filled, like a reservoir, with joy? It is because his heart is brimming with good things and experiences that God is able to love and forgive and suffer so long for mankind. The same holds true for us. Are you a delight to be with after an hour in traffic? No wonder we are so short on grace and mercy. Life drains us dry—and we just accept it as the normal way to live.

We were really burned out, Stasi and I, when we headed off to this year's annual family vacation. Before we left, she told me she was "done with people." I was too. Even a short conversation felt draining. Neither of us wanted to see anyone. We gave some serious thought to becoming hermits. Enough of this community stuff. Living alone in a hut in the Kalahari sounded like paradise. God's remedy was eight days in southeast Alaska, photographing grizzly bears, sea kayaking with humpback whales, eating more than our share of great food, and drinking in breathtaking views in every direction. We got home late on a Saturday night; I woke Sunday morning to hear Stasi chatting away on the phone with a friend. She called another and another all day long. "Just catching up," she said with a smile.

AS AN ACT OF LOVE

Caring for our own hearts isn't selfishness; it's how we begin to love.

Yes, we care for our hearts for the sake of others. Does that sound like a contradiction? Not at all. What will you bring to others if your heart is empty, dried up, pinned down? Love is the point. And you can't love without your heart, and you can't love well unless your heart is well.

When it comes to the whole subject of loving others, you must know this: how you handle your own heart is how you will handle theirs. This is the wisdom behind Jesus' urging us to love others *as we love ourselves* (Mark 12:31). "A horrible command," as C. S. Lewis points out, "if the self were simply to be hated." If you dismiss your heart, you will end up dismissing theirs. If you expect perfection of your heart, you will raise that same standard for them. If you manage your heart for efficiency and performance, that is what you'll pressure them to be.

"But," you protest, "I have lots of grace for other people. I'm just hard on myself." I tried the same excuse for years. It doesn't work. Even though we may try to be merciful toward others while we neglect or beat up ourselves, they can *see* how we treat our own hearts, and they will always feel the treatment will be the same for them. They are right. Eventually, inevitably, we will treat them poorly too.

You know this without knowing that you did. There are certain people you would never go to with a problem, would never call at 2:00 A.M. when you were struggling under some burden or loss. Why not? You know they would not handle your heart well. Some folks I know won some airline tickets good for travel to anyplace in the world. That was fifteen years ago. They still haven't used them. Would you ask them for advice on caring for your heart? Don't you sense they would say, "There's no time for that"?

Yes, there is a place for sacrifice. And yes, I know, a lot of very selfish things have been done under the excuse that "I'm taking care of my heart." I've heard divorces and affairs justified that way. But the fact that someone abuses an idea doesn't make it a bad idea. People overeat too. Does that mean you shouldn't enjoy eating? Some pretty awful things have been done in the name of Christianity. Does that mean you shouldn't be a Christian? Don't let others' bad choices shape your life. Care for your heart. Above all else. Not only for your own sake; not even primarily for your own sake. Do it in order to love better, for the sake of those who need you. And they need you. Remember—this is our most desperate hour.

AS AN ACT OF DEVOTION

Caring for your heart is also how you protect your relationship with God.

Now there's a new thought. But isn't our heart the new dwelling place of God? It is where we commune with him. It is where we hear his voice. Most of the folks I know who have never heard God speak to them are the same folks who live far from their hearts; they practice the Christianity of principles. Then they wonder why God seems distant. *I guess all that intimacy with God stuff is for others, not me.* It's like a friend who hates the telephone. He neglects to pay the bills, could care less when the phone company disconnects the service. Then he wonders why "nobody ever calls." You cannot cut off your heart and expect to hear from God.

The same holds true for those folks who cannot seem to find the abundant life that Christ promised. Your heart is where that life flows into you. "On the last and greatest day of the Feast, Jesus stood and said in a loud voice, 'If anyone is thirsty, let him come to me and drink. Whoever believes in me, as the Scripture has said, streams of living water will flow from within him'" (John 7:37–38). "Flow from within" means "from your inmost being," from your heart, that wellspring of life within you. God *wants* to give you his life; your part is to keep the channel open. You do that by caring for your heart.

Clairvaux describes Christian maturity as the stage where "we love ourselves for God's sake," meaning that because he considers our hearts the treasures of the kingdom, we do too. We care for ourselves in the same way a woman who knows she is deeply loved cares for herself, while a woman who has been tossed aside tends to "let herself go," as the saying goes. God's friends care for their hearts because they matter to *him.*

WHAT WILL YOU DO?

So, let me ask again: How would you live differently if you believed your heart was the treasure of the kingdom?

What does your heart need? In some sense it's a personal question, unique to our makeup and what brings us life. For some it's music; for others it's reading; for still others it's gardening. Our friend Lori loves the city; I can't wait to get out of one. Bart reads articles on flying; Cherie loves a good novel. Bethann loves horses, and Gary needs time working in the woodshop. You know what makes your heart refreshed, the things that make you come alive. I don't get the thing with women and baths, but I know that Stasi loves them and finds a little retreat in a fifteen-minute tub: "He leads me to soak in bubbly waters." For me and the boys it's the dirtier, the happier.

Yet there are some needs that all hearts have in common. We need beauty; that's clear enough from the fact that God has filled the world with it. He has given us sun and rain,

> wine that gladdens the heart of man,
> > oil to make his face shine,
> > and bread that sustains his heart. (Ps. 104:15)

We need to drink in beauty wherever we can get it—in music, in nature, in art, in a great meal shared. These are all gifts to us from God's generous heart. Friends, those things are not decorations to a life; they bring us life.

> The skies of blue
> The fields of green
> Are all for you

> The silver moon
> The shining sea

All for you

For you, the wind blows
For you, the river flows

And everything you dream about
Even the love you dream of, too,
Is all for you. (John Smith and Lisa Aschmann, "All for You")

I don't think I could have finished this book if it weren't for the walks I take each day in the woods. Last night it began to snow. It is still snowing now. It, too, is a gift to my heart. Early this morning I just sat and watched it fall; so quiet and beautiful, it felt like a balm to my soul.

We need silence and solitude. Often. Jesus modeled that, though few of us ever follow his example. Not even one full chapter into the gospel of Mark, there's quite a stir being created by the Nazarene. "The whole town gathered at the door," which is to say, Jesus is becoming the man to see. Let's pick up the story there:

> That evening after sunset the people brought to Jesus all the sick and demon-possessed. The whole town gathered at the door, and Jesus healed many who had various diseases . . . Very early in the morning, while it was still dark, Jesus got up, left the house and went off to a solitary place, where he prayed. Simon and his companions went to look for him, and when they found him, they exclaimed: "Everyone is looking for you!" Jesus replied, "Let us go somewhere else." (1:32–38)

"Everyone is looking for you!" Surely you can relate to that. At work, at home, at church, aren't there times when everything seems to come down on you? Now this is a tremendous opportunity. I mean, if Jesus really wants to launch his ministry, increase sales, expand his audience, this sure looks like the chance to do it. What does he do? He leaves. He walks away. Everyone is looking for you! Oh, really . . . then we'd better leave. It cracks me up. Wendell Berry might have been writing of Jesus when he said, "His wildness was in his refusal—or his inability—to live within other people's expectations." We are just the opposite; our entire lives are ruled by the expectations of others, and when we live like that, the heart is always the first thing to go.

Let me ask again: What does *your* heart need? A simple starting place would be to ask God: *What do you have for my heart?* You'll be stunned by what he guides you into.

My parents recently came for a visit. It was a good time, but it fell during a lot of other demands on me, and by the time the week was over, I was wiped out physically, emotionally, spiritually. I hadn't had a moment to myself. As I was driving them to the airport, my dad mentioned that he'd read in the local sports section that the fishing had been good up at one of my old favorite spots. I passed it over with a "huh." On the way home, God whispered, *Go fishing.* What? I haven't time to do that. It was the last thing on my mind. *Take your canoe, call Morgan, and go to the lake.* Now, you need to understand my reluctance. For one thing, the canoe was serving as a storage bin for every piece of flotsam and jetsam in my garage. It was buried. For another, I hadn't been to that lake in four years . . . not since the day my best friend died.

But I've learned to trust God on these urgings, and so I called my buddy, dug out the canoe, found my gear, and went. It was a gorgeous scene. The waters were completely calm, like glass, and there wasn't another soul around. We pushed out, and within a few minutes we were catching these enormous rainbows, one after another, laughing and whooping and having a ball. I'm a little embarrassed to admit it, but I was stunned. Simply stunned. *Really, God? My heart matters to you?*

You might not think God wants this for you . . . but have you asked him? I think I've missed thousands of little promptings over the years, simply because I wasn't open to the fact that they occur. But I am astounded and more than humbled by the number of gifts he has given my heart since I've begun to give even partial heed to Proverbs 4:23. And I know I'm not some special case. Just this week, on Tuesday night, the people in our home fellowship were reviewing some notes from an exercise we'd done together at the first of the year. We'd taken an evening to write down the things we'd love to see happen in our lives in the coming year. It's a simple way of listening to what your heart needs: What do you want? What is your heart longing for?

Ten months had passed when Jenny suggested we have a look at what we'd jotted down. Reviewing our desires was astounding in two ways. First, most of us had completely forgotten what we were longing for. (The sign of an abandoned heart: we didn't even remember our own dreams.) Stasi hadn't recalled wanting to speak to women. I'd forgotten that I wanted to go to Alaska. Leigh had forgotten wanting to dance. Joni had forgotten her desire to visit the Tetons. But what was even more astounding was that *God* had not forgotten. We'd gone to Alaska. Joni had gone to the Tetons. Leigh had danced—and beautifully. Stasi spoke at her first women's retreat—and gloriously. On every single person's list—in more cases than not—God had given us our heart's desire. Wow. Our hearts *do* matter to God.

Now, the Enemy will tell you this is foolish. *There are so many more important things to do. You can get to it some other time. You're being selfish. This isn't even what you want, anyway.* Remember: he fears you—fears your heart's coming alive and full and free. Caring for your heart is an act of obedience. It is an act of love, an act of faith, an act of war.

As an Act of War

Caring for your heart is your first blow against the Enemy's schemes.

The heart that is weak is vulnerable. Are you able to fend off accusation when you are wiped out from a hard week? It seems so true at that point, and who really cares anyway? You know how draining the holidays can be. Are you overflowing with prayer the day after Christmas? Listen—the first wave of any strike against us is to rob us of the heart to fight it. It always starts that way, with that sense of being too tired or overwhelmed. Heads up—the main assault is coming on the heels of it. Facing an overwhelming enemy at Agincourt, King Henry prays for his men, that the opposing numbers will not "pluck their hearts from them."

It works like this: hyenas cannot bring down a lion in its prime. What they do is run it and taunt it and wear it down to the point of exhaustion. Once they see it cannot defend itself, then they close in. The strategy of our Enemy in the age we live in now is *busyness* or *drivenness*. Ask the people you know how things are going. Nine out of ten will answer something to the effect of "really busy." Every time I call another ministry I get voice mail. "They're busy right now, can I put you into voice mail?" The deadly scheme is this: *keep them running. That way, they'll never take care of their hearts. We'll burn them out and take them out.*

I don't want to be taken out. Others are counting on me. I must care for my heart as my first line of defense.

Also, an empty heart is more vulnerable to temptation. Isn't it when you're sad and discouraged that a bag of donuts looks like salvation? When you're bored and lonely that the adult cable channel seems irresistible? A heart that has been cared for is like a man or woman deeply in love—an affair isn't even appealing when you have the real deal. It's the famished heart that falls for seduction. There's a great picture of this in the film *Chocolat*. The mayor of the town is a Pharisee, a legalist bound to rules. He denies his heart, hates it, fears it. He goes in one night to destroy the chocolate shop and ends up binging himself into a coma, his starving heart taken out by some fudge.

Be kind to yourself. Take care of your heart. You're going to need it.

AND WE ARE AT WAR, DEAR FRIENDS

If you have raced with men on foot
> and they have worn you out,
> > how can you compete with horses?
If you stumble in safe country,
> how will you manage in the thickets by the Jordan? (Jer. 12:5)

Look—it's going to get worse before it gets better. Jesus warned us about that. So let me say, one more time, *we are at war.* The worst scenes in *The Lord of the Rings* or *The Matrix* or *Gladiator* are merely trying to wake you to the reality in which you now live. The Ransom of your life commands you to *take care of your heart . . . now.* He knows what's coming.

Something like the battle for Iwo Jima is coming—spiritually, in our own lives, and in the life of the body of Christ around the world. To say it was one of the bloodiest, ugliest, most heroic battles in the history of war is true, but hardly captures it. John Wayne's movie doesn't even come close to what really happened there. It was . . . horrifying beyond words. Picture the opening scenes from *Saving Private Ryan,* and multiply them by a factor of three. The Japanese had studied the Allied victory at Normandy to prepare against this invasion. They transformed the little island, a tiny scrap of rock out in the Pacific, into a fortress maze of tunnels, bunkers, pillboxes, and underground caverns to conceal 22,000 Japanese soldiers who had, like crazed kamikazes, pledged themselves to die defending the island.

The young marines who landed on Iwo Jima were forced to drive out the Japanese inch by inch, battling an enemy they could not see while being exposed to every sort of weapons fire from every possible direction. Mortars, machine guns, mines, grenades. Some survivors reported that they never saw one living Japanese soldier in all those days of combat. (Sounds just like spiritual warfare.) Military analysts thought the battle could be won in seventy-two hours. It took thirty-six days and cost nearly seven thousand American lives. More medals of honor were awarded for action there than in any other battle in U.S. history. On the second day of the invasion, one war reporter, leaving the field, warned a colleague, "I wouldn't go in there if I were you. There's more hell in there than I've seen in the rest of the war put together."

The men of Easy Company were among the first to descend into that hell, and among the last to pull out after fighting more than five straight weeks. Their unit suffered 85 percent casualties. Easy landed on the far left end of Green Beach One, the end of the line. They led the assault on Mount Suribachi. Two thousand entrenched Japanese began firing everything they had at the totally exposed marines. Not just for hours or days, but *weeks*. On the fifteenth day of battle, Easy was pulled off the front line for a breather. Their captain removed the company to a secured beach on the west side of the island. Their orders?

Take a swim.

Take Heart

We now are going to war. This is the beginning of the end. The hour is late, and you are needed. We need your heart.

If there were something more I could do to help you see, I wish to God I could have done it. Tears fill my eyes for fear I have not done enough. You must turn, then, back to myth—tomorrow and the next day and the next. Read the battle of Helm's Deep; it's chapter 7 of *The Two Towers*. Watch any of the trilogy of those films. And the opening of *Gladiator*. That is where we are now. Or if you can bear it, watch the battle of the Ia Drang Valley in *We Were Soldiers*. It is so deeply true to what we must face, will face. Linger over the climax of *The Prince of Egypt*, where God goes to war against Egypt to set his people free. If the images of the Exodus do not move you, I don't know what will.

Read Lewis's last installment in *The Chronicles of Narnia*, titled *The Last Battle*. I don't think even he knew all he was saying there. These stories and images are among the stories that God is giving to his people for this hour. They are gifts to us from his hand, clarity and strength for our hearts. Apparently, we need them. They will do you a great good. And then . . . you will do a great good. Remember our friends from the Emmaus Road? Well, the story ends with their eyes wide open. They go tearing back to Jerusalem, their hearts bursting. "They found the Eleven and those with them, assembled together and saying, 'It is true!'" (Luke 24:33–34). It is true. All of it.

We are now far into this epic Story that every great myth points to. We have reached the moment where we, too, must find our courage and rise up to recover our hearts and fight for the hearts of others. The hour is late, and much time has been wasted. Aslan is on the move; we must rally to him at the stone table. We must find Gepetto lost at sea. We must ride hard, ride to Helm's Deep and join the last great battle for Middle Earth. Grab everything God sends you. You'll need everything that helps you see with the eyes of your heart, including those myths, and the way they illumine for us the words God has given in Scripture, to which "you will do well to pay attention . . . as to a light shining in a dark place, until the day dawns and the morning star rises in your hearts" (2 Peter 1:19).

Yes. Until the day dawns, my friends, and the Morning Star rises in all our *hearts*.

Wake up, O sleeper,
rise from the dead,
and Christ will shine on you.
—THE APOSTLE PAUL
(Eph. 5:14)

A Daily Prayer
for Freedom

My dear Lord Jesus, I come to you now to be restored in you—to renew my place in you, my allegiance to you, and to receive from you all the grace and mercy I so desperately need this day. I honor you as my sovereign Lord, and I surrender every aspect of my life totally and completely to you. I give you my body as a living sacrifice; I give you my heart, soul, mind, and strength; and I give you my spirit as well.

I cover myself with your blood—my spirit, my soul, and my body. And I ask your Holy Spirit to restore my union with you, seal me in you, and guide me in this time of prayer. In all that I now pray, I include (my wife, and/or my children, by name). Acting as their head, I bring them under my authority and covering, and I come under your authority and covering. Holy Spirit, apply to them all that I now pray on their behalf.

Dear God, holy and victorious Trinity, you alone are worthy of all my worship, my heart's devotion, all my praise and all my trust and all the glory of my life. I worship you, bow to you, and give myself over to you in my heart's search for life. You alone are Life, and you have become my life. I renounce all other gods, all idols, and I give you the place in my heart and in my life that you truly deserve. I confess here and now that it is all about you, God, and not about me. You are the Hero of this story, and I belong to you. Forgive me, God, for my every sin. Search me and know me and reveal to me any aspect of my life that is not pleasing to you, expose any agreements I have made, and grant me the grace of a deep and true repentance.

Heavenly Father, thank you for loving me and choosing me before you made the world. You are my true Father—my Creator, my Redeemer, my Sustainer, and the true end of all things, including my life. I love you; I trust you; I worship you. Thank you for proving your love for me by sending your only Son, Jesus, to be my substitute and representative. I receive him and all his life and all his work, which you ordained for me. Thank you for including me in Christ, for forgiving me my sins, for granting me his righteousness, for making me complete in him. Thank you for making me alive with Christ, raising me with him, seating me with him at your right hand, granting me his authority, and anointing me with your Holy Spirit. I receive it all with thanks and give it total claim to my life.

Jesus, thank you for coming for me, for ransoming me with your own life. I honor you as my Lord; I love you, worship you, trust you. I sincerely receive you as my redemption, and I receive all the work and triumph of your crucifixion, whereby I am cleansed from all my sin through your shed blood, my old nature is removed, my heart is circumcised unto God, and every claim being made against me is disarmed. I take my place in your cross and death, whereby I have died with you to sin and to my flesh, to the world, and to the Evil One. I am crucified with Christ, and I have crucified my flesh with all its passions and desires. I take up my cross and crucify my flesh with all its pride, unbelief, and idolatry. I put off the old man. I now bring the cross of Christ between me and all people, all spirits, all things. Holy Spirit, apply to me (my wife and/or children) the fullness of the work of the crucifixion of Jesus Christ for me. I receive it with thanks and give it total claim to my life.

Jesus, I also sincerely receive you as my new life, my holiness and sanctification, and I receive all the work and triumph of your resurrection, whereby I have been raised with you to a new life, to walk in newness of life, dead to sin and alive to God. I am crucified with Christ, and it is no longer I who live but Christ who lives in me. I now take my place in your resurrection, whereby I have been made alive with you, I reign in life through you. I now put on the new man in all holiness and humility, in all righteousness and purity and truth. Christ is now my life, the one who strengthens me. Holy Spirit, apply to me (my wife and/or my children) the fullness of the resurrection of Jesus Christ for me. I receive it with thanks and give it total claim to my life.

Jesus, I also sincerely receive you as my authority and rule, my everlasting victory over Satan and his kingdom, and I receive all the work and triumph of your ascension, whereby Satan has been judged and cast down, his rulers and authorities disarmed, all authority in heaven and on earth given to you, Jesus, and I have been given fullness in you, the Head over all. I take my place in your ascension, whereby I have been raised with you to the right hand of the Father and established with you in all authority. I bring your authority and your kingdom rule over my life, my family, my household, and my domain.

And now I bring the fullness of your work—your cross, resurrection, and ascension—against Satan, against his kingdom, and against all his emissaries and all their work warring against me and my domain. Greater is he who is in me than he who is in the world. Christ has given me authority to overcome all the power of the Evil One, and I claim that authority now over and against every enemy, and I banish them in the name of Jesus Christ. Holy Spirit, apply to me (my wife and my children) the fullness of the work of the ascension of Jesus Christ for me. I receive it with thanks and give it total claim to my life.

Holy Spirit, I sincerely receive you as my Counselor, my Comforter, my Strength, and my Guide. Thank you for sealing me in Christ. I honor you as my Lord, and I ask you to lead me into all truth, to anoint me for all of my life and walk and calling, and to lead me deeper into Jesus today. I fully open my life to you in every dimension and aspect—my body, my soul, and my spirit—choosing to be filled with you, to walk in step with you in all things. Apply to me, blessed Holy Spirit, all of the work and all of the gifts in pentecost. Fill me afresh, blessed Holy Spirit. I receive you with thanks and give you total claim to my life (and my wife and/or children).

Heavenly Father, thank you for granting to me every spiritual blessing in the heavenlies in Christ Jesus.

I receive those blessings into my life today, and I ask the Holy Spirit to bring all those blessings into my life this day. Thank you for the blood of Jesus. Wash me once more with his blood from every sin and stain and evil device. I put on your armor—the belt of truth, the breastplate of righteousness, the shoes of the readiness of the gospel of peace, the helmet of salvation. I take up the shield of faith and the sword of the Spirit, the Word of God, and I wield these weapons against the Evil One in the power of God. I choose to pray at all times in the Spirit, to be strong in you, Lord, and in your might.

Father, thank you for your angels. I summon them in the authority of Jesus Christ and release them to war for me and my household. May they guard me at all times this day. Thank you for those who pray for me; I confess I need their prayers, and I ask you to send forth your Spirit and rouse them, unite them, raising up the full canopy of prayer and intercession for me. I call forth the kingdom of the Lord Jesus Christ this day throughout my home, my family, my life, and my domain. I pray all of this in the name of Jesus Christ, with all glory and honor and thanks to him.

ACKNOWLEDGMENTS

My love and thanks to Travis, to Sealy and his team, to my allies at Thomas Nelson, to my friends at Ransomed Heart, to Jenny, and to my family. We did it.

ABOUT THE AUTHOR

John Eldredge is the founder and director of Ransomed Heart Ministries in Colorado Springs, Colorado, a fellowship devoted to helping people recover and live from their heart. John is the author of numerous books, including *Epic*, *Wild at Heart*, and *Walking with God*, and coauthor of *Captivating* and *The Sacred Romance*. John lives in Colorado with his wife, Stasi, and their three sons, Samuel, Blaine, and Luke. He loves living in the Rocky Mountains so he can pursue his other passions, including fly-fishing, mountain climbing, and exploring the waters of the West in his canoe.

For the Journey

Developing a Conversational Intimacy with God

Developing a Conversational Intimacy with God explores why it is part of the normal Christian life to walk intimately with Christ. He longs to speak, and it is our right and privilege to hear His Voice. If you long for more in your relationship with God, you will understand "how" and "why" we are invited into the closest of fellowships with Him.

The Hope of Prayer

Things Can be Different.

Every one of us can point to things in our lives that we'd sure like to see change. Lots of things. Relationships that need some help. Health issues. A need for guidance and direction. Financial woes . . .

The list for most of us is pretty long. And to help us bring about that change, God has given us prayer.

The Scriptures talk a lot about prayer, but we're not really sure what to do with it, or, more importantly, how to do it. At least, how to do it in a way that works. Meaning, it actually brings about change.

But that's what prayer is supposed to do! Bring about change. When Jesus teaches us to pray "Thy Kingdom come, thy will be done," he means precisely that—that our prayers somehow enable the Kingdom of God to come and his will to be done "on earth as it is in heaven."

Meaning, here, now, in our lives.

In *The Hope of Prayer* series John shares how to pray with hope and confidence—how to apply prayer to the various dilemmas of life. A live audience recording, this 8 CD set includes the question and answer period at the end of each session, as well as, John fielding prayer requests and praying—providing a mini prayer clinic.

There are few thoughts as hopeful as the thought that things can be different. And so the disciples said, "Teach us to pray." We hope through this series you will find answers to many of the questions you have longed to ask.

The Utter Relief of Holiness

"Long before he laid down earth's foundations, God had us in mind, had settled on us as the focus of his love, to be made whole and holy by his love." (Ephesians 1: 3–4, *The Message*)

Whole and holy. Have we ever put those two words together before? We've thought of wholeness as something for which we hope . . . that remains elusive. And as for holiness, doesn't the word sound sort of heavy and disciplined and hard?

It's not.

When we discover what the salvation of Jesus Christ means for our own restoration, we'll find that holiness is an expression of the healing of our humanity. What a relief it would be to be set free from all that plagues us: the inner struggle with anger or contempt—the struggle with habitual sins.

We can! We can be set free . . . through the healing work of Christ in our lives.

In this four-part CD series, John Eldredge explores the beauty of the genuine goodness available to us in Jesus Christ and guides us through the process whereby God makes us whole and holy by his love.

You will be relieved. Utterly.

Only Available at RansomedHeart.com!

GOD IS TALKING TO YOU.
LISTEN—IT WILL CHANGE YOUR LIFE.

In his most personal book ever, John Eldredge opens up his own
life and heart to share what a conversational intimacy with God can
be like. *Walking with God* reveals how talking and listening to
God will open up an unending and inexhaustible source of guidance,
comfort, and protection. Every moment of every day.

AVAILABLE WHEREVER BOOKS ARE SOLD.

FOR ADDITIONAL RESOURCES, VIDEOS, AND TEACHING FROM
JOHN, VISIT WALKINGWITHGOD.NET

Listening to God

If only I had listened.

We have a family tradition of going out into the woods each year after Thanksgiving to cut down our Christmas tree. It's something we started when the boys were small, and over the years it became the event to help us inaugurate the Christmas season. We bundle the boys up and head off to the snowy woods on a Saturday morning. Stasi brings hot cocoa in a thermos; I bring the rope and saw. Inevitably, I think there's a better tree "just over the next hill," which is always one more hill away, and family members start peeling off and heading back to the car while I cut down a tree that's always three feet too tall and drag it a mile. It's all part of the tradition.

Now, you get a pretty funky-looking tree, sort of a Charlie Brown tree, when you go out to find one on your own. But it's *our* tree, with a story that goes along with it. We love it. Most of the time.

Last year we headed out for the tree the weekend *after* Thanksgiving weekend. There was new excitement to the adventure—we'd bought some land way out in the mountains, and this would be the first time we'd ever been able to cut a tree down on our own property. I envisioned a family hike on snowshoes up through the forest, hot drinks by the fire afterward, board games, rich memories. That's not exactly how it turned out.

A blizzard came upon us during the night and dumped about two feet of snow on the back roads. We decided we'd better get out while we could, but in the first five minutes of our journey home, we slid off into a ditch. It took us more than an hour to dig out.

We had no shovel. We used the boys' plastic sled, with repeated failures. Finally, the only way we could get the Suburban to climb up onto the road was to have the whole family on the right side of the truck, outside on the running boards, riding it like a catamaran while I gunned it for all it was worth.

Slowly we made it back out to the highway. I got out to check the tree (we did get the tree, three feet too tall) and discovered that we now had two flat tires. Not one, but two. It was ten degrees outside, and the wind was howling down from the north, bringing the windchill to minus ten—as in ten below zero. I knew I had one spare tire, but not two. (Who carries two? Who gets two flat tires at the same time?) I did have a can of Fix-A-Flat—maybe that would get us into town. Nope, it was frozen. When I got out to deal with the situation, I left the flashers on to warn oncoming traffic of our condition. Now the battery was dead.

The word that comes to mind is *ordeal.* It was an ordeal.

And now here is my confession: we weren't supposed to go.

We'd prayed about the weekend, asking God when would be a good time to head out. This was the day after Thanksgiving (Friday), and both Stasi and I sensed God saying we were to go up the following day. But it didn't make sense to us. We were tired, and the boys wanted to see their friends. There were all sorts of "reasons" not to go, but more so there was that lingering unbelief that often passes for weariness, that thing in us that sort of whines, *Really? Do we really have to do this now, God?* So we ignored the counsel and went the following weekend. Now, the weekend God told us to go was a gorgeous weekend—no snow, sunny skies, no wind. The whole event would have been delightful.

But no. We had to do things our way.

How does the old hymn go? "Trust and obey, for there's no other way to be happy in Jesus, but to trust and obey." The whole ordeal could have been avoided had we simply listened.

The Power of Assumptions

I ran into an old acquaintance at the bookstore today.

Actually, I was nearly out the door when he called my name, so I turned back in to say hello and chat for a few moments. He seemed . . . not well. Half the man he used to be. I wondered why. I expected him to say that he had suffered some major loss. A loved one, I feared. Or maybe it was a prolonged illness. Not that he was visibly deteriorating as some do in the late stages of cancer. But there was something about his countenance, a loss of some essential part of himself. You know the look. Many people have it, actually. It's a confused and disheartened look. As we talked, it became clear that he had simply been eroded by a number of confusing years strung together by disappointment.

As I left the store, I found myself thinking, *He held such promise. What happened?*

It has to do with assumptions.

He assumed that God, being a loving God, was going to come through for him. In the sense of bless his choices. His ministry. Make his life good. He looked sort of dazed and hurt that it hadn't happened. He was trying to put a good face on it, but you could see that he had lost heart. This may be one of the most common, most unquestioned, and most naive assumptions people who believe in God share. We assume that because we believe in God, and because he is love, he's going to give us a happy life. A + B = C. You may not be so bold as to state this assumption out loud—you may not even think you hold this assumption—but notice your shock when thing don't go well. Notice your feelings of abandonment and betrayal when life doesn't work out. Notice that often you feel as though God isn't really all that close, or involved, feel that he isn't paying attention to your life.

Now, it's not fair to diagnose someone else's life without having some intimate knowledge of their situation, the story leading up to it, and what God is after. But I *do* have enough information to say that this man assumed the Christian life was basically about believing in God and doing good. Be a good person. That's good. That's a beginning. But it's just a beginning. It's sort of like saying that the way to have a good friendship is not to betray the other person. That will certainly help. You certainly want to have that going. But there's a whole lot more to friendship than simply not committing a betrayal, wouldn't you say? I know this fellow also holds the assumption that God doesn't really speak to his children. And so, when he found himself assaulted and undermined by all that had unfolded in his life, he had no source of guidance or explanation. It was sad to see the toll it had taken.

I left the store thinking about assumptions—how they are either helping us or hurting us, every single day of our lives. Our assumptions control our interpretation of events, and they supply a great deal of the momentum and direction for our lives. It's important that we take a look at them. And life will provide hundreds of opportunities to take a look at our assumptions in a single week. Especially as we walk with God.

I'll tip my hand to one assumption I am making. I assume that an intimate, conversational walk with God is available, and is meant to be normal. I'll push that a step further. I assume that if you *don't* find that kind of relationship with God, your spiritual life will be stunted. And that will handicap the rest of your life. We can't find life without God, and we can't find God if we don't know how to walk intimately with him. A passage from the gospel of John will show you what I'm getting at. Jesus is talking about his relationship with us, how he is the Good Shepherd and we are his sheep. Listen to how he describes the relationship:

"I tell you the truth, the man who does not enter the sheep pen

by the gate, but climbs in by some other way, is a thief and a robber. The man who enters by the gate is the shepherd of his sheep.
The watchman opens the gate for him, and the sheep listen to his
voice. He calls his own sheep by name and leads them out. When
he has brought out all his own, he goes on ahead of them, and his
sheep follow him because they know his voice." . . .

"Whoever enters through me will be saved. He will come in
and go out, and find pasture. The thief comes only to steal and
kill and destroy; I have come that they may have life, and have it
to the full." (John 10:1–4, 9–10)

The sheep live in dangerous country. The only way they can
move securely in and out and find pasture is to follow their shepherd closely. Yet most Christians assume that the way to find the
life God has for us is to (A) believe in God, (B) be a good person,
and (C) he will deliver the rest. A + B = C. But Jesus says no,
there's more to the equation. I *do* want life for you. To the full. But
you have to realize there is a thief. He's trying to destroy you. There
are false shepherds too. Don't listen to them. Don't just wander off
looking for pasture. You need to do more than believe in me. You
have to stay close to me. Listen to my voice. Let me lead.

Now there's a thought: if you don't hold the same assumptions
Jesus does, you haven't got a chance of finding the life he has for you.

Does God Still Speak?

I was talking on the phone yesterday with a young woman who was
interviewing me for an article of some sort. She asked what this
book was about, and I tried to explain it in this way: "This is a sort
of tutorial on how to walk with God. And how to hear his voice."
I told her several stories (including the one about the Christmas

tree ordeal). There was a long pause, that pregnant sort of pause that tells me I've just hit upon a great need and a great doubt. Finally, she asked, "What do you say to people who say, 'God isn't that intimate with us?'" I had a hunch—it was something in the tone of her voice—that she hadn't experienced the Christian life in the ways I was describing. Maybe because she'd never been told this is available; maybe it's as simple as the fact that no one had ever shown her how.

Is God really that intimate with us? That's a good place to begin.

It might seem trivial that I'm bothering the God of the universe with a family outing for a Christmas tree. Does God really care about that kind of stuff? Is he really that intimate with us? Let's start with this much—God certainly knows *us* that intimately.

> O LORD, you have searched me
> and you know me.
> You know when I sit and when I rise;
> you perceive my thoughts from afar.
> You discern my going out and my lying down;
> you are familiar with all my ways.
> Before a word is on my tongue
> you know it completely, O LORD.
>
> You hem me in—behind and before;
> you have laid your hand upon me.
> Such knowledge is too wonderful for me,
> too lofty for me to attain.
>
> Where can I go from your Spirit?
> Where can I flee from your presence?
> If I go up to the heavens, you are there;
> if I make my bed in the depths, you are there.
> If I rise on the wings of the dawn,

if I settle on the far side of the sea,
even there your hand will guide me,
   your right hand will hold me fast.

If I say, "Surely the darkness will hide me
   and the light become night around me,"
even the darkness will not be dark to you;
   the night will shine like the day,
     for darkness is as light to you.

For you created my inmost being;
   you knit me together in my mother's womb.
I praise you because I am fearfully and wonderfully made;
   your works are wonderful,
     I know that full well.
My frame was not hidden from you
   when I was made in the secret place.
When I was woven together in the depths of the earth,
   your eyes saw my unformed body.
All the days ordained for me
   were written in your book
   before one of them came to be.

How precious to me are your thoughts, O God!
   How vast is the sum of them!
Were I to count them,
   they would outnumber the grains of sand.
When I awake,
   I am still with you.

(Psalm 139:1–18)

Whatever else we might believe about intimacy with God at this point, the truth is that God knows us *very* intimately. He knows what time you went to bed last night. He knows what you dreamed about. He knows what you had for breakfast this morning. He knows where you left your car keys, what you think about your aunt, and why you're going to dodge your boss at 2:30 today. The Scriptures make that very clear. You are known. Intimately.

But does God seek intimacy *with* us?

Well, start at the beginning. The first man and woman, Adam and Eve, knew God and talked with him. And even after their fall, God goes looking for them. "Then the man and his wife heard the sound of the LORD God as he was walking in the garden in the cool of the day, and they hid from the LORD God among the trees of the garden. But the LORD God called to the man, 'Where are you?'" (Genesis 3:8–9). What a beautiful story. It tells us that even in our sin God still wants us and comes looking for us. The rest of the Bible continues the story of God seeking us out, calling us back to himself.

> The LORD is with you when you are with him. If you seek him, he will be found by you. (2 Chronicles 15:2)

> I will give them a heart to know me, that I am the LORD. They will be my people, and I will be their God, for they will return to me with all their heart. (Jeremiah 24:7)

> This is what the LORD Almighty says: "Return to me," declares the LORD Almighty, "and I will return to you," says the LORD Almighty. (Zechariah 1:3)
> Come near to God and he will come near to you. (James 4:8)

> Let us draw near to God. (Hebrews 10:22)

Intimacy with God is the purpose of our lives. It's why God created us. Not simply to believe in him, though that is a good beginning. Not only to obey him, though that is a higher life still. God created us for intimate fellowship with himself, and in doing so he established the goal of our existence—to know him, love him, and live our lives in an intimate relationship with him. Jesus says that eternal life is to know God (John 17:3). Not just "know about" like you know about the ozone layer or Ulysses S Grant. He means know as two people know each other, know as Jesus knows the Father—intimately.

But does God speak to his people?

Can you imagine any relationship where there is no communication whatsoever? What would you think if you met two good friends for coffee, and you knew that they'd been at the café for an hour before you arrived, but as you sat down and asked them, "So, what have you been talking about?" they said, "Nothing." "Nothing?" "Nothing. We don't talk to each other. But we're really good friends." Jesus calls us his friends: "I'm no longer calling you servants because servants don't understand what their master is thinking and planning. No, I've named you friends because I've let you in on everything I've heard from the Father" (John 15:15 MSG).

Or what would you think about a father if you asked him, "What have you been talking to your children about lately?" and he said, "Nothing. I don't talk to them. But I love them very much." Wouldn't you say the relationship was missing something? And aren't you God's son or daughter? "Yet to all who received him, to those who believed in his name, he gave the right to become children of God" (John 1:12).

Now, I know, I know—the prevailing belief is that God speaks to his people *only* through the Bible. And let me make this clear: he does speak to us first and foremost through the Bible. That is the basis for our relationship. The Bible is the eternal and unchanging Word of God to us. It is such a gift, to have right there in black and white God's thoughts toward us. We know right off the bat that any other supposed revelation from God that contradicts the Bible is not to be trusted. So I am not minimizing in any way the authority of the Scripture or the fact that God speaks to us through the Bible.

However, many Christians believe that God *only* speaks to us through the Bible.

The irony of that belief is that's not what the Bible says.

The Bible is filled with stories of God talking to his people. Abraham, who is called the friend of God, said, "The LORD, the God of heaven, who brought me out of my father's household and my native land and who spoke to me . . ." (Genesis 24:7). God spoke to Moses "as a man speaks with his friend" (Exodus 33:11). He spoke to Aaron too: "Now the LORD spoke to Moses and Aaron about the Israelites" (Exodus 6:13). And David: "In the course of time, David inquired of the LORD. 'Shall I go up to one of the towns of Judah?' he asked. The LORD said, 'Go up.' David asked, 'Where shall I go?' 'To Hebron,' the LORD answered" (2 Samuel 2:1). The Lord spoke to Noah. The Lord spoke to Gideon. The Lord spoke to Samuel. The list goes on and on.

I can hear the objections even now: "But that was different. Those were special people called to special tasks." And we are not special people called to special tasks? I refuse to believe that. And I doubt that you want to believe it either, in your heart of hearts.